Production Planning, Scheduling, and Inventory Control: Concepts, Techniques, and Systems

Second Edition

Edited by

Vincent A. Mabert
Operations and Systems Department
Indiana University

Colin Moodie
School of Industrial Engineering
Purdue University

Production and Inventory Control Division
Institute of Industrial Engineers
American Institute of Industrial Engineers

Additional copies can be obtained by contacting:
Industrial Engineering and Management Press
Institute of Industrial Engineers
25 Technology Park/Atlanta
Norcross, Georgia 30092
(404) 449-0460

Quantity discounts available on request.

Contents

Preface

Douglas C. Montgomery and William L. Berry edited the first volume of **Production Planning, Scheduling, and Inventory Control: Concepts, Techniques, and Systems** in 1974. Their objective was to indicate how computers and operations research techniques could be used in (1) preparing production and capacity, (2) controlling inventory levels, (3) forecasting product demand, and (4) scheduling operations. They included readings that focused upon presenting basic concepts and techniques, with some applications.

This publication continues with the same spirit but with a shift in focus. In the 1970s a number of new techniques and systems have become popular, and have been applied in manufacturing and service organizations. The papers selected for inclusion in this publication illustrate some of these procedures and applications. In fact, the majority of the papers selected represent actual applications, which provide the reader with a good balance of conceptual, technical, and practical information.

In selecting the papers for inclusion, we reviewed only the literature of the 1970s. Montgomery and Berry included many fine papers written prior to 1970, which lay a foundation for formal planning and control systems. This publication updates and expands by illustrating new procedures and applications. Therefore, both books complement each other and provide a useful source of documented material in the area of production planning and inventory control. The contents should be beneficial to practitioners and students of industrial engineering, operations research, management science, industrial management, and systems engineering.

We want to express our thanks to the authors of the papers included in the book and to the editors of the respective journals in which the papers originally appeared. There were many fine papers published during the 1970s and we selected a set which provides a reasonable balance of theoretical value and practical experience.

The appendix of the book provides an extensive list of other publications in production planning and inventory control. Many of the papers concentrate in greater detail some of the concepts we have selected for inclusion in this publication.

Vincent A. Mabert — Bloomington, Indiana
Colin L. Moodie — West Lafayette, Indiana

1/Overview

Production planning and inventory control systems are concerned with the effective management of an organization's limited resources. This is true whether the organization manufactures a product or provides a service, operates in the public or private sector, or is profit or non-profit in orientation. The planning task determines the allocation of the limited resources (men, equipment, energy, etc.) to meet an expected demand. The control system oversees the execution of the allocation within the guidelines of the developed plan. If changes occur due to unanticipated events, the control system must respond to these new conditions. Therefore the planning and control systems operate within limits that are set by the organization's goals, but must be flexible to accommodate changes which occur in a dynamic society.

The planning and control system is really a combination of subsystems. These subsystems are designed to gather data on a timely basis, and convert it to useful information. For example, forecasting customer demand for specific products over a known planning horizon or collecting shop floor status information to determine critical jobs are two commonly used subsystems. The examples reflect two necessary elements of a system: 1) looking into the future to anticipate events for effective planning and 2) updating to determine the current status relative to the plan. Today, many organizations are using a combination of manual and computerized subsystems, which comprise the whole system.

The design of the production and inventory system is critical, since it reflects many factors existing both internal and external to the organization. Internal factors like manufacturing lead time, worker productivity, and capital equipment availability impact on meeting specified output levels. External elements like laws, customer expectations, and technology limit many of the organization's options to effectively **design** and **deploy** limited resources.

The first reading by Harvey Wagner presents a framework for the design of planning and control systems. He suggests a five step procedure for evaluating different system configurations. For the typical manufacturing firm, he states there are six functions that need to be linked by the planning and control system. They are: Sales Forecasting, Production Planning, Materials Ordering, Production Scheduling, Distribution Planning, and Customer Order Processing. The paper poses key questions that must be answered when designing a system. Even though Wagner bases his discussion on the design of a system for a manufacturing firm, many of the concepts presented are appropriate for services.

The second reading provides a description of a production planning and control system in use at the Statistics Canada Department, the Canadian national statistical agency. The paper presents the main production stages required by the agency and the planning and control system utilized. The discussion indicates that organizations in the public sector can utilize formal systems to complete their required missions.

The interested reader may want to review the article "Production Planning and Control Integrated" by William K. Holstein. It was originally published by the **Harvard Business Review** (May - June 1968) and reprinted in Vol. 1 of **Production Planning, Scheduling, and Inventory Control: Concepts, Techniques, and Systems**, edited by D.C. Montgomery and W.L. Berry. It suggests a way to integrate many systems into an effective unit. In the remaining sections of the monograph, the specific subsystems of production planning, forecasting, inventory control, and scheduling will be covered.

The Design of Production and Inventory Systems for Multifacility and Multiwarehouse Companies*

Harvey M. Wagner

Yale University, New Haven, Connecticut, and McKinsey & Co., New York, N.Y.

(Received October 29, 1973)

This paper presents an overall structure for the design of combined production and inventory systems. The suggested approach is a synthesis of several recent applications in large-scale manufacturing companies. The paper lists a comprehensive set of questions whose answers serve to characterize the complete systems design. A three-phase program is outlined for conducting an inventory and production systems analysis, design, and implementation project. The paper treats in some detail the component steps to be followed at each phase, the management functions that must be included in a workable design, and the usefulness of operations-research techniques in such computer-based systems.

WHEN THE OPERATIONS RESEARCH SOCIETY OF AMERICA and The Institute of Management Sciences were founded in the United States about 20 years ago, considerable optimism was voiced that mathematical approaches to production scheduling and inventory control would bring about great progress in making these management activities more efficient. To illustrate, the first two volumes of *Management Science* carried over 15 research articles on inventory and production scheduling. The research interest in this topic has continued to this very day. In Volume 18 of *Management Science*, over 20 articles studied various aspects of inventory and production systems.

Of course, during this period thousands of pages have been printed in scholarly books and in operations-research journals that are published by the many professional societies all around the world. These books and articles deal with methods and approaches to improving the planning and execution of manufacturing schedules.

It is paradoxical, then, that so few of these techniques have been implemented in real manufacturing companies. Only rarely have companies been able to adopt the approaches that have appeared in the scientific literature. And usually when the methods have been accepted, the adopted approaches are simplified approximations to the original technique.

In this paper, I shall explain why such a gap exists between real-life production-scheduling and inventory-control systems and the vast scientific literature on this area that has been written over the past two decades. I shall describe several concepts that have actually proved successful in the design of practical production-and inventory-planning systems. Finally, I shall suggest further systems research that would help to close the present gap between science and enlightened management.

* * *

To begin, I shall describe in brief the kind of company that I shall deal with in my subsequent discussion. Specifically, I shall enumerate ten characteristics of the company that have critical bearing on the requirements for an effective production-scheduling and inventory-control system:

1. The company manufactures a large number of different items—anywhere from several hundred to several thousand. I am counting as different items possible differences due to specifications, size, finish, color, weight, and packaging. To illustrate, the company may produce canned (or tinned) foods, or automobile and truck nylon tires, or men and women's work clothing, or steel rods and standard-sized rolled steel plates.

2. The line of products that the company supplies its customers is standardized at least during a selling season or a year. I shall *not* discuss manufacturing firms that produce items made to each individual customer's particular specifications. Hence, I shall not treat companies that only produce to customer order or that operate a purely job-shop plant.

3. From one selling season to the next, or from one year to the next, some old products are dropped from the line and other new ones are added. The added products may be substitutes for, or improvements on, the older products, or they may be entirely new items.

4. The company's customers may be consumers, that is, households, or they may be other firms.

5. The demand for the company's products cannot be perfectly forecast, and sales may fluctuate in a random-like way from week to week, and possibly even from year to year. Demand for some of the items may be seasonal and not steady over a 12-month period, cyclic over a longer time, and directly affected by the state of the economy.

6. The productive capacity of the company is limited. By this I mean that the company cannot change its rate of production from week to week or over a selling season so as to match the fluctuations in its customer demand. Because the company wants to maintain a stable labor force, it is limited in the amount it can increase production in any short period of time. And because of limited machine capacity, the company cannot produce at the peak rate of seasonal demand even if it has a sufficiently large labor supply.

7. The manufacturing lead time is sufficiently long that the company cannot quickly increase the amount of finished product available to meet large and unexpected increases in sales.

8. In addition, the company may have to order raw materials and components far in advance of its own needs because of the long lead times required by its suppliers. These suppliers are not always completely reliable, in that they do not always deliver the ordered amount of raw materials when they promise.

9. The manufacturing processes for the different items share common machinery and facilities. For example, in a food-processing company, different tinned foods use the same preparation and cooking facilities. In a steel plant, different sizes of steel plates are made from rolled steel produced in common furnaces. In an auto-

* An invited address given on September 11, 1973, at a plenary session of a seminar on "Algorithms for Production Control and Production Scheduling" at Karlovy Vary, Czechoslovakia, sponsored by the International Federation of Operational Research Societies and the Czechoslovak Ministry of Iron, Steel, and Engineering.

mobile-manufacturing company, different color automobiles are painted in the same paint shops.

10. Finally, the finished items may be sent from the plant to storage in a factory warehouse and subsequently shipped from the warehouse to customers. Or, for some companies, the items may be shipped to one or more distribution warehouses, and then sent to customers. And, for some large manufacturing firms, the items may be sent from the factory to intermediate storage locations, and then shipped again to field warehouses that serve local customers. In this kind of company inventories are kept at the factory, at intermediate depots, and at district warehouses. Usually transportation and storage costs are sufficiently high so that it is important for the company to decide carefully where to locate its inventories and from which warehouse to serve each of its customers.

The preceding description fits manufacturing companies in many major industries, and therefore represents an important segment of most nonagrarian economics.

For this kind of a company, I shall now pose all the basic questions that must be answered in order to describe completely any real production and inventory-planning system. In other words, the answers to the following questions yield a characterization of all the basic elements of an entire production and inventory system for such a company. And since each of these questions *must* be answered for any particular system, that is, for a company's existing system as well as for any proposed revision of that system, we can refer to these questions to obtain helpful comparisons among alternatives. The nine sets of questions that must be answerable at any arbitrary moment are:

1. How much of each product is to be manufactured over the entire planning horizon used by the company? Of course, the response to this question depends in part on answering the questions: What is forecast customer demand? and, What is forecast available productive capacity?

2. When is the plant to produce each individual item, on what facility or equipment, and in what amount? The response to this question obviously depends on the answer to the first question. It also requires the definition of a planning time interval, such as a week, two weeks, or a month, for the separate production-plan targets. The factory is expected to sequence production on the machinery in an efficient way within these stated planning intervals so as to meet the interval target quantities.

3. When are raw materials to be ordered and in what quantities? How are the shortages removed?

4. How much inventory buildup of each individual item is planned in anticipation of future peak sales?

5. During each time interval, what are the target inventory levels for all the items at every stocking point within the system? In other words, given targeted aggregate inventory for each time interval, where is this inventory to be positioned? Under what circumstances is inventory to be shipped from one stocking point to another?

6. If customer orders exceed stock availability at any time, who is allocated the available supply? How are the backlogs managed?

7. What record-keeping, status-reporting, and cost-gathering information systems are required to provide the data inputs for the production- and inventory-planning system?

8. When and under what circumstances are the plans subject to revision? What information is used to make the revision and how often is this information made available? What are the feasible options for plan revision? How far into the future are the revised plans to be made?

9. Who in the organization is responsible for setting management policy governing the answer to all the preceding questions? Who is responsible for carrying out the planning process and the daily decisions that are made within the management guidelines and the production and inventory plan? And who is responsible for monitoring the system to tell whether management policy is being observed, whether the plans are being well formulated, and whether the execution of these plans is being efficiently accomplished?

Having this list of critical questions, we can readily see why the impact of scientific advances in production- and inventory-planning methods has been so limited. Consider, for example, the use of linear programming models to provide answers to the questions of how much of each product to manufacture, at what week, on which facility, and in how large an amount. I personally have seen in operation successful applications of this sort of model in several process industries, namely, aluminum, pulp and paper, and lubricants and chemicals. Such models, however, do not provide complete and detailed answers to the questions I pose because the combined computational and data requirements for dealing with all the manufactured items to be produced over 52 weekly periods on several dozens of machine groupings are far too great. The cost of trying to use linear programming to plan at this extensive level of detail far exceeds any benefits that would accrue. Successful applications must strike a compromise. To illustrate, such models may not look at all 52 weekly periods, but instead treat only a single three-month interval. Or they may group the many different items into only a few large categories. These compromises in the model do not eliminate the necessity for the company to do detailed planning, and hence, as valuable as the linear programming models are, they contribute only partially to the entire planning and control system. Further, the linear programming models assume the existence of reliable data on forecast demands, capacities, and costs. Hence, to put such models into operation, the company usually has to design a special information system that collects and summarizes the data needed by the models.

For another illustration of how operations research so far has provided only limited insight, consider the question of how much inventory of each item is to be positioned at each stocking location week by week over the sales season. Surprising as it may seem, there do not seem to be any scientifically derived formulas that give good estimates of the costs and customer services associated with different allocation strategies for system-wide inventories. The theoretical results that have appeared usually make far too many restrictive assumptions to give reasonable approximations to reality, and involve far too many calculations to be used on a regular basis in a company that stocks at least hundreds and possibly thousands of items.

As a third example, although operations researchers have a good conceptual grasp of feedback mechanisms and control, and therefore understand the need to build into a production-planning and inventory-control system the opportunities for revising plans and policies, they nevertheless have almost no knowledge of how their feedback devices will actually behave in a real dynamic environment. Let me be more specific. Most linear programming models assume that future demand is known, and therefore must hedge against uncertainty by adding in extra restrictions on minimal inventory levels and maximum production levels. But we have no scientific knowledge about how well such models behave from week to week, or month to month, when they are repeatedly reapplied with updated future forecasts. Similarly, most inventory stockage models that treat demand probabilistically assume that the distribution of customer demand is known. In reality, when the operations-research analyst postulates the form of the demand distribution, he then must estimate the parameters of the distribution using past data, which introduce further error and uncertainty. And, as the operations researcher periodically reestimates the parameters, the inventory and service levels may behave quite differently than predicted by the original mathematical model in which the demand distribution is assumed to be known. Only recently has research been directed toward this topic.

To summarize my position, then, I believe that the production-and-inventory-systems designer for the kind of firm that I have described can get only very limited help from the available scientific literature on production and inventory analysis. Nevertheless, as I shall explain in more detail later, I do think it is possible to use formal, science-like approaches for designing improved systems. Prior to illustrating how a formal approach can be successful, I shall outline the major steps that must be followed in designing and implementing an improved production- and inventory-planning system.

* * *

The *first phase* of a systems study must assess whether there exist sufficient improvement opportunities over the current system to warrant the cost of developing and installing a new system. Since designing and installing a new system may require a large investment of money and staff time, a company must first examine whether its present system can be substantially improved. An experienced inventory- and production-systems analyst, working with a team of company staff, can usually obtain useful estimates of potential savings and possible service improvements within one or two months. This diagnostic task involves the team's examining the current system to determine where better information and better coordination among decision makers would lower the company's costs and improve its service. The task must identify the specific sources and natures of the benefits. For example, frequently a diagnosis shows that inventories are too high at several stocking points. The savings from reducing these inventory levels will occur only once—when the inventories are diminished—and hence may be obtainable by a special one-time program that is aimed solely at the purpose of inventory reduction. Other similar improvements may be possible by implementing a simple management program to eliminate inefficiencies in the current system, inefficiencies that usually are the result of the current system having grown in size and complexity over a period of time without having been carefully watched by the company's senior management.

Additional savings may be available by improving the customer demand forecasts used for production planning. This benefit is recurring, and may entail installing a new computerized management-information system. Thus, one opportunity identified by a diagnosis involves improving only one part of the current system, and making only minor changes elsewhere to accommodate the limited change.

In a company where the current production and inventory system operates badly, as evidenced by high inventories of some items, too frequent stockouts of other items, a large number of revisions in scheduled production quantities, frequent shortages in raw materials and supplies, and high transportation and warehousing costs due to poor forward planning, the most attractive remedy often is a complete redesign of the entire production- and inventory-planning system.

In this diagnostic phase of study, I have found that tools of statistical and economic analysis can be helpful in demonstrating current inefficiencies and estimating possible monetary benefits. Only rarely have I found production and inventory models in the operations-research literature of much assistance as diagnostic tools. Suppose we now assume that the outcome of the initial diagnostic phase is the recommendation to redesign the entire system.

The *second phase* of the study, then, must provide a new system's design. This design phase can be conducted by employing formal procedures and consists of five major steps:

Step 1. Using a graphic descriptive presentation, or an equivalent, to capture the essential management processes required by the new system.

Step 2. Specifying in realistic terms the management functions to be performed.

Step 3. Selecting the approaches for carrying out these management functions.

Step 4. Defining the information files to be used by decision makers within the system, and preparing requirements and a development timetable for new procedures and computerized information systems.

Step 5. Testing the design and estimating the economic results.

I shall expand next on each of these steps of the design phase.

Even for large manufacturing companies, I have found it feasible and essential to describe any proposed system's design by means of a flow chart that resembles that used for a computer program, or by an equivalent tabular form. On this single diagram I show each major management function to be performed and identify the decisions that must be made. I shall enumerate each of these functions and decisions in a moment. I also display who in the organization is responsible for the management function. The diagram must indicate the data information to be supplied for making each type of decision, who receives the results of the decisions in the form of information, and what files are needed for these purposes. The graphical display can be laid out along a time axis to show the timing and sequencing of information flow and decision making. Finally, the diagram must also contain the information feedback that occurs when the system operates in a real-time environment.

The second step of the design phase is to specify the management functions to be performed by the production and inventory system. For the type of manufacturing company that I have described, I find it useful to define six management functions:

• Sales forecasting
• Production planning
• Materials ordering
• Production scheduling
• Distribution planning
• Customer order processing

Defining each of these functions requires listing the decisions to be made and tasks at the plant is higher than anticipated owing to equipment breakdowns or labor shortages, and raw-materials supplies are insufficient to produce the items because of suppliers' inabilities to ship on time or to erroneous procurement decisions. The item-by-item and facility-by-facility detailed status information already mentioned is needed to provide the necessary feedback for responding to these phenomena.

The materials-ordering function must purchase supplies, that is, determine when and how much to purchase, negotiate delivery dates with suppliers, monitor the status of purchase orders outstanding, and control the inventory levels of raw materials held by the company. Inputs to this function are the production plan and its revisions, a bill of materials for each item, current raw-materials inventory levels, current production schedules, a record of performance for on-time delivery for each supplier, and other supplier information relating to quantity discounts, minimum order sizes, and shipping options. The outputs of this management function include an up-to-date status report of raw-materials stocks and a schedule of raw materials due in. The primary recipient of this information is the production-scheduling function. Errors in procurement decisions arise from unanticipated revisions in production plans requiring new timing for delivery or new supply quantities needed, and from poor supplier performance. The need for detailed record keeping is most severe with reference to the use of the bill of materials. Given a production plan for each standard item, the bill of materials task must calculate the requirements for all of the different raw materials. Since many of the raw materials may be common to the production of several items, the materials-ordering function must aggregate the total requirements for each item to be ordered.

The production-scheduling function must develop daily schedules at the factories. This task is usually performed weekly, and sometimes for two to four weeks ahead, with revisions made daily as unforeseen circumstances arise. The information inputs are the production plan, the availability of raw materials, the amount and location of work in process within the factory, the available work force, and the status of the machinery. Notification of the availability of finished product each day must be sent to the distribution-planning function, and shortfalls in production targets must be sent to the production-planning function. Notification of withdrawals of raw materials must be sent to the materials-ordering function. Errors in scheduling consist of creating bottlenecks within the plant and not having the necessary combination of available raw materials and in-process inventory, labor, and machinery to achieve the targeted production. Production-scheduling management must have a close familiarity with the methods of production and the equipment options in order to load plant facilities efficiently.

The distribution-planning function must monitor product inventories throughout the system so that at each location adequate stocks are held in anticipation of forecast demand. For a company that maintains a factory warehouse, intermediate distribution centers, and field warehouses, this management function must decide on a daily basis where to place the production currently coming available at the factory, and whether to move stocks from one location to another. It must also determine daily the method of shipping the product—for example, by truck or by railroad— and must take account of the monetary savings from shipping in large quantities. If customers' orders can be filled from more than one stocking location, the distribution-planning function must select the best source. In some companies, the source point of an item differs from customer to customer and from item to item. And

to be performed. It is necessary to describe the possible causes for making erroneous decisions, and the information feedback that is needed to identify and then respond to the impact of such decisions. And it is also important to make clear the amount of detail involved in making the decisions and performing the tasks. I next give a brief definition of these management functions to explain the process.

The sales-forecasting function must produce both long-term and short-term projections of sales for each standard item sold. The long-term forecasts are usually made for a 12- to 18-month period and updated quarterly; the time intervals can be monthly or quarterly. (Sometime these forecasts are called intermediate-term.) The short-term forecasts are usually made for weekly or biweekly intervals, extending over the next six to thirteen weeks, depending in part on the production lead time, and updated weekly. The forecasts require maintaining an historical sales file as well as up-to-date sales statistics. In many American and Western European companies, special sales promotions are utilized to increase sales, and such promotion plans must also be factored into the future forecasts as well as netted out of the past historical sales patterns. The forecasts themselves become information input to the production-planning and distribution-planning management functions. When customer demand is not perfectly forecastable, errors in projections commonly occur, especially on a week-to-week basis. Cumulative sales also may be substantially off plan owing to a change in the company's market share, or an expansion or contraction of industry-wide demand. The impact of these forecast errors is immediately felt in terms of unplanned excesses of inventory or unplanned shortages and possibly lost sales. For large companies it is essential that the information feedback on realized sales versus forecast sales not only be on an item-by-item basis, but also by sales regions or districts, and perhaps even by customer categories. All in all, a considerable amount of data is required for a comprehensive forecasting system.

The production-planning function must provide the anticipated dates (usually by weekly intervals) and run quantities for each item at each factory over the planning horizon, such as thirteen weeks. The horizon itself must be long enough to permit early order of raw materials and supplies, unless the lead time for ordering raw materials is so long that the company keeps large inventories of these materials at all times. The plan is updated monthly, although the up-to-date interval may be longer or shorter, depending in part on the magnitude of sales-forecasting errors and raw-materials lead times. The production plan also calculates target levels for system-wide inventories. As part of the regular planning process, the management of this function may determine the need to expand capacity or improve facility capability. Inputs to this planning process include forecasts (or assumptions about) sales, capacity availability, raw-materials availability, production efficiencies, and equipment requirements. For the purpose of revising the plans periodically, this function must receive information about actual production and factory schedules, and current system inventories. The plans and their revisions become input information to the production-scheduling, materials-ordering, and distribution-planning management functions. Errors in production planning arise because, owing to poor forecasting, too little or too much production is scheduled (that is, inventories are too low or too high) relative to actual customer demand, sufficient capacity at the plant is not available to produce all the targeted amounts because of poor planning-efficiency and equipment-utilization factors, down time of equipment finally, the distribution-planning function has responsibility for deciding on the number, locations, and sizes of warehouse facilities. The ongoing data inputs for this function are the production plan, the production schedule, up-to-date inventory stock status, and forecast demand. The information must be available by item and for each stocking point. Errors in distribution decisions give rise to situations of excess supplies in some locations and shortages in others, and too high expenditures on transportation and storage. The errors of inventory imbalance usually can be detected from the stock-status and sales reports, but errors in transportation and storage decisions are much harder to determine, unless a special diagnostic study is made of the current decision rules. An important information output of the distribution-planning function is the availability of items in stock to meet customer demand.

This brings us to the sixth management function that must be part of a production- and inventory-system design, namely, the customer order-processing function. The responsibility of this function is to enter and record the customer's order, transmit the information to the appropriate distribution center so that the items may be shipped, keep the status of the entire customer order current (that is, whether it is awaiting shipment, whether some items requested must be backordered, when the order is likely to be delivered, etc.), and eventually bill and invoice the customer for the items that are shipped. The customer-order-processing function keeps an up-to-date file of each customer's orders, and also prepares the sales statistics that are to be used by the sales-forecasting function. Aside from bookkeeping mistakes, which I shall not discuss, errors in the order-processing function involve informing a customer that an item is not available when it really is, and promising delivery to a customer when the stock actually is not available. A well managed function processes orders promptly to minimize delays in shipment to customers, and bills promptly to collect revenues owed by customers.

Having defined each of the management functions that comprise the entire system, I now shall return to the third step of the design phase, namely selecting the proper approaches for carrying out these management functions. I shall describe some practical design alternatives, and indicate the degree to which operations-research approaches have proved useful in dealing with the design requirements that I have just enumerated.

I hope that my discussion of the six management functions to be performed, and in particular, of the way they impact each other, has made clear that a total-system design is required. Trying to design each function by looking at it in isolation is not likely to result in an improvement over a company's present system. Rather, the functional interdependencies are so many and so complex that a designer must choose a place in the system to start, and then proceed in a logical fashion from one function to the next until the entire system fits together. The interactions among the functions require building two devices into the system design: one consists of information-feedback mechanisms that can cause a function to alter its proposed plans on the basis of the response of other functions; the other consists of decouplers or buffers that permit the functions to operate on a day-to-day basis without having to coordinate every single decision among all functions. The most common example of a buffer device is inventory. A criterion of good design is that the system will not come to a crashing halt if there is a minor malfunction in one of its parts, and will give an early warning when serious trouble lies ahead.

Based on my own experience with several companies of the type that I have described, I shall explain a design approach that I find successful. The initial point of entry into the total-system design is the task of long-term sales forecasting. Given historical sales information and other relevant data, the forecasting function provides annual projections of potential company-wide sales by item, possibly aggregated into product lines. Typically these annual sales projections are broken down by month, sometimes only by quarter. When a product can be made at more than one factory, regional sales breakouts are also needed.

On the basis of these sales forecasts and forecasts of productive capacity over the same intervals of time, a long-term production plan is developed. This plan shows the anticipated quantities by item and by factory that will be manufactured for each month, and frequently for each week. The plan also should examine, for each stockage point, minimum inventory targets desired to maintain adequate customer service. Changes in these minimums throughout the year can affect the amount of production required. Actually, the specific dates and production quantities in this plan are of much less importance than the implied figures for weekly capacity utilization of each factory and facility and for the system-wide inventory levels throughout the year. At this stage of analysis, the production planners must examine the production economies and annual demand for each item to determine targeted run quantities and time intervals between successive runs.

The output of the long-term production plan, and more specifically, the targets for system-wide inventory levels, are then used by the distribution-planning function to devise policy guidelines for where to position inventory stock at different periods during the year. To illustrate, as inventory builds up prior to peak sales, the stocks may be shipped out to district or field warehouses that serve customers directly. Then, as stocks diminish as sales exceed production, more stock may be kept back at central warehouses and shipped to a sales region only after a customer order has been received. The distribution-planning function also must decide which warehouses are to receive additions to stock based on a central review of system inventories and which warehouses are permitted to replenish inventory based on their own calculations of stock requirements. The terminology sometimes used to distinguish these two alternatives is a 'push' system and a 'pull' system. Linear programming models for production and inventory planning typically imply a push system, whereas standard probabilistic inventory models for inventory replenishment typically imply a pull system.

Having determined targeted capacity-utilization figures, recommended run quantities and frequencies, and inventory build-up plans, as well as the minimum inventory levels desired for adequate customer service, one can then make short-term production plans. The long-term plan is usually made annually for 12 to 18 months, with revisions that occur every three months to extend the plan so that it continues to look ahead for the same time span. The short-term plan is made and revised much more frequently, often every week or two, looking ahead for enough weeks into the future to permit the production-scheduling and materials-ordering function to plan adequately. The short-term plan, in brief, is achieved by looking at forecast sales over the short-term planning horizon, such as thirteen weeks, and the current and projected levels of inventory, given the production already scheduled. Thus, the planner can project the amount of inventory for each item measured in weeks of supply beyond the factory's firm production schedule, that is, beyond the manufacturing lead time. Typically, some items will be in short supply, but during a period of inventory build-up, most items may be in ample supply. Depending on the relative amounts of inventory held for each item, it is usually necessary to again measured in weeks of supply, items are selected for production so as to utilize the targeted capacity fully; that is, items in shortest supply (earliest to run out) are scheduled for production. The production quantities depend on the economies of run length and the anticipated date for next producing the item. Recall that the targeted capacity and the run length and frequency figures are taken from the long-term production plan.

The production-scheduling function bases its decisions on the short-term production plan. The immediate two to four weeks of the schedule are held firm to avoid costly disruptions at the factory. The materials-ordering function must distinguish between supplies that require a long lead time and those that are readily available. For long-lead-time goods, the long-term production plan is needed. For the other supplies, the short-term plan is sufficient, unless there are substantial economies for ordering in large quantities that provide supplies beyond the short-term planning horizon. The materials-ordering function can frequently make its decisions guided by the inventory-replenishment procedures that have appeared in the operations-research literature.

The design that I have outlined does not treat all the tasks that I mentioned previously, but the remaining ones can be designed separately so as to operate consistently with the suggested structure.

Please note that what I have described is really a design type for a production and inventory system in the kind of manufacturing company that I have assumed. In other words, what I have suggested is a time sequence for each of the planning tasks and the type of rules to be used. In any actual application, the systems designer must select the specific parameter values for the design, such as the planning intervals, the revision frequencies, the timeliness and frequency of the information reports, the level of customer service to provide, the amount of inventory build-up to permit, the amount of raw-materials safety-stock to allow, and so forth. For the most part, operations-research techniques and tools have been useful in setting some of the design parameters, mostly in conjunction with long-term planning, and only occasionally in providing the system rules themselves. I shall now elaborate on this claim.

As I mentioned earlier, linear programming models have proved practical in formulating a long-term production plan. By dealing with product lines or families, such models can provide an initial aggregate plan, compute the appropriate inventory build-up, and allocate production to alternative plants and facilities. Sometimes it is feasible to include within a linear programming production-planning model the decision options regarding which warehouses ought to serve as supply sources for customers. On other occasions, the question of sourcing customer orders, as well as the locations and sizes of warehouses, can be treated by a separate mathematical programming model. I must hasten to add that there are many companies that do not require using linear programming models for these analyses, although some formal model that systematically compares costs for different production and distribution choices is usually essential. A common by-product of having a formal model for long-term production planning is that it can be used to test the impact of adding different kinds of capacity, and can help show when capacity additions are required.

The operations-research literature on determining economic run quantities provides workable first approximations that can be used in both long- and short-term production planning. In real situations, however, it is usually necessary to modify the quantities found by textbook formulas to take account of the many special circumstances that govern feasible choices for run quantities.

Similarly, the operations-research literature on inventory replenishment and safety-stock levels that yield desired customer service can be applied, oftentimes without much modification, to determining minimum inventory levels to hold at the various stocking points, and to specifying raw-material and supply reordering rules.

The area of sales forecasting has received considerable attention by operations researchers, who have developed some helpful approaches. But it is unrealistic, in my opinion, to expect that any mechanical methods for forecasting will ever relieve the company's management of the necessity of reviewing and modifying mechanically produced forecasts. Thus, the scientific sales projections from forecasting methods have to be viewed as only an intermediate piece of information to the forecasting function and not the output.

Of course, I do not wish to minimize the importance of all these operations-research contributions to the design of improved production- and inventory-planning systems. But, as you can see from the description that I gave of the management functions comprising such a system, all the tasks that they must perform, their information needs, the amount of detail that they must handle economically, and the feedback devices that they require to correct errors, we should hold no illusions as to how extensive the impact of such operations-research approaches has been.

The fourth step in the design phase of the entire study deals in part with defining the information files to be used by the decision makers. I have already mentioned many of the information files required in discussing the functions to be performed and in suggesting an approach for a system design; hence, I shall not repeat them again. This particular step is usually performed by data-processing analysts within a company working as a team with the system designers.

The fourth step also involves preparing the requirements and a development timetable for new manual operating procedures and computerized information and control systems. Depending on how advanced the company's present production- and inventory-planning system is, and on how talented its data processing staff is, this step may produce a development timetable extending from six months to two years with a staff effort of as many as five to ten system programmers. It has been my observation that companies that plan too large a development program usually fail to obtain the desired results. The time-table can be represented by a Gantt chart, and must show, for each system to be developed, the timing, the number of full-time staff required, and the skill levels of this staff. It is useful to make a 'most likely,' an 'optimistic,' and a 'pessimistic' time-table, each of which differs in its assumptions of staff availability and task development time.

Recall that the fifth step in the design phase consists of testing and estimating the economic results of the proposed design. Some companies actually choose to skip this step. They are persuaded by the force of their own logic in the development of the system that it must be an improvement worth making, and go directly to the implementation phase. My own attitude is more conservative, and I usually recommend that the design be pretested prior to implementation to determine design deficiencies.

For example, we need a better understanding of when a 'push' system operates better than a 'pull' system, when inventories should be built up at district warehouses instead of central warehouses, and how often to revise plans.

4. It would be insightful to examine approaches of behavioral scientists that could facilitate the implementation of new management planning and control systems.

I hope that some readers will turn their attention to these vital and difficult research areas.

REFERENCE

1. Michael M. Connors, Claude Coray, Carol J. Cuccaro, William K. Green, David W. Low, and Harry M. Markowitz, "The Distribution System Simulator," *Management Sci.* **18**, 425–453 (1972).

At this step, the analyst should use a powerful operations-research technique, namely, computer simulation. Actually, it is about the only tool that we have for evaluating the full impact of a total-system design. The most sophisticated simulation model that I know is described in the April 1972 issue of *Management Science*.[1] This model, developed under IBM sponsorship, permits the analyst to describe his own company by means of answering a long, detailed questionnaire. The computer program then develops a full simulation model that can be used to test a proposed design. It is my understanding that an American company desiring to use this program would have to spend over $32,000 to purchase it from IBM. Regardless of whether a company chooses to use the sophisticated IBM program or develop a simpler version for itself, computer simulation can be an expensive approach to testing a system design. But at this time I know of no approach other than computer simulation that will give equally reliable estimates of the service and inventory levels for a proposed system design for a multi-item, multiwarehouse system.

The entire design phase, consisting of the five steps that I outlined, is at least a three-to-five-person effort over a period of four to six months.

The *third* and final *phase* of the entire study is the implementation stage of the recommended new system. There are three important elements in this phase. The first is, if possible, beginning the implementation with a pilot test, that is, trying the new approaches with only part of the system so as to work out any unforeseen difficulties. Of course, this possibility is not always available or practical, but, when it is possible, it usually serves to make the remaining tasks of implementation much easier.

The second element is the adoption of information-reporting systems that can monitor how well the new system is performing. Frequently these systems coincide with the information needs of the new approaches themselves, such as measurements of customer service. But problems of communication delays, for example, are not always captured by the routine information-gathering systems and can have a large impact on the system's success.

The third element of the implementation phase is often critical, but equally often overlooked by technical specialists. It may be necessary to implement key organizational changes within the company to make the new system work well and be an improvement over the old system. To illustrate, it may be necessary to name managers of new functions, or to combine several functions under a single manager. Most of the feedback devices that operate within a production and inventory system are affected by the organizational-responsibility arrangements.

* * *
* * *

Before closing, I want to mention four problems that operations researchers could usefully study to advance today's state of the art.

1. It would be helpful to have some practical analytic models that could be used to diagnose how much improvement potential exists in an existing production- and inventory-planning system, before designing and testing an alternative system.

2. It would be valuable to have analytic approximations that could estimate the operating characteristics and economic results of a proposed system without having to resort to lengthy computer simulation.

3. It would be worthwhile to have some rules of thumb, developed from analytic studies, to guide the basic design of a production- and inventory-planning system.

OMEGA, The Int. Jl of Mgmt Sci., Vol. 2, No. 6, 1974

Production Planning and Control in a National Statistical Agency

DAVID P DEZIEL

DAVID M CARLILE[1]

Bureau of Management Consulting
Department of Supply and Services, Ottawa

(Received August 1973; in revised form November 1973)

The collection, analysis and dissemination of national statistical information can be likened to a manufacturing process. Despite obvious differences, the strength and extent of the analogy is such that it provides a powerful argument for the organisation of the production of statistics along industrial lines. This paper describes the implementation of this approach in Statistics Canada, the Canadian national statistical agency. It discusses the problems which indicated the need for action and the proposed activities of the centralised Production Planning and Control Branch (now in operation).

INTRODUCTION

THE COLLECTION, analysis, and dissemination of statistics can be likened in many aspects to a production process. In controlling this process, managers are concerned with matters of throughput time, quality, resource balancing and production efficiency. This paper describes work carried out in one national statistical agency, Statistics Canada, to develop and implement OR techniques for production planning and control. An analogy is drawn between the operations of a statistical agency and those of a typical industrial operation. Borrowing from this analogy, procedures for scheduling and production planning in a statistical agency are outlined.

Government managers are not accustomed to thinking in industrial terms nor to using the terminology of the factory. This paper describes the problems encountered, first in gaining acceptance for the industrial analogy and second in collecting valid data with which to develop and test the production planning and scheduling system. The resolution of these problems is indicated and steps

leading to the implementation of a system for production planning and control are described.

In Canada, statistical information is collected, analysed and disseminated by a centralized statistical agency known as Statistics Canada. Formed in 1918, this agency is charged with developing and operating a centralized and fully co-ordinated statistical system to provide statistical information essential to the activities of government, industry, labour, universities and other bodies. The demand for such information has grown enormously in recent years due mainly to the increased complexity and sophistication of our institutions, but also as a result of advances in data handling technology, and improved statistical sampling and analysis techniques.

While the demand for statistical services has expanded rapidly, there has been a relatively less rapid increase in the availability of resources. Thus, there exists an imbalance between supply and demand so that statistical resources must be viewed as a scarce commodity to be carefully rationed [3]. For this reason, the question of how to allocate resources among competing demands and how to ensure the maximum return from a given allocation are matters of utmost concern to any statistical office. Indeed, the argument for centralizing statistics-gathering activity rests partly on the need to achieve higher operating efficiency through operating economies associated with large-scale operation. Of course, such economies only accrue if the activities of a central organization are fully integrated and this problem is being addressed on two fronts in Statistics Canada. On the one hand, data and information that flow through the statistical system need to be integrated across the various statistical programs and rendered coherent. This task constitutes one of the main challenges for planning [2], and forms part of the ongoing developmental activity in any large statistical office. On the other hand, there is the need to integrate and co-ordinate the internal activities which act in concert with the flow of statistical data and information. This is the task of production planning and control; the need for such a system will now be outlined.

The need

By 1971, Statistics Canada had grown to a staff of more than 3500 employees with an annual budget of 38 million dollars. Of the total workforce, over 1000 were professionals with the remainder employed in technical and administrative support functions. Professional effort was organized along subject matter lines, that is to say, separate groups were employed in producing the various kinds of statistics (financial, economic, socio-economic and economic accounts). Within each subject matter area there was a requirement for both professional and service activities. However, whereas the professional expertise was supplied from experts working within the group, service functions (such as typing, printing, data processing, field services and so forth) were obtained from a central pool of so-called 'common services'. At that time, no overall system of

---

[1]Now with R.T.Z. Consultants Limited.

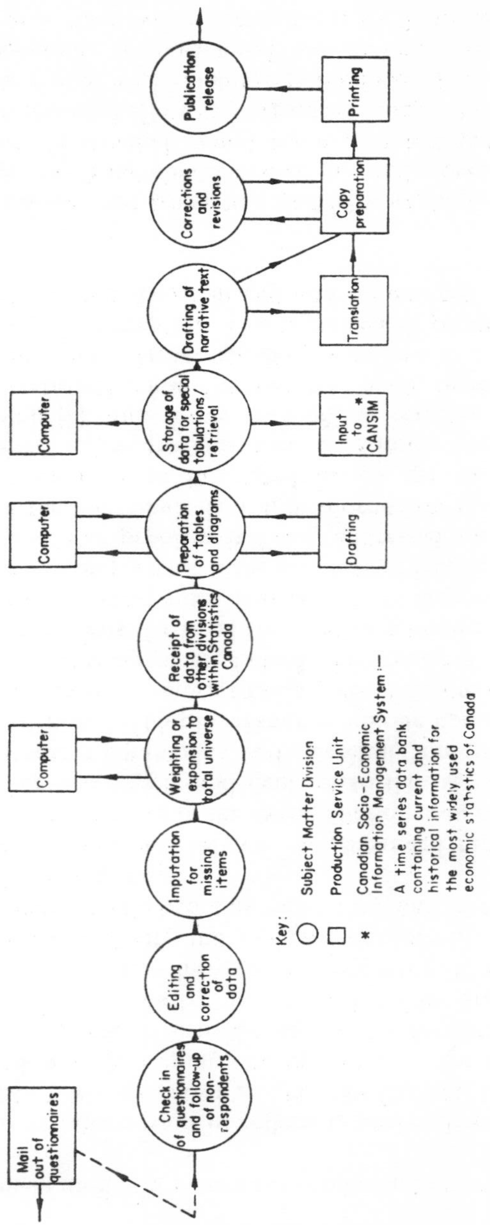

Fig. 1. *Work steps in producing a publication.*

production planning and control existed; although several systems were in operation, each functioned within a given subject matter area with little control or planning authority in relation to the common services.

The difficulties inherent in such a system were manifest. Bottlenecks and lengthy delays resulted from the uneven workload on common services. These in turn led to additional production costs through overtime payments, while during slack periods facilities were idle and valuable productive capacity was lost. Production techniques were not standardized, and innovations carried out in one part of the organization often were not translated to other areas. But worst of all, the entire process seemed to be getting out of hand. Attempts to dislodge one piece of work caught up in the system only served to delay others. Studies carried out to assess the capacity requirements for selected common services provided only temporary respite, and while efforts to expedite highly important surveys on a routine basis were partly successful, it was recognized that this had been achieved at the expense of other important work and that further gains could only be achieved if all parts of the statistical system were considered simultaneously.

Thus, in 1970, a study was undertaken to develop a system for production planning and control in Statistics Canada. This study began by devising a framework to describe Statistics Canada activities, formulating a scheme to deal with the problems, testing it and drawing up a plan for implementation. In what follows, each of the above steps will be outlined.

THE FRAMEWORK

While Statistics Canada is primarily a professional organization, there are many ways in which its operations closely resemble those of a manufacturer [1]. Where a typical manufacturer takes in raw material and processes it to produce a finished product, Statistics Canada takes in raw data and through a series of operations, many of them complex and interrelated, converts these to finished statistics. As in manufacturing, much emphasis is placed on quality, timeliness and work efficiency, also there are often severe difficulties associated with measuring quality and some aspects of work output.

The analogy can be extended further: The publication itself can be thought of as the output from the production process. Raw data correspond to raw materials; the activities of procurement, production, quality control and distribution have counterparts in data collection, manipulation/analysis/presentation, quality control and distribution. Figure 1 shows these worksteps in some detail.

In a production operation, certain raw materials (or components) can be brought together to form sub-assemblies. These, in turn, assembled in various configurations lead to different end products. In a statistical office, the raw

TABLE 1. MANAGEMENT ACTIVITIES OVER A LIFE CYCLE

Activity	Manufacturing firm	Statistical office
Market research	Identification of gaps in market which organization can fill. Measurement of market for products organization has developed.	Identification of new or changed information needs.
Research & development	Research into ways of satisfying known market need. Development of products with possible market potential.	Research into—type of data —availability —collection problems —statistical methodology
Product design	Definition of product in terms which satisfy known market need.	Determination of publication content and layout.
Production planning	Methods—design of production processes. Estimating—calculation of production times. Equipment—planning and designing of tools, jigs and fixtures. Facilities—adjustment of facilities in light of new product. Layout and routing—translation of production plans into detailed instructions. Materials records—allocation of material to a particular work order. Scheduling—the time allocation of jobs to processes.	Design of data collection methods (including questionnaire) and statistical methodology. Design of processing methods (clerical and automated). Same as for manufacturing. Same as for manufacturing. Same as for manufacturing. Same as for manufacturing.
Production control	Initiation—release of production orders. Expediting—shop floor monitoring and control, maintenance of communications. Transportation—movement of men and material within the plant.	Same as for manufacturing. Same as for manufacturing. Same as for manufacturing.
Inventory control	Stores management. Purchasing and receiving. Quantity control. Simplification.	Mail out survey. Receipt. Follow-up.
Quality control	Inspection of incoming goods. Process control. Inspection of outgoing goods.	Checking incoming surveys. Cut-off decision. Clerical quality control. Rationality check on results. Quality of publication.

data are manipulated into time series which constitute the sub-assemblies for the finished product, the publication.

A statistical office operates on a batch production basis, with its outputs (publications) scheduled according to the reference period (monthly, quarterly, annually, etc.). In addition, there is a certain amount of job-shop production (special publications) and even component manufacture—in the form of special surveys. There are prototypes (surveys and publications conducted initially on an experimental basis), production models, and obsolescence (statistical publications no longer required by users). The parallel is strong enough to suggest that the operations of a statistical office should be regarded as production with management of this activity organized along industrial lines.

Figure 2 shows the sequence of management activities that take place over

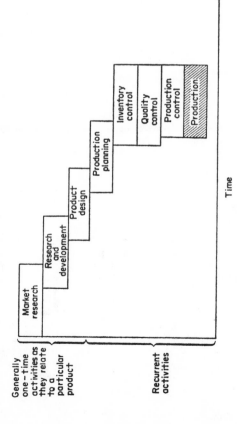

FIG. 2. *Management activities over a product life cycle.*

the life cycle of a typical manufactured product. For the most part terms used are self-explanatory; however, a brief account of each is contained in Table 1. In a statistical office a similar activity sequence takes place over the life cycle of each publication. Table 1 lists these activities and highlights their relationship to corresponding activities in a manufacturing operation. With this framework as a basis, the study proceeded to re-cast the activities for production planning and control in a manufacturing environment into a form suitable for implementation in a statistical office.

THE SYSTEM

(A) Production control

The system for controlling production can be characterized by the flow of information and authorizations that govern the operation of the production

11

system. The information cycle begins with schedule information fed from the "subject matter divisions" to the Production Planning and Control unit which then combines the schedules to determine the total workload requirement and to signal the need for adjustments where necessary.

The basic schedules are then used to provide a separate breakdown of work requirements for each production service and this information is fed back to the production services. At the same time, schedule information fed to subject matter divisions enables them to set their own deadlines for providing work to common service areas. Monitoring of production progress allows Production Planning and Control to arrange short-term schedule changes and also to periodically report to all levels of management the performance of production units.

These information flows are described in greater detail in Fig. 3. Basic schedules, provided by the subject matter divisions to Production Planning and Control, can be prepared annually and updated as necessary at the end of each reference period. These basic schedules are then combined to provide a permanent Master Schedule of all production operations for all publications. From this Master Schedule, weekly production schedules for each production service unit are split out. In addition, monthly forecasts of future workload are prepared

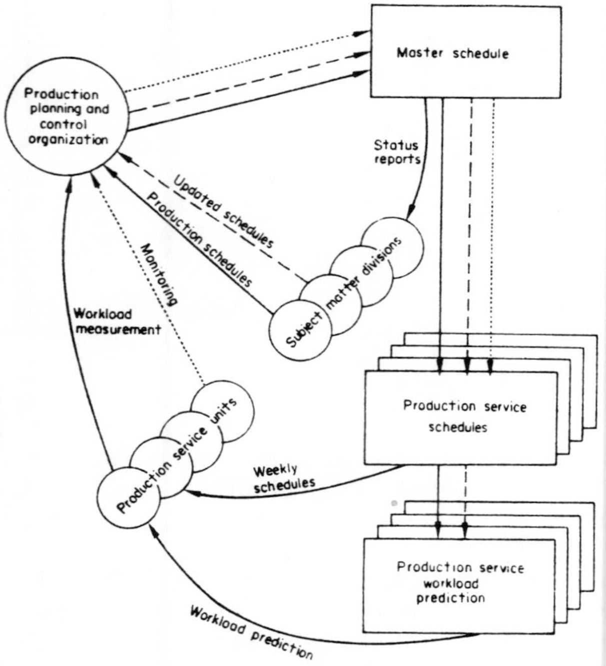

FIG. 3. *Detailed information flows.*

(in lesser detail than the weekly schedule) and submitted to each production service.

By means of daily formal reporting (and informal liaison) the progress of each publication through the production process is monitored. This information is used to create a permanent record of performance and the master schedule, to arrange short-term re-scheduling if target dates are missed or reached early, and to provide periodic performance summaries to both production service management and subject matter division staffs.

(B) *Production planning*

This activity comprises five elements as follows:

(*i*) *Process evaluation and improvement*

This involves evaluating each component of the production process to assess its effectiveness in terms of its ability to meet stated goals, and its efficiency in terms of the required resources, as well as exploring new ways of performing production tasks and assessing the impact of technological innovation.

(*ii*) *Work measurement*

Measurement or estimation of each component of the production sequence will be a regular review activity, so that the data bank of times will be constantly updated.

(*iii*) *Production design*

This function ensures that publications are designed in the most economical and effective manner (accepting that these may at times be conflicting criteria) from the production standpoint. The appearance of a publication, as well as the way in which data are collected and analysed, determine the production processes to be used and can have a strong influence on the cost of production. Recognition of this requires the involvement of Production Planning and Control staff with an interdisciplinary statistical design team at the stage in the development of a publication where decisions are made as to how the publication is physically to be produced.

(*iv*) *Output analysis*

This function affords a continual monitoring of the nature and characteristics of the output workloads on the production system. Because forward planning requires an accurate forecast of likely future production workloads, and since the nature of the workload is liable to change over time as the nature and characteristics of the output change, it is important to maintain a clear picture of the characteristics of this output.

Perhaps the most important contribution of output analysis is in measuring the existing level of production output to help estimate future output levels.

(v) Resource allocation

This function ensures that a balance is maintained among the production capacities at all stages in the production process. It determines for each stage the appropriate quiescent capacity and the most economical means of increasing capacity temporarily. Also, as part of long term planning, the resource allocation function determines the most economical expansion policy for each process stage, taking account of costs of adding capacity, the need to maintain a capacity balance, and the leadtimes involved in purchasing equipment and training personnel.

TESTING AND IMPLEMENTATION

The introduction of a Production Planning and Control system was not without its difficulties in an organization consisting largely of professionals, who already felt overburdened with bureaucratic procedures. Nevertheless, it could be demonstrated that planning and controlling production would do much to relieve this burden, and that while some early re-adjustment might be required, the system would lead to universal improvement in the long term. This message had an intrinsic appeal to workers at all levels of Statistics Canada, and to lay the groundwork for implementation phases it was advanced energetically at senior levels of the organization. Following formal approval, implementation proceeded in three phases:

Phase I (a) Test pilot scheduling system
(b) Brief Statistics Canada staff
(c) Take action to recruit staff

Phase II (a) Expand pilot system to include all Statistics Canada publications
(b) Establish a Methods unit
(c) Establish an Estimating unit

Phase III (a) Expand system to include all production activity (i.e. products which are not publications)
(b) Assign overall responsibility to Production Planning and Control (up to this point, it operates in parallel with existing procedures)
(c) Complete analysis to determine the optimal balance of resources

Since Phases II and III are now being carried forward by the Production Planning and Control Branch which has been established in Statistics Canada, we shall confine our remarks to the problems encountered in Phase I.

Phase I

The Pilot Scheduling System consisted of the collection of schedule information for a selection of publications from subject matter divisions and the develop-ment of methods for consolidating that information, transmitting it to production service units and monitoring progress. To begin with, the collection of schedule information presented some difficulties. Although some subject matter divisions maintained records of historical events relating to the production of their publications, fewer used these to draw up target schedules for future work. Working with divisional staff, we established such target schedules for the selected publications, but the information used was a mixture of fact, intent and aspiration. The validity of the information was, therefore, suspect, and had to be carefully watched during the pilot project.

All subject matter divisions think of units of production as publications, hence the consolidation of schedule information was straightforward. Problems arose, however, in transmitting workload information to the production service units prior to the preparation and printing of the final manuscript.

There were two linked reasons for these problems. Firstly, any publication may draw on a number of incoming streams of surveys (sub-components) for the information it prints. As a result, since survey streams tend to maintain their identity through mail-out and computation procedures, those production units tend to use work-reference codes associated with the survey form itself (not, alas, identical associations in every case!). Secondly, in the case of the computer unit, the reference code was the identifier of program(s) developed to handle one or several surveys or information streams coming from surveys. These problems were solved by using one publication trigger to mail several surveys, maintaining cross-indexed lists of the surveys which feed publications, setting up 'master' and 'slave' schedules for minor publications, and starting a study aimed at rationalizing the multiplicity of work reference codes in operation.

During the pilot project, a start was made on establishing the production information needs of various levels of management. Obviously, the level of aggregation of data on the timeliness of publications has to be different for different levels of management. Further, the performance of production units should perhaps be expressed in terms of both workload handled and timely completion of jobs.

The results of this pilot project were to demonstrate that the proposed production planning and control scheme was workable, that meaningful schedules could be obtained, that progress reporting was feasible and that a range of performance reports could be developed from the monitoring information collected.

Formal briefings of all Statistics Canada senior management were then held to outline the principles of the System being adopted and to provide a continuing dialogue between the project team and the executives who would ultimately be responsible for the success of the system.

The problems encountered at the working level were no different to those one would expect when introducing change into any organization. There was no problem at all with speaking of Statistics Canada's operations in terms of a manufacturing operation, this being the production-oriented end of the management spectrum.

At more senior levels, however, when dealing with the professional statistician it was in some cases necessary to dispel the impression that we regarded Statistics Canada as just another production line mindlessly churning out plastic daffodils. Once this was done, a strong measure of acceptance was accorded to the industrial analogy.

CONCLUSION

This paper focusses on the need to develop a systematic means for planning and controlling the activities and internal resources of a statistical office, and draws on the analogy with a manufacturing operation as blueprint for this purpose. The weight of this analogy has helped to provide a powerful argument in favour of the need for formal production management while at the same time providing guidance in the design of such a system. This represents an early attempt to translate the experiences of industry into the operations of a government agency, and the results of this attempt suggest that a wide range of government activities might be amenable to such an approach.

ACKNOWLEDGEMENTS

The authors wish to gratefully acknowledge the participation of senior staff of Statistics Canada whose assistance and support contributed to the success of this study, in particular, Mr. W E Duffett, former Chief Statistician of Canada, and Dr. S A Goldberg, former Assistant Chief Statistician of Canada. We are also indebted to the following members of Statistics Canada staff who, as part of the project team, assisted in every phase of the study; they are Mr. G A Richardson, Mr. R W Collins, Mr. B J Lynch, Mr J M Routhier, and Mr. E J Wilhelm. Finally, we wish to thank Dr. S Ostry, Mr. D A Worton and Mr. R E J Rose for having taken on the burden of implementation and for having given us permission to publish this paper.

REFERENCES

1. DUFFETT WE and GOLDBERG SA (1971) *Planning and Co-ordination in a Central Statistical Office.* Paper presented at the 38th Session of the International Statistical Institute, Washington, D.C.
2. EILON S (1962) *Elements of Production Planning and Control.* Macmillan, London.
3. GOVERNMENT OF CANADA (1962) *Report of the Royal Commission on Government Organization.*

2 / Production Planning

Production planning, in a mass production or job shop environments, is of great importance from profitability and service view points. This planning allows the best possible use of facilities within the constraints of policies regarding hiring, firing, inventory, subcontracting, and shop loading. The economic importance of these decisions are by no means minor, because they represent broad operating decisions that are implemented for planning horizons 6 to 12 months in the future. Inventories can be used to absorb seasonal changes in demand. However, this can be an expensive alternative when high interest rates exist. Changing the work force can allow an organization to accommodate seasonal demand swings, but again there are many costs existing when work force adjustments are made.

The first paper by Eilon provides an excellent survey of mathematical work done to date in this area. First, the paper outlines the basic planning problem, discussing relevant costs and problem structure. Second, he presents five approaches to assist in making decisions: linear decision rules, management coefficients method, mathematical programming, minimize production changes rule, and production switching heuristics. And third, he comments on the implementation and usefulness of all five methods.

The paper of Mellichamp and Love illustrates how to apply in detail production switching heuristics. The advantage of the approach is a reduction in the amount of period to period adjustment. This approach is quite consistent with a manager's natural inclination to maintain reasonable stability in his operations. It is a simpler approach than some others, increasing ease of implementation.

The paper by Glover et al illustrates an application of systematic planning for production, distribution, and inventory for Agrico Chemical Co. They illustrate an integrated planning system for not only production and distribution decisions, but also purchasing. The system allows an evaluation of production and purchase sizing decisions, distribution location points, transportation needs, and long term inventory investment.

Five Approaches to
Aggregate Production Planning

SAMUEL EILON

Department of Management Science
Imperial College of Science and Technology
Exhibition Road
London SW7 2BX ENGLAND

Abstract: Production scheduling problems are reviewed briefly and the smoothing problem is defined as planning the aggregate production level for each period in a given horizon to meet forecast demand. Five approaches to the problem are reviewed: (1) the HMMS linear decision rule for production and employment; (2) the DE rule for production, in which time lag is incorporated; (3) the management coefficients method; (4) the use of LP models; (5) the production switching method. The assumptions and objectives inherent in each approach are discussed and certain shortcomings are indicated.

■ Planning of aggregate production within a given framework of facilities is concerned with determining the level of production in each period over a specified horizon. To see this problem in its proper context, it is convenient to identify three types of production systems:

1. *Job production*—where a stream of orders have to be processed on common facilities or production centres, each job having its own unique specifications and requirements in terms of production resources. A job may consist of a single item or a batch of identical items. The scheduling problem here is concerned with setting the sequence with which jobs should be processed at each production centre.

2. *Batch production*—where a continuous demand for certain products exists, but because the rate of production exceeds the rate of demand, there is a need to produce products in batches. The scheduling problem here is concerned with determining the batch sizes for products and the order in which they should be produced.

3. *Continuous production*—where the demand for a product justifies its production on a continuous basis, but because of fluctuating demand it is desirable to adjust the production level from time to time.

Received November 1974, revised February 1975.

By definition, the first two categories are concerned with multi-products, since the single product case is meaningless in job production and trivial in batch production. Continuous production, on the other hand, may well involve only a single product, or at least a product with such minor variations from the production or inventory viewpoint, that considering the production problem on an aggregate level is justified. In the case of multi-products in continuous production the conflict between products competing for limited production resources is essentially the same as in batch production.

Perhaps a more important distinction is between problems concerned with sequencing and those concerned with production levels, as illustrated in Fig. 1. When jobs need to be processed on several machines in some given sequence, as in Fig. 1(a), the production system consists of several queues in tandem, where a job proceeds from one queue to another until processing is complete and the job leaves the system. Here the question of production levels does not arise, since the processing requirements for each job are specified in advance. The problem is to steer the job through the system, where alternative routes exist, and to determine the queueing discipline at each queue, namely to order the jobs in the sequence in which they are to be processed by each machine [9].

In Fig. 1(b) each product proceeds through a single processing facility and then leaves the production system. The problem of sequencing encountered in case (a) does not

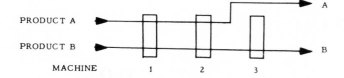

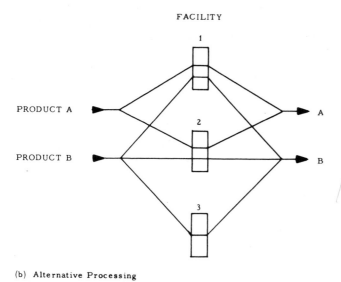

(a) Sequential Processing

FACILITY

(b) Alternative Processing

Fig. 1. Sequential and alternative processing

arise or is considered irrelevant. If a product can be processed on alternative facilities, as in the example shown in Fig. 1(b), the question of allocating facilities to products needs to be resolved, as well as the question of the production level for each product.

Table 1 summarises the type of problems that management scientists have been considering in recent years. In continuous production a distinction is made between the single and the multi-product case. The former is a special case of the example shown in Fig. 1(b) and has been called in the literature *the production smoothing problem.* The multi-product case may be regarded either as an aggregate production smoothing problem, in which the global production level for the system as a whole is determined (with subsequent disaggregation routines), or as a variant of the batch production problem, and these alternative approaches provide the basis for some of the models proposed for solving the problem.

Table 1 is intended as a guide and not as a comprehensive classification system for production scheduling problems. It

Table 1: Types of problems [9].				
	No. of products		Control concerned with	
	one	several	sequencing	production level
Job shop	-	✓	✓	•
Batch	-	✓	-	✓
Continuous $\begin{cases} a \end{cases}$	✓	-	-	✓
	-	✓	-	✓
*a*This is the production smoothing problem.				

shows certain features common to batch and continuous production and it distinguishes between the sequencing problem and the production-level problem. This is not to say that in practice both cannot occur in the same production environment. Indeed they frequently do. The proposed distinction between them is merely a matter of convenience, which reflects the methods of analysis employed in the study of these problems.

In this paper we are largely concerned with the production smoothing problem, in which it is assumed that essentially there is a single product processed through the plant, and we are required to specify the production and manpower levels for each period over a given horizon.

The Problem

The production system is considered as a single facility which handles a single product. Time is divided into discrete periods and demand forecasts for future periods are given. Demand is stochastic, so that discrepancies between forecasts and actual demand values may occur.

Figure 2 shows cumulative and production demand curves. The vertical difference between them denotes inventory (which turns into a "runout" or shortage when cumulative demand exceeds cumulative production) and the horizontal difference denotes storage time (assuming depletion on a first-in-first-out basis).

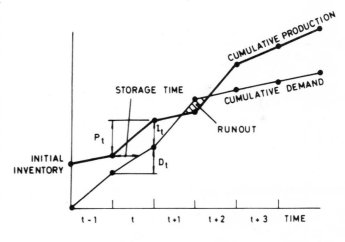

Fig. 2. Production and demand.

Three possible strategies may be considered for production planning to handle this case [7]:

(a) *Have a static production programme,* coupled with an inventory large enough to satisfy the fluctuating demand. The inventory level would fluctuate according to the demand pattern, replenishment being provided by a constant flow from the plant. This method is greatly favoured by the production department, since it simplifies planning, ensures higher machine utilisation, allows better supervision and control, and promotes a sense of security among the workers. Average stock level is high, however, thus tying up capital and involving high carrying costs.

(b) *Have a fluctuating production programme*, to cater for the changing demand, and keep a constant inventory level to provide a safety cushion between production and marketing. Any change in the demand pattern requires a certain time lag before production can follow suit, and the safety stock enables management to satisfy demand in the interim period. The stock level does not, strictly speaking, remain constant, but the fluctuations and the average stock level are fairly low, compared with the previous method.

(c) *Have a combination of the two systems*, so as to bring the total costs to a minimum. The problem is, therefore, to achieve a proper balance between the amount of fluctuations in the production programme and those of the stock level.

This problem of production for fluctuating demand may be illustrated graphically as a network flow [17]. Sales forecasting and production planning are broken down into periods. The network consists of a chain of identical units, each unit representing one for production and the other for inventory. The flow in the network is as indicated by the arrows in Fig. 3 (in which the *ith* time period is shown), and the flow must always be positive. A certain amount of

At any point of intersection in the network we must have equilibrium of flow; namely, the flow into the intersection is equal to the flow coming out of it. On the production flow line: (previous capacity) + (any increase) − (any decrease) = (output) = (capacity carried over to the next period). On the inventory line: (previous inventory) + (output) = (sales) + (inventory carried over to the next cycle). Bearing in mind these conventions, we can omit the arrows in the network (leaving the quantities in each link) and represent the three strategies listed earlier in graphical form as shown in Fig. 4.

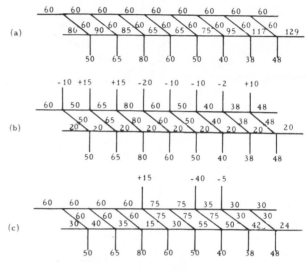

(a)   A static production programme
(b)   A static inventory programme
(c)   A combination of (a) and (b)

Fig. 4. Policies in analysing production smoothing problems

The problem before us can be formulated as follows: Given the demand forecast F_t for any period t in the planning horizon, which extends over T periods, determine the production level P_t and the work force W_t for time t (where $t = 1, \ldots, T$).

Various methods for solving this problem have been suggested in the literature, ranging from simulation to search procedures, heuristic rules, and explicit mathematical solutions. In this paper we confine our discussion to the following five methods:

A. The HMMS decision rule

B. The DE decision rule

C. The management coefficients method

D. Mathematical programming

E. Production switching.

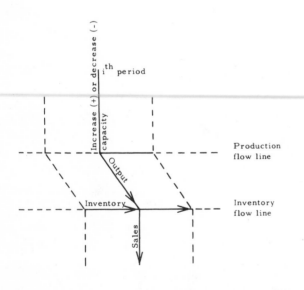

Fig. 3. A network presentation of production and inventory (see [17]).

production capacity is carried over through the productive flow line from the preceding period. At the beginning of the period one can plan to increase the capacity (by adding labour, machines, overtime, subcontracting) or to reduce it (by lowering the labour force, etc.). The output flows into the inventory line, from which a certain quantity is tapped for sale.

The smoothing problem was studied extensively by Holt, Modigliani, Muth and Simon (hence their method is called *the HMMS decision rule*), who suggested that four cost factors should be accounted for [2, 16]. (The parameters c_1, c_2 etc. below are constants):

(1) *Regular production costs in period* t

$$c_t(1) = c_1 W_t \qquad (1)$$

The assumption here is that the cost is linearly related to the size of the workforce W_t. An additional fixed cost term can be added to Eq. (1), but that would not affect the solution.

(2) *Hiring and firing*

The cost of increasing or decreasing the work force is assumed to take the form of the quadratic function

$$c_t(2) = c_2(W_t - W_{t-1})^2 \qquad (2)$$

where $W_t - W_{t-1}$ is the change in the level of the work force from interval $t - 1$ to t. Here the cost is assumed to be symmetrical, namely an increase or a decrease in the work force by a given amount incurs the same cost. Asymmetry in the cost function can be introduced, for example, by

$$c_t(2) = c_2(W_t - W_{t-1} - c_{10})^2 \qquad (3)$$

but HMMS state [16, p53] that this additional constant "proves to be irrelevant in obtaining optimal decisions."

(3) *Cost of overtime*

It is assumed that for a given production level there is a corresponding desirable level of labour requirements and that the cost of overtime and undertime is

$$c_t(3) = c_3(P_t - c_4 W_t)^2 + c_5 P_t - c_6 W_t. \qquad (4)$$

This function has a point of minimum where the production level matches the work force. HMMS add that c_5 turns out to be irrelevant in making the scheduling decisions because in the long term the cumulative production is unaffected by the decision rule [16, p53].

(4) *Cost of inventory*

If the inventory level at the end of period t is I_t then

$$I_t = I_{t-1} + P_t - S_t \qquad (5)$$

where I_{t-1} = inventory level at the end of period $t - 1$

P_t = the production in period t

S_t = the sales or shipment from the manufacturing plant in period t

The minimum cost inventory level is assumed to be linearly related to the demand, taking the form

$$c_8 + c_9 F_t$$

where F_t is the forecast demand for period t. In fact, it is known from inventory theory that the optimal inventory level is proportional not to demand but to its square root, while in the HMMS model it is assumed that the linear relationship is an adequate approximation.

The total cost of inventory, including holding costs and runout costs, are then assumed to take the quadratic form

$$c_t(4) = c_7[I_t (c_8 + c_9 F_t)]^2 . \qquad (6)$$

The Solution

The total cost for period t is then

$$c_t = c_t(1) + c_t(2) + c_t(3) + c_t(4) \qquad (7)$$

and over T periods

$$C_T = \Sigma c_t \qquad (8)$$

where henceforth Σ stands for $\Sigma_{t=1}^{T}$ unless stated otherwise.

The problem posed by the HMMS model is as follows: Find the values of P_t and W_t that will minimise the total cost function (8). When derivatives of the quadratic cost function are taken, linear expressions are obtained and the solution can finally be reduced to the following form:

$$P_t = a_0 F_t + a_1 F_{t+1} + a_2 F_{t+2} + \ldots + g_1 W_{t-1} - h_1 I_{t-1} + e_1 \qquad (9)$$

$$W_t = b_0 F_t + b_1 F_{t+1} + b_2 F_{t+2} + \ldots + g_2 W_{t-1} - h_2 I_{t-1} + e_2. \qquad (10)$$

These are the production and employment linear decision rules, where all the lower case coefficients are constants. Each expression consists of a series of terms that include the forecasts for a given number of future periods and each rule takes account of the present (i.e. at the end of period $t - 1$) levels of employment and inventory.

In the example of a paint factory, which the authors quote in connection with their study, production planning was carried out on a monthly basis and forecasts were available for twelve months. The results[1] suggest that:

---

[1] The results cited in [2] are only marginally different from those given in [16, p. 61].

- All the a's and all the b's are smaller than 1.
- The a's and the b's decline rapidly, so that forecasts for the immediate future are weighted more heavily than those for the more distant future; in the example quoted, half the forecasts (for the latter periods) could be ignored without any significant effect on the results
- $g_1, g_2 > 0$, i.e. the higher the present level of the work force, the higher the future level of activity
- $h_1, h_2 > 0$, i.e. a high level of inventory has the effect of reducing the values of P_t and W_t but too low a level of inventory has the opposite effect because of the positive value of the last term in these decision rules.
- HMMS studied the effect of errors in estimating the cost parameters and say: "we conclude that an estimating accuracy of, say, $\pm 50\%$ is probably adequate for practical purposes. This accuracy will yield decision rules whose cost performance is tolerably close to the minimum possible" [16, p165]. This conclusion is supported by other writers [22]
- The HMMS decision rules are based on demand forecasts, unbiased forecasts being treated exactly as if they were perfect forecasts [16, p60]; the variance of the demand distribution has no effect on the decisions. Actual orders (as opposed to forecasts) are accounted for only indirectly by the effect they have on the inventory level I_{t-1} which is included in the decision rules
- A comparisor of the HMMS rules for alternative forecasting procedures with the hypothetical case of perfect forecasts provides an indication of the desirability to improve forecasting in any given situation.

Comments on the HMMS Rule

Criticisms of the HMMS model fall into several categories. The first relates to the assumptions of the cost functions. Their quadratic form is clearly a matter of mathematical convenience (in that the derivatives of these functions lead to the linear decision rules in Eqs. (9) and (10)) and this may be justifiable over a narrow range; nevertheless, it is arbitrary and may be a source of serious errors.

What is the justification, for example, for assuming that the cost of hiring and firing is a quadratic function? HMMS suggest [16, p53] that the plausibility of this assumption rests on the argument that "reorganization costs are more than proportionately larger for large layoffs than for small layoffs; and similarly the efficiency of hiring, measured in terms of the quality of the employees hired, may fall when a large number of people are hired at one time," but why should this increase costs? Such an argument defeats the notion of economies of scale, which is intuitively far more plausible.

The quadratic form of overtime costs in Eq. (4) is, in some ways, even more baffling. In practice overtime rates are paid in direct proportion to the amount of overtime; sometimes a further higher rate applies above a certain

level of overtime, for example in the case of third shifts or weekend working. A piecewise linear cost function is perhaps a better description of such a situation, so that a quadratic form can only be regarded as an approximation. Another objection is that Eq. (4) also expresses the cost of undertime, namely the cost of the work force being idle when the scheduled production rate is too low. It may be argued that the cost of the labour force, whether it is gainfully employed or not, is already included in the regular payroll in Eq. (1) and that to impose a further penalty for undertime is not appropriate.

Similarly, the justification for a quadratic function for inventory costs is dubious. Since inventory is a major factor in designing an aggregate production schedule, alternative strategies over a wide range need to be considered and this implies that the use of a quadratic function, which may provide a reasonable fit over a short range, may generate wide margins of error.

It is interesting to quote in this context some results (see Table 2) from the case study of the paint factory

Table 2: Cost comparisons (x 10^3 dollars).			
	Company performance	HMMS	
		Moving av.	perfect forecast
Regular payroll	1940	1834	1888
Overtime	196	296	167
Inventory holding	361	451	454
Back orders	1566 }1927	616 }1067	400 }854
Hiring and layoffs	22	25	20
Total	4085	3222	2929
Total excluding back orders	2519	2606	2529
Hiring and layoffs as % of total	0.5	0.8	0.7

reported by HMMS [16]. The company's performance for 1949-53 was compared with the linear decision rule, first based on a moving average forecast and secondly on the assumption of having perfect forecasts.

Several interesting features of these results should be noted:

(1) The regular payroll is not greatly affected by the introduction of the HMMS rule.

(2) The cost of hiring and firing is so small (well under 1% of the total costs) that the advantage of including this cost term in the model is rather questionable.

(3) The reduction in costs envisaged by the HMMS rule is almost entirely due to reduction in total inventory costs, and this is achieved in the main by drastically reducing the cost of back orders through an increase in the average inventory level. In fact, if the cost of back orders were ignored altogether, the results for the HMMS

rule would prove to be no better than the company performance (Table 2). Bearing in mind the somewhat arbitrary manner in which runout costs are sometimes evaluated in practice, this result is certainly one which management is likely to view with some reservation.

The HMMS rule triggered off several investigations into the production smoothing problem and many of these studies are reviewed elsewhere [5, 21]. An interesting point is made by Peterson [20] regarding the basic assumption in the HMMS model that the amount S_t shipped by the manufacturer to the wholesaler in period t is the same as the amount ordered D_t (i.e. $S_t \equiv D_t$ and he suggests that if the manufacturer were to disregard this identity, he would have three decision variables at his disposal (P_t, W_t and S_t) instead of the two considered by the HMMS rule (P_t and W_t). In this way the manufacturer introduces an additional degree of freedom into his decision matrix and it may sometimes be possible to determine cheaper production plans than those obtained by the HMMS rule, even though the manufacturer must be prepared to pay some penalty (in the form of compensation to the wholesaler) for not meeting the precise amount specified in the order. Peterson suggests that a term be added to the cost function (8), so that the total costs become

$$C_{TOT} = \sum (c_t + k Z_t^2) \qquad (11)$$

where

$$Z_t = \sum_{i=1}^{t} (D_t - S_t) \qquad (12)$$

is the cumulative imbalance between demand and shipment during the first t periods and k is a cost parameter. He goes on to show that a linear decision rule for S_t similar in structure to the rules for P_t and W_t, can be derived.

Peterson puts forward this idea as an alternative to the one indicated by Abramovitz [1], who suggests a tax on inventories in order to encourage the smoothing of orders. Another possibility is for the manufacturer to give the wholesaler a positive incentive to keep his orders constant [15], but there are some doubts as to whether the idea of an incentive or Peterson's idea of a deliberate imbalance Z_t between orders and shipments can be implemented in practice without changing fundamentally the structure of the production smoothing problem [8].

Rather than introduce a new decision variable Z_t it may be pertinent to consider a model where W_t is not independent of P_t In such a model a penalty would be imposed on increasing or decreasing the rate of production from P_{t-1} to P_t and this penalty would absorb the adjustments that need to be made in this level of the work force (this is discussed later).

The DE Decision Rule
The Model

A different approach to the production smoothing problem suggests that it is not the minimisation of an overall cost function that should be the planner's objective, but the minimisation of the fluctuations in production and inventory levels. This approach is exemplified by the method investigated by Deziel and Eilon [6], which will be referred to as the DE rule. Their model is based on the following assumptions:

1. The decision variable is the production quantity Q_t and this decision is made at the beginning of period t. There is no separate decision for the work force level.

2. There is a lead time of L periods for implementing the production decision, so that the production level P_t in period t is

$$P_t = Q_{t-L}$$

3. Production orders already in the pipeline cannot be altered.

4. Orders that cannot be filled at the end of a period are backlogged.

The decision rule takes the form

$$Q_t = k \left[R - I_{t-1} - \sum_{i=t-L}^{t-1} (Q_i - \bar{D}) \right] + \bar{D} \qquad (13)$$

where Q_t = decision made in period t for reorder quantity

R = safety stock

I_{t-1} = stock level at end of period $t-1$

$\bar{D}$ = expected demand level

k = a smoothing constant ($0 \leqslant k \leqslant 1$)

$R - I_{t-1}$ describes the amount by which the stock level falls below the safety stock requirement and the third term in the square brackets represents the cumulative excess of production over demand during the lead time. The smoothing factor k gives a weight to the total inventory balance in the square brackets. If $k = 0$ is taken then the decision rule is reduced to ordering an amount equivalent to the expected demand.

If in place of the expected demand $\bar{D}$ the forecast F_t is substituted into (13) the decision rule becomes

$$Q_t = k \left[R - I_{t-1} - \sum_{i=t-L}^{t-1} Q_i \right] + (1+kL)F_t \ . \quad (14)$$

Here F_t represents the forecast for demand per period and it may be derived from some forecasting procedure; for example, if simple exponential smoothing is used then

$$F_t = \alpha D_{t-1} + (1 - \alpha) F_{t-1} \qquad (15)$$

where F_t = updated demand forecast

F_{t-1} = previous demand forecast

D_{t-1} = actual demand in period $t-1$

α = the smoothing constant in forecasting $(0 \leqslant \alpha \leqslant 1)$.

Thus, the decision involves two smoothing parameters k and α. The performance of the system can be described by several measures, such as the following:

(1) Fluctuations in the inventory level, measured by the standard deviation σ_I

(2) Fluctuations in the reorder level, measured by the standard deviation σ_Q

(3) If a sudden increase in demand occurs, the level of stock runout increases. The *additional* amount of stock that cannot be supplied as a result of this sudden impulse in the demand is defined as

$$\gamma = q' - q$$

where q is the expected level of future runout when demand is stationary and q' is the level of future runouts when the mean demand is subject to a sudden increase (both q and q' are measured over a given horizon). Thus γ expresses (in terms of runouts) the consequence of a "disturbance" in the demand pattern.

(4) If a disturbance occurs (for example, a discrete increase in the demand level), the system reacts by supplying the demand from stock and by issuing orders to increase the production level (see Fig. 5, derived by simulating the system on an analogue computer). After a while the stock is replenished sufficiently for the production level to settle down to the expected demand level. The time that it takes the system to re-establish the inventory level I_t to a value within a given margin of the level prior to the disturbance is called the "rise time" T_r.

Thus, the purpose of the proposed control procedure is to provide a mechanism that will respond quickly enough to abrupt changes in the mean demand level and yet protect the production rate from being affected by spurious demand fluctuations, and this is the essence of the smoothing problem.

Three alternative objectives are considered in the DE model:

(a) Minimise $C = a\sigma_I + b\sigma_Q$ (16)
where a and b are constants

(b) Minimise $C = a\sigma_I + b\sigma_Q + c\gamma$ (17)
where a, b and c are constants

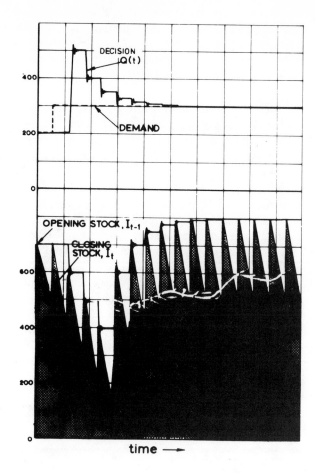

Fig. 5. Linear system response to a demand step [6] (for $\alpha = 0.5$, $k = 1.0$, $L = 3$).

(c) Same as (a) and subject to a given maximum value of T_r to ensure that the system recovers from an abrupt disturbance within a reasonable period.

Comments on the DE Model

One interesting result from this study [6] is the symmetry of results with respect to α and k: Figs. 6 and 7 show examples of isomers for σ_Q and σ_I respectively, the latter being a saddle shaped space with the saddle point at $\alpha = k = 0.4$. An example of a cost function which follows objective (c) is shown in Fig. 8 (where a sudden increase ΔD in demand is considered, the step being equal to the standard deviation of demand σ_D) and in general one finds that the optimal solution for any of the three alternative objectives listed above lies either at $\alpha = k$ or sometimes at $k = 0$ (or alternatively $\alpha = 0$). This result substantially reduces the search (which often follows a simulation approach) required to establish the optimal value of the decision parameters α and k, since only a range of values for one parameter needs to be scanned.

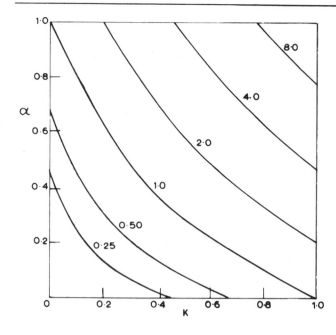

Fig. 6. Isomers of σ_Q (where L = 1) [6].

The fact that the DE model is essentially reduced to determining a single decision variable is an obvious advantage for the sake of simplicity; also, the model takes account of the lead time L, a feature which is missing from the HMMS model.

But a direct comparison with HMMS is difficult to make, as the two models are based on different structures and assumptions. DE dispenses with the need to determine the numerous cost parameters required by HMMS and avoids many of its problems which were discussed earlier. On the other hand, for DE one needs to specify the two or three weighting parameters used in objective functions such as in

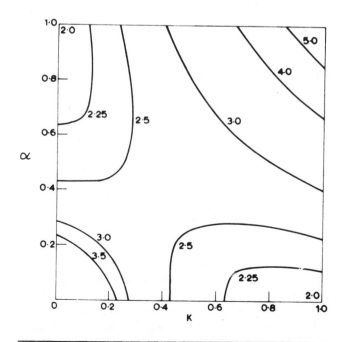

Fig. 7. Isomers of σ_I (where L = 1) [6].

Fig. 8. The cost function of $C = a\sigma_I + b\sigma_Q + c\gamma$ [6]
(for a = 2, b = 1, c = 0.5, L = 3, $\Delta D = \sigma_D$.

Eqs. (16) and (17); these parameters imply costs, and yet are difficult to derive directly from conventional accounting procedures. Another shortcoming of the DE model is that it incorporates the demand forecast for the forthcoming period, but not for subsequent periods.

Management Coefficients Approach
The Model

This method, which is due to Bowman [4], seeks to establish coefficients that describe the management's decision-making behaviour in a given environment. Using statistical regression analysis the scheduling rules are fitted to simple expressions [13], such as

$$P_t = a_1 F_t + a_2 W_{t-1} - a_3 I_{t-1} + a_4 \qquad (18)$$

$$W_t = b_1 F_t + b_2 W_{t-1} - b_3 I_{t-1} + b_4 \qquad (19)$$

where the a's and the b's are derived from the regressions. The assumption here is that management's decisions are in the main governed by the current work force, by the forecast for demand in period t and by the inventory level.

There are, of course, many alternative multiple regression models that may be examined. For example, an attempt to account for the forecast in period $t + 1$ as well may take the form

$$P_t = a_1 F_t + a_2 F_{t+1} + a_3 W_{t-1} - a_4 I_{t-1} + a_5 \qquad (20)$$

and indeed extended expressions like Eqs. (9) and (10) may be tried, although Bowman remarks that in the cases that he studied such regressions gave poor results because of the high correlation between the forecast estimates.

The axiomatic notion of this approach is that, as Bowman puts it [4], "experienced managers are quite aware of and sensitive to the criteria of a system" and that managerial decisions are "more erratic than biased". He proceeds to argue that managerial decisions are basically sound and that what is needed is to eliminate the "erratic" element by making them more consistent.

Comments

Criticisms of this approach are manifold:

1. The form of the multi-regression function is arbitrary and particularly regression of past decisions over a narrow range may lead to erroneous conclusions.

2. The test of goodness of fit is self-defeating. If the fit is poor, the regression model is rejected, because it does not sufficiently describe the behaviour pattern of the manager; if the fit is good, the model is accepted. But the better the fit and the more confidence we have in the model, the smaller is the erratic element in managerial decisions and hence the smaller the potential benefit from removing inconsistencies through the use of this approach.

3. The regression model relies on decisions made by a manager or by a group of managers. Changes in personnel may render the model invalid.

4. Last, but not least: The fundamental assumption that managers are good decision makers and that what is needed is just to eliminate inconsistencies in their behaviour is rather questionable. Such a philosophy is tantamount to suggesting that we should endeavour to make contributions only of a second order magnitude, whereas many believe that management scientists should pose more penetrating questions about the performance of an industrial enterprise.

Mathematical Programming
General

In the mathematical programming approach the demand forecasts are assumed accurate, so that a production plan for the complete horizon of T periods may be determined at the outset. The plan may then be updated period by period as more information becomes available. Several alternative mathematical programming models can be constructed, depending on the complexity of the assumptions that are made, and a few examples are discussed below [9].

Model 1: Production and Inventory Costs

In addition to notation introduced later, let

P_t = production rate in period t (where $t = 1, \ldots, T$)
   $= x_t + y_t + z_t$

x_t = production rate in regular time in period t

y_t = production rate in overtime in period t

z_t = production rate from subcontracting (or from third shift working) in period t

c_1 = cost per unit in regular time

c_2 = cost per unit produced in overtime

c_3 = cost per unit subcontracted

I_t = inventory level at end of period t

c_4 = cost per unit of closing inventory level

F_t = forecast demand for period t

S_t = shipment or sales in period t

Thus the costs of production are piecewise linear and if

$$c_3 > c_2 > c_1$$

the solution will ensure that regular time is fully used before overtime is employed and similarly that no subcontracting takes place before all available overtime is used. The cost parameters c_1, c_2, c_3 are assumed here to be time independent, but the model can equally handle the case where each of these parameters has different values in different periods.

The inventory level at the end of period t is computed by Eq. (5) and an initial inventory I_0 at the beginning of the planning horizon can be accounted for. Thus

$$I_t = I_0 + \sum_{i=1}^{t} (P_i - S_i) \qquad (21)$$

in the case of backlogged demand, and the inventory holding costs are $c_4 I_t$ for period t.

The total cost function then becomes

$$C = \sum (c_1 x_t + c_t y_2 + c_3 z_t + c_4 I_t). \qquad (22)$$

Several constraints may have to be observed, such as

$$\left. \begin{array}{c} A_t^* \leqslant x_t \leqslant A_t \\[2mm] B_t^* \leqslant y_t \leqslant B_t \\[2mm] C_t^* \leqslant z_t \leqslant C_t \end{array} \right\} \qquad (23)$$

where A_t^* and A_t are the lower and upper bounds for the production rate in regular time in period t and the other limits B_t^*, B_t, etc. are similarly defined. The lower bounds may often be zero, but sometimes certain prior commitments in terms of a minimum level of employment or a minimum undertaking to contractors may result in lower bounds assuming given positive values. The upper bounds simply reflect the production capacities of the available facilities, and account can be taken of the changing level of the work force by making the upper bounds period-dependent.

Stock Runouts

So far in this LP (linear programming) formulation no reference has been made to stock runouts and it is not difficult to see that the minimum cost solutions for equation (22) is achieved by producing quantities equal to the lower bounds. There are two ways to guard against excessive runouts:

(a) *Model 1.1* A constraint is imposed on the inventory level, for example, in the form

$$I_t \geqslant I^* \qquad (24a)$$

where I^* is the absolute lowest level that must be maintained (and in this context I^* may even be negative; also if it is desirable to allow I^* to vary from period to period then I_t^* will substitute I^* in expression (24a)). Alternatively

$$I_t \geqslant k F_{t+1} \qquad (24b)$$

where k is a constant. This expression suggests that the closing stock of period t must be at least a given proportion of the forecast demand in the next period. The LP model may therefore be defined as follows: Find the values of x_t, y_t and z_t that will minimise the objective function (22), subject to the constraints and requirements as stated.

(b) *Model 1.2* A penalty is imposed on runouts, say c_5 per unit. The inventory level I_t is replaced by

$$I_t = u_t - v_t \qquad (25)$$

where u_t is the closing physical stock at the end of period t and v_t is the amount of runout; both u_t and v_t are non-negative. Thus, if $u_t > 0$ then $v_t = 0$ and if $v_t > 0$ then $u_t = 0$. The inventory cost term in the cost Eq. (22) is now replaced by

$$\text{Inventory costs} = c_4 u_t + c_5 v_t \qquad (26)$$

and we now regard u_t and v_t as decision variables. Since $c_4 \neq c_5$ and since there are no upper bounds to u_t and v_t the solution to the linear programme will include either u_t or v_t for each time period.

Model 2: The Work Force

In Model 1 the work force does not appear as a decision variable. If an assumption is made that a certain relationship must be maintained between the available work force

and the possible rate of production in regular time, then the model needs to be modified accordingly. Let W_t be the work force in period t and let production be constrained by

$$x_t \leqslant \alpha_1 W_t - \alpha_0 \qquad (27)$$

where α_0 and α_1 are non-negative parameters; α_1 is the output per man and α_0 is proportional to some minimum level of manning that may be required before production can commence.

If $c_1 = $ cost per man per period for regular time

$c_6 = $ cost for hiring a worker

$c_7 = $ cost for layoff per worker when the work force is reduced,

then similar to Eq. (25) we introduce

$$W_t - W_{t-1} = U_t - V_t \qquad (28)$$

where $U_t = $ number of people hired to increase the work force to W_t

$V_t = $ number of people fired to reduce the work force to W_t

Here, too, U_t and V_t are non-negative and if $U_t > 0$ then $V_t = 0$ while if $V_t > 0$ then $U_t = 0$. The total cost function now becomes

$$\qquad (29)$$
$$C = \sum \left(c_1 W_t + c_2 y_t + c_3 z_t + c_4 u_t + c_5 v_t + c_6 U_t + c_7 V_t \right)$$

where the penalty for runouts is assumed as in Model 1.2 and the constraints are given in (23), (25), (27) and (28). A variant of Model 2 may be constructed to account for costs incurred by increasing or decreasing *production* (rather than the work force).

Comments on LP Models for Production Smoothing

The fundamental assumption in these models that cost functions are linear may be challenged, and where such an assumption cannot be sustained there is a need to construct nonlinear programming models, which are more intricate and take much longer to solve than LP problems.

A more serious issue is the tacit assumption that we are dealing with a deterministic problem; all demand forecasts are treated as if they were accurate, and they all carry equal weight. Admittedly, a procedure for updating the solution to the LP model, say every period, helps to take account of new information, but the fact remains that the production level for the forthcoming period can be significantly affected by demand forecasts for the more distant future, even though they are far less reliable than forecasts for the immediate future. This difficulty can be alleviated to a certain extent by reducing the planning horizon, but the fundamental criticism of this point remains valid.

The planning horizon also raises the problem of the end conditions. If none are stated, the model will produce a solution where the final inventory will be zero at the end of the planning period, it may also drastically reduce resources (such as manpower) towards the end of the horizon in an attempt to minimise overall costs. This "end effect" can be eliminated either by specifying minimum end conditions for inventory and production that must be met, or by planning for a longer horizon than that considered for implementation, so that the end effect is thereby diffused.

It is, of course, possible to subject expected costs for future periods to a discounting procedure, so that both the problems of equal weighting for forecasts and the end effect become less significant, but then the final results may well depend on the value of the discounting factor.

The advantage of LP for solving the production smoothing problem lies in the simplicity of the model and in the comparative ease with which it can handle constraints on availability of resources. Also, it provides some useful information about shadow prices to indicate profitable ways in which limited resources may be expanded.

It is precisely because of these advantages that in cases where cost parameters are not linear, attempts are often made at linearisation. There are many forms which such attempts can take (see, for example, [14]); one interesting approach is to aim at minimising the value of nonlinear cost parameters by a goal-programming formulation [12]. It is impossible, however, to make general statements about the effectiveness of such methods, whose performance appears to depend on the degree of nonlinearity involved, so that the justification for adopting any particular approach must rest with a comparative examination in any given case.

Production Switching
The Switching Model

In many production systems adjustment of the production level incurs two types of costs: a discrete fixed cost associated with the fact that a change in level is to take place, and a variable cost proportional to the amount by which the level is adjusted. If any production level may be considered (with upper constraints reflecting plant capacity), a mathematical model can be formulated with zero-one variables, where in each period such a variable takes the value of 0 when no change in production is introduced and value 1 when a change is made.

Another approach to solve the problem for the stationary demand case is based on dynamic programming [3, 18], resulting in a solution illustrated in Fig. 9, where P and I are the production level and inventory respectively. The shaded area shows the domain where no action is called for, but when a point representing the current production and inventory lies outside the shaded area, the production

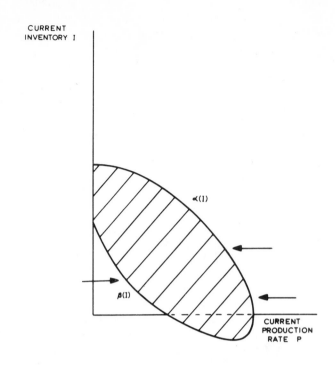

Fig. 9. Dynamic programming solution to the production smoothing problem (Beckman's Method [3]).

is adjusted by the amount needed to bring the point to the envelope of this area. The computations involved in this method are very time-consuming and it is not amenable to handling non-stationary demand distributions.

If production is confined to a relatively small number of prescribed levels (so that adjustment in production is achieved by given discrete steps), experience of performance and scheduled activities at each level provide good opportunities for controlling costs and minimising the effects of change. The total cost model is then expressed as [19]

$$C = \sum [c_1 P_t + c_2 z_t + c_3 I_t \, (I_t > 0) + c_4 I_t (I_t < 0)] \qquad (30)$$

where P_t and I_t are the production rate and inventory level in period t and

c_1 = unit cost of production

c_2 = production changeover cost

c_3 = unit carrying costs for leftover inventory (when $I_t > 0$)

c_4 = unit runout cost (when $I < 0$)

z_t = number of step changes made in period t

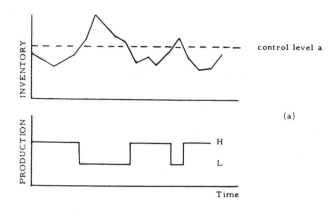

(a)

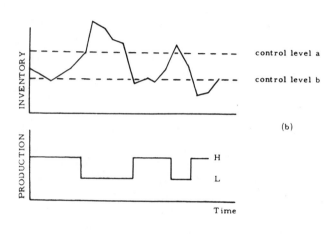

(b)

Fig. 10. The two-production-level case.

    (a) Single control level
    (b) Two control levels.

The control mechanism is illustrated by the simple two-production-level case, described in Fig. 10: the levels H and L represent the high and low production rates at which the system can operate. The inventory level is monitored and when it crosses a control level a, this determines when production is to switch from H to L and vice versa. A more elaborate control mechanism would involve two control levels a and b (when $a > b$) and switching from L to H will take place when the inventory level crosses the control limit a from below. The rationale for such switching policies is similar to the two-bin or (s, S) inventory control system. In the three-production-level case, where three production rates H, N, L (with $H > N > L$) are possible, three control limits a, b and c may be defined (where $a > b > c$), and the production rule will then follow the operating instructions:

$$P_t = \begin{cases} H \text{ if } I_t \text{ passes } c \text{ from above} \\ N \text{ if } I_t \text{ passes } b \\ L \text{ if } I_t \text{ passes } a \text{ from below} \end{cases}$$

Clearly, the introduction of multi-production/control levels provides more degrees of freedom and added protection to the system when demand is very volatile or unpredictable.

An effective way for analysing such a model for any given demand pattern is by simulation. An example for results obtained in one case with two-production-levels [11] is given in Fig. 11; each of the points shown is based on 1000 simulation runs. In Fig. 11(a) the lower production level $L = 0$ and the three curves correspond to the upper production level $H = 300$, 400 and 500 respectively. The control level a is shown on the abscissa scanning the range from L to H. The costs for changing the production level consist of a fixed cost per change plus a cost proportional to the magnitude of change, but the costs of inventory

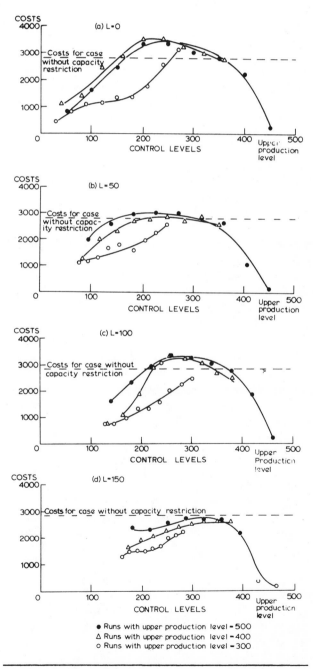

Fig. 11. Production changeover costs against control levels [11].

holding are ignored here. The demand is sampled from a normal distribution (truncated at zero) with lead times assumed for processing as well as for the supply of raw materials. A horizontal dotted line in the figure shows the costs incurred when no production capacity restrictions are imposed and when the quantity scheduled for production can be adjusted to attain an optimal solution for the inventory system on its own (designed to meet demand with minimum inventory, provided no runouts are allowed). Such a policy would incur frequent adjustments in production levels (and thereby high changeover costs) and clearly these costs can be reduced by a switching method. The results in this case also suggest that the costs decline when the control level a approaches either L or H. Figs. 11 (b-d) show similar results for $L = 50, 100, 150$.

Comments on the Switching Model

When production operations are preferably carried out at certain predetermined levels (such as the opening or shutting of a production line), it is not appropriate to treat the production level as a continuous variable, and the model described here is a convenient way for analysing alternative values of control parameters for switching purposes. In addition, the model can be used to determine desirable fixed production levels (if a decision to that effect is open to the management) and to carry out sensitivity analyses.

Since this is a simulation model, there are no constraints on the type of demand pattern that can be handled (it may involve a series of deterministic demand forecasts, in which case the questions posed by the planning horizon often remain, or sampling from a stationary or nonstationary distribution), and the objective cost function given in (30) may be easily extended as appropriate, for example to include inventory holding costs of raw materials. Alternative cost functions may also be considered. For example, a function similar to Eq. (16) may be constructed to incorporate the standard deviations of inventory and work in progress respectively; simulation results for these standard deviations in an example involving a three-level-production case [11] are shown in Fig. 12, and such results allow the cost function to be computed for various values of the control parameter. Mean values for inventories of raw materials, work in progress and finished goods may also be derived from simulation and fed into similar cost functions.

For a simple control procedure, involving one or two control levels, this simulation model is an effective analytical tool, but the obvious danger in the system described in Fig. 10 is that when a drastic change in demand takes place (for example, following an upward or a downward trend), production will lock into a single high or low level which may prove to be inadequate to deal with a persistently depleted or soaring stock level. To guard against such extreme situations, additional monitoring is needed to tell management when the two-level-production system ceases to be effective and needs to be replaced (for example, by new prescribed levels).

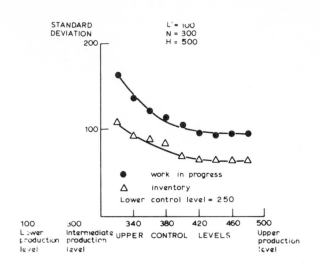

Fig. 12. **Standard deviation of inventory and work in progress** [11].

Such an elaboration of the control system may take the form of specifying multi-production and control levels, and clearly the amount of computational work required for such simulation models rises very rapidly, particularly when—in addition to determining the optimal control levels—investigations are carried out for several alternative production levels. The greater the number of levels incorporated in a switching system, the more degrees of freedom are introduced and the greater is therefore the potential for finding a lower cost solution than the optimal solution for the two-level case. However, as the control system increases in complexity, the advantages of simplicity imbedded in the two- or three-level methods are eroded, the frequency of switching is expected to increase, and management becomes less able to gear the plant to an effective use of resources during a relatively shorter production spell at any given level.

Conclusion

Each of the five approaches reviewed in this paper for solving the production smoothing problem has certain strengths and weaknesses. The HMMS rule, the switching method and the LP model are concerned in the main with minimising costs (or maximising profit in some LP formulations), the DE rule also has cost minimisation as an objective (but of a different structure than the HMMS model), while the management coefficients approach strives to maintain consistency in scheduling decisions and costs are only quoted as a justification. Because of the differences in the assumptions and the objectives of the five approaches, a direct comparison is difficult, particularly as other factors—such as the accuracy of the forecasting system employed by the organisation and problems of implementation—may be crucial. For example, if cost functions are indeed found to be quadratic in form, the HMMS rule may be most suitable;

if the objective of the production scheduler is to strike a balance between fluctuations in production and fluctuations in inventory, while avoiding a direct evaluation of many of the cost parameters considered in the HMMS model, then the DE rule or the switching method may be effective and simple to use; the management coefficients method appears to be the least disruptive to implement and also perhaps the least rewarding; LP models are powerful, for the most part quite satisfactory in spite of the linear cost assumptions, but vulnerable when demand forecasts are relatively inaccurate. The switching method is flexible in the type of assumptions and cost functions that can be entertained and is based on a simple control mechanism, whose performance can be repeatedly and closely monitored by simulation.

References

[1] Abromovitz, M., *Inventories and Business Cycles with Special Reference to Manufacturer's Inventories*, National Bureau of Economic Research, New York (1950).

[2] Anshen, M., Holt, C. C., Modigliani, F., Muth, J. F. and Simon, H. A., "Mathematics for Production Scheduling," *Harvard Business Review*, 36 pp 51-58 (1958).

[3] Beckman, M. J., "Production Smoothing and Inventory Control," *Operations Research*, 9 pp 456-467 (1961).

[4] Bowman, E. H., "Consistency and Optimality in Managerial Decision Making," *Management Science*, 9 pp 310-321 (1963).

[5] Buffa, E. S., *Production-Inventory Systems: Planning and Control*, Irwin, chapters 5-7 (1968).

[6] Deziel, D. P. and Eilon, S., "A Linear Production-Inventory Control Rule," *The Production Engineer*, 46 pp 93-104 (1967).

[7] Eilon, S., *Elements of Production Planning and Control*, Macmillan, New York (1962).

[8] Eilon, S., "On Smoothing Shipments—A Comment," *Management Science*, 17 pp 608-609 (1971).

[9] Eilon, S., "The Production Smoothing Problem," *The Production Engineer*, 52 pp 123-129 (1972).

[10] Elmaleh, J., "Integrated Production-Inventory Control Systems," PhD thesis, Imperial College, London (1968).

[11] Elmaleh, J. and Eilon, S., "A New Approach to Production Smoothing," *International Journal of Production Research*, 12 pp 673-681 (1974).

[12] Goodman, D. A., "A New Approach to Scheduling Aggregate Production and Work Force," *AIIE Transactions*, 5 pp 135-141 (1973).

[13] Gordon, J. R. M., "A Multi-Model Analysis of an Aggregate Scheduling Decision," PhD dissertation, Sloan School of Management, MIT (1966).

[14] Hanssmann, F. and Hess, W., "A Linear Programming Approach to Production and Employment Scheduling," *Management Technology*, 1 pp 46-51 (1960).

[15] Holt, C. C., "Dynamic Pricing and Economic Instability," *Management Science*, 17 pp 609-611 (1971).

[16] Holt, C. C., Modigliani, F., Muth, J. F. and Simon, H. A., *Planning Production, Inventories and Work Force*, Prentice Hall, (1960).

[17] Hu, Te Chiang and Prager, W., "Network Analysis of Production Smoothing," *Naval Research Logistics Quarterly*, 6 pp 17-23 (1959).

[18] Mills, E. S., "The Theory of Inventory Decisions," *Econometrica*, 23 pp 46-66 (1955).

[19] Orr, D., "A Random Walk Production-Inventory Policy: Rationale and Implementation," *Management Science*, 9 pp 108-122 (1962).

[20] Peterson, R., "Optimal Smoothing of Shipments in Response to Orders," *Management Science*, 17 pp 597-607 (1971).

[21] Silver, E. A., "A Tutorial on Production Smoothing and Work Force Balancing," *Operations Research*, 15 pp 985-1010 (1967).

[22] Van de Panne, C. and Bose, P., "Sensitivity Analysis of Cost Coefficient Estimates: the Case of Linear Decisions Rules for Employment and Production," *Management Science*, 9 pp 82-107 (1962).

Dr. Samuel Eilon is Professor and Head of Department, Management Science, Imperial College, London. He received his DSc(Eng.) and PhD both from London University. Dr. Eilon is a member of the Institution of Mechanical Engineers, Institution of Production Engineers and Operational Research Society.

MANAGEMENT SCIENCE
Vol. 24, No. 12, August 1978
Printed in U.S.A.

PRODUCTION SWITCHING HEURISTICS FOR THE AGGREGATE PLANNING PROBLEM*

JOSEPH M. MELLICHAMP† AND ROBERT M. LOVE‡

A number of approaches to the aggregate planning problem have been proposed in the literature, yet experience suggests that industrial concerns seldom use these models in actual planning situations. This paper describes a modified random walk production-inventory heuristic for the problem which should appeal to managers on the basis of simplicity as well as efficiency. The proposed approach is contrasted with linear programming, parametric programming, and linear decision rule optimal and near optimal solutions for several well known production situations. The simple production switching heuristic produces schedules which exceed optimal schedules by only 1 to 2 percent of total production costs in all cases.
(PLANNING; PRODUCTION/SCHEDULING; INVENTORY/PRODUCTION-PRODUCTION SMOOTHING)

1. Introduction

The aggregate production planning problem is: given the demand forecast F_t for each period t in the planning horizon which extends over T periods, determine the production level P_t, inventory level I_t, and work force level W_t for periods $t = 1, 2, \ldots, T$ which minimize relevant costs over the planning horizon. The production system is considered to be a single production facility that produces a single product (multi-product firms are treated by aggregating individual products to some common unit such as cost, contribution, or direct machine hours). Time is divided into discrete periods and demand forecasts for each period are obtained by some appropriate forecasting technique [5, p. 119–120].

In response to fluctuations in demand, management may follow one of three pure strategies, namely:

1. Change the production level by altering the size of the work force through hiring or layoffs,

2. Change the production level through the use of overtime or idletime holding the work force constant, or

3. Maintain a constant production level absorbing fluctuations in demand through changes in the inventory level.

Alternatively, management may adopt some combination of the pure strategies [4, p. 171] and [16, p. 987].

Recognition of the widespread existence of the problem has led to publication of a number of different approaches for solving the aggregate planning problem. An early approach that has become a standard for comparison is the linear decision rule (LDR) proposed by Holt, Modigliani, Muth, and Simon [9], [10]. A linear programming (LP) approach has been advanced by Hansmann and Hess [8]. Extensions to the linear programming approach have included a transportation formulation by Bowman [1] and, more recently, goal programming formulations proposed by Lee and Moore [13] and Goodman [7]. Elmaleh and Eilon have suggested a switching procedure for use in industries in which production is limited to discrete levels [6]. Other approaches which have been presented include the management coefficients model (MCM) developed by Bowman [2], parametric production planning (PPP) by Jones [11], and the search

---

* Accepted by David G. Dannenbring; received December 20, 1977. This paper has been with the authors 6 weeks for 1 revision.
† University of Alabama.
‡ Army Logistics Management Center, Fort Lee.

decision rule (SDR) suggested by Taubert [3], [17]. Comparisons of these and other models may be found in Eilon [5] and Silver [16].

Unfortunately, even with the modest number of approaches available to managers, aggregate planning methods have not had a significant impact on operating practice. Taubert states that, "Simplified aggregate scheduling models have not found widespread use in industry [17, p. B–343]." Lee and Khumawala agree, " . . . reported examples of successful applications are rare, and a cohesive methodology for implementation of these models is lacking [12, p. 903]." Buffa and Taubert have identified the alternative many firms are taking, "It is not surprising, therefore, that there has been a lack of actual industrial applications. Firms have preferred to rely on the judgment of a manager, or executive committee, for such decisions [3, p. 252]."

Given this rather lackluster record, one has to wonder what has hindered the assimilation of aggregate planning techniques into management practice. Several reasons are apparent.

For one thing, the analytical models—linear programming, goal programming, transportation techniques, and the LDR approach—all incorporate various simplifying assumptions which limit their applicability. For example, the mathematical programming approaches require that all cost functions be linear. While it is true that piecewise linear approximations may be used to represent non-linear cost functions, the additional complexity is certainly a deterrent to wide application. The LDR approach, on the other hand, utilizes quadratic cost functions for mathematical convenience. Unfortunately, actual cases in industry are rarely either/or situations; we might expect to observe in the same situation some costs which are linear and some costs which are of higher order. A second example of unrealistic assumptions involves the way demand is treated in the mathematical programming approaches. These methods all incorporate the tacit assumption that demand forecasts are accurate and are equally weighted over the planning horizon. The result is that the production level for the forthcoming period can be significantly affected by forecasts for future periods even though forecasts for distant periods are less reliable than forecasts for the immediate future [5, p. 127].

Simulation approaches, including parametric production planning and the SDR approach, overcome some of the problems associated with analytical approaches. Complex cost functions which accurately describe actual costs may be embodied in most simulation models. Stochastic demand characteristics can be incorporated in simulation models, permitting analysis of the impact of forecast errors on strategy development. However, simulation models suffer from a limitation that also applies to analytical models. That is, most models produce a different set of decision variable values—P_t, W_t, and I_t—for each period in the planning horizon. This may very well be the most important factor in limiting the application of aggregate planning models. It may be argued that a large set of decision variable values is inconsistent with management practice. Orr [15, p. 113] has suggested that an implied goal of management in production planning is to avoid rescheduling too frequently. Thus, as long as demand is being met, i.e., stockouts do not occur too frequently and inventory levels do not increase drastically, managers are often inclined to maintain the same production and work force levels, making minor adjustments when necessary.

It would appear from these and other arguments that an aggregate planning methodology which utilizes simulation methods to select a small number of decision variable values that are efficient over most levels of demand would have much potential. Interestingly, the basic theory of such a method has been developed and the method has been applied to a limited set of production problems. Orr [15] has suggested that certain production-inventory problems can be treated with random walk inventory policies. Furthermore, Elmaleh and Eilon [6] have demonstrated how switching heuristics are useful in industries such as food and chemical industries in which production must be carried out at discrete levels.

The objectives of this research are to suggest a simple modification to the production switching heuristic which renders the methodology appropriate for aggregate planning problems in general and to demonstrate that production schedules produced by the modified approach are cost efficient relative to other aggregate planning techniques. §2 of the paper describes the modified production switching heuristic. §3 presents the results of applying the heuristic to four production situations for which optimum solutions are available. Some conclusions and comments are given in §4.

2. Development of the Production Switching Heuristic

The random walk approach to aggregate production planning proposed by Orr [15] and adapted by Elmaleh and Eilon [6] is formulated as follows:

Specify three inventory levels, $a > b > c$, and three production levels, $H > N > L$, with the operating instructions

$$P_t = \begin{cases} H & \text{if } I_{t-1} \text{ passes } c \text{ from above,} \\ N & \text{if } I_{t-1} \text{ passes } b, \\ L & \text{if } I_{t-1} \text{ passes } a \text{ from below.} \end{cases} \tag{1}$$

Values for a, b, c and H, N, L are obtained by simulating various combinations of these control parameters over a historical demand series and choosing the set for which costs are minimum [6, pp. 675, 676].

We propose incorporating F_t, the demand forecast for period t, in the rule for determining P_t as follows. The estimated closing inventory $\hat{I}_t$ in period t is

$$\hat{I}_t = I_{t-1} + P_t - F_t. \tag{2}$$

Since we are attempting to control both production and inventory costs, we replace $\hat{I}_t$ by B where B represents a target inventory level to be determined. Rearranging equation 2 such that the input variables I_{t-1} and F_t are on the left side of the equation and the decision variables P_t and B are on the right yields:

$$F_t - I_{t-1} = P_t - B. \tag{2'}$$

The left side of the equation represents the amount of anticipated demand in period t which cannot be met with on-hand inventory, while the right side of the equation reflects the production from period t available to meet demand after satisfying the target inventory requirement.

We now suggest the following rule for P_t.

$$P_t = \begin{cases} L & \text{if } F_t - I_{t-1} < L - C, \\ H & \text{if } F_t - I_{t-1} > H - A, \\ N & \text{otherwise,} \end{cases} \tag{3}$$

where A = Minimum acceptable target inventory, C = Maximum acceptable target inventory.

The heuristic suggests that if the net production required after taking on-hand and target inventories into account is less than the low level of production, produce at the low level. If the net production requirement is greater than the high level of production, produce at the high level. If the net production requirement is between the low and high levels of production, produce at the normal level of production.

The problem is to determine values for the control parameters H, N, L and A, B, C which generate a set of production, work force, and inventory decisions (P_t, W_t, and I_t) that will be cost efficient over the planning horizon. Once appropriate values have been determined, planning decisions for each period are made using (3)—the computational effort required is hardly more than simple inspection.

The procedure used in this research for selecting values for the control parameters of the heuristic is an iterative simulation approach utilizing a historical demand series and including the following steps:

Step 1.   Obtain input data as follows:

  1. Demand history: $\{S_t\}$ and $\{F_t\}$ for $t = 1, 2, \ldots, T$.
  2. Initial values: P_0, W_0, and I_0.
  3. Productivity function: $W_t = f(P_t, G)$ where G is the percent increase or decrease in the work force required to achieve high or low levels of production.
  4. Cost functions: C_{it} for $i = 1, 2, \ldots, n$. Where n is the number of cost functions included.[1]

Step 2.   Specify various values of control parameters that are to be evaluated. Any one of several different search options including various grid and gradient procedures may be used.[2]

Step 3.   Initialize control parameters.

Step 4.   Calculate P_t, W_t, I_t, and $C_t = \sum_{i=1}^{n} C_{it}$ for $t = 1, 2, \ldots, T$ using (3).

Step 5.   Calculate total cost $TC = \sum_{t=1}^{T} C_t$.

Step 6.   Repeat Steps 4 and 5 for all combinations of the control parameters H, N, L and A, B, C.

Step 7.   Select those values for H, N, L and A, B, C for which TC is minimum.

3.   Applications of the Production Switching Heuristic

In order to demonstrate the production switching heuristic (PSH) described in the preceding section and to evaluate its performance relative to other aggregate production planning approaches, we applied PSH to four variations of two production situations described in the literature. Since optimal or near optimal solutions are available for each of the four cases, the comparisons will convey some idea of the cost of using the simpler PSH in planning activities.

The first production situation to which PSH was applied was the paint factory described by Holt, Modigliani, and Simon [9]. Cost relationships for this firm as described by the authors are quadratic and include regular production costs, overtime and hiring costs, and inventory costs. The first comparison between PSH and the optimum LDR plan was based on the assumptions that the cost approximations were actual costs and that perfect forecasts were available to the firm. The second

---

[1] The basic costs involved in aggregate production planning have been fully covered in the literature [3] [14], and [17].

[2] This research utilized a simple grid procedure in which initial values, increments, and ranges were specified for N, B, D, and E. Then using the relationships

$H = N + E$,

$L = N - E$,

$A = B - D$,

$C = B + D$,

the grid was systematically searched. Improvements in both computer run time and total cost could possibly be obtained by using a more sophisticated procedure; however, in view of the research objectives, a simple search procedure was selected.

comparison reflects the relative merits of PSH and LDR under conditions of uncertainty in the form of errors between forecasts and actual sales.[3]

The second production situation to which PSH was applied was the hypothetical Company X described by Jones in [11]. Optimal plans for Company X which has all linear cost functions are available through linear programming. The first comparison has PSH against both LP and PPP when perfect forecasts are available to the company. The second comparison shows the results of applying PSH, LP, and PPP to Company X in the face of forecast uncertainty.

The Paint Factory

The cost relationships used for the paint factory were:

$C_{1t} = 340.0 W_t$	(Regular Payroll),	(4)
$C_{2t} = 64.3(W_t - W_{t-1})^2$	(Hiring and Layoffs),	(5)
$C_{3t} = 0.20(P_t - 5.67 W_t)^2 + 51.2P_t - 281.0W_t$	(Overtime),	(6)
$C_{4t} = 0.0825(I_t - 320.0 - 0.0S_t)^2$	(Inventory, Back-order and Setup).	(7)

And the objective is to minimize total costs

$$TC = \sum_{t=1}^{T} \sum_{i=1}^{4} C_{it}. \qquad (8)$$

(6) yields negative overtime costs for certain values of P_t and W_t. Whenever this occurred in the calculations, C_{3t} was set to zero.

The normal production level N was set at the average level of demand forecasted for the planning period ($N = 382.417$). Average worker productivity k was set at the same level used in Holt et al. [10, p. 54] ($k = 5.67$).

A computer search routine incorporating the steps described earlier for determining values for the PSH control parameters produced the following

$H = 452.417$,
$N = 382.417$,
$L = 312.417$,
$A = 300$,
$B = 320$,
$C = 340$,

Table 1 gives the component and total cost values for the paint factory for LDR, PPP, and PSH. The total cost value of $299,889 obtained with the switching heuristic is only 1.30 percent greater than the optimum value of $296,036 generated by LDR.

TABLE 1

Paint Company Results with Perfect Forecast

Cost Component	LDR	PPP	PSH
Regular Payroll	282,642	285,141	276,325
Overtime	8,518	7,810	13,211
Hiring and Layoff	3,514	3,229	8,860
Inventory	1,362	1,865	1,593
Total Cost	296,036	298,045	299,889

[3] Forecast errors were generated by computing sales in each period as
$S_t = F_t + z\sigma_t$ where
$\sigma_t = 0.05N$,
$z =$ standardized normal random variable.

TABLE 2

Comparison of PSH, LDR, and PPP Production, Work Force, and Inventory Decisions for the Paint Company with Perfect Forecasts

Month	Forecast	Sales	Production Switching Heuristic			Linear Decision Rule			Parametric Production Planning		
			Production (Gallons)	Work Force (Men)	Inventory (Gallons)	Production (Gallons)	Work Force (Men)	Inventory (Gallons)	Production (Gallons)	Work Force (Men)	Inventory (Gallons)
0				81.00	263.00		81.00	263.00		81.00	263.00
1	430	430	452.42	70.82	285.42	467.72	78.63	292.72	461.26	78.56	286.26
2	447	447	452.42	70.82	290.83	441.32	75.32	289.08	440.50	75.37	281.76
3	440	440	382.42	67.45	233.25	414.88	72.24	263.92	417.11	72.44	258.88
4	316	316	382.42	67.45	299.67	379.83	69.55	328.75	380.38	69.82	324.25
5	397	397	382.42	67.45	285.09	375.28	67.21	309.03	379.80	67.98	309.06
6	375	375	382.42	67.45	292.50	367.09	66.29	301.12	371.34	66.74	305.39
7	292	292	382.42	67.45	382.92	358.51	65.66	369.64	360.91	66.13	376.30
8	458	458	382.42	67.45	307.34	380.57	65.87	295.21	390.73	66.53	312.03
9	400	400	382.42	67.45	289.75	376.80	66.49	270.01	385.71	67.25	297.74
10	350	350	382.42	67.45	322.17	366.70	67.68	283.71	372.14	68.39	314.88
11	284	284	312.42	64.07	350.59	366.59	69.67	365.30	367.31	70.17	397.19
12	400	400	382.42	67.45	333.00	405.95	72.62	366.24	408.72	72.93	400.91

TABLE 3

Paint Company Results with 5% Forecast Error

Cost Component	LDR	PPP	PSH
Regular Payroll	282,141	284,615	276,325
Overtime	9,155	8,617	13,211
Hiring and Layoff	3,657	3,381	8,860
Inventory	1,531	1,950	1,428
Total Cost	296,484	298,563	299,824

TABLE 4

Comparison of PSH, LDR, and PPP Production, Work Force, and Inventory Decisions for the Paint Company with 5% Forecast Error

Month	Forecast	Sales	Production Switching Heuristic			Linear Decision Rule			Parametric Production Planning		
			Production (Gallons)	Work Force (Men)	Inventory (Gallons)	Production (Gallons)	Work Force (Men)	Inventory (Gallons)	Production (Gallons)	Work Force (Men)	Inventory (Gallons)
0				81.00	263.00		81.00	263.00		81.00	263.00
1	430	434	452.42	70.82	281.42	467.65	77.84	296.65	457.59	77.78	286.59
2	447	419	452.42	70.82	314.83	444.00	74.74	321.64	441.43	74.83	309.02
3	440	415	382.42	67.45	282.25	403.84	71.51	310.48	403.73	71.77	297.75
4	316	299	382.42	67.45	365.67	363.25	68.58	374.73	361.66	68.91	360.41
5	397	454	382.42	67.45	294.09	358.96	66.47	379.69	362.59	66.94	269.00
6	375	386	382.42	67.45	290.50	385.03	65.72	378.72	392.02	66.42	275.02
7	292	275	382.42	67.45	397.92	374.57	65.45	378.29	377.57	66.22	377.59
8	458	459	382.42	67.45	321.34	382.58	65.57	301.87	390.83	66.53	309.42
9	400	397	382.42	67.45	306.75	377.96	66.10	282.83	385.36	67.17	297.78
10	350	338	382.42	67.45	351.17	364.49	67.14	309.32	368.57	68.19	328.35
11	284	293	312.42	64.07	370.59	358.95	68.91	375.27	358.38	69.78	393.73
12	400	402	382.42	67.45	351.00	404.31	71.84	377.58	407.11	72.56	398.84

Table 2 compares the period by period production plans resulting from PSH, LDR, and PPP when perfect forecasts are available to the firm.

Using the same PSH control parameters for determining aggregate production plans for the paint factory but allowing errors between forecasted and actual sales produced the costs given in Table 3. The total cost of $299,824 exceeds the LDR optimum total cost of $296,484 by 1.13 percent. Table 4 compares the period by period production decisions obtained with PSH, LDR, and PPP.

Company X

The total cost function for the hypothetical Company X is:

$$C_t = 120.375 I_t + 1500.0 E_t + 20.0625 P_t + 200.0 H_t$$
$$+ 1067.53 W_t + 50.0 L_t - 9028.125 S_t \qquad (9)$$

where

E_t = overtime in period t measured in full-time worker equivalents.

H_t = workers hired in period t.

L_t = workers layed-off in period t.

And the other variables are as defined previously in this paper. The objective is to minimize total costs subject to thirteen production constraints specified in Jones [11, p. 856].

In order to comply with the production constraints imposed on Company X, the PSH rule was reformulated slightly. Production for Company X was measured in units equivalent to the output of one experienced worker in one period; thus, productivity was unity. The switching heuristic is

$$W_t = \begin{cases} L & \text{if } F_t - I_{t-1} < L - C, \\ H & \text{if } F_t - I_{t-1} > H - A, \\ N & \text{otherwise.} \end{cases} \qquad (10)$$

To assure compliance with Company X inventory constraints, the production rule is

$$P_t = 1.1F_t - I_{t-1}. \qquad (11)$$

The production capability in period t is constrained by the work force level in the prior period as

$$P_t \leqslant 1.32W_{t-1} + 1.32E_{t-1} - 0.66H_{t-1}. \qquad (12)$$

Thus, if the required production from (11) exceeded the production capability given by (12), W_{t-1} was revised to the next highest level, E_{t-1} was set at zero, and the new period t production level was set at

$$P_t = W_{t-1} - 0.5H_{t-1} \qquad (13)$$

based on the revised values for W_{t-1} and H_{t-1}.[4]

The simulation search routine produced the following PSH control parameter values:

$H = 293.886$,

$N = 253.886$,

$L = 213.886$,

$A = 20$,

$B = 20$,

$C = 20$.

Table 5 shows total revenue, cost, and profit values for Company X resulting from LP, PPP, and PSH.[5] The total cost of $3,546,616 produced by PSH exceeds the LP

TABLE 5

Company X Results With Perfect Forecast

	LP	PPP	PSH
Total Revenue	27,505,356	27,505,356	27,505,356
Total Cost	3,493,325	3,501,244	3,546,616
Total Profit	24,012,031	24,004,112	23,958,740

---

[4] Company X had a maximum work force size of 296. Thus, if W_{t-1} was already at H, it would be reset to 296.

[5] Results given for LP and PPP are slightly different than those reported in [11] because of rounding and differences in coding the algorithm used to treat the non-symmetric production rule and simultaneous layoffs and overtime [11, p. 858]. The reported values were $3,493,227 for LP and $3,500,326 for PPP, while our coding yields $3,493,324 and $3,501,244.

TABLE 6

Comparison of PSH, LP, and PPP Production, Work Force, and Inventory Decisions for Company X with Perfect Forecasts

			Production Switching Heuristic				Linear Programming				Parametric Production Planning			
Month	Forecast	Sales	Workers	Over-time	Produc-tion*	Inventory	Workers	Over-time	Produc-tion	Inventory	Workers	Over-time	Produc-tion	Inventory
0	195.03	195.03	200.08	47.56	247.64	52.61	200.08	47.56	247.64	52.61	200.08	47.56	247.64	52.61
1	217.81	217.81	253.89		226.98	61.78	259.93	6.30	236.30	71.10	264.92		232.41	67.21
2	300.94	300.94	253.89	15.38	269.25	30.09	259.93		259.93	30.09	264.92	.22	263.83	30.09
3	285.75	285.75	253.89	30.35	284.23	28.58	259.93	24.30	284.23	28.58	264.92	19.31	284.23	28.58
4	208.21	208.21	213.89		200.46	20.82	243.75		243.75	64.11	241.70		242.00	62.36
5	224.47	224.47	253.89		226.10	22.45	243.75		243.75	83.38	242.54		242.25	80.15
6	282.19	286.19	253.89	38.48	292.36	28.62	243.75		243.75	40.93	253.64		247.93	41.88
7	258.80	258.80	253.89	2.17	256.06	25.88	256.77		250.26	32.39	257.10		255.34	38.42
8	217.78	217.78	213.89		213.89	21.78	263.33		260.05	74.67	259.89		258.46	79.11
9	244.44	244.44	293.89		253.89	31.22	263.33		263.33	93.55	257.29		257.16	91.83
10	324.44	324.44	293.89	31.78	325.67	32.44	263.33		263.33	32.44	268.97	2.26	265.06	32.44
11	268.89	268.89	253.89	9.45	263.33	26.89	263.33		263.33	26.89	263.33		263.33	26.89
12	208.90	208.90	213.89		202.90	20.89	260.56		260.56	78.56	258.80		259.10	77.10

* Production is measured in units equivalent to the output of one experienced worker in one period.

TABLE 7

Company X Results with 5% Forecast Error

	LP	PPP	PSH
Total Revenue	27,505,274	27,505,274	27,435,974
Total Cost	3,524,529	3,505,464	3,579,659
Total Profit	23,980,747	23,999,810	23,856,315

TABLE 8

Comparison of PSH and PPP Production, Work Force, and Inventory Decisions for Company X with 5% Forecast Error

			Production Switching Heuristic				Parmetric Production Planning			
Month	Forecast	Sales	Workers	Overtime	Production	Inventory	Workers	Overtime	Production	Inventory
0	195.03	195.03	200.08	47.56	247.64	52.61	200.08	47.56	247.64	52.61
1	217.81	220.77	253.80		226.98	58.82	240.31		220.19	52.03
2	300.94	282.36	253.89	18.33	272.22	48.68	252.49	32.60	279.00	48.68
3	285.75	269.67	253.89	11.76	265.65	44.66	252.49	13.16	265.65	44.66
4	208.21	197.32	213.89		184.38	31.72	233.98		233.98	81.31
5	224.47	262.59	293.89		253.89	23.01	228.84		228.84	47.56
6	286.19	294.12	253.89	37.91	291.80	20.69	247.19	29.23	267.25	20.69
7	258.80	248.10	253.89	10.10	263.99	36.60	258.09	11.35	263.99	36.58
8	217.78	218.89	213.89		202.98	20.66	254.61		254.61	72.30
9	244.44	242.66	293.89		253.89	31.90	249.52		249.52	79.16
10	324.44	316.76	293.89	31.11	324.99	40.13	251.71	27.12	277.73	40.13
11	268.89	275.14	253.89	1.77	255.65	20.63	253.35	3.13	255.65	20.63
12	208.90	210.56	213.89		209.15	19.22	256.21		254.78	64.85

optimum value of $3,493,325 by 1.53 percent. The resulting production schedule is given in Table 6. Notice that the work force is relatively stable; however, slight adjustments in production through overtime and undertime are necessary. Schedules generated by LP and PPP are also shown in Table 6.

Table 7 reflects revenue, cost, and profit values resulting from scheduling production under conditions of uncertainty with LP, PPP, and PSH. The PSH cost value differs from the . optimum value by 1.56 percent. Table 8 gives the detailed schedules resulting from PSH and PPP.[6]

4. Comments and Conclusions

The production switching approach described in preceding paragraphs offers several clear advantages over other approaches for treating the aggregate production

---

[6] Corresponding values for the LP schedule were not reported in [11] and are therefore not shown.

planning problem. The principal advantage being that it produces production, work force, and inventory decisions which necessitate a minimum amount of period to period adjustment—a characteristic that is quite consistent with the natural inclinations of operating managers. The approach is sufficiently flexible as to permit incorporation of most cost functions that are likely to be encountered in practice. In addition, computational requirements of the approach are minimal; the search procedure is relatively straightforward and computational requirements are modest—decisions for the Paint Company and Company X reqiure less than 30 seconds per run on a UNIVAC 1110 time-sharing system.

The major disadvantage of the PSH approach is the impact of nonstationary or extremely seasonal demand patterns on production costs generated by the heuristic. Either condition could cause production to peg to the high or low production level and could lead to continuing demand shortages or inventory surpluses [5, p. 130]. More decision levels could be employed to hedge against such possibilities, but this would increase the complexity of the approach thus reducing its advantage of simplicity. An alternative is to review the control parameters periodically to determine whether selection of new levels is appropriate.

From the examples presented herein, the production switching approach offers considerable benefits in simplicity and flexibility for only a slight sacrifice in cost—in the range of 1 to 2 percent. Since the clear verdict on aggregate production planning methods is that they are not enjoying wide use in industry, the implication is that many firms are not pursuing optimal scheduling policies. Adoption of production switching scheduling procedures, thus, might offer substantial savings for many of these firms.

References

1. BOWMAN, E. H., "Production Scheduling by the Transportation Method of Linear Programming," *Operations Res.*, Vol. 4, No. 1 (February 1956), pp. 100–103.
2. ———, "Consistency and Optimality in Managerial Decision Making," *Management Sci.*, Vol. 9, No. 2 (January 1963), pp. 310–321.
3. BUFFA, ELWOOD AND TAUBERT, WILLIAM H., *Production-Inventory Systems: Planning and Control*, Richard D. Irwin, Inc., Homewood, Ill., 1972.
4. EBERT, RONALD J., "Aggregate Planning and Learning Curve Productivity," *Management Sci.*, Vol. 23, No. 2 (October 1976), pp. 171–182.
5. EILON, SAMUEL, "Five Approaches to Aggregate Production Planning," *AIIE Transactions*, Vol. 7, No. 2 (June 1975), pp. 118–131.
6. ELMALEH, J. AND EILON, S., "A New Approach to Production Smoothing," *Internat. J. Production Res.*, Vol. 12 (1974), pp. 673–681.
7. GOODMAN, D. A., "Goal Programming Approach to Aggregate Planning of Production and Work Force," *Management Sci.*, Vol. 20, No. 12 (August 1974), pp. 1569–1575; Vol. 22, No. 6 (February 1976), pp. 708–716.
8. HANSMANN, FRED AND HESS, SIDNEY W., "A Linear Programming Approach to Production and Employment Scheduling," *Management Technology*, Monograph No. 1 (January 1960), pp. 46–51.
9. HOLT, C. C., MODIGLIANI, F. AND SIMON, H., "A Linear Decision Rule for Production and Employment Scheduling," *Management Sci.*, Vol. 2, No. 1 (September 1955), pp. 1–30.
10. ———, ———, MUTH, J. F. AND SIMON, H., *Planning Production, Inventories, and Work Force*, Prentice-Hall, New York, 1960.
11. JONES, CURTIS H., "Parametric Production Planning," *Management Sci.*, Vol. 13, No. 11 (July 1967), pp. 843–867.
12. LEE, W. B AND KHUMAWALA, B. M., "Simulation Testing of Aggregate Production Planning Models in an Implementation Methodology," *Management Sci.*, Vol. 20, No. 6 (February 1974), pp. 903–911.
13. LEE, SANG M. AND MOORE, LAURENCE J., "A Practical Approach to Production Scheduling," *Production and Inventory Management*, Vol. 15, No. 1 (First Quarter 1974), pp. 79–92.
14. McGARRAH, R. E., *Production and Logistics Management*, Wiley, New York, 1963.
15. ORR, D., "A Random Walk Production—Inventory Policy: Rationale and Implementation," *Management Sci.*, Vol. 9, No. 1 (October 1962), pp. 108–122.
16. SILVER, EDWARD A., "A Tutorial on Production Scheduling and Work Force Balancing," *Operations Res.*, Vol. 15, No. 6 (November-December 1967), pp. 985–1010.
17. TAUBERT, WILLIAM H., "A Search Decision Rule for the Aggregate Scheduling Problem," *Management Sci.*, Vol. 14, No. 6 (February 1968), pp. B343–B359.

INTERFACES
Vol. 9, No. 5, November 1979

AN INTEGRATED PRODUCTION, DISTRIBUTION, AND INVENTORY PLANNING SYSTEM

Fred Glover

University of Colorado, Boulder, Colorado 80309

Gene Jones

Agrico Chemical Company, Tulsa, Oklahoma 74103

David Karney

The Williams Companies, Tulsa, Oklahoma 74103

Darwin Klingman

University of Texas at Austin, Austin, Texas 78712

John Mote

Analysis, Research, and Computation, Inc., Austin, Texas 78765

ABSTRACT. The critical importance of integrating production, distribution, and inventory (PDI) operations has long been recognized by top management of many companies. Now, using the latest advances in Management Science modeling and solution technology, an integrated computer-based PDI system has saved approximately $18 million dollars during its first three years of implementation for a major national firm, Agrico Chemical Company. According to the Vice-President of Agrico Supply and Distribution, an additional $25 million savings is anticipated over the next two years.

Brought about by close cooperation between company officials and an outside staff of Management Science consultants, the PDI system has been used extensively to evaluate the benefit/cost impact of alternative capital investments in both short-term and long-term planning decisions. The development of the system underscores the value of recent Management Science innovations that have made it possible to analyze interacting influences too numerous and complex to be analyzed adequately only a few years ago.

Advanced network methodology incorporated into the PDI system required only one one-hundredth of the computer time and cost of methodologies previously used. The power and flexibility of the new Management Science tools have also brought about increased communication and understanding of key company operations. This increased communication and understanding stems from the inherent ''pictorial'' nature of network-based models, which facilitates interpretation of these models and policy recommendations based upon their solution.

INVENTORY/PRODUCTION; NETWORKS/GRAPHS

Overview

Agrico Chemical Company, with annual sales exceeding half a billion dollars, is one of the nation's largest chemical fertilizer companies. A subsidiary of The Williams Companies, Agrico mines, manufactures, and markets eight principal chemical products domestically and internationally. The company's success story, based on aggressive and forward-looking management, is typical of others in which a relatively small firm has been transformed into a leader in its field in less than a decade.

In the mid-1970's Agrico encountered unexpected difficulties. The seasonal demand characteristic of the chemical fertilizer industry was creating a chain of intricate and far reaching effects that could not be responded to adequately. As a result, the company's profit margins were being seriously eroded by steeply escalating distribution costs. It became apparent that a multitude of interdependent factors made it impossible to find a remedy through customary methods, such as studying cost figures and charts. The web of interacting influences which spanned the company's principal activities — production, distribution, and inventory — required an integrated computer-based planning system to uncover the appropriate decisions.

In 1976, David Wilson, Vice-President of Agrico Supply and Distribution, in coordination with Herb Beattie, Vice-President of The Williams Companies Information Services, created a project team to develop such a planning system. The principal objective of this team, headed by the authors, was to develop a computer-based production, distribution, and inventory (PDI) planning system which integrated the three major segments of Agrico's business decisions:

(1) the Supply Segment, consisting of production, purchases, and product exchanges with other chemical corporations (coproducers);

(2) the Storage and Customer Distribution Segment, involving sizing and locating bulk distribution centers; and

(3) the Demand Segment, involving customer demand throughout the eastern two-thirds of the United States, and locations where the product must be supplied to coproducers due to product exchange agreements.

The project team designed and implemented a PDI system utilizing recent advances in network modeling and solution technology [1], [2], [5—10], [12], [14—16]. The system was given the capability to provide planners with insight into the system-wide ramifications of their decisions. Its integrated framework allows the system to consider the relevant environmental impacts of all decisions simultaneously, thereby equipping it to provide analyses for long- and short-range planning and operational decisions.

Long-range planning summary

In long-range planning, the system is used primarily for decisions associated with the sizing and configuration of the distribution system. This helps to answer such questions as:

— Where should distribution centers be located and what should be their size?
— How much long-term inventory investment should be made?

INTERFACES November 1979

— How much transportation equipment is needed?

— What supply/purchase/exchange opportunities should be exploited?

In the short time that the integrated network PDI planning system has been in use at Agrico, it has already proven to be an extremely valuable decision aid for long-range planning and its effect in cutting the steeply rising distribution costs has been dramatic. Further, the system has uncovered several entirely unanticipated areas of cost savings, primarily through the evaluation of capital investment decisions.

One of Agrico's long-range studies, using this system, showed that by locating a distribution center on the upper Ohio River, $100,000 could be saved on transportation costs. Another study revealed that it was worth $175,000 to obtain the early completion of a new distribution center. The PDI planning system was also used to evaluate the long-range impact of changing the distribution pattern of a particular nitrogen chemical solution plant. Prior to the analysis using the PDI system, Agrico management had planned to build an additional 100,000 square foot storage facility to accommodate the forecasted growth in demand over a five-year period. The PDI planning system revealed that the additional storage facility was not cost effective. By not expanding the storage capacity Agrico realized a capital savings of $800,000. In addition, the distribution plan suggested by the PDI system reduced the annual transportation costs for the plant by $12,000.

Other long-range planning studies, using the PDI system, have been carried out by Agrico management, but the financial impact of the resulting decisions is more difficult to quantify. One such decision involved the closing of three small distribution centers in the midwest. The resulting capital was reinvested in rolling transportation equipment. In light of the current freight car shortage and energy cost increases, it is virtually impossible to accurately gauge the long-range affect of this decision.

The total quantifiable impact of Agrico's long-range planning studies using the PDI system is a cost savings in excess of $1 million. However, the most substantial results have come from the usage of the PDI system for short-range planning and operational decisions.

Short-range planning summary

For short-range operational decisions, Agrico uses the integrated network-based PDI system to aid in answering questions dealing with the *allocation* of a defined supply of product through a specific distribution center configuration. For such decisions, the system is used to avoid unnecessary production, distribution, and inventory costs by providing the capability to evaluate alternatives on a systemwide basis. To illustrate, the model is used to decide what, where, and how much product should be produced as well as when, where, and how much product should be shipped.

Since 1976, Agrico has used the PDI planning system for operational decisions to supply its products to customers at the right time and at the least possible cost consistent with good customer service. During its first year of implementation, the PDI planning system enabled management to reduce Agrico's total distribution costs by $3.7 million. *But this is not the bottom line*.

During the first year, Agrico was unable to adopt completely the decision alternatives suggested by the PDI planning system. This partial implementation was anticipated, and is natural, since the task of rescheduling production and distribution activities is formidable.

The overall impact of the planning system is best illustrated by Figure 1. This figure shows the growth in the total cost of distribution over the past few years as well as the anticipated growth through 1980. In the figure, the projected distribution costs are those that Agrico would have expected to incur if the PDI planning system had not been developed. The projected distribution costs are based on a conservative 7% annual inflation rate applied to the known point-to-point freight rates prior to the development of the PDI system. These inflated freight rates are multiplied by the anticipated distribution tonnage to obtain the projected costs. The actual incurred distribution costs through 1978 are also shown in Figure 1. These are projected forward for 1979 and 1980 by applying the same 7% annual inflation rate of the 1978 point-to-point freight rates obtained by the PDI system. A total distribution cost savings of nearly $17 million was made from 1976 to 1978. It is projected that by 1980 the PDI planning system will be providing Agrico with an *annual* distribution cost savings in excess of $13 million. Clearly the impact of this planning system is becoming more pronounced as the cost of energy increases.

FIGURE 1. Distribution Cost Trends.

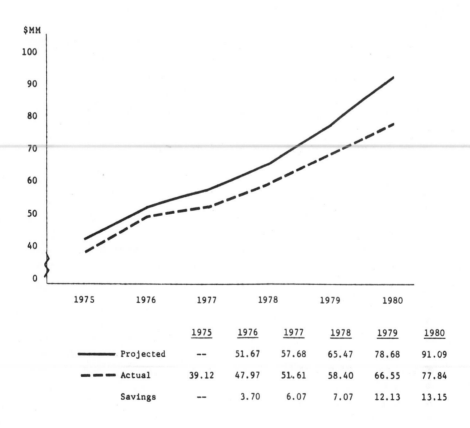

		1975	1976	1977	1978	1979	1980
———	Projected	--	51.67	57.68	65.47	78.68	91.09
– – –	Actual	39.12	47.97	51.61	58.40	66.55	77.84
	Savings	--	3.70	6.07	7.07	12.13	13.15

INTERFACES November 1979

Agrico's commitment to use the PDI planning system necessitated the development of an on-line automated freight rate system. Although initially designed simply to provide input data to the PDI system, the automated freight rate system has radically altered the way Agrico rates its orders from customers. The use of the freight rate system has reduced the average billing time by approximately one day. In 1978 alone, the corresponding reduction of accounts receivable produced a working capital interest savings of $50,000.

The system has also enabled Agrico to reduce the number of stockouts suffered by its clients by more effectively prepositioning its products in the marketplace. As a result, Agrico was able to sell nearly 50,000 more tons of product during 1978 than anticipated. This increased sales volume resulted in an additional $850,000 of working capital.

Another outcome of the usage of the PDI system for short-range planning is improved coordination and information flow between key departments. Although it is hard to quantify the impact of this improved departmental communication, in the long run this is potentially as important as the more quantifiable cost reductions.

The fundamental features of Agrico's integrated network computer-based PDI planning system and additional benefits from using this system are detailed in the following sections.

Agrico study

Background of company operations

Agrico's eight principal chemical products are produced continuously throughout the year. However, the demand for these agricultural products is highly seasonal with approximately one-third of the annual demand occurring within a four-week span. (See Figure 2.) This graph is fairly typical of all the principal chemical products.

FIGURE 2. 1976 Ammonia Fertilizer Sales.

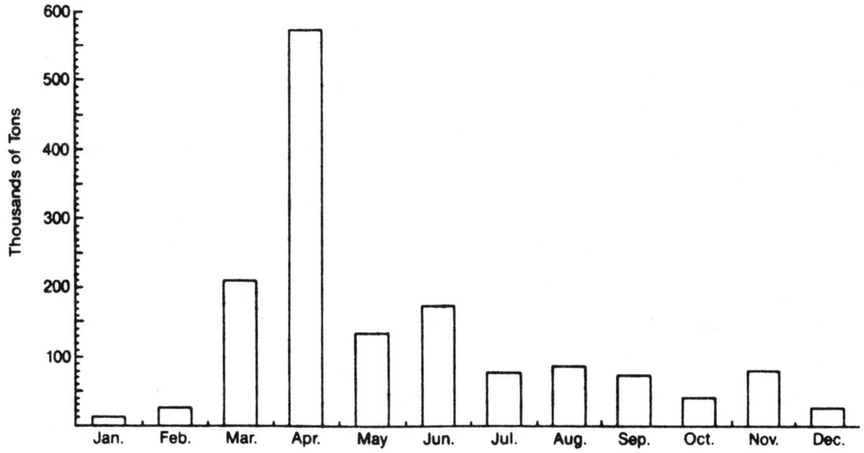

Managerial decisions relating to the distribution and inventory functions require evaluation of the following questions:

- Where should products be shipped?
- Which demand should be met?
- Which company-owned distribution centers should be used?
- Where should new distribution centers be leased and what should be their size?
- Where and how much product exchange should be made?
- How many railroad cars should be leased and purchased?
- What level of customer service provides the most cost-effective results?
- Which plants or distribution centers should service which clients?

As the size and complexity of the organization increased, it became apparent that answers to these important questions required more powerful analytical tools than previously employed. This realization was abruptly accentuated by the crisis of steeply escalating distribution costs in the mid-1970's. This led management to seek an effectively designed computer-based PDI planning system. The virtues of this decision are becoming more important due to the current energy and rail car shortages.

Model development

The interdisciplinary team, created by management to develop the PDI system, was composed of high-level company personnel and an outside staff of Management Scientists and computer specialists. It undertook as its initial effort to thoroughly analyze Agrico's existing facilities and on-going operations. Agrico has 4 production plants, 78 distribution centers, and approximately 2000 clients. The bulk distribution of product from plants to distribution centers is primarily by pipeline, barge, and rail. Shipments from distribution centers to clients also include truck and client-arranged pickup. The total bulk storage capacity of the 78 distribution centers is about 1.6 million tons, or approximately 40% of sales of the major products marketed.

A number of the distribution centers are owned and operated by Agrico and the remainder are leased on an annual basis. The centers provide a buffer between the constant production rate at the plants and the highly seasonal demand pattern of the clients. In addition, their storage capability allows Agrico to strategically preposition its products in order to provide its clients with faster deliveries at a lower cost.

The project team ascertained that Agrico had available or could obtain the following data:

- The production rates, capacity limitations, and variable operating costs at each supply point.

- Transportation costs from plants to distribution centers, inventory storage, capacity by product, transportation equipment loading and unloading limitations, variable throughput and operating costs, and the cost of stocking by mode of shipment for each distribution center in the system.

- Mode of shipment, demand to be served, and transportation costs from distribution centers for each client.

Overall model strategy

Based on the information obtained in the initial evaluation effort, a 12-month planning horizon was selected, since Agrico's distribution center leases are on an annual basis and uncertainties in sales forecasts diminish the value of a longer planning horizon. In addition, the project team decided to partition the planning horizon into monthly time periods in order to capture the highly seasonal demand pattern.

The critical task at this stage was to identify a model that exhibited a useful degree of realism, in view of the decision objectives, yet which was efficiently solvable. The early history of Management Science applications contains numerous examples of elaborate decision-making systems which were either designed to solve the wrong problems, or designed to solve the right problems, but which utilized a model structure that could never be solved with existing solution technology. In addition, the interpretations of these models and their outcomes were often completely opaque to anyone other than the highly technical "experts" who designed them.

To avoid these pitfalls, the project team devoted special consideration to the intricate task of designing a mathematical model which could effectively incorporate all the details of Agrico's PDI problems and, at the same time, satisfy the other two important criteria of *solvability* and *understandability*. Investigation showed that a network-based model was the most useful and effective for this task because:

(1) Network models are highly solvable. Advances in network modeling and solution technology [1]—[18] have occurred over the past several years whereby problems that previously cost $1000 to solve can now be solved for less than $10 [8], [9]. Further, it is now possible to solve network problems vastly larger than could be solved a few years ago [1].

(2) Network models facilitate communication between specialists and nonspecialists, due to their pictorial (diagrammatic) nature [8], [9].

(3) The visual aspects of network models also contribute to increased insights into the problem structure and enable meaningful interpretation of problem solutions.

With the decision to use a network-based model, the steps of the model development could be undertaken in a manner which allowed all members of the project team to actively participate, regardless of their Management Science background. Each member was encouraged to contribute to the team effort according to his own area of expertise.

The integration of the modeling effort, with the organizational levels and branches it affected, was an extensive and demanding task. Inputs required were the distribution history and modes of shipment, geographical demand patterns, process characteristics, plant capacities, variable operating costs, transportation costs and constraints, and inventory configurations, costs, and constraints. These were fed into the model and processed by an optimization routine that produced plans for top management's analysis and review. On the basis of this review, revised projections and "what if" questions were formulated which were again presented to the model, thereby establishing a dynamic feedback process that provided still more refined and useful information. The overall design of the project team's strategic effort is shown in Figure 3.

FIGURE 3. Project Design.

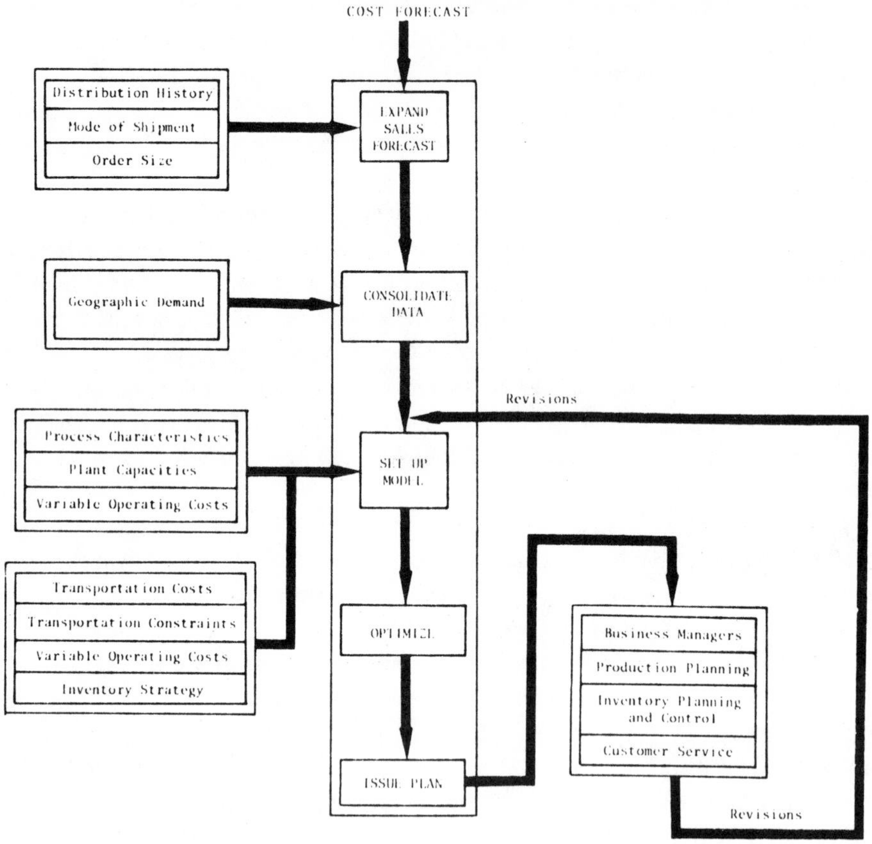

Special network model considerations

To make possible the dynamic feedback process of model review and revision, it was necessary to begin by charting Agrico's existing and proposed operations on a map of the United States. First, the existing and proposed supply sites were located on the map. They included Agrico's four production plants as well as points of potential product purchases and exchanges with coproducers. Next, existing and potential sites for bulk distribution centers were located on the map. They included the 78 distribution centers owned and operated by Agrico as well as the ones leased on an annual basis. Finally, all of the points of demand were located on the map. They included Agrico's 2000 clients as well as the points of potential product sales and exchanges with coproducers.

After constructing a map of Agrico's domestic operations, the project team transformed it into a more workable network model format. The two principal components of a network formulation are *nodes* and *arcs*. In this case, nodes (depicted by points, or circles) were used to represent the supply sites, distribution centers, and demand sites. The arcs (depicted by arrows) connect pairs of nodes, and indicate the possible ways to ship goods from supply sites to distribution centers and from these to demand sites. The orientation of an arc (direction of the arrow) indicates the allowable direction of shipment.

INTERFACES November 1979

In addition to the nodes and arcs, network models commonly have five data components: *Supplies, Demands, Costs, Lower Bounds,* and *Upper Bounds.* Supplies and demands are associated with nodes while costs, lower bounds, and upper bounds are associated with arcs. A simplified network diagram illustrating these data elements is presented in Figure 4. This diagram illustrates the feasible shipping routes between two supply sites (S1 and S2), two distribution centers (D1 and D2), and three demand sites (C1, C2, and C3). The supplies and demands in Figure 4 appear in triangles attached to the associated nodes. For example, supply site 1 has a supply of 29 tons of product, and demand site 2 has a demand of 28 tons of product. In this illustration, none of the distribution centers has any supply or demand. The marginal shipping cost between a pair of nodes is given in the rectangle attached to the arc that connects the nodes. The lower and upper bounds indicate the allowable size of the shipment between a pair of nodes and are given in parentheses beside the corresponding arc. For instance, it costs $2 per ton to ship from supply site 1 to distribution center 2. The minimum shipment is 8 tons and the maximum is 20 tons.

FIGURE 4. Network Diagram of Agrico Facilities.

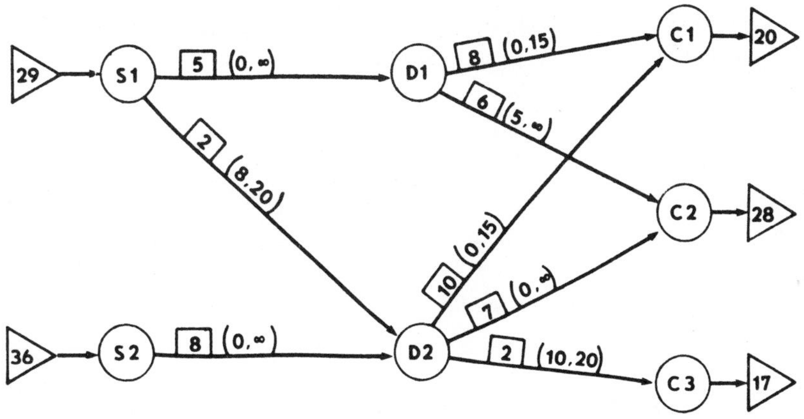

The lower bound on an arc in the network formulation allows the model to incorporate such features as contractual agreements to ship at least a certain amount of product between locations. The upper bound on an arc can be used to capture such things as management policies on shipment sizes or physical rate of movement limitations (e.g., pipeline limits).

Elaborating the basic model form

Once the fundamental network model form was understood by members of the project team, the next step was to elaborate it in order to handle the special considerations that applied to the real-world structure of Agrico's problem. For example, it was desired to give the model the ability to accommodate management's practice of setting lower and upper limits on supply quantities. This ability allows the model, instead of the manager, to select the exact levels of production, purchase, and exchange. The manager is required only to specify feasible ranges for these decisions. In the network formulation, this feature was implemented by adding a *supply policy node* and *supply policy arcs* to each of the supply sites.

This added construction provided an increased model capability that made it possible to handle the variable costs of production, purchase, and exchange. In an analogous fashion, the model was extended to enable fixed levels of demand at each demand site to be replaced by an estimated demand range. *Demand policy arcs* from each demand site to a *demand policy node* can be used to capture the variable revenue associated with selling the product or exchanging with a coproducer.

Additional problem considerations required somewhat more complex augmentations to the model. Analyses conducted with the aid of Agrico's production, distribution, and marketing staffs led to identifying the least cost alternatives for modes of transportation from the supply sites to the distribution centers. These were incorporated into the model by means of appropriate network constructions. Safeguards on the quality of customer service were provided by a preliminary culling of transportation links from distribution centers to demand sites and imposition of bounds on appropriate arcs.

Agrico's marketing staff raised the further consideration that many clients expressed a preference for certain modes of transportation during certain times of the year. Consequently, the project team decided to represent these clients by a *set* of demand site nodes instead of by a single node. A set of nodes made it possible to handle variances in distribution cost depending on the mode of transportation.

Further augmentations of the model were developed to handle the seasonal demand patterns, inventory capacities, and holding costs, beginning and ending inventory levels, and transportation equipment loading and unloading limitations. A simplified three-month "snapshot" of the overall model structure is provided in Figure 5. The supply sites are modeled in this figure by the nodes labeled S_{it}. For instance, S_{21} represents supply site 2 in period 1. The complex nature of the distribution centers requires that three nodes, D_{jAt}, D_{jBt}, and D_{jCt}, be used to represent distribution center j during period t. The movement of product from supply site i to distribution center j during period t is handled by the arc connecting S_{it} to D_{jAt}. The unloading (loading) dock at distribution center j in period t is modeled as the arc from D_{jAt} to D_{jBt} $(D_{jBt}$ to $D_{jCt})$. The long term storage of product during period t at distribution center j is captured by the arc connecting D_{jBt} to D_{jBt+1}. The clients (by mode of transportation) are represented by the nodes labeled C_{kmt}. The shipment of product from the distribution centers to the clients is handled by the arcs from D_{jCt} to C_{kmt}. For example, the rail shipments from distribution center 2 to customer 1 during period 3 are modeled by the arc from D_{2C3} to C_{1R3}. The supply (demand) policy arcs are those that are connected to the node labeled SP (DP).

FIGURE 5. Agrico PDI Network Model.

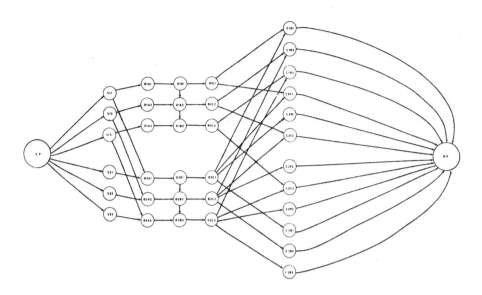

LCD model

One of the fundamental model components of Agrico's PDI system is the *Least Cost Distribution* (LCD) model. This basic model is used for many different types of analyses and policy evaluations and is sometimes augmented by additional variables and constraints. At other times, portions of the basic model are dropped from consideration. For instance, Agrico has used the model, so far, with no revenue values associated with the demand policy arcs. Thus, the LCD model has been used strictly to minimize costs.

For short-range planning, it is assumed that the plant and distribution center configuration is fixed. Consequently, for short-range analysis, the objective of the LCD model is to minimize the following "laid-in" costs:

- variable production costs,
- primary costs to move product to distribution center storage,
- secondary costs to move product to the client,
- variable costs associated with holding inventory,
- variable distribution center throughput costs.

The sum of these costs is minimized subject to the following constraints:

- demand volume of clients,
- supply availability at supply points,
- distribution center input-output capacity,
- inventory capacity,
- opening inventory levels,
- minimum closing inventory requirements,
- mode of shipment required.

For long-range planning, the LCD model is used to determine the optimal plant and distribution center configuration and size. For these types of analyses, the objectives are augmented to include minimization of plant expansion and fixed distribution center lease costs. The constraint set is expanded to include various distribution center location and plant expansion options.

The inputs and outputs of the LCD model are shown in Figure 6. Two of the especially important outputs of this model are the *least cost distribution zone maps* and the *distribution center report summary*. The zone maps are prepared directly from the solution to the network model. They show the counties that can be supplied at least cost from each distribution center and are used daily to manually control the placement of orders.

FIGURE 6. LCD System.

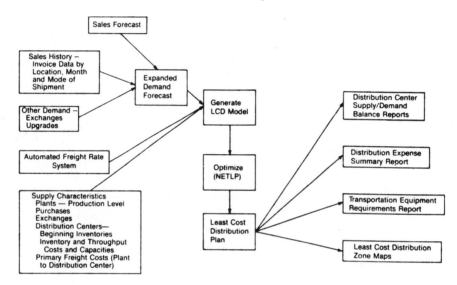

The distribution center report summary gives a full breakdown, by month and by transportation mode (truck, rail, barge, etc.) for each client. Clients are also grouped on the basis of type of sales, i.e., Agrico retailers, non-Agrico retailers, and national wholesale executive accounts.

The foregoing outputs, together with the others indicated in Figure 6, contribute markedly to the ease of implementing this model. The outputs also facilitate the companywide coordination essential to model review and updating. The success of the LCD model rests in no small part on the effectiveness of this coordination.

Solving the LCD model - no small task

The inclusion of multimodal shipping aspects and partitioning the planning horizon greatly increased the size and complexity of the LCD model. For this reason, the project team was careful to capture the production, inventory, and distribution constraints of the system in a network formulation for short-range planning. Even so, the typical size of the short-range LCD problem involves approximately 6000 equations and more than 35,000 variables.

INTERFACES November 1979

In fact, the apparently formidable task of solving this problem almost caused the study to be aborted before it began. To test the feasibility of solving the problem, Agrico obtained access to a primal simplex-based network code from its parent, The Williams Companies. Attempts to solve a problem with this code on a large-scale AMDAHL V-6 computer required approximately two and a half hours. This outcome was severely negative, due to the need for reasonable turnaround time to perform iterative solution analyses. As a result, the project was on the brink of being scrapped.

Fortunately, however, major recent innovations in network solution technology [5], [9], [10] came to the rescue. The project team recommended that Agrico undertake to solve the problem with an advanced and highly efficient code developed by Analysis, Research, and Computation (ARC), Inc. With management's approval, ARC's network code, ARCNET, was obtained and tested. ARCNET was able to reduce the solution time from two and a half hours to only 50 seconds! Because of the need to solve the short-range LCD model repeatedly, in order to answer "what if" questions concerning different demand structures and production/distribution scenarios, this occurrence was a vital element in the success of the project.

The project team's network expertise was also utilized to obtain highly efficient solution software for the long-range LCD model. This model is a large-scale, mixed integer, linear programming problem whose linear programming (LP) portion involves a large embedded network structure. Members of the project team had previously played a fundamental role in developing mathematical procedures [11], [16] for solving LP problems with embedded networks efficiently. However, at that time such procedures had never been implemented for use on a computer. Since management had faith in the project team, they authorized the team to negotiate a contract with ARC to develop such an LP system. This was the second and most crucial decision made by Agrico management for the solution of their models.

ARC developed a new LP solution system, called PNET/LP, which has proven to be far superior in performance to even the team's most optimistic expectations. The system, when compared against one of the fastest state-of-the-art LP systems, APEX-III, proved to be at least 75 times faster on medium size prototypes of Agrico's problems. PNET/LP normally solves Agrico's long-range LCD problems, involving 6250 equations and 23,000 variables, in less than 5 minutes, including all input and output. The value of this solution capability, in terms of providing management with a tool — the LCD model — which can be used on a routine basis to evaluate planning alternatives, is difficult to overstate.

Concluding remarks by Agrico management

The following remarks regarding the success of this Management Science application at Agrico Chemical Company are given by David Wilson, Vice-President of Agrico Supply and Distribution:

> The PDI planning system has had a widespread impact at Agrico. In addition to cost savings that exceed $8 million in 1978 alone, the system has brought about improvements in nearly every phase of our production, distribution and inventory operations.

We have recently used the PDI system, for example, to evaluate the benefit/cost impact of resizing an ammonia pipeline system and to determine the effects of pipeline tariff rate changes. Additionally, we have used the system to evaluate long-term conversion/exchange agreements affecting operations companywide. Also, the use of the model to assist in sizing our UAN solution distribution system has provided new insights on size and location of storage tanks.

A major nonquantifiable benefit has been a better and more thorough understanding of our Supply and Distribution operations. The PDI system has been particularly valuable to Agrico in the areas of marketing (by more clearly identifying the end-point demands of our customers and the transportation modes best suited to satisfy them) and supply and distribution (by more effectively relating distribution center operations to the most profitable shipping alternatives).

The ability to investigate the impact of various decision alternatives, *before they are implemented*, provides us with information to manage more intelligently. The "whys" of a particular solution are often more valuable than the "what" of an optimal solution, as optimal solutions are typically modified during implementation due to changes in real-world conditions. Insights into the "whys" of system behavior, gained through the investigation of alternative scenarios with the PDI system, have enabled us to respond more effectively to our operating environment.

The use of the LCD system has been so successful and encouraging that we are in the process of incorporating revenue data into the model and are considering extensions of the model to encompass our manufacturing and mining activities. These extensions of the model will enable marketing to evaluate the impact of new areas of demand and allow Agrico to gain the benefits of the PDI planning system in additional areas of management.

REFERENCES

[1] Barr, R. and Turner, J.S., "A New, Linear Programming Approach to Microdata File Merging," *1978 Compendium of Tax Research*, Office of Tax Analysis, Department of the Treasury, Washington, D.C.

[2] Bartholdi, J., III, and Ratliff, H.D., "A Field Guide to Identifying Network Flow and Matching Problems," Research Report No. 77-12, Department of Industrial and Systems Engineering, University of Florida, Gainesville, Florida.

[3] Bazaraa, M. and Jarvis, J., *Linear Programming and Network Flows*, John Wiley & Sons, New York, 1977.

[4] Bradley, G., "Survey of Deterministic Networks," *AIIE Transactions* 7, 1975, pp. 222—234.

[5] Bradley, G., Brown, G., and Graves, G., "Design and Implementation of Large-Scale Primal Transshipment Algorithms," *Management Science* 24, 1977, pp. 1—35.

[6] Cunningham, W., "A Network Simplex Method," *Mathematical Programming* 11, 1976 pp. 105—116.

[7] Dennis, J., "A High-Speed Computer Technique for the Transportation Problem," *Journal of the Association for Computing Machinery* 8, 1958, pp. 132—153.

[8] Glover, F., Hultz, J., and Klingman, D., "Improved Computer-Based Planning Techniques, Part I," *Interfaces* 8, 1978, pp. 16—25.

[9] Glover, F., Hultz, J., Klingman, D., and Stutz, J., "Generalized Networks: A Fundamental Computer-Based Planning Tool," *Management Science* 24, 1978, pp. 1209—1220.

[10] Glover, F., Karney, D., and Klingman, D., "Implementation and Computational Study on Start Procedures and Basis Change Criteria for a Primal Network Code," *Networks* 4, 1974, pp. 191—212.

[11] Glover, F. and Klingman, D., "Models and Methods for Network-Related Problems," *Proceedings of NATO Advanced Study Institute on Computer Methods in Practical Applications*, Sogesta, Urbino, Italy, July 1977.

[12] Helgason, R. and Kennington, J., *Algorithms for Network Programming*, to be published.

[13] Jensen, P. and Bhaumik, G., "A Flow Augmentation Approach to the Network with Gains Minimum Cost Flow Problem," *Management Science* 23, 1977, pp. 631—643.

[14] Johnson, E., "Flows in Networks," in *Handbook of Operations Research*, ed. by J. Moder and S. Elmaghraby, Van Nostrand Rineholt Co., 1978, pp. 183—205.

[15] Klingman, D. and Russell, R., "On Solving Constrained Transportation Problems," *Operations Research* 23, 1975, pp. 91—107.

[16] Maier, S., "A Compact Inverse Scheme Applied to a Multicommodity Network with Resource Constraints," Technical Report No. 71-8, Operations Research House, Stanford University, 1971.

[17] Mulvey, J., "Testing of a Large-Scale Network Optimization Program," *Mathematical Programming* 15, 1978, pp. 291—315.

[18] Srinivasan, V. and Thompson, G., "Benefit-Cost Analysis of Coding Techniques for the Primal Transportation Algorithm," *Journal of the Association for Computing Machinery* 20, 1973, pp. 194—213.

3 / Inventories

Inventories have existed in our society in many forms for many years and for many purposes. One can think of an inventory of automobiles at an automobile rental agency or an inventory of cattle at a food processor's stockyard. In an industrial manufacturing sense, inventories have been broadly classified into those which include raw materials, in-process materials, and finished goods. In almost all cases we can see inventories as something which management uses as a hedge against uncertainty; something which helps to insure smooth operation of the system, whatever it may be.

The security which inventories offer for specific systems may be costly however. Many years of study and research by industry, research institutes and universities has yielded a wealth of analytical techniques which enable the user to determine the size of an inventory he needs in order to run a specified risk of a stockout and utilize the amount of money he wishes to tie up in inventory.

Inventories offer managerial flexibility (scheduling, planning, etc.) to the administrator of a firm and security and/or service to the customer primarily in socio-economic systems which deal with discrete ports. It is to systems such as these which we have directed the collection of articles on inventory contained in this publication.

The initial paper in this collection, by Berry, Marcus and Williams, addresses an inventory problem in an industrial manufacturing setting. A statistical sampling procedure is described which enables the determination of potential inventory cost savings which will accrue from the acquisition of specific processing equipment. Raw materials inventory could be reduced by this proposal.

The second article, by Whybark, considers the inventory maintained by a distribution center (warehouse). A major concern here is the amount of inventory which is maintained and the level of service which is offered to the customer. A demand generation procedure which borrows from the straightforward logic of material requirements planning is proposed here. An implosion rather than an explosion procedure is utilized to generate the demand. Whybark shows how this method could be most effective.

As a final inventory oriented article we have included a work by Brodheim and Prastacos. An inventory of blood in a medical environment offers a significant challenge to the analyst who attempts to develop a suitable control model. The demand patterns and shelf life of the product are severe restrictions here. One will be able to see, however, many of the ingredients that are present in the typical industrial inventory problem.

MANAGEMENT SCIENCE
Vol. 23, No. 12, August 1977
Printed in U.S.A.

INVENTORY INVESTMENT ANALYSIS USING BIASED SAMPLING TECHNIQUES*

WILLIAM L. BERRY†, MYLES MARCUS‡ AND J. GREG WILLIAMS§

This paper describes the use of Biased Sampling to solve an inventory planning problem at a firm which produces plastic coated steel products. In this application, the Biased Sampling solutions provided an estimate of the inventory investment savings to be obtained from a major capital investment proposal. The problem structure, the development of biasing procedures to guide the solution process, and the computational results are presented.

Inventory Investment Analysis Using Biased Sampling Techniques

Biased Sampling, involving the random generation of solutions to complex combinatorial problems using computer techniques, has been suggested as an analytical method for solving a variety of operating problems, e.g. in balancing assembly lines [1], [7], scheduling production [2], [3], and in locating and laying out facilities [4], [6]. This paper describes an application of Biased Sampling to solve an inventory planning problem at a company that produces plastic coated steel products. This problem was encountered in the course of evaluating a major capital investment proposal involving the purchase of steel sheeting equipment to cut steel coils into flat sheets, thereby enabling the company to buy steel coils instead of individually cut sheet stock items (of a specified width and length). The economic justification of the proposed equipment derives from both purchasing and inventory savings (balanced against trim loss since the purchase of steel coils would reduce the total number of items to be stocked as raw material). The determination of the total operating savings involves the solution of an inventory planning problem to determine which coil sizes should be stocked as raw material in order to produce the more than 300 sheet stock items currently being purchased from steel suppliers.

While this inventory planning problem can be structured and solved using integer or dynamic programming methods (as shown in the Appendix), it is important to note several advantages of the Biased Sampling solution methodology that were considered to be important in this application. First, Biased Sampling exploits the power of the computer to produce optimum or near optimum solutions. Since management was primarily interested in determining whether the level of savings from the proposed equipment was sufficient to provide a minimum return on the investment, optimal solutions were not of primary importance in this situation. Second, Biased Sampling provides an analytical method that can be easily used and understood by operating personnel. In this case a series of example problems were analyzed with the company managers during the process of structuring the inventory planning problem for analysis. Since the logic in the Biased Sampling computer program was similar to that used in solving the example problems, the method and the results were easily interpreted by the company personnel. Finally, Biased Sampling has the flexibility to accommodate a wide variety of problem assumptions regarding the cost structure and restrictions. Moreover, the Biased Sampling computer program can be easily modified to accommodate changes in these problem elements that are suggested during the

* Accepted by Samuel Eilon, former Departmental Editor for Production Management; received December 1, 1975. This paper has been with the authors 11 months, for 1 revision.
† Indiana University.
‡ Travenol Laboratories, Inc., Morton Grove, Illinois.
§ Bell Helicopter Textron, Fort Worth.

course of the analysis. What this means is that Biased Sampling permits a considerable breadth of analysis in situations where the time for analysis is limited.

We begin by describing the important elements of the inventory planning problem, and then turn to structuring the problem for analysis with special attention to the requirements for using Biased Sampling. This structuring includes (1) the specification of an objective function and the problem variables, (2) the determination of the operating data required for the analysis, and (3) the development of two probability setting procedures to guide the sampling process (Constant Probability and Demand Biasing). Finally, the computational results for the inventory planning problem are discussed. These results include an analysis of the solution quality of the two biasing procedures. This analysis (obtained by solving a small example problem as a zero-one integer linear programming problem, and comparing the results with those obtained using Biased Sampling) is intended to illustrate the quality of the Biased Sampling solutions in this application.

The Problem Setting

The plastic coating plant currently buys pre-cut steel sheet in sizes ranging from 30 to 60 inches in width, 50 to 147 inches in length, and 0.020 to 0.032 inches thick. Subsequently, a plastic coating is applied to one or both sides of the sheet stock. More than 300 different sizes and grades of steel sheet are carried in the raw material inventory, representing an investment exceeding $1,000,000. An example of the types of sheet stock items purchased by this plant is shown in Table 1. The production of any of these items from coil stock eliminates the need to carry sheet stock inventory for these items, since the proposed coil cutting process and the plastic coating process would be scheduled as a single operation.

TABLE 1

Example Sheet Stock Data

Item Number	Sheet Stock Item Description				Annual Usage[3]	Average Inventory[3]	Order Quantity[3]
	Material Grade[2]	Thickness	Width	Length			
1	CQ	0.032 in.	40 in.	145 in.	250,000	15,000	30,000
2	CQ	0.032	40	80	330,000	15,000	30,000
3	CQ	0.032	39	100	50,000	15,000	30,000
4	CQ	0.032	38	110	300,000	15,000	30,000

Notes: [1] Example Costs: Sheet Stock Purchasing Cost = $0.15/lb.
Coil Stock Purchasing Cost = $0.14/lb.
Annual Inventory Carrying Cost = $0.04/lb.[4]
Variable Processing Cost = $0.005/lb.[5]

[2] CQ stands for one of the high usage grades of sheet steel—Commercial Quality Steel.

[3] Measured in lbs.

[4] In order to simplify the calculations for this example, the same inventory carrying cost has been assumed for both coils and sheet. In actual fact, the inventory carrying cost for steel coils is slightly less than that for sheet.

[5] The estimated cost of cutting coils into sheet on the proposed equipment includes the variable portion of the combined labor and overhead cost.

Currently, the raw material inventory of steel sheet is controlled manually using an Order Point System. Incoming finished product sheet requirements are netted against the current inventory balance on a daily basis, and when the order point is reached an order is placed on a steel supplier. Sheet stock orders are accepted by the steel suppliers for a minimum order quantity of an ingot load (or in ingot load multiples). The ingot weight depends on the material width and thickness of the finished item.

and varies from 18,000 to 43,000 pounds for the different types of sheet stock items. As an example, the items shown in Table 1 have an ingot weight and a minimum order quantity of 30,000 pounds, since they are of the same material grade and thickness and are of similar widths. In the past sheet stock orders have usually been placed for the minimum order quantity. This is largely explained by the fact that the cost of placing an order with a steel supplier is negligible at this company, causing the economic order quantity generally to be smaller than the minimum order quantity specified by the steel suppliers.

The Inventory Planning Problem

The decision to purchase the steel sheeting equipment depends on the amount of purchasing and raw material inventory savings that can be obtained. Although the purchasing savings is easily determined from forecasts of production volume and sheet stock usage, these savings were not sufficient to justify the proposed equipment. Hence, management questioned the impact of purchasing steel coils instead of sheet on the size of the raw material inventory investment.

The determination of the amount of raw material inventory savings involves the solution of an inventory planning problem to decide which coil sizes and grades should be stocked as raw material to provide the more than 300 different sheet stock items used in the plastic coating process. The decision of which coil sizes and grades are to be stocked involves determining the best trade-off between inventory savings (obtained by reducing the number of coil types to be stocked) and trim loss (resulting from a decision to make smaller width sheet stock items from wider coil types). An expression measuring the total savings to be obtained by stocking a particular set of coils is given in (1).

$$\text{Total Savings} = (\text{Purchasing Savings}) + (\text{Inventory Carrying Cost Savings})$$
$$- (\text{Trim Loss}), \tag{1}$$

where:

$$\text{Purchasing Savings} = \sum_i \left[\sum_{j \in \Phi_i} V_j S_j - V_i(C_i + P_i) \right].$$

$$\text{Inventory Carrying Cost Savings} = \sum_i \left[\sum_{j \in \Phi_i} I_j(Q_j/2) - I_i(Q_i/2) \right].$$

$$\text{Trim Loss} = \sum_i \left[\sum_{j \in \Phi_i} [(W_i - W_j)/W_j] C_i V_j \right],$$

where $i =$ a coil type to be stocked.

$j =$ a sheet stock item.

$\Phi_i =$ the subset of the individual sheet stock items (j) to be produced from coil type i.

$V_j =$ the annual volume for sheet stock type j.

$V_i =$ the annual volume for coil type i ($V_i = \sum_{j \in \Phi_i} V_j$).

$S_j =$ the purchasing cost for sheet stock item j.

$C_i =$ the purchasing cost for coil type i.

$P_i =$ the processing cost for coil type i on the proposed equipment.

$I_j =$ the inventory carrying cost for sheet stock j.

$I_i =$ the inventory carrying cost for coil type i.

$Q_j =$ the purchase order quantity for sheet stock type j.

$Q_i =$ the purchase order quantity for coil type i.

$W_j =$ the width of sheet stock item j.

$W_i =$ the width of coil type i.

56

(1) was used to evaluate the various solutions produced by the Biased Sampling procedure. In this case, each solution represented a different mapping of sheet stock items to coil types (Φ_i, for the $i = 1, n$ coil types in a particular solution). Several examples which illustrate the use of (1) to evaluate the total savings for individual coil stocking plans are presented next. These examples use the data shown in Table 1. In these examples, the average inventory level is assumed to be one half of the order quantity. Several alternative assumptions concerning the average inventory figure, including the use of historical inventory data, were considered in this study, and will be discussed further in the data gathering section of this paper.

Sources of the Inventory Savings

The inventory savings that are determined by (1) are obtained from two sources. First, several different items involving the same sheet thickness, width, and material grade, but differing lengths, could be produced from a single coil. Items 1 and 2 in Table 1 (the $40'' \times 145''$ and the $40'' \times 80''$ items) illustrate this source of savings. That is, the production of items 1 and 2 from a single coil would cause a reduction in the inventory investment of \$2250 (\$0.15/lb. $\times$ 15,000 lbs.) and a reduction in the annual inventory carrying cost of \$600 (\$0.04/lb. $\times$ 15,000 lbs.).

The second source of inventory savings is obtained by reducing the number of coils that are stocked by slitting smaller width sheets from a larger width coil on the proposed equipment.[1] For example, consider the three widths shown in Table 1 (40'', 39'' and 38''). The 39 inch item could be produced from either a 39 or a 40 inch wide coil. When this item is produced from a 40 inch coil, a one inch trim loss is incurred. Likewise, there are three alternatives for producing the 38 inch wide item. All of these alternatives are summarized in Table 2, where the columns denote the sheet widths to be produced and the rows denote the coil widths that could be stocked as raw material. In using Table 2 it is important to note that further inventory savings, obtained by reducing the number of coils stocked, involves a trade-off between trim loss and inventory savings. This trade-off between inventory savings and trim loss can be illustrated by considering several of the alternative solutions suggested by the data in Table 2.

TABLE 2
Savings Calculations

Alternatives Make From:	Sheet Stock Widths		
	40 in. Wide Item	39 in. Wide Item	38 in. Wide Item
40 in. Coil	Inventory Savings* \$ 600 Purchasing Savings 2900 Trim Loss — Total Annual Savings \$3500	Inventory Savings \$ 600 Purchasing Savings 250 Trim Loss − 179 Total Annual Savings \$ 671	Inventory Savings \$ 600 Purchasing Savings 1500 Trim Loss − 2211 Total Annual Savings \$ − 111
39 in. Coil		Inventory Savings — Purchasing Savings \$250 Trim Loss — Total Annual Savings \$250	Inventory Savings \$ 600 Purchasing Savings 1500 Trim Loss − 1105 Total Annual Savings \$ 995
38 in. Coil			Inventory Savings — Purchasing Savings \$1500 Trim Loss — Total Annual Savings \$1500

* Obtained by combining items 1 and 2 in Table 1.

[1] The maximum coil width that can be produced on the proposed equipment is 60 inches.

Example Solutions

One possible solution to the inventory planning problem is that of stocking a different coil for each material width, thickness, and grade produced as sheet stock. An example of such a solution is suggested by the diagonal elements in Table 2 (moving from the upper left-hand to the lower right-hand corner of the table). That is, a separate coil could be stocked for each product width, i.e., the 40", 39", and 38" items. This solution would only provide purchasing savings in this example, since the same inventory carrying cost is used in this example for both coil and sheet stock. A second solution would involve producing the 39 inch sheet from a 40 inch coil and stocking the 38 inch wide coil. Since a 39 inch coil would not be stocked in this case, a $600 annual inventory carrying cost savings is produced, but a $179 trim loss is incurred.[2]

Although the second solution (stocking both the 40" and 38" wide coils) provides the largest total savings in this example (of $5,671), two additional solutions could be constructed from the data shown in Table 2. All of these solutions must meet two conditions. First, each final product sheet width must be produced from a coil. This condition is satisfied by assuring that one element in each column is included in the solution. The second condition involves assuring that all of the coil widths required to implement a given solution are stocked. For example, the 39 inch wide sheet in Table 2 must be produced from a 39 inch wide coil in order to make the 38 inch wide sheet from a 39 inch wide coil. This means that the diagonal element in a given row in Table 2 must be in the solution *if* any other element in the same row is in the solution.[3]

Biased Sampling Approach

Biased Sampling provides a means for intelligently generating solutions to combinatorial problems such as the inventory planning problem. However, only a small fraction of the solutions generated are of interest, i.e., those which are near optimum.[4] To increase the probability of finding optimum or near optimum solutions, special procedures (called Biasing Procedures) are needed to guide the sampling process. Three steps were involved in solving the inventory planning problem using Biased Sampling: (1) data gathering, (2) writing a short computer program that would perform the savings calculations for any given problem solution, and (3) developing two different Biased Sampling procedures to be used with the computer program. These steps were taken after the company managers involved had reviewed several example problems (similar to the one shown in Tables 1 and 2) that illustrated the savings calculations to be performed by the computer program.

Data Gathering

Since gathering data such as that shown in Table 1 is expensive, one of the early problems was that of determining which of the 300 sheet stock items should be included in the analysis. An ABC analysis inicated that four different sheet stock thickness and material grades represented 68% of the annual production volume, involving 156 different inventory items. Since these items provided the largest savings potential (and would permit the determination of a lower limit on the overall savings), the data gathering effort was directed at these items. Three parameters were estimated

---

[2] While the trim loss calculation in this example does not provide for a scrap credit, such an allowance could easily be included in determining the savings figures in Table 2.

[3] These conditions form the basis for the integer programming formulation in the Appendix.

[4] Clearly, the number of optimum (or near optimum) solutions which are produced depends on the size of the sample obtained.

TABLE 3

Sample Sheet Stock Input Data Report

Material				Annual Usage*	Order Quantity*	No. Weeks Between Orders	Average Inventory Level*	Average Inventory Investment	Annual Inventory Carrying Cost
Thickness	Grade	Width	Length						
0.032 in.	CQ	40 in.	145 in.	250,000	30,000	6.2	15,000	$2250	$ 600
0.032	CQ	40	80	330,000	30,000	4.7	15,000	2250	600
0.032	CQ	39	100	50,000	30,000	31.2	15,000	2250	600
0.032	CQ	38	110	300,000	30,000	5.2	15,000	2250	600
Total				930,000			60,000	9000	2400

TABLE 4

Sample Computer Program Results

Material Thick/Grade/Width	Coil Stock Code	Order Quantity*	Average Inventory Level*	Average Inventory Investment	Annual Inventory Carrying Cost	Coil Annual Usage*	Number of Weeks Between Orders	Trim Loss Percentage	Annual Purchasing Savings	Total Savings
0.032in./CQ/40 in.	1	30,000	15,000	$2100	$ 600	630,000	2.5	—	$1250	$1250
0.032/CQ/40	0	—	—	—	—	—	—	—	1650	2250
0.032/CQ/39	0	—	—	—	—	—	—	2.56%	250	671
0.032/CQ/38	1	30,000	15,000	2100	600	300,000	5.2	—	1500	1500
Total			30,000	$4200	$1200	930,000			$4650	$5671

* In lbs.

Note: In order to be consistent with the data shown earlier in Table 1, the average inventory figures shown here equal one-half of the order quantity.

for each item: (1) the annual usage, (2) the average inventory level, and (3) the order quantity. These parameters were determined by reviewing the inventory record for each item. The annual usage was estimated from an average of the previous 13 weeks demand and an average inventory level was determined by averaging the ending inventory value at the close of each of the previous four quarters. The order quantity was taken directly from the inventory record for each item.

Management personnel reviewed the resulting data to insure that the figures reflected the business forecasts for the coming year. The average inventory figure was the most difficult parameter to estimate, and three different assumptions were considered: (1) the use of the average cycle stock ($\frac{1}{2}$ of the order quantity), (2) the average cycle stock plus an estimate of the safety stock, and (3) the historical average inventory value. The historical average inventory level was used in the analysis presented here. The use of the other alternatives to determine the inventory savings involved minor changes to the computer program, but indicated very little change in the estimated inventory savings.

The Computer Program

The computer program was developed to serve two purposes: (1) to evaluate the solutions generated randomly by each of the Biased Sampling procedures, and (2) to provide a means of evaluating specific solutions that are input to the program by management personnel. The program simply reads the detailed data which were gathered on the 156 sheet stock items, and prints out two separate reports. Examples of these two reports are shown in Tables 3 and 4, using the example problem data from Table 1. The first report (shown in Table 3) provides a listing of the input data and some summary statistics. The second report (Table 4) describes an individual solution. As an example, the savings results for the solution involving the stocking of 40 inch and 38 inch wide coils in the example problem is shown in Table 4.

Several items should be noted in the solution shown in Table 4. First, all of the sheet stock items considered in the study are listed, including those items which only involve differing lengths of the same raw material. For example, item number two in Table 1 is included in this listing, and the savings figure totals include the inventory savings contributed by making two items, which differ only in length, from a single width coil. Second, the coil stocking code shown in the second column of Table 4 indicates which items are to be stocked as coils (a 1 indicates that the line item is to be stocked as a coil and a 0 indicates that the item is to be made from the next wider coil type). For example, the 0.032"/CQ/39" item in Table 4 is to be produced from a 40 inch wide coil. Finally, the computer printout provides an easy means of communicating the inventory savings results to the managers involved in the study. The savings calculations can be easily verified using the data in this report. Also, it facilitates changes in the problem assumptions. For example, if the average time between orders for the 40 inch wide coil in Table 4 is judged to be too short, the order quantity for this item can be increased, to say 60,000 pounds, and the solution re-evaluated.

Biased Sampling Procedures

Two different techniques were developed to bias the random generation of solutions by the computer program toward solutions with large annual savings. These two procedures, referred to as Constant Probability and Demand Biasing, determine whether a particular product width/grade/thickness item is to be stocked as a coil in a given solution or not. These biasing procedures are utilized by the computer program in the following manner. First, one of the two biasing procedures is selected for use with the computer program. Next, the computer program proceeds by (1) using the biasing procedure to generate a specific coil stocking solution (i.e., determining either a 0 or a 1 coil stocking code for each item, as is illustrated in column two of Table 4), (2) evaluating the total savings of the current solution, and (3) checking to determine whether the desired number of solutions (i.e., the sample size) has been generated. The computer program continues in this manner until the desired sample size has been reached.

Constant Probability Procedure

This procedure develops a complete coil stocking solution in two steps. First, a fixed coil stocking probability (P_C) is assigned to each product width/grade/thickness item. For example, a coil stocking probability value of $P_C = 0.2$ might be used for lines 3 and 4 in Table 4.[5] In the Constant Probability procedure the same coil stocking probability value (P_C) is used for all items (except line 1), and this value remains fixed in generating all of the solutions in a given sample size. Next, the coil stocking code is set to either 0 or 1 for every line item, indicating whether each item is to be purchased as a coil (1) or made from a larger width coil (0). This is accomplished by generating a random number (between 0 and 1) for each line item, and comparing this value with the coil stocking probability (P_C). If the random number for an item is less than its coil stocking probability value (P_C), the item is to be stocked as a coil. Otherwise, the item is to be produced from the next larger width coil. For example, the random numbers 0.30 and 0.10 for line items 3 and 4 respectively and a coil stocking probability of $P_C = 0.20$ would have produced the sample results shown in Table 4.

In the Constant Probability biasing procedure, the same coil stocking probability was used for all line items, and the coil stocking probability value (P_C) was varied in a series of computer runs to explore the trade-off between the trim loss and inventory savings. We bias the expected number of coils to be stocked with this procedure by changing the level of the coil stocking probability value, and it is treated as a parameter to be studied. (Note that more coils are stocked with a 0.9 stocking probability than with a 0.1 probability value.) In the experiments which follow the coil stocking probability value (P_C) was varied from 0.10 to 0.90.

Demand Biasing

In the second procedure, Demand Biasing, a change was made in the method used to determine the coil stocking probability values.[6] Here, the individual coil stocking probabilities (P_D) are determined for each line item. In this case, the stocking probability (P_D) for each product width/grade/thickness item is set in proportion to its annual usage rate. This was done to reduce the chance of generating solutions where high usage items are produced from a coil for a low usage item, thereby creating a large trim loss. An example of this would involve producing the 38″ width from a 39″ wide coil in Table 1.

The stocking probabilities under Demand Biasing were determined by normalizing the annual usage figures between a lower limit (P_L) of, for example 0.0, and an upper limit of 0.9. That is, the item having the largest annual usage would have a stocking probability of 0.9, and the item with smallest annual usage would have a stocking probability of, for example, 0.0. Thus, even the highest usage item has a small probability of not being stocked as a coil. In addition, the lower limit on the stocking probabilities (P_L) was treated as a parameter in the experiments and was varied from 0.0 up to 0.9. This was done to determine the impact on inventory savings obtained by differentiating between items on the basis of their annual usage.

---

[5] The Coil Stocking Probability (P_C) for the largest product width (e.g., line 1 in Table 4) is set to 1.0 since this item will always be purchased as a coil.

[6] Otherwise the computer processing for the two procedures is identical.

Computational Results

Nineteen sets of Biased Sampling results were produced. A random sample of 200 solutions was generated for each set of coil stocking probability values investigated, using both Biased Sampling procedures. The Constant Probability results, shown in Figure 1, were produced by using nine different coil stocking probability settings (P_C ranging from 0.1 to 0.9) for all items. Likewise, Figure 2 presents the results obtained with the Demand Biasing procedure when the minimum coil stocking probability value (P_L) was varied from 0.0 to 0.9 in 0.1 increments. Several results are plotted in Figures 1 and 2: (1) the average total savings for each sample of 200 solutions (the solid line), (2) ±2 standard deviation limits around the mean savings values (the dashed lines), and (3) the best solution observed in each 200 observation sample (denoted as ⊙). While many solutions were generated at each probability setting in Figures 1 and 2, the best solution value is of particular interest. These points all lie on or above the $+2_\sigma$ line in each graph.

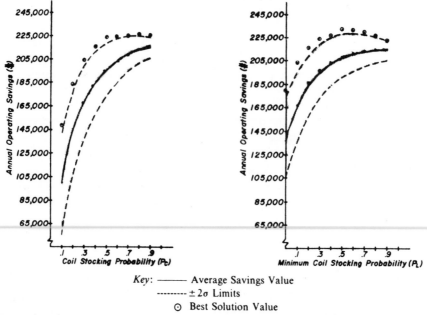

Key: ———— Average Savings Value
      --------- ±2σ Limits
          ⊙ Best Solution Value

FIGURE 1. Constant Probability Results.   FIGURE 2. Demand Biasing Results.

Inventory Savings Estimates

Very little difference was observed in the best solutions produced by the two biasing procedures. In both cases the best solution value increases slightly as the coil stocking probability is reduced from the maximum value, and the number of coils stocked decreases. A maximum savings of $231,542 was found when $P_L = 0.5$ for Demand Biasing, while the maximum savings of $226,704 was found at $P_C = 0.8$ for the Constant Probability procedure. Subsequent decreases in the coil stocking probability values yield smaller annual savings figures. The underlying trade-off between trim loss and inventory savings explains the general shape of the savings curves shown in Figures 1 and 2. As an example, in Figure 2 the reduction in the coil stocking probability (and thus the number of coils stocked) yields greater inventory savings than trim losses until a coil stocking probability of $P_L = 0.5$ is reached. Thereafter, the trim loss exceeds the inventory savings gained by stocking fewer coils, and the total savings decline.

Solution Quality

An important question in reviewing the computational results shown in Figures 1 and 2 concerns the quality of the solutions produced. To provide a check on solution quality, a small version of the inventory planning problem was solved using the integer programming formulation described in the Appendix and the two biased sampling procedures. This problem involved ten product widths of the same material grade and thickness. The results of this analysis are presented in Table 5. These results indicate that, within the range of stocking probabilities where the best solutions were observed, a penalty of as much as 8% may have been incurred with a sample size of 200.

TABLE 5
Small Problem Results (0.020″ CQ Material Items)

Coil Stocking Probability Parameter Value	Constant Probability Procedure		Demand Biasing Procedure	
	Best Solution	Percent Below Optimum Solution	Best Solution	Percent Below Optimum Solution
0.1	$4500	43%	$6537	18%
0.2	4943	38	7144	10
0.3	7953	0	7518	5
0.4	7953	0	7953	0
0.5	7953	0	7518	5
0.6	7518	5	7518	5
0.7	7518	5	7953	0
0.8	7348	8	7783	2
0.9	7348	8	7348	8

Computational Efficiency

The computer time required by the biased sampling procedures in this application was quite small. A sample size of 200 required between 17 and 20 seconds on a CDC6500, depending mainly upon the coil stocking probability setting. In addition, the biased sampling procedures required 2 seconds per 200 observation run for the smaller ten item problem versus 337 seconds for the integer programming code to produce the optimum solution. All of the biased sampling analysis, including the program debugging, required less than nine minutes of computer time.

Conclusions

Biased Sampling can be a practical tool for solving operating problems. In this application it provided an easily understood means of evaluating a vast number of potential solutions to the inventory planning problem with a minimal computational effort. The results provided management with an estimate of the annual operating savings for the proposed capital investment, and indicated that the raw material inventory investment could be reduced by approximately $500,000 by stocking coils instead of sheet stock.

This application also suggests that Biased Sampling can be easily applied to produce near optimum solutions to actual operating problems. Further, Biased Sampling provides a much more flexible problem solving methodology. Changes in the problem assumptions, such as the method of estimating the average inventory level for the inventory items, can be easily accommodated, requiring minimal changes to the computer program. Moreover, the development of biasing procedures proved to be a relatively simple task for this problem. The two biasing procedures became obvious in working with the early example problems (similar to the one shown in Table 1) that were solved for management prior to the development of the computer program. A final advantage of Biased Sampling involves the transparency of the results. The fact that the Biased Sampling program produced results which looked similar to the early example problems (such as the one shown in Table 1) helped in communicating the results to the management personnel involved in this work.

Appendix

Optimal solutions to the inventory planning problem can be produced using integer or dynamic programming methods.

Zero-One Integer Linear Programming

$$\text{Maximize:} \quad \sum_i \sum_j C_{ij} X_{ij} \tag{1}$$

$$\text{Subject to:} \quad \sum_j X_{ij} = 1 \quad \text{for each } i, \tag{2}$$

$$(n - j)X_{jj} - \sum_{i=j+1}^{n} X_{ij} \geqslant 0 \quad \text{for } j = 1, 2, \ldots, n - 1, \tag{3}$$

$$X_{ij} = 0, 1, \tag{4}$$

where C_{ij} = Total operating savings for making the ith finished product from the jth coil width.

X_{ij} = 1 if the ith finished product is to be produced from the jth coil width, and 0 otherwise.

n = The number of finished product widths. (The n items are arranged in descending order of the finished product width.)

The objective function involves maximizing the operating savings subject to two types of constraints: (1) meeting the final product demand (equation (2)) and (2) assuring that a coil is stocked for a given width before permitting smaller width items to be produced from that coil (3). The problem variables involve either making a given product width from a particular coil ($X_{ij} = 1$) or not ($X_{ij} = 0$). This formulation requires $\frac{1}{2}(n^2 + n)$ variables and $2n - 1$ constraints, and can be solved for small problem sizes, e.g. up to 12 product widths, using available Zero-One Integer Programming Codes [5].

Dynamic Programming

The inventory planning problem can also be solved using the Wagner-Whitin Algorithm by viewing the problem as a "one-way temporal feasibility" (assortment) problem similar to the steel beam problem described in [8]. Instead of ordering a steel beam of strength g_i to satisfy the demand for a beam of strength g_{i+k} (where $g_i > g_{i+k}$ with $i = 1, n$ different strength beams), we consider the use of coil width i for the production of a smaller width sheet stock item $i + k$. This problem involves the purchasing and inventory savings from buying steel coils instead of sheet, and a trim loss (which is analogous to the wasted steel cost in the steel beam problem).

The dynamic programming recursive equation for finding the maximum savings for a set of sheet widths 1 through j (arranged in descending order by width) is

$$F(j) = \text{Max}\left\{ \underset{1 < i < j}{\text{Max}}\left[V_i(S_i - C_i - P_i) + \left(I_i' \cdot \frac{Q_i'}{2} - I_i \cdot \frac{Q_i}{2} \right) \right.\right.$$

$$\left.+ \sum_{i < k \leqslant j}\left(V_k(S_k - C_k - P_k) + I_k' \cdot \frac{Q_k'}{2} - \frac{W_i - W_k}{W_k} C_k \cdot V_k \right) + F(i - 1) \right],$$

$$\left. V_j(S_j - C_j - P_j) + I_j' \cdot \frac{Q_j'}{2} - I_j \cdot \frac{Q_j}{2} + F(j - 1) \right\}. \tag{5}$$

This formulation is consistent with the dynamic programming formulation of the dynamic lot sizing problem in [8]: i.e. (7) in [8, p. 92]. (5) uses the notation defined previously in the third section except:

$F(0) = 0.$

I'_j = the inventory carrying cost per unit per period for sheet stock width j.

I_j = the inventory carrying cost per unit per period for coil stock width j.

Q'_j = the purchase order quantity for sheet stock width j.

Q_j = the purchase order quantity for coil stock width j.

i, j, and k are index values.

The results of the calculations, using (5), can be presented in a table similar to the one shown in Table 2 which illustrated the various coil stocking alternatives. It should be noted that the added volume obtained by combining several sheet stock items of the same widths (but with differing lengths) is included in the V_j and Q_j values.

References

1. ARCUS, A. L., "Comsol: A Computer Method of Sequencing Operations for Assembly Lines," *International Journal of Production Research*, Vol. 4, No. 4 (1966).

2. GIFFLER, B., THOMPSON, G. L. AND VAN NESS, V., "Numerical Experience with the Linear and Monte Carlo Algorithms for Solving Production Scheduling Problems," Chapter 3 in *Industrial Scheduling*, Prentice-Hall, Englewood Cliffs, New Jersey (1963).

3. HELLER, J. AND LOGEMANN, G., "An Algorithm for the Construction and Evaluation of Feasible Schedules," *Management Science*, Vol. 8, No. 2 (1963).

4. MABERT, V. A. AND WHYBARK, D. C., "Sampling as a Solution Methodology," *Decision Science Journal*, Vol. 8, No. 1 (January 1977).

5. McMILLAN, C., *Mathematical Programming*, Appendix C, John Wiley & Sons, Inc., 1970.

6. NUGENT, C. E., VOLLMANN, T. E. AND RUML, J., "An Experimental Comparison of Techniques for the Assignment of Facilities to Locations," *Operations Research* (January-February 1968).

7. TONGE, F. M., "Assembly Line Balancing Using Probabilistic Combinations of Heuristics," *Management Science* (May 1965).

8. WAGNER, H. M. AND WHITIN, T. M., "Dynamic Version of the Economic Lot Size Model," *Management Science*, Vol. 5 (1958).

MRP: A PROFITABLE CONCEPT FOR DISTRIBUTION

by

D. Clay Whybark
Graduate School of Business
Indiana University

INTRODUCTION

As a person who frequently becomes involved in the development or evaluation of "decision making" procedures for computers, I'm occasionally distressed to find that people themselves are pretty effective as decision makers. A. M. Geoffrion perhaps had a useful perspective on decision making procedures when he used the words "computer-assisted methods" in his guide to distribution systems planning procedures[1]. The same philosophy might well be applied to many operating decisions as well, although much of our development and software work is pointed toward machine decision making.

In the same article Professor Geoffrion sets forth some criteria for evaluating computer procedures. The criteria listed include the ability of the procedure to reach "optimum" solutions, and to easily perform sensitivity analyses. While agreeing with the latter, I feel there are many instances where I would forsake optimality for clarity of method, availability of information and transparency of assumptions. In this paper, I will describe a system which has these attributes and which has the capability of providing useful information to distribution planners. After relating some of the observations that motivated this paper, I'll present the elements of the system which is currently making important contributions in improving the performance of manufacturing operations, and show how we might exploit some of these ideas to take some of the inventory out of distribution systems without jeopardizing customer service levels.

AN INVENTORY MANAGEMENT SAGA

One of the situations that brought me up short and started me thinking about providing information instead of producing decisions concerns the management of inventories for a major catalog sales company. In this firm the product line consisted of several thousand items divided into classes, each of which was managed by a buyer. Typically, something like 50 percent of the line items were obsolete within six months and were dropped from the next catalog. Many were high fashion items and/or items that required long lead times. Obviously the buyers had a difficult job in correctly determining the quantities to buy and locating the inventories for rapid response to customer orders.

This company knew some inventories were excessively high and yet customer service was declining. The response was to hire a man with a Ph.D. (specializing in inventory), put him in charge of the buyers and give him ultimate responsibility for inventory and customer service. What a great opportunity!

This meant that the new manager could put all his inventory procedures to the test. In order to do this, he first needed to clean up the order and inventory data, centralize it and take stock of where the company was. He did this, and in order to keep things functioning while he implemented the new techniques, he provided CRT terminals which displayed sales, order and inventory position information to his buyers.

Then a surprising thing happened. Before the inventory techniques were completely designed, a major improvement in both the inventory position and customer service levels occurred. The reason is obvious, in retrospect, but came as a surprise to the manager. The buyers were very capable, experienced people. When they were given good, complete and accurate information, their decisions improved substantially. The result was that the manager stopped work on the inventory techniques and turned his attention to providing better and more useful information for the buyers.

This is not an isolated example of the utility of quality information. During the recent shortage economy, many firms with good customer order and inventory status information systems, were able to do a more effective job of allocating inventories than would have been possible without that information. Several firms in the food processing industry have developed methods of capturing and sharing information up and down the distribution channel, even though these activities mean interfirm coordination. In fact, one manager in this industry declared that, among the firms along their distribution channel, the information system had "entered the era of computer-to-computer conversation".

In a look at the "new era" in distribution, Jim Heskett identifies several activities that will be required to make increased gains in efficiency in distribution.[2] One of these activities is to seek situations where coordination can produce gains for both parties and a second is to establish mechanisms for capturing and transmitting information along the channel. Material requirements planning (MRP) is a system for capturing and transmitting planning information that can help disclose opportunities for profitable coordination. Before turning to the application of the MRP concept in distribution, we will look at an application in manufacturing, where the technique was developed, and see how it operates in that environment.

WHAT'S HAPPENING IN MANUFACTURING?

What's happening in manufacturing is material requirements planning. Since the American Production and Inventory Control Society (APICS) mounted its educational "MRP Crusade" a few years ago, the number of companies using MRP systems has grown rapidly. The benefits from using MRP are quite varied and have not been the sole province of a few unique companies. For example:

A $200 million sales midwestern manufacturing firm was able to change their product line from 25,000 relatively simple products to more than 100,000 complex products while holding inventories to 25% less than would have been possible without the information available from their MRP system.

A small Eastern firm supplying industrial and residential hardware was able to increase sales from $20 million to $30 million while reducing the work force slightly, improving their customer service and increasing inventory turnover from 2.5 to 3.5 turns per year.

A $1.4 billion sales, multi-national, multi-divisional firm reports a reduction in the space required for one division's manufacturing facilities after installing an MRP system. The reduction enabled them to avoid a $1 million plant expansion program and, after some time, they were running 200% more volume through the original space.

MRP is based upon a very straight-forward concept: the demand for parts and components used in manufactured products depends upon the quantities in which those products are produced. The concept has been called the principle of dependent demand.[3] Despite the fact that the concept, once stated, appears obvious, part and component production scheduling and inventory control are sometimes conducted as though the parts' demand was independent of the production of those products on which they were to be used. Reorder points and order quantities are set on the basis of past usage and decisions on the production of parts are made independently of the planned production of their parent products.[4] The advent of the computer has now provided enough information processing power to enable manufacturing to exploit the principle of dependent demand.

An MRP system uses the information which relates a manufactured product to its components (for example, how many of each component are required for the product, how long does it take to make each one, etc.) and current information on the status of the components (such as, how much inventory is on hand, how many units are in process, etc.) to project the number of each component required to support planned future production of the product. Thus, the system can be viewed as a manufacturing information system, though many firms have learned through experience to use the MRP system to do much more than simply provide information. In this article I want to concentrate on the information aspects of the system, however, and how the various components of a product are related.

A simple molded plastic toy car will be used as the example product for illustrating the information aspects of MRP. The product structure tree that is presented in Figure 1, shows the relationships and quantities of the parts and subassemblies required to make the toy car. Each car requires one body-axle mount assembly and two wheel-axle subassemblies. At the next level, the wheel-axle subassembly, for example, requires two axles and four wheels. (This same information is often captured in the manufacturing bill of materials.) Thus a plan to produce one finished toy car

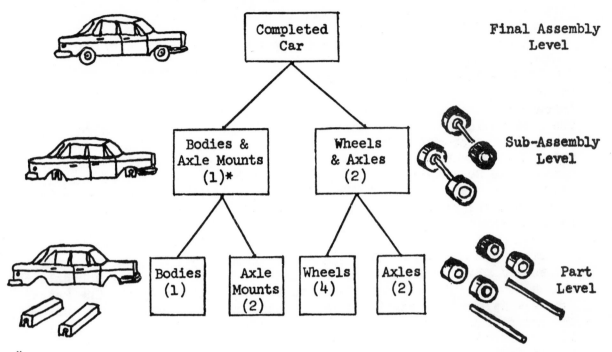

Figure 1
Product Structure Tree Showing the Relationships
of the Components of a Toy Car

*Note: (1) indicates the number required on the next higher item.

in the future implies that we will need to manufacture four wheels in time to assemble them to axles which need to be ready for the planned production of the complete car. If it takes two weeks to manufacture wheels and one week for making the wheel-axle subassembly, we must start to make wheels three weeks before the finished car is scheduled for final assembly.

THE MRP SYSTEM

The determination of production requirements starts from a master schedule of production for the end item and is carried (exploded) down through the product structure to the fabricated or purchased parts level. The process involves first determining the gross requirements for a particular item. The gross requirements are the number of units of that item which will be needed in each period in the future to support the production plan at the next higher level. The next step is to determine what the net requirements are (net of any inventory and outstanding orders) and when orders will be released for fabrication or sub-assembly (called offsetting for lead time).

This process can be illustrated using the toy car. We will start with an assumed production plan for the finished item, the master schedule that states how many finished cars we plan to produce and when. The master schedule is shown in Figure 2. Since each car requires two axle assemblies, the gross requirements for this subassembly are twice the figures listed in the master schedule. This is also shown in Figure 2. That is, if we plan to assemble ten toy cars in week 1, we must have 20 wheel-axle sub-assemblies available for use in week 1. The gross requirements then, show when the completed units must be available to support the production planned for the next highest level item.

Figure 2
Master Schedule for the Toy Car and
Gross Requirements for the Wheel-Axle Subassembly

Week	1	2	3	4	5	6
Master Schedule (Toy Cars)	10	20	5	0	15	10
Gross Requirements Wheel-Axle Subassembly	20	40	10	0	30	10

To translate the gross requirements information into net requirements, we need to take into account any inventory on hand and/or orders that may be outstanding. This is illustrated in Figure 3. Since 30 units are in inventory and the gross requirements are 20 in period 1, no additional subassemblies need to be produced to meet the final assembly schedule. In the second period, however, there will only be 10 units in inventory and we have a gross requirement of 40 units; so there is a net requirement of 30 units. The remaining net requirements are equal to the gross requirements, as no more orders are outstanding and the inventory has been exhausted.

Figure 3
MRP Records for the Wheel-Axle Subassembly

Week	1	2	3	4	5	6
Gross Requirements	20	40	10	0	30	10 .
Inventory/On Order	30	0	0	0	0	0
Net Requirements	-	30	10	0	30	10
Planned Orders	30	10	0	30	10	

Lead Time = 1 week

Also illustrated in Figure 3 is the lead-time offset for planning orders when the lead time to produce a subassembly is one week. That is, since 30 wheel-axle subassemblies are required in week 2, an order for 30 units should be sent to the subassembly department in week 1. This gives them the required time (1 week) to produce the subassemblies.

This process can be carried one step further for our example. If 30 wheel-axle subassemblies are required in week 1, we must have 60 wheels available in week 1 for the subassembly department to use in making the subassemblies. Thus the planned orders for the wheel-axle subassembly represent one-half the gross requirements for the wheels. The gross requirements are shown in Figure 4. Note that only 5 periods of data are available,

Figure 4
MRP Records for the Wheels

Week	1	2	3	4	5	6
Gross Requirements	60	20	0	60	20	
Inventory/On Order	70	20	0	0	0	
Net Requirements	-	-	-	50	20	
Planned Orders	-	50	20			

Lead Time = 2 weeks

because of the one week lead time to make the subassemblies. After calculating the net requirements and offsetting for lead time, three periods of planned orders are available. No planned orders are called for in week 1, indicating that a sufficient inventory or orders for more wheels exist to cover the subassembly requirements for the next three weeks and final assembly of toy cars for the next four weeks.

We have only looked at an example for a simple product and many more complex considerations, missing here, can be included in an MRP system. The essence, though, of the information processing aspects of the system are shown in Figures 2, 3, and 4. The principal advantage of this information is that it makes transparent the dependent relationships between the production plans for the finished product and the requirements for the components of the product. By periodically rerunning the MRP system, incorporating changes in plans and component status, it becomes possible to determine the impact of the changes on each component in the system, assess the feasibility of the new plans and reestablish priorities for manufacturing the necessary components. Having current information on the plans at the finished product level, as reflected in the gross requirements, makes it possible for the manufacturing personnel responsible for operating decisions to do a better job of utilizing their resources to meet those plans. The task now before us is to see if we can exploit the MRP information structure to provide better information for distribution decisions.

TURNING TO DISTRIBUTION

In order to relate the MRP structure to distribution we need only make two small changes. The first is to rotate the product structure tree of Figure 1 90° and change some names. This gives us the distribution system shown in Figure 5. The second change is to recognize that

Figure 5
A Three Stage Distribution System

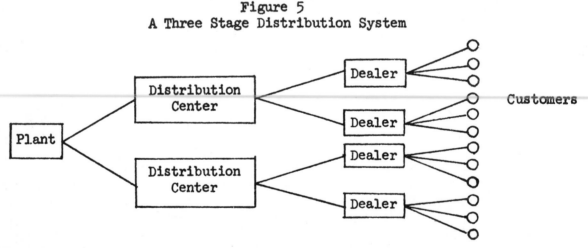

the demand implodes (rather than explodes) from the dealers through the distribution centers back to the plant, but the principle of dependent demand still holds. It is evident that the distribution centers' demand is dependent upon what the dealers do and the plant's demand depends upon what the distribution centers do. However, many actual distribution systems are operated today as though the demand at any point was independent of that for any other component of the system. In such cases, historical data is used to determine order points and order quantities. But, the specific requirements which are placed on the distribution centers are determined by the dealers' operating decisions. For example, the orders that the dealers place might be in economic order quantities or quantities related to transportation economies (e.g., full car load) rather than for weekly replenishment. A similar effect may be seen between a distribution center and the plant. Capturing this information in an MRP type system makes possible considerably more rational management of the distribution inventories. An example will help illustrate this point.

We will use the system depicted in Figure 5 as the basis for our example. Suppose that each dealer has an average and fairly constant demand of 20 units a week and that it takes one week to ship between the plant and a distribution center or between a distribution center and a dealer. Some economic data will enable us to compute economic order quantities, so let us say it costs $.10 a week to store the product in any location and $9.00 to place an order at any location. The implications of all this data are summarized in Figure 6.

Figure 6
Demand and Order Quantity Data for
Example Distribution System

	Plant	Distribution Center	Dealer
Weekly Demand	80	40	20
Economic Order Quantity	120	80	60
Weeks Supply per Order	1½	2	3

The dealer demands of 20 units per week imply 40 units per week for the distribution centers and 80 units per week for the plant. These demand averages, coupled with the economic data permit the calculation of economic order quantities for each stage considered independently. However, these don't match with those of the next stage in the system. If acting independently, the dealers would order every three weeks while the distribution centers would order every two weeks. Figure 7 shows how the information on the dealers' ordering plans can be incorporated in an MRP record framework to coordinate the ordering decisions at a distribution center with those of the dealers.

The ordering plans of the dealers become the gross requirements for a distribution center. These orders can be planned taking into account the forecasts of customer demand, economies of transportation, seasonal build-up and so on. In this sense the order planning is very similar to the master scheduling of production. The process of determining net requirements and developing planned orders for the distribution center is the same as that illustrated for the toy car example. The information in Figure 7 shows clearly that there are two possible ordering decisions for the distribution center; an order of 60 units in each of two successive periods with no order the following period or a single order of 120 units

Figure 7
MRP Records for a Distribution Center

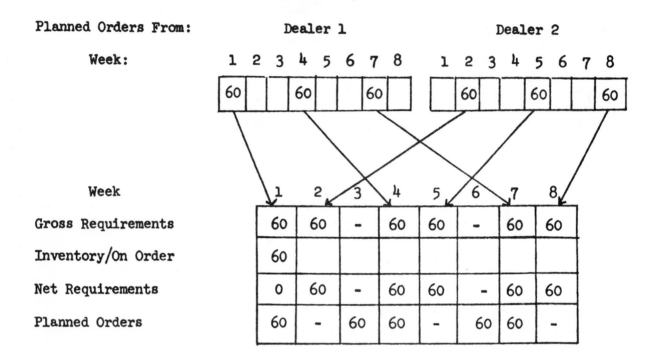

Planned Orders From: Dealer 1   Dealer 2

Week: 1 2 3 4 5 6 7 8   1 2 3 4 5 6 7 8

Week	1	2	3	4	5	6	7	8
Gross Requirements	60	60	-	60	60	-	60	60
Inventory/On Order	60							
Net Requirements	0	60	-	60	60	-	60	60
Planned Orders	60	-	60	60	-	60	60	-

every three periods. Although it works out to be slightly less expensive for the distribution center to order quantities of 120 units in this example, we will compare the use of the planned orders shown in Figure 7 to the use of the economic order quantity shown in Figure 6

The brief simulation in Figure 8 shows the opening inventories and closing inventories for the alternative ordering decisions at the distribution center. The inventory carrying cost of $.10 per week per unit is charged against whatever is left in inventory at the end of the week, since shipments to the dealers must be made very soon after the distribution center receives shipments from the plant. This means that the inventory is in the distribution center only a very short time when the distribution center's orders match the dealers' requirements of 60 units. In contrast, the orders of 80 units every two weeks necessitate the carrying of additional inventory in order to have enough available to meet the dealers' requirements, due to the mismatch of quantities and timing.

Acknowledging its simplicity, the example of applying the MRP framework to a distribution system still serves to illustrate two important points. First, it is possible to use the MRP information framework and logic to indicate the dependencies between plans at different stages in a

Figure 8
A Comparison of Ordering Decisions for
a Distribution Center

Using MRP Records

Week	1	2	3	4	5	6	7	8
Order Receipts	60	60	-	60	60	-	60	60
Opening Inventory	60	60	-	60	60	-	60	60
Requirements	60	60	-	60	60	-	60	60
Closing Inventory	0	0	0	0	0	0	0	0

Average cost per period: inventory $ 0
                          ordering   6.00

                          total $6.00

Using Order Quantities

Week	1	2	3	4	5	6	7	8
Order Receipts	-	80	-	80	-	80	-	80
Opening Inventory	80	100	40	120	60	80	80	100
Requirements	60	60	-	60	60	-	60	60
Closing Inventory	20	40	40	60	0	80	20	40

Average cost per period: inventory $4.00
                          ordering   4.50

                          total $8.50

distribution system. Secondly, there are potential economic advantages from using this information to match the operating decisions at each stage with requirements of successive stages. In our example we only considered the case where plans were not subject to change over time but MRP is perhaps even more useful when the plans are changing. In the work with MRP in manufacturing it has become clear that using even imperfect information about future plans is preferable to using past information. The analogy is old, but true, that when driving in the rain it is preferable to look out through a rain-splattered windshield, than it is to look through a perfectly clear rear window.

CONCLUSIONS

It is apparent from our review of the elements of an MRP system, that MRP is not a sophisticated decision making procedure, but rather a framework for providing useful information for decision makers. The key, then, to realizing the benefits of any MRP system, is the ability of the inventory or distribution planners to use the information well. Inventory planners in manufacturing firms with MRP systems, as they gained experience with their systems, have become quite adroit at using the planned order information to stay on top of changing conditions. Changing market or supplier conditions often necessitate modified production plans which are reflected in new planned orders. The inventory planners use this planned order information to modify manufacturing priorities or purchasing due dates in time to meet the new plans. They have learned to accommodate changing plans with information rather than expediting and inventory. The same can be expected of experienced distribution planners as they meet the shifting requirements along the distribution channel while maintaining customer service levels.

The appeal of the MRP logic has not gone unnoticed in distribution. Many firms, that supply companies with MRP systems, use planned purchase order information from their customers' systems for their own planning purposes. Other examples of the growing interest in MRP for distribution include:

· A midwestern manufacturer makes direct use of the requirements of its largest customer in developing the production plans for their MRP system.

· A major pharmaceutical firm has started an extensive project to develop an MRP system for its entire distribution network.

· One division of a multi-division company has installed an MRP system that integrates manufacturing and the distribution centers.

In many other firms the necessity of interfacing the distribution system with an existing manufacturing MRP system has at least brought MRP to the attention of distribution management.

The MRP framework provides a potential channel coordination mechanism of the kind that Jim Heskett suggested was necessary for entering the new era in distribution. Further, its use may help disclose opportunities for substantial savings from increased coordination along the channel.[5] In our example distribution system, the minimum total costs for <u>all</u> stages considered together are achieved when all stages order two weeks of requirements in a coordinated fashion. In order to reap the benefits of this reduction in cost, however, all dealers would need to give up their independence and place their orders simultaneously every other week. Similarly, the distribution centers would need to order simultaneously to permit the plant to order every other week. This would require coordination along the channel and an acceptable method of sharing the benefits. As we provide the information for coordination and learn to share the benefits, we can look forward to significant increases in distribution productivity.

FOOTNOTES

1. A. M. Geoffrion, "A Guide to Computer-Assisted Methods for Distribution Systems Planning", <u>Transportation and Distribution Management</u>, Sept./Oct. 1974.

2. J. L. Heskett, "Sweeping Changes in Distribution", <u>Harvard Business Review</u>, March-April 1973.

3. This principle was identified by Joe Orlicky some ten years ago and is elabroated in his book, <u>Materials Requirements Planning: The New Way of Life in Production and Inventory Management</u>, New York: McGraw-Hill, 1975.

4. See P. H. Thurston, "Requirements Planning for Inventory Control", <u>Harvard Business Review</u>, May-June 1972, for a good example of the implications of using independent logic in a dependent demand situation.

5. Some indication of the potential for coordination and new methods for accomplishing it are described in W. F. Friedman, "Physical Distribution: The Concept of Shared Services", <u>Harvard Business Review</u>, March-April 1975.

INTERFACES
Vol. 9, No. 5, November 1979

THE LONG ISLAND BLOOD DISTRIBUTION SYSTEM
AS A PROTOTYPE FOR REGIONAL BLOOD·MANAGEMENT

Eric Brodheim

Lindsley F. Kimball Research Institute, The New York Blood Center, New York, New York 10021

and

Gregory P. Prastacos

Department of Decision Science, The Wharton School, University of Pennsylvania,
Philadelphia, Pennsylvania 19104

ABSTRACT. Each year over two million hospitalized Americans depend upon the timely availability of the right type of blood products at 6,000 hospital blood banks (HBB's) in the United States. If the right blood products are not available at the HBB when required, then medical complications or postponements of elective surgery can result which translates to extra days of hospitalization and expense. On the other hand, since most blood products may only be administered to a patient of the same blood type within 21 days of collection, overstocking at HBB's leads to low utilization, which increases costs and is wasteful of the scarce blood resource.

The Long Island blood distribution system was set up as a prototype of a regional blood center and the hospital blood banks that it services collaborating to preplan regional blood flow. It maximizes blood availability and utilization according to a Programmed Blood Distribution System (PBDS) model and strategy that has been shown to be generally applicable. PBDS schedules blood deliveries according to statistical estimates of the needs of each HBB and monitors actual requirements to adjust deliveries when indicated by control chart techniques. In addition, it provides a daily forecasting of short-term shortages and surpluses for the next several days that results in controlled movement of blood to and from adjoining regions. Finally, the system is able to adjust the regional strategy so that availability is reduced uniformly at all HBB's during periods of seasonal, regional shortages.

PBDS has drastically improved utilization and availability of blood on Long Island: wastage has been reduced by 80%, and delivery costs by 64%. This prototype is acting as a model for other regional blood centers in the United States and for other national blood services as a basis for planning and controlling blood flow in a geographic area. It usually replaces preexisting procedures where a regional blood center collects blood based upon gross estimates and reacts to requests for blood by individual HBB's on the basis of experience and on the currently prevailing inventory situation.

Introduction

The Operations Research Laboratory of the New York Blood Center, in collaboration with the Long Island Blood Services (LIBS) division of the Greater New York Blood Program (GNYBP), has been studying the problem of providing a high availability of perishable blood products at each of the hospitals in a region, while

HEALTH CARE—BLOOD BANK

assuring that the maximum number of these products are utilized during their 21-day lifetime. This problem requires that the dual and seemingly conflicting concerns about availability and utilization be reconciled. It also requires a radical change in management decision concepts so that the regional blood center (RBC) that is responsible for collecting and distributing blood and the hospital blood banks (HBB's) that stock it for possible use recognize common objectives and collaborate in implementing a strategy that optimizes the regional utilization and availability of these scarce products.

The first section of this paper describes the national problem. The Management Science techniques that were utilized to create a transferable model for a distribution plan with near-optimal characteristics are described in the second section. This is followed by a description of the implementation of this model by the Programmed Blood Distribution System (PBDS) and of its testing at LIBS as a regional prototype for the evolution of a national blood distribution network and operation. The managerial and economic impact and the implications and extensions of this prototype model are then discussed in the concluding sections.

Background

The national problem

Most blood products in the United States are derived from whole blood that is collected in units of one pint from volunteer donors by approximately 200 RBC's. After laboratory processing and testing, blood products derived from the whole blood are distributed to the HBB's in the region where they are stored to be available for transfusion when requested. This paper is restricted to whole blood and red blood cells (i.e., whole blood from which plasma and other components have been separated), which together account for over 95% of all transfusions. Both have a lifetime of only 21 days during which they can be transfused to a patient of the same type and after which they have to be discarded.

Historically, HBB's have maintained high inventories of most of the eight different types of each of these products in order to provide high availability to satisfy patient needs and have accepted the low utilization resulting from spoilage. Consequently, the national utilization rate of whole blood and red blood cells prior to expiration was estimated to be only 80% in 1974. At that time, the federal government adopted a national blood policy that called for an all volunteer blood supply to be accessible to all segments of the public. The blood supply was to be efficiently administered through the formation of regional associations of blood service units in each of which a RBC and the HBB's that it serves would collaborate to achieve these objectives.

The role of Management Science

It had long been recognized that Management Science techniques were required to improve blood utilization and availability. Strategies with desirable characteristics were formulated for individual hospital blood banks and pragmatic regional approaches that improved performance in a certain region had been implemented and reported. The National Heart, Lung and Blood Institute Resources Panel in its 1973 recommendations, which were a major factor in formulating the National Blood Policy [4], stated that:

> One of the strongest arguments favoring the introduction of systems management to blood service is that it will result in improved service, in more economical utilization of the blood resources, and most important, in improved effectiveness and efficiency. For these reasons it is recommended that emphasis be placed on developing measures of activity and relating these to objectives. Only in this way will it be possible to obtain secure and credible evaluation of the changes to be made.

This study addressed these issues by:

(1) creating a model for relating measures of blood banking activity to availability and utilization;

(2) developing a management tool called the Programmed Blood Distribution System (PBDS) to implement a regional blood distribution strategy that is based upon this model;

(3) evaluating the effectiveness of PBDS in a prototype region (LIBS).

Complexity of the problem

The complexity of the blood distribution problem is primarily due to the perishable characteristics of blood, to the uncertainties involved in its availability to the RBC, and in the variable daily demand and usage for it at each of the HBB's. The situation is complicated by the large variation in the size of the HBB's supplied, the incidence of the different blood groups, and the requirements for whole blood and red blood cells at individual hospitals.

Since it is a national policy for blood to be derived from volunteer donors, its availability is uncertain and is a function of a number of factors that cannot be controlled by the RBC. The demand and usage of blood at HBB's are also uncertain and vary from day to day and between hospital facilities. The HBB's within a region may range from those transfusing a few hundred units per year to those transfusing tens of thousands of units per year. The most frequently occurring blood type (0 positive) occurs in approximately 39% of the population, while the least frequently occurring blood type (AB negative) occurs in only about 0.5% of the population. While most medical authorities agree that at least 90% of all blood transfusions could be in the form of red blood cells, some hospitals transfuse almost entirely red blood cells while others transfuse entirely whole blood with the ratio of whole blood to red blood cells frequently changing with time as transfusion practices improve.

Approach

The transfusion services throughout the nation are characterized by diversity. Each RBC has independently evolved its own philosophies and techniques for blood distribution. Each region strives for "self-sufficiency" in supplying the blood needs of the hospitals in its region from donors who also reside in approximately the same area. Because of these factors, it is essential that any strategy devised be defensible from the point of view of both the RBC and each of the wide range of HBB's that it serves. Furthermore, any strategy that involves interactions between RBC's must provide for clearly defined benefits for all participants. In addition, it is desirable that the implemented strategy be characterized by two management concepts: rotation of blood products between HBB's, and prescheduled deliveries to the HBB's.

Any strategy that allocates blood products to be retained until transfused or outdated will result in low utilization, especially in the case of the small usage HBB's which, in aggregate, account for the largest part of overall blood usage. Consequently, some form of blood "rotation" is required whereby freshly processed blood is sent to a HBB, from which it may be returned, some time later, for redistribution according to the regional strategy. It is also desirable that a significant portion of the periodic deliveries to the HBB's be prescheduled. This way the uncertainty of supply faced by the HBB's is reduced, with a resulting improvement in the planning of operations, and the utilization of their resources.

The model

The blood needs of a HBB can be expressed in terms of the *demand* for blood (i.e., the number of units required to be on hand for possible transfusion to patients) and the *usage* of blood (i.e., the number of units transfused to patients). A model is required that translates demand and usage to availability and utilization as functions of the RBC blood distribution policy and the HBB's blood stocking policy. Such a model was established by a combination of statistical analysis and Markov chain modeling. This model was then used to derive regional allocation strategies with desirable properties regarding availability and utilization.

Availability

The availability rate (i.e., fraction of days when the inventory of a given blood type on hand is sufficient to meet the demand) at the HBB depends only upon the statistical pattern of demand and the total inventory level. To establish this relationship, data were collected on the daily demands for each blood type at a number of HBB's. These data, together with comparable information published by other researchers, provided a total of 49 data sets, each containing the daily demands for one blood type at one HBB for a period of at least six months.

Statistical analysis [2] established a "universal" piecewise linear relationship between inventory level (I) and mean daily demand (D)* with availability rate as a parameter as is illustrated in Figure 1. The ability of the model to predict the availability rate was verified by collecting additional daily demand data from 21 HBB's in collaboration with five RBC's throughout the country. The model predicted the availability rate to within approximately 10% of actual experience for availability rates in the range of 80% to 99%. This model was then utilized to establish the "acceptable" range of availability rates for HBB's. This was done by requesting a number of HBB's to concurrently provide estimates of their mean daily demand and of the inventory levels in each of the eight blood types which they considered adequate. In almost all cases, the levels that the HBB's considered adequate turned out to correspond to availability rates of between 90% and 95%.

---

*The mean daily demand is computed as 1/6th of the mean weekly demand based upon the observation that the mean demand for the three-day weekend (i.e., either for Friday, Saturday, and Sunday or for Saturday, Sunday and Monday) is close to twice the mean demand for each of the other four days in all instances.

FIGURE 1. Availability Rate Model.

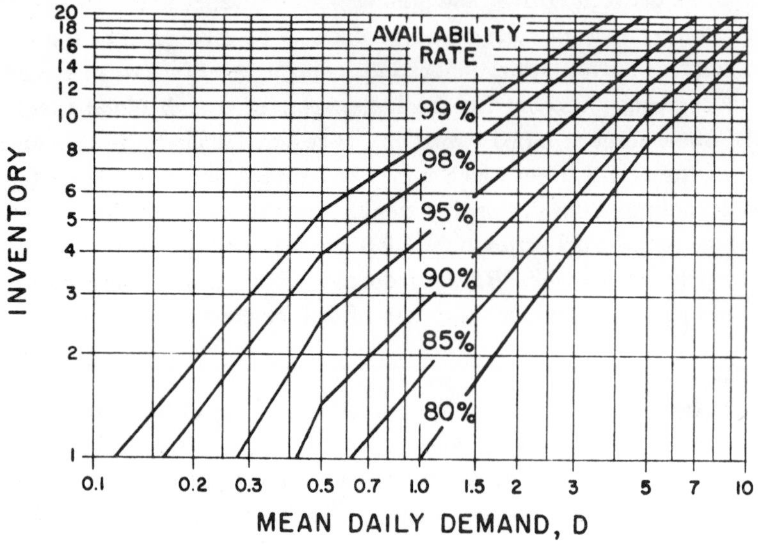

It was similarly established that the daily usage could be modeled as an exponential-type distribution whose parameter is related to the mean daily usage (U). The demand-to-usage ratio (D/U) was found to vary between 1.5 and 4.0 for most HBB's with an average value of about 2.5 in most regions. These analyses showed that the parameters for the models of demand and usage could be readily estimated from records maintained by HBB's and further that availability rate could be reliably estimated by the model.

Utilization

The utilization rate (i.e., fraction of the periodic supply which is transfused) at an HBB depends on the size as well as the age mix of its blood supplies. In order to derive a model for utilization rate, the following basic distribution strategy was developed, based on the premise that periodic shipments are made to each HBB. At the beginning of every "period" the RBC ships a fixed number of fresh (1-2 days old) rotation units and a fixed number of older (6-9 days old) retention units to each HBB. The retention units are permanently retained by the HBB until transfused or discarded at the end of their useful life. The rotation units that are in excess of a fixed "desired inventory level" at the end of the period are returned to the RBC for redistribution as retention units. Since the rotation units are not subject to spoilage, the utilization rate is determined by the behavior of the retention inventory.**

The number of retention units in inventory at a HBB immediately after each delivery can be represented by a finite-state Markov chain, whose transition probabilities are a function of the fixed periodic input (i.e., the fixed retention shipments), and of the variable demand and usage. Under the assumption that the oldest unit in inventory is transfused first, the steady state solution of the system can be computed and related to the utilization rate. This model was examined in [3], where

**Utilized Units = Total Supply − Units Spoiled.

analytical approximations were derived for Poisson usage, relating the number of retention units in each shipment to the resultant utilization rates with the desired inventory level as a parameter.

This relationship is illustrated for a fixed utilization rate of 98% by the family of broken lines in Figure 2 where the scheduling factor ρ is the fraction of mean daily usage that is replaced by retention shipments. As an example, if a HBB's mean daily usage for a given blood product is 1.5, then the HBB can achieve a utilization rate of 98% by any of the following combinations: desired inventory $I=1$ and $\rho =0.89$, or $I=3$ and $\rho =0.82$, or $I=5$ and $\rho =0.70$.

FIGURE 2. Utilization Rate Model.

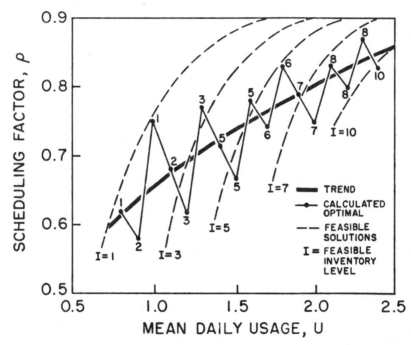

It was shown that this stocking procedure maintains the mean inventory close to this desired inventory level most of the time. It was also shown that adding additional stages of returns and redistribution would make only slight improvements in the availability rate and utilization rate achieved. Since multiple redistributions introduce severe logistical problems and significant transportation costs, distribution strategies involving more than two stages of distribution were not investigated.

Properties of desirable regional allocation strategies

Having derived models enabling us to predict the availability and utilization rates of a HBB for any rotation/retention policy implemented by the RBC, the regional allocation problem was examined. It was assumed that some fixed penalty costs were associated with every nonavailable unit and every nonutilized unit, and the objective was to determine the distribution policy parameters so as to minimize the total expected regional cost.

INTERFACES November 1979

First, the policy that minimizes the total expected one-period cost was derived [5]. It was shown that this policy involves the following operations:

(1) first allocate all available retention units so as to equalize the utilization rates at all HBB's;

(2) then allocate all available rotation units (which are not subject to spoilage) so as to equalize the availability rates at all HBB's.

It was shown that this policy is independent of the unit penalty costs, and that is maximizes both the availability and the utilization of blood in the region, simultaneously. That is, any deviation from the policy that would reduce utilization would also result in reduced availability for the next period, and vice versa. It was next shown [6] that this policy was not only myopically optimal but also approximately optimal in the long run. Further, in a large number of cases that were tested by computer, the utilization and availability rates computed from the myopic results also corresponded to the absolute optimal values computed.

This result established the principle that a distribution policy should seek to equalize utilization rates and availability rates. This is also a policy that has the essential elements of "fairness" in equally spreading the nonavailability and nonutilization risks among hospitals regardless of their relative size and is consequently a highly defensible policy.

Finally, it was shown that the highest possible regional availability and utilization rates are achieved when the desired inventory level for each blood type in each HBB is at the value that minimizes the total number of rotational units that are required to achieve these availability and utilization rates.

It is a straightforward effort by computer to calculate the combination of inventory level and scheduling factor that requires the minimum number of rotational units. The minimum number of rotational units required to achieve a fixed utilization rate of 98% and an availability rate of 95% are indicated by the points connected by the straight line segments in Figure 2. The irregular behavior of this solution is due to the fact that inventory levels must be integer values and rounding occurs on very small absolute values. As an example, the minimum rotational shipments required to an HBB of mean usage of 1.5 units daily to obtain the target goals above occur when the desired inventory is 5 units, and the scheduling factor is set to 0.67. The trend line which is drawn in the heavy line in Figure 2 is meant to indicate simultaneously the optimal values in inventory level and scheduling factor for given values of mean usage.

Adding operational constraints

The above distribution model of equalizing availability rates and utilization rates among the HBB's is illustrated by the two curved lines in Figure 3. The upper curved line shows the minimum total shipments required to achieve a fixed availability rate at a HBB of a given mean usage. The lower curved line shows the maximum retention shipments to achieve a fixed utilization rate. The area between the curves would have to be met by rotational shipments. As can be seen from the right end of the curves where the tails meet, this results in a situation where the larger usage HBB's receive almost all of their shipments in older retention units, while the smaller usage HBB's receive almost all of their shipments in fresh rotation units.

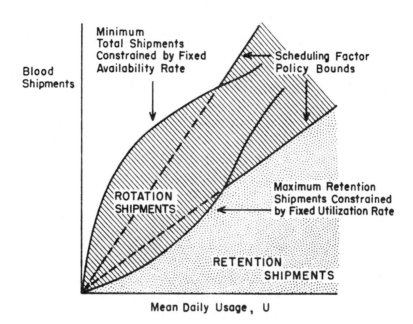

FIGURE 3. Shipping Policy Constraints.

To alleviate this situation, and provide all HBB's with a reasonable mix of fresher and older bloods in inventory, an upper bound was placed on the scheduling factor (the proportion of mean usage replaced by retention shipments). The total amount delivered to each HBB was further constrained to exceed the mean usage by at least the complement of the scheduling factor. These constraints are represented by the "scheduling factor policy bounds" in Figure 3. It can be seen from this figure that this policy modification acts to equalize the mix of fresh to older bloods between HBB's. The scheduling factor was left as a decision parameter since the mix of larger and smaller HBB's varies as a function of the region; this also provides an extra degree of freedom to adjust regional blood distribution in times of overall blood shortages.

Finally, the effect of varying the interval between deliveries was investigated using the mean number of units on rotation as a basis of comparison. The week is divided into six delivery days with Saturday and Sunday counting as a single delivery day. It was determined that for blood types where mean daily usage is small, the mean required number of units on rotation is independent of whether the delivery interval is one, two or four delivery days. For higher values of mean daily usage, the difference between one-day and two-day delivery intervals remains slight, but increasing the delivery interval to four days causes significant increases in the mean number of rotational units required to achieve the policy objectives.

As a result of these observations, HBB's that transfuse less than approximately 1,500 units per year are receiving deliveries every four delivery days. Since analyses showed little distinction in the number of rotational units required between one-day and two-day intervals between deliveries, all larger HBB's were encouraged to utilize two-day intervals between shipments.

INTERFACES November 1979

The final model

On the basis of the above, the final model was formulated as a mathematical program [7]. The decision variables determined by the program are the distribution parameters: size of rotation and retention shipments, frequency of deliveries, and desired inventory levels for each HBB.

The objective of the program is to achieve the set "target" values for availability and utilization rates, while conforming to the operational constraints, with the minimum possible amount of total fresh rotational blood needed in the region. Even though the model is highly nonlinear, its structure is decomposable, and the optimal solution is readily obtained by parametric enumeration.

Implementation and operation

The Programmed Blood Distribution System (PBDS) is the tool used to implement the above model in any region. The system is broken down into three interrelated functions which are:

(1) to *plan* the regional distribution and to forecast performance measures;

(2) to *implement* the regional distribution plan;

(3) to *evaluate* the actual performance with respect to forecast and to indicate changes required in the distribution plan when appropriate.

The interrelationship between these functions is illustrated in Figure 4 which acts as the basis for the discussion which follows. The planning and evaluation functions involve the top management while the implementation function is intended to be carried out by middle level management.

The Long Island Blood Services prototype

LIBS was set up as a prototype regional association of blood service units to demonstrate and evaluate the effectiveness of PBDS. LIBS is approximately the median size of existing regional associations and processes approximately 100,000 units of blood per year. It serves a diverse area ranging from the rural parts of Suffolk County to urban parts of New York City with a combined population of two million persons. LIBS is one of four divisions of the GNYBP which serves approximately eighteen million people in the greater New York area. This facilitates interaction between these regions for such purposes as to smooth out local short-term shortages and surpluses.

The implementation of the program was carried out in a series of planned stages. At first only four hospitals were invited to join the program. These were provided support to rapidly correct the start-up problems that occurred. Once these were working to the satisfaction of the HBB supervisors, they described the system to supervisors of other HBB's at seminars where the Operations Research staff, wherever possible, played a passive role of providing information when requested to do so. By this technique, all but four very small HBB's in Long Island have voluntarily joined the program over the past two years, and none have dropped out.

Overview

The initial planning starts with collecting the initial estimates of demand and usage for each of the HBB's in the program. This information, together with additional data required for shipping and other purposes, is used to create data files. From these data files, and using the model described above, "policy selection tables" are generated. These tables indicate the minimum total fresh supply needed to be distributed on rotation in the region over a two-week period, in order to achieve certain "acceptable" values for availability and utilization. On the basis of these tables, of the amount and the stability of the collections, and of the reserve to be kept at the RBC, the attainable values are determined, and the "target" values are selected for these performance measures.

FIGURE 4. Programmed Blood Distribution Flowchart.

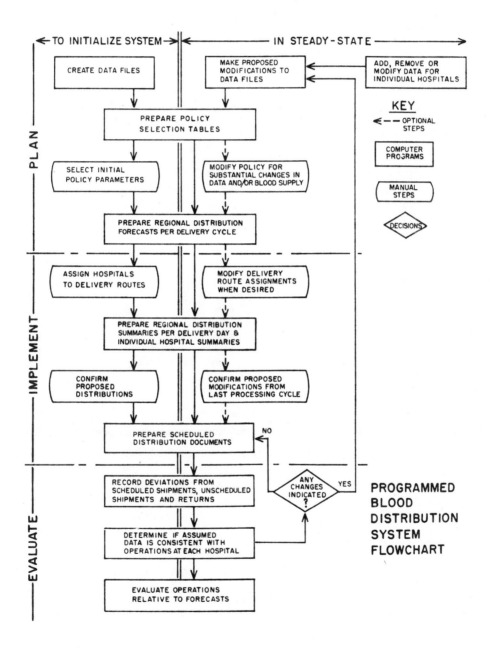

Once the planning phase is completed, hospitals are assigned to delivery routes. These delivery routes are constrained to provide for deliveries to all hospitals at a fixed time each delivery day. Delivery day intervals are either one, two, or four days, depending on the size of the hospital and special requirements or strong preferences expressed. From these assignments "regional distribution summaries" per delivery day are prepared for evaluation. These are revised as needed to equalize the amount of blood distributed each day as far as possible. Individual hospital "summaries of delivery schedules" and of "desired inventory levels" are then prepared and sent to all HBB's. After discussions during which the above distribution schedules are confirmed or modified as required and extensive educational sessions with the HBB's' management and operational personnel take place, the operation is ready to start. The final step is the preparation of packing documents which are prepared in the order in which deliveries are to be made.

Once operational, data files or distribution schedules are modified by one of two means. As new hospitals are added, as hospitals are removed, as changes in usage occur, such as those from increased bed capacity, or as changes in usage are detected by the control procedure, the data files are modified. The policy selection tables are revised each time there are revisions in usage estimates. The revised tables are then manually evaluated to determine if the changes are substantial enough to require a change in targets. A change in targets may also be required if a substantial increase or decrease in the blood supply is anticipated from other information. If such changes are required, then the regional distribution forecasting procedure is performed again as described above.

Scheduling deliveries

A major advantage of PBDS, both to the RBC and to the HBB's, is the ability to preschedule most deliveries. Prior to PBDS being implemented, a number of delivery vehicles were dispatched as orders came in. For urgent orders, vehicles were dispatched immediately, while for more routine orders an attempt was made to hold vehicles back until several deliveries in the same geographical area could be combined. This procedure was expensive and, perhaps more importantly, resulted in situations where even urgent orders were delayed, since delivery vehicles were not always available during peak delivery hours.

With the PBDS most deliveries are prescheduled, and take advantage of known traffic patterns in order to minimize delivery time. An interactive, computer-aided procedure was devised which assigns HBB's to delivery routes so as to meet their time and frequency of delivery requirements. The twelve delivery day planning cycle is split into three groups of four delivery days, after which the delivery cycle repeats. In each four-delivery-day cycle each HBB receives either one, two, or four deliveries. The procedure tries to satisfy the delivery requirements without leaving gaps in consecutive time slots, since an empty time slot indicates idle time.

An opportunity to test the flexibility of this delivery scheme occurred recently when the LIBS Blood Center was moved from one location to another several miles away. It was found that the delivery routes could be adjusted rapidly and the required reassignment of the HBB's was determined conveniently.

Controlling the system

The shortage deliveries and the rotational returns for each hospital are monitored in order to detect changes in hospital requirements. Every two weeks the "discrepancy" between the hospital's estimated† and expected usage during these two weeks is computed. This discrepancy is added to the cumulative discrepancy from prior weeks to form an updated cumulative discrepancy, which, together with the number of weeks included in it, and the value of the hospital's expected usage, are used to compute the "normalized cumulative discrepancy" of this week. This last value is compared with a statistically established "limit;" if it exceeds the limit, it is concluded that a shift in usage level has occurred. New usage estimates are computed, and new distribution schedules are prepared. Otherwise, no action is taken.

Since the mix of the eight blood types is a function of the ethnic mix of the population, which is in a state of transition for some of the hospitals tested, the above control procedure was established for each of the blood types as well as for all types of whole blood and all types of red blood cells. Adjustments were made either by blood type or for all blood types. It was found that this had the unfortunate characteristic that if overall usage was increasing or decreasing, individual blood types tended to go out of control in consecutive evaluation cycles before the total usage chart went out of control. This caused an excessive number of distribution changes. For this reason, the concept of "warning limits" and "action limits" was set up. A change is only made if one of the blood types exceeded the action limits. However, at that time if any other blood type also exceeded the warning limits, then that distribution would also be changed at the same time.

Daily inventory adjustment

The resulting regional blood flow is illustrated in Figure 5. In this figure the aging of the RBC inventory is indicated down the center of the figure with the scheduled movement of blood to HBB's indicated to the left of the figure and the nonscheduled movement to the right. The long-dated, stock-dated, and short-dated RBC inventories refer to blood units that are suitable respectively for rotation shipments, for retention shipments, and solely for supplemental shipments — which are filled by the oldest available units. The arrows indicate the blood flow that is normalized to 1,000 units collected.

On the basis of this anticipated regional blood flow, the RBC's inventory is evaluated and adjusted daily. Stock-dated inventory balancing is performed late each afternoon after all rotational returns have been received. It involves the part of the flow circled towards the bottom of Figure 5. The available stock-dated inventory is compared to the retention shipments that are scheduled, the anticipated supplemental shipments plus a small reserve for unusual circumstances which is shown as becoming short-dated inventory. When the inventory for any product exceeds these requirements, the excess units are designated as surplus, and transshipped to the New York Blood Services (NYBS) division of GNYBP. When stock-dated inventory is

---

†The usage is determined by combining the known weekly scheduled distributions with the recorded supplemental deliveries and rotational returns to form an estimate of actual usage.

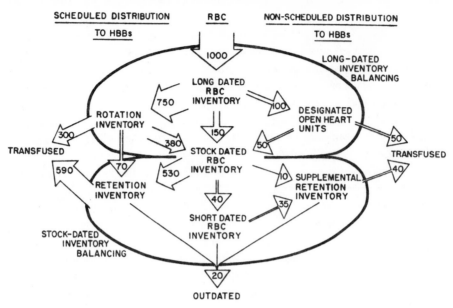

FIGURE 5. Regional Blood Flow Balancing.

below requirements then either surplus long-dated units (if available) will be retained, or the shortage will be made up from the other divisions of GNYBP if possible.

Long-dated inventory balancing is performed each morning after the bulk of the bloods collected the previous day have been typed. It involves the part of the flow circled at the top of Figure 5. The long-dated regional inventory which is expected to become available during that day is compared to the commitment of units for scheduled rotation shipments plus units required to meet open heart surgery needs (which is a specialized procedure where only fresh blood units are suitable). Any units in excess of these requirements are either retained to make up for shortages in stock-dated inventory as discussed above, or are made available for transshipment to other divisions of GNYBP. Since LIBS collects in excess of its needs, there is generally a surplus of rotation units especially in the more common blood types.

Computer operation

The effectiveness of PBDS depends upon accurate and timely data on operations, which is achieved in part by running the system on a minicomputer, and by utilizing machine-readable bar codes on blood products and on test samples [1]. The machine-readable codes on test samples are used in conjunction with automated equipment which performs blood type determinations and links the data concerning the unit and its test results directly in the computer. This provides the earliest possible indication of what products will be reaching inventory during that day. The bar codes, which indicate product, blood type, identification numbers, etc., are also scanned as blood units are shipped out and returned, to maintain perpetual inventory. In this manner, the total inventory picture at the RBC is accurately maintained in real time.

The light pen techniques are also utilized to control computer operations and to identify the locations to which blood products are shipped or from where they were received. This is done by scanning bar codes on menu sheets that list all shipping locations, all types of transactions, and all available types of computer operations. This way, the computer is effectively used by nontechnical personnel, and any errors in entering data are minimized.

In order to maintain a modular approach that can be utilized by all RBC's regardless of size, a network of minicomputers is being used to handle all the RBC blood processing needs. In a larger operation, such as LIBS, the operations are split functionally (i.e., separate minicomputers in the laboratory and distribution areas), while in the smaller centers a single minicomputer would handle all functions.

Impact, implications, and extensions

Scientific impact

The successful operation of PBDS at LIBS has demonstrated the ability to set performance measures on the basis of regional planning. It establishes the first quantitative management guide for the selection of feasible targets and strategies, for the evaluation of options within a class of strategies, and for establishing the best possible performance within that class as a reference for the strategy selected. It further demonstrates the ability to identify deviations from anticipated performance and, consequently, the ability to manage by exception.

An example of this is the analysis of reported utilization by 28 HBB's that was performed recently. Statistical techniques indicated that the utilization rate pattern for 18 of the 28 HBB's were statistically not differentiable and showed an average utilization rate of 96%, which is close to the 98% value predicted; 6 HBB utilization rates were indicated as significantly below this norm and 4 utilization rates were indicated as significantly above the norm. Since the same utilization rate is achievable for all HBB's under PBDS, deviations from the statistical norm can be confidently attributed to assignable causes. The utilization rates above the norm are attributed to sophisticated techniques such as holding the same blood unit for several possible recipients concurrently. The poorer utilization performance of the 6 HBB's is attributed to poor blood banking practices such as failure to return untransfused units to inventory promptly, or to special hospital practices.

Management decision implications

PBDS implies major changes in management decision models both for the RBC and the HBB's. Most regions follow a procedure characterized by a decentralized and reactive distribution. In this mode of operation, the HBB checks its inventory status one or more times per day and, if it deems it to be low, places an order for additional blood. The RBC makes a decision whether its inventory is sufficient to fill the order. If it is, it delivers the requested quantity. If it is not, then it seeks to modify the order to a lesser amount, to substitute red blood cells for whole blood, etc. This "discussion" results in a modified order which is actually delivered. Both the HBB and the

RBC are making short-term decisions regarding each delivery, sometimes with conflicting objectives and are reacting to a situation more than anything else.

PBDS allows the system to operate in a predictive distribution mode. In this mode the RBC assumes responsibility for the long-term scheduling decisions, while each HBB assumes responsibility for the daily fine adjustments. The RBC starts with a distribution strategy as described above. A copy of this, in the form of a shipping schedule and recommended inventory levels to be maintained, is furnished to each HBB. The HBB inventory checking is then reduced to two steps. First, before each scheduled shipment is due, any inventory above the desired levels is returned and second, whenever the inventory is insufficient to meet demand, a supplemental order is placed which is automatically filled under normal situations since it is assumed that it is needed immediately.

The supplemental deliveries and the returns are monitored over a two-week period, at the end of which period a decision is made based on the control statistics on whether or not to revise the distribution. This is a further example of how PBDS has achieved a management by exception principle.

Economic impact

The economic impact of PBDS can be most directly measured in terms of improvement in blood utilization. Prior to the implementation of PBDS, the utilization rate in the LIBS region was 80%, which was also then the national average. Since the implementation of PBDS, the utilization rate for LIBS has improved by 16%, while the national average has improved little if at all during the same interval. The improvement in utilization at LIBS translates to 80% reduction in wastage, and therefore, to annual savings of $500,000 per year.

Of lesser economic impact is the reduction in the number of deliveries. Before PBDS was implemented, an average of 7.8 weekly deliveries were made to each hospital, all of which were unscheduled; after PBDS was implemented, the number of deliveries dropped to 4.2, but of which only 1.4 are unscheduled. By associating a $10 cost to an unscheduled delivery to an HBB and a $5 cost to a scheduled delivery (which is part of a route), PBDS has achieved a 64% reduction in delivery costs. This translates to annual cost savings of $100,000. Additional important, though less tangible, costs savings are achieved by the implementation of sounder blood banking practices to reduce discrepancies between actual and achievable performance for individual HBB's.

Probably the most important savings in the national health care bill brought about by PBDS is realized by improved blood availability to patients. Since deliveries to the hospitals are mostly prescheduled, elective surgeries can be prescheduled also, so as to minimize the number of surgeries postponed because of lack of the right blood products. However, savings from this improved availability are extremely difficult to estimate and quantify.

National implications

It can be seen from the model of Figure 3 that, in order to achieve high availability and utilization rates for the rarer blood types (small usage), most of the shipments have to be on rotation. In practice, however, RBC's can only schedule between 70% and 85% of the average blood collections for rotation shipments because of uncertainties in blood availability, and the need to keep an RBC reserve. Therefore, if the amount of rotational blood available for distribution is approximately equal to that which will be utilized within the region (i.e., if a strict self-sufficiency criterion is applied), then for these blood groups either very low availability or alternatively a very significant reduction in utilization must be accepted. Since neither of these alternatives is desirable, an alternative is to rotate more blood units in this blood group than will be eventually transfused in the region and redistribute some portion of the returned blood units to another region utilizing the inventory balancing techniques that were described earlier. This is a feasible approach in LIBS since, like most regions that are primarily suburban and rural in nature, it has the capacity for collecting blood significantly in excess of the overall regional needs.

LIBS collects approximately 20% more blood than will be ultimately transfused in the region. Virtually all of the rarer bloods are first rotated to HBB's in the region, while the excess collection in the more common bloods are mostly immediately sent to the New York Blood Services (NYBS) division of GNYBP. This division encompasses the metropolitan New York area and, like most large urban areas, has difficulty in collecting enough blood to meet the needs of the major medical centers and other hospitals in this area. The influx from LIBS is of significant help and the small fraction of older, rarer bloods that are received as stock-dated units can readily be absorbed. Thus the units collected in LIBS in excess of its own transfusion needs improves the quality of blood services in LIBS as well as in NYBS. On the other hand, the major medical centers in the New York Division of GNYBP also serve the needs of much of the population residing in the area covered by LIBS.

It should be noted that not all major regions such as LIBS require interaction with larger regions. A planning exercise performed for the regional blood center in Richmond, Virginia, which services only seven HBB's, indicated that this region was remarkably self-sufficient. This is primarily because it includes a major medical center which accounts for a significant part of the regional usage. However, for the most part there is a mutually beneficial interaction feasible between the smaller RBC's serving mainly suburban and rural areas and the larger ones which will mostly service larger urban areas.

These conclusions suggest that the concept of total regional self-sufficiency which has long prevailed in blood banking is in conflict with the goals of the National Blood Policy that calls for high availability with efficiency. Rather, a modest level of resource sharing between regions as outlined above will work to the benefit of all participants.

Extensions

The success of PBDS has fostered a favorable climate for the further application of Management Science techniques both on a national and international basis. The International Society of Blood Transfusion Expert Committee on Automation has recently endorsed the concepts inherent in PBDS and the Swiss Red Cross Transfusion Service is studying it as a basis for the creation of a national blood distribution system for that country.

On the national level, as the PBDS strategy is expanded to the other three divisions of the GNYBP, it will provide an opportunity to more thoroughly investigate a broader regional network. Concurrently, other regional blood programs are investigating the use of PBDS. The American Red Cross Blood Services — Northeast Region has already implemented a distribution plan for its six RBC's based upon the PBDS concept. These implementations represent broader geographic groupings of RBC's which, together with other such groupings, could eventually interact through a hypothetical national blood clearinghouse.

Such developments would contribute significantly towards meeting the objectives of the National Blood Policy. It would act to alleviate the "national blood shortage" which, in part, at least is thought to be not so much a national blood shortage but rather the lack of a national logistical system for moving blood from where it is available to where it is needed. They would thus contribute to a reduction in the consumer's hospitalization costs and the delivery of higher level health care.

Acknowledgements

We are indebted to Aaron Kellner, M.D., President of the New York Blood Center, Inc.; Johanna Pindyck, M.D., Director; Robert Hirsch, M.D., Medical Director of the Greater New York Blood Program; and Theodore Robertson, M.D., Director of Long Island Blood Services, for their wholehearted collaboration and encouragement. We are also grateful for contributions made by Professors Cyrus Derman, Ed Ignall, Peter Kolesar, and Donald Smith of Columbia University, at various phases of this work, and for helpful comments and encouragement provided by Professors Howard Kunreuther, William Pierskalla, and Morris Cohen of the University of Pennsylvania.

This research was supported in part by the National Institutes of Health, National Heart, Lung and Blood Institute Grant No. HL 09011-16 at The New York Blood Center.

REFERENCES

[1] Brodheim, E., "Regional Blood Center Automation," *Transfusion*, Vol. 18, 1978, pp. 298—303.

[2] Brodheim, E., Hirsch, R., and Prastacos, G. P., "Setting Inventory Levels for Hospital Blood Banks," *Transfusion*, Vol. 16, 1976, pp. 63—70.

[3] Brodheim, E., Derman, C., and Prastacos, G. P., "On the Evaluation of a Class of Inventory Policies for Perishable Products such as Blood," *Management Science*, Vol. 21, 1975, pp. 1320—1326.

[4] National Blood Policy, Department of Health, Education and Welfare, Vol. 39, 1974, 176.

[5] Prastacos, G. P., "Optimal Myopic Allocation of a Product with Fixed Lifetime," *Journal of the Operational Research Society*, Vol. 29, 1978, pp. 905—913.

[6] Prastacos, G. P., "Allocation of Perishable Inventory," forthcoming in *Operations Research*. Also available as Technical Report No. 70, Operations Research Group, Columbia University, 1977.

[7] Prastacos, G. P. and Brodheim, E., "A Mathematical Model for Regional Blood Distribution," Working Paper 79-02-91, Department of Decision Sciences, The Wharton School, University of Pennsylvania, 1979.

4 / Forecasting

Forecasts are necessary inputs for many production and operating decisions. They are used for such problems as production planning, manpower requirements, scheduling, and inventory control. The accuracy, time horizon, and forecast interval needed may vary substantially from one problem area to another, as well as the use of the most appropriate forecasting technique for use in the forecasting subsystem.

Exponential smoothing has found widespread usage as a method for projecting requirements in an inventory control system. These systems must manage thousands of parts, providing good accuracy at a reasonably low cost. Exponential smoothing represents a useful procedure easily converted to a computer based routine for short range forecasting. This procedure was thoroughly presented in the first volume of **Production Planning, Scheduling, and Inventory Control** edited by Montgomery and Berry.

Three forecasting papers have been included in this section to provide the reader with exposure on recent advances in forecasting methodology and their usefulness. The first paper by Roberts and Whybark provides a comparison of four adaptive forecasting techniques. Since forecasting must be done in a dynamic environment, the forecasting system must be capable of first identifying when a change has occurred and second, make the appropriate corrections to future forecasts. The authors provide a useful classification and description of the techniques for the reader, and an evaluation of the form procedures under study.

The second paper by Mabert is an introductory tutorial on the Box-Jenkins methodology. This procedure attracted substantial attention in the 1970s as a useful forecasting technique for short range forecasting. Since that time many applications have occurred with the recent availability of computer software programs to complete the data analysis. The paper introduces the basic methodology and then illustrates its application on a case study data set.

The third paper by Mabert and Hill illustrates the problem in a non-manufacturing environment, banking, where demand behavior does not follow completely reoccurring patterns. The authors describe procedures for combining two methodologies, dummy variable regression and Box-Jenkins procedure to adequately model customer behavior. They demonstrate that each forecasting problem can be potentially a unique occasion and must reflect each situation's unique elements. Therefore, strictly applying a single model universally may be inappropriate. The forecast analyst must take care and understand the forecasting situation before modeling. "Look before you leap" communicates the key idea.

For the reader interested in a more detailed discussion of forecasting procedures, the following two references are suggested. They are written for a reader with limited mathematical background. Both provide many examples to illustrate the methodology.

1) Vincent A. Mabert, **An Introduction to Short Term Forecasting Using the Box-Jenkins Methodology**, American Institute of Industrial Engineers, Atlanta, Georgia, 1975.

2) Spyros Makridakis and Steven C. Wheelwright, **Forecasting: Methods and Applications**, John Wiley & Sons, Santa Barbara, CA, 1978.

INT. J. PROD. RES., 1974, VOL. 12, NO. 6, 635–645

Adaptive forecasting techniques

STEPHEN D. ROBERTS* and D. CLAY WHYBARK†

The class of exponential smoothing models which vary the values of their parameters to adapt to changing conditions in a time series are referred to as adaptive forecasting techniques. In this article criteria for evaluating forecasting models are presented and the features of a simple exponential smoothing model that are exploited by the adaptive techniques are discussed. Several adaptive forecasting schemes are described and classified, and examples of the performance of these techniques are presented.

Introduction

Nearly every business and economic decision relies on a forecast to reduce the uncertainty involved in decision making. The need for forecasts arise from short-term and long-term requirements. Short-term forecasts, which span a period from a few days to a few months, are frequently more pressing and will be the principal emphasis of this paper.

Problems requiring short-term forecasts include inventory control, production scheduling, purchasing, short-term investments, and labour assignments. In many cases forecasts are routinely needed for a large number of individual items. For example, in an inventory control system it is not uncommon to find several thousand products or parts which require forecasts. Thus, in addition to accuracy, the forecasts must be inexpensively and quickly computed while not requiring large amounts of data and storage.

In discussing the merits of several forecasting techniques, Chambers, Mullick and Smith (1971) identified the class of techniques that meets these criteria for short-term forecasts. The class is time series analysis and projection. Because forecasts using these methods are formed just from past data, economists often classify the techniques as ' naive ' since there is no attempt to explain or determine the factors which are shaping the time series or how these factors are causing fluctuations in the data (Spencer *et al.* 1961). Motivations for using a naive technique may include lack of understanding of the basic theory causing the time series, the inability to justify a more sophisticated approach economically, or insufficient time to pursue other approaches. Hence, while the more econometric approaches are very useful in describing the influences that shape economic time series, it is believed that the projection or time series analysis method very often provides sufficient short-term accuracy and can be implemented on a routine basis.

Of the many methods of short-term forecasting using time series analysis or projection, the technique of exponential smoothing seems to be a widely

Received 22 November 1972.
* Indiana University, School of Medicine, Indiana, U.S.A.
† Purdue University, Indiana, U.S.A.

Published by Taylor & Francis Ltd, 10–14 Macklin Street, London WC2B 5NF.

accepted and proven short-term forecasting technique. It is attractive computationally because one need not retain a lot of data from one forecast period to another, and the computations are very simple. Although this technique has been widely accepted and frequently applied, it does suffer from some limitations. Specifically, when forecasts rely on characterizing and projecting past history it is possible that some short term shifts or changes may be missed. As will be seen, subsequently, the exponential smoothing model's ability to track changes in the time series is critically dependent upon the values of the smoothing constants or parameters chosen. Also, the smoothing constants determine the stability of the forecasting system while undergoing various changes in the time series.

If one is willing to assume certain critical characteristics of a time series, then 'optimal' parameters may be determined, e.g. Brown (1963), Cox (1961), and Nerlove and Wage (1964). However, in spite of the fact that it may be possible to mathematically derive optimal smoothing constants for certain kinds of time series, frequently one will not be able to make such rigid assumptions. Usually, some intuitive approach based on past experiences must be employed.

An alternative to an intuitive approach would be one in which the forecast parameters were controlled in an adaptive fashion based on the data presented. This procedure will not require making rigid assumptions for determining forecast parameters. We will call these techniques which involve the adaptive control of the exponential smoothing models 'adaptive forecasting techniques'. Adaptive smoothing, then, attempts to overcome the difficulties of exponential smoothing while still preserving the accuracy, low cost and data sparsity requirements for producing the forecast. This paper presents a discussion of the various criteria for evaluating forecast accuracy, some features of the simple exponential smoothing model, a classification and explanation of some of the adaptive smoothing techniques, and examples of the performance of adaptive smoothing approaches. By reviewing the essential features of adaptive forecasting techniques, one should be able to tailor the techniques to particular applications.

Forecast criteria

The ultimate evaluation of the quality of a forecasting technique is, of course, how well it performs in the application for which the forecasts are developed. More specifically, one needs to balance the cost of imperfect forecasts with the cost of improving the forecast for the specific application. In order to judge the merits of each forecast routine, criteria are presented which, while they are by no means universally accepted, do represent the general nature of the evaluation problem and are satisfactory for most applications. To determine a 'good' forecasting technique four basic aspects of the forecasts must be considered. These are : information and computational requirements, forecast accuracy, rate of response, and cost. The value of each aspect must be considered in light of the specific application being considered.

Information and computational requirements

If forecasting technique is to be acceptable in an industrial environment it must provide forecasts economically, thus, computing time and information storage are important. The computing time and information storage reflect costs of the forecasting system. Unfortunately these two criteria are inextricably tied to the computing system, and cannot objectively be separated from the equipment being used.

Forecast accuracy

On the other hand, forecast accuracy is independent of the equipment and can be measured in a variety of ways. Each measure is based on the forecast error in any period, which can be written:

$$e_t = F_t - X_t, \tag{1}$$

where X_t is the time series value for period t. Four of the more common measures follow.

A measure of the bias of the forecasting technique is given by the mean forecast error, defined as:

$$\bar{e} = \sum_{t=1}^{n} e_t / n, \tag{2}$$

where n denotes the number of periods forecast. Two measures related to the variability of forecast error are the mean absolute error deviation (used frequently in the forecasting literature and called MAD) and the forecast error variance, S_e^2, both defined below:

$$\text{MAD} = \sum_{t=1}^{n} |e_t| / n, \tag{3}$$

$$S_e^2 = \sum_{t=1}^{n} (e_t - \bar{e})^2 / (n-1). \tag{4}$$

The variance measure is important since it reflects the degree of uncertainty that must be accommodated by the decisions that are based on the forecasts.

Finally, because many industrial time series are influenced by some common set of factors rather than by a completely independent or random set of influences, it is necessary to determine the presence of correlation in the forecast errors. The measure which reflects the correlation between successive forecast errors is the autocorrelation coefficient, AC_e, and is defined as

$$AC_e = \left[\sum_{t=1}^{n} e_t e_{t-1} - n\bar{e}^2 \right] \bigg/ \left[\sum_{t=1}^{n} e_t^2 - n\bar{e}^2 \right].$$

Ideally one would like a forecasting system which, in terms of forecast accuracy, yields all measures as close to zero as possible. Unfortunately, it is very difficult to determine a technique which simultaneously satisfies all criteria because these measures frequently conflict. For example, it may be possible to reduce to a minimum the variability of the forecast error by minimizing MAD or the error variance. In doing so, however, one may increase the mean error in the forecast or the autocorrelation. Again, the question of which type of criterion to minimize or whether additional studies of the forecasting alternatives is warranted, must be evaluated in light of the expected benefits from improved forecasts for each individual application.

2 x 2

Rate of response

The third aspect of a good forecasting system is its rate of response. A fundamental assertion in the development of adaptive smoothing techniques is that time series are not stationary but change with time. Therefore, the forecasting system must track these changes as quickly as possible. To test the forecasting technique reaction to various changes in the basic time series, the response to several standard signals is usually analysed. The signals chosen are those which are typical of true changes in the time series. These include impulse, step, ramp, and trigonometric signals. Through the use of these functions the dynamic characteristics of the forecasting technique may be experimentally determined.

Costs

The fourth measure of good forecasts is probably the most essential. This measure reflects the cost associated with a forecasting technique by determining the cost implication for each forecast error. For example, in an inventory system the cost of overestimating the demand is different to that when demand is underestimated. The cost measure, while being perhaps the most comprehensive, is the most difficult to obtain. Only a few applications of this measure have been reported (Whybark 1970).

Exponential smoothing

Philosophically, exponential smoothing is appealing as it is consistent with the belief that, for a changing process, more recent data is more representative than older data. It is attractive computationally because it is not necessary to retain a lot of data from one forecast period to another and computations are very simple. For the purpose of introducing the basic exponential smoothing model, the time series will be assumed to consist of a slowly changing constant component plus some random variations. In exponential smoothing the forecast can be written :

$$F_{t+1} = F_t + \alpha e_t, \tag{6}$$

where α is a fraction ($0 \leqslant \alpha \leqslant 1$) reflecting the forecasters belief in the validity of the newer data. Performing the appropriate algebra gives the formula for exponential smoothing :

$$F_{t+1} = \alpha X_t + (1 - \alpha) F_t. \tag{7}$$

The result of these adjustments is the development of a ' smoothed average ' which gives actual values geometrically decreasing weights with increasing age.

Importance of the smoothing constant

The ability of the forecasting system to track changes in the time series is critically dependent upon the weight or smoothing constant, α. Also the smoothing constant determines the stability of the forecasting system by smoothing random changes in the time series. The importance of the smoothing constant can be understood by noting the changes the smoothing constant has on the forecast itself. When the smoothing constant is close to 1 nearly all the weight is placed on the current observation. As the smoothing constant decreases, more of the weight will be concentrated on the past data.

Selection of the smoothing constant is a difficult and complex problem. This parameter determines the responsiveness of the forecasts and will determine the accuracy and stability for the forecasting system. Exponential smoothing forecasts are often referred to as adaptive systems since the forecast will change in response to observed changes in the time series. The sensitivity of the forecasting system to changes in the smoothing constant can be illustrated by examining the response of the basic exponential smoothing model to a step input. If the step input was short lived, the smoothing constant of 0·1 might be appropriate, but were it permanent the higher smoothing constant would provide a quicker response to the change. Similar arguments can be made for other pure inputs like a step, as shown in Fig. 1. Thus, the basic exponential smoothing model can be made to be quite sensitive to changes in the basic time series or can be made to be insensitive to such changes in the time series by choice of the smoothing constant. The problem is to choose α so that the forecasting system responds only to real changes in the time series and ignores random variation.

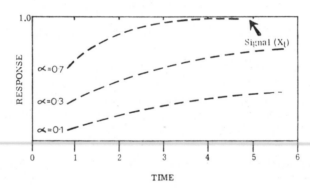

Figure 1. Response to a unit step at time = 0 for various smoothing constants.

Adjusting the smoothing constant

One obvious way to accomplish improved response would be simply to alter manually the smoothing constant as changes are detected in the time series. However, such a procedure would involve continuously monitoring the forecasting system and would require managerial interaction with the forecasting programme. A more attractive alternative than this administrative interference would be to develop a system of automatically monitoring and controlling the smoothing constant in a self-contained fashion. These systems are what we shall refer to as ' adaptive forecasting techniques ' and will be the subject of the latter portion of this paper.

In addition, to the basic forecasting model other more complicated models which represent a greater variety of time series can be developed. Most of the developments follow one of two schools of thought on how to extend the basic model to time series having additional complications such as seasonality, etc. One school is that which is presented and developed by R. G. Brown (1963) while the other is that developed by P. R. Winters (1960). Brown's methods are probably more attractive mathematically because of their sophistication and the fact that they closely resemble popular techniques of regression and moving averages. On the other hand, Winter's techniques are much simpler to understand and possibly have more practical applicability. A third approach which is gaining wide popularity is that developed by Box and Jenkins (1970).

Classification of adaptive techniques

The smoothing constant establishes the balance between rapidity of response to basic changes and stability in the face of random fluctuations. A high value will produce rapid responses but exhibit 'nervousness' in the forecasts when there are random fluctuations. A low value of the smoothing constant 'smooths' the random fluctuations but reacts slowly to basic changes in the time series. Each of the adaptive forecasting techniques to be discussed attempts to capitalize on the virtues of high and low values while minimizing their limitations. Implementation is accomplished by using high values of the smoothing constant when changes are occurring and low values when there are random fluctuations to be smoothed out.

	Periodic evaluation	Continuous evaluation
Unconstrained or computed value of smoothing constant	Eilon and Elmaleh (1970)	Trigg and Leach (1967)
Constrained or prespecified choice of smoothing constant	†Roberts and Reed (1969)	Whybark (1970)

† Note, this classification is not consistent with the original work of Roberts and Reed but reflects the experimental findings presented in this paper.

Table 1. Classification of adaptive smoothing models and examples of each class.

The principal adaptive forecasting techniques can be broadly classified into four categories as shown in Table 1. The two basic divisions are the review period and the method by which the smoothing constant is chosen. Some of the approaches to adaptive forecasting use a periodic evaluation of the model's forecasting performance (using one of the forecast criteria discussed earlier) and then appropriately adjust the smoothing constant. Other techniques continuously review the forecasting performance and can change the smoothing constant each period. The second classification concerns the choice of the smoothing constant when a change is required. Some techniques require the new smoothing constant to be equal to a prespecified amount or to change by a specified amount. Other models permit the smoothing constant to take on any of a number of prespecified values or is computed as a result of the forecast performance review.

One of the adaptive forecasting techniques based on periodic evaluation of performance is that developed by Eilon and Elmaleh (1970). In their approach to adaptive forecasting, they set initial parameters and make forecasts for a specified number of periods (the evaluation interval) with a fixed value of the smoothing constant. The evaluation interval was 100 periods in their work, but was considered a parameter to be predetermined in the experiments reported here. At the end of the evaluation interval, the forecast errors are computed for the time series during the evaluation interval for every permitted value of the smoothing constant ($\alpha = 0.1$, 0.2, ..., 0.9). The value of the smoothing constant which minimizes forecast error over the evaluation interval is then used for making forecasts until the next evaluation is made. This model does not constrain the choice of α at any evaluation, apart from the initial specification of the permitted values, in that any of the permitted values can be chosen as the smoothing constant for the next set of forecasts.

A method which constrains the choice of smoothing constants was developed by Roberts and Reed (1969). In their original work, the model evaluated performance each period (continuous evaluation). The experiments reported here treated the model as a periodic evaluation model with the evaluation interval a parameter to be set and indicated that other intervals than one period gave better performance, hence the classification as a periodic evaluation model. The procedure attempts to minimize error variance by adjusting the smoothing constant in accordance with a technique called evolutionary operation. The forecasting model, for the evaluation interval, computes the sample error variance resulting from a specified smoothing constant and the error variance which would have resulted if the smoothing constant had been 0.05 greater or less than the central value. If it can be shown by a statistical test that a larger or smaller smoothing constant would have produced smaller error variance then the central value is changed to that higher or lower value. The procedure is repeated at the end of the next evaluation interval and the smoothing constant is re-evaluated and adjusted, if indicated. But the adjustment does not exceed more than ± 0.05. Two similar approaches to the Roberts–Reed method are Chow (1965) and Montgomery (1970).

The Trigg and Leach (1967) approach continuously evaluates forecasting performance and calculates an unconstrained value for the smoothing constant each period. Other approaches of this type are proposed by Dudman (1966) and D'Amico (1971). Trigg and Leach perform the evaluation of the forecasts with a tracking signal of the form :

$$T = \tilde{e}_t / |\tilde{e}_t|, \tag{8}$$

where

T = tracking signal,
$\tilde{e}_t$ = smoothed forecast error,
$|\tilde{e}_t|$ = smoothed absolute forecast error.

The forecast error and absolute error are exponentially smoothed with a smoothing constant γ :

$$\left. \begin{aligned} \tilde{e}_t &= \gamma e_t + (1 - \gamma)\tilde{e}_{t-1}, \\ |\tilde{e}_t| &= \gamma |e_t| + (1 - \gamma)|\tilde{e}_{t-1}|, \end{aligned} \right\} \tag{9}$$

where γ = tracking signal smoothing constant ($0 \leqslant \gamma \leqslant 1$).

102

In the Trigg and Leach approach, the smoothing constant for the forecasting equation is set equal to the absolute value of the tracking signal each period. The tracking signal compares the exponentially smoothed current error to the smoothed absolute error. It is a measure of how closely the current errors compare to the ' expected ' errors. When the smoothed absolute error is large the tracking signal tends to be small (i.e. near zero). It is desirable to have the smoothed error near zero as well, since this indicates that the forecasts are closely scattered around the actual values. This would also produce a tracking signal near zero. But when large forecast errors occur, relative to what is expected, the value of the smoothing constant moves from zero toward one.

Another approach, developed by Whybark (1970), also involves continuous evaluation of the forecast error but changes the smoothing constant to pre-determined values only when deemed necessary. Two other continuous evaluation, constrained α change approaches are found in Rao and Shapiro (1970), who make use of evolutionary spectra, and Farley and Hinich (1970), who use smoothed past data. The essential notion involved in these three approaches is to set control limits around forecast error. The discovery of forecast errors that are outside these limits in any period indicates that a shift in the mean value has been detected.

Two control limits were used by Whybark for monitoring the forecast error, one for the error in a single period and another limit for errors in two periods in sequence. For single periods, the control procedure would signal for a change in the smoothing constant when the forecast error was found to lie outside a range of ± 4 standard deviations around zero. Also, a change in the smoothing constant would be requested when two consecutive forecast errors were in the same direction outside $\pm 1\cdot2$ standard deviations.

Once the forecast errors are determined to be outside the limits for either of these conditions, the smoothing constant is set to a high value for making the forecast the period after the detection of the shift and then is reduced somewhat for the following period. The smoothing constant is then returned to a base value until another shift is detected.

Testing the adaptive forecasting techniques

Some example simulation runs were performed by Whybark (1973) to provide samples of the performance of these four adaptive forecasting techniques. The simulations involved forecasting the demand for an item in an inventory control situation. The simulated demand for the item was generated using a constant mean with normally distributed fluctuations. The mean of the demand distribution was stable for a uniformally distributed random number of periods and then shifted to a uniformly distributed random new level. Demand forecasts for the inventory item were used in a decision rule for ordering replenishment inventory. The mean forecast error, standard deviation of forecast error and the total cost of the inventory control system were recorded for each of the four adaptive approaches and, in addition, two simple models for comparison purposes.

Four hundred periods of demand were used in the simulations. The first 200 of these periods were used for setting the parameters of the various techniques to their best values. The criteria used for setting these parameters was the minimization of the total cost of the inventory control system. These parameters were then used in each technique for forecasting the next 200 periods of simulated demand. The results are recorded in Table 2.

Model	Cost	Mean forecast error	Standard deviation of forecast error
1. Constant forecast	$668·50	0·000	5·012
2. Constant $\alpha = 0·2$	670·24	0·118	3·871
3. Eilon–Elmaleh (EI = 40)†	659·38	−0·321	4·477
4. Roberts–Reed (EI = 5)†	663·02	0·061	3·632
5. Trigg–Leach	648·12	−0·004	3·204
6. Whybark	655·90	0·143	3·070

† EI indicates the best evaluation interval (in periods) found over the first 200 periods of data.

Table 2. Results for comparison runs (200 periods) with parameter values from initialization runs.

Although these results are based on an experiment of limited scope (200 periods, step function only, one set of cost parameters) they are consistent with the other research findings cited. Generally, the results indicate that one can improve the forecast error deviations and total costs from exponential smoothing models, using adaptive forecasting techniques. Some insights can be gained from looking at typical forecasts versus actual demands for the various techniques. Figures 2 and 3 plot some of these results for a typical portion of the time series. The two periodic evaluation models both show something of a lag in responding to the demand shifts. This is explained by the fact that these adaptive models must wait a specified number of periods (the evaluation interval) before determining whether the smoothing constant should be changed even though, in both cases, the best evaluation interval was greater than one

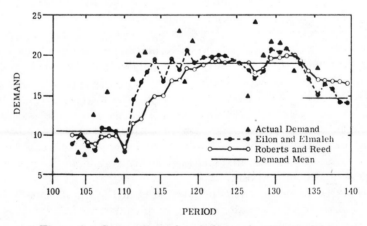

Figure 2. Comparison of periodic evaluation models.

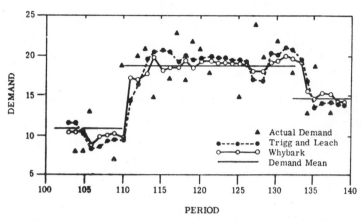

Figure 3.   Comparison of continuous evaluation models.

period.   The continuous review models both show quite rapid responses to the basic changes and relatively stable forecasts during periods of a constant demand.

Conclusions

The adaptive forecasting techniques hold promise for increased forecast accuracy under conditions of short-term shifts in the time series.   The adaptive models do require some additional computation and this cost must be balanced by substantially improved forecasts.   Also there is some evidence to recommend the continuous review approaches over those based on periodic review for time series data characterized by random step inputs.   Of course, the final evaluation of appropriateness of adaptive forecasting technology must rest in the content of the forecasting environment.

On appelle techniques de prévisions adaptives la variété de modèles à aplanissement exponentiel qui varient la valeur de leurs paramètres pour s'adapter aux conditions variables d'une série de temps.   Dans cet article, on présente les critères utilisés pour évaluer des modèles de prévisions et on discute les caractéristiques d'un simple modèle à aplanissement exponentiel exploitées par les techniques adaptives.   On décrit et on classe plusieurs projets de prévisions adaptives et on donne des exemples du fonctionnement de ces techniques.

Die Gruppe von Exponentialglättungsmodellen, die die Werte ihrer Konstanten in einer Zeitfolge verändern, um sich veränderlichen Verhältnissen anzupassen, wird den anpassungsfähigen Prognoseverfahren zugeordnet.   Dieser Artikel führt Gesicht‑ punkte an zur Bewertung von Prognosemodellen, und die Eigenschaften eines einf‑ Exponentialglättungsmodelles, die durch das anpassungsfähige Verfahren wurden, werden diskutiert.   Mehrere anpassungsfähige Prognosesyste‑ beschrieben und klassifiziert, und Beispiele über die Arbeitsweise di‑ werden demonstriert.

REFERENCES

BOX, G. E. P., and JENKINS, G. M., 1970, *Time Se* Holden-Day).
BROWN, R. C., 1963, *Smoothing Forecasting an* (New Jersey : Prentice-Hall).
CHAMBERS, JOHN C., MULLICK, CATIND the right forecasting techni

CHOW, WEN M., 1965, Adaptive control of the exponential smoothing constant, *J. Ind. Engng*, **16,** 314–17.

COX, D. R., 1961, Prediction by exponentially weighted moving averages and related methods, *J. roy. Stat. Soc.*, (Series B), **23,** 414–22.

D'AMICO, PETER, 1971, Forecasting system uses modified smoothing, *Ind. Engng.* **3,** 15–20.

DUDMAN, R. S., 1966, Forecasting with three-factor adaptive smoothing. A paper presented at the Thirteenth International Meeting of The Institute of Management Sciences, Philadelphia, Pennsylvania, September.

EILON, S., and ELMALEH, J., 1970, Adaptive limits in inventory control, *Mgmt Sci.*, **16,** B 533–48.

FARLEY, JOHN U., and HINICH, MELVIN J., 1970, Detecting 'small' mean shifts in time series. *Mgmt Sci.*, **17,** 189–99.

MONTGOMERY, DOUGLAS C., 1970, Adaptive control of exponential smoothing parameters by evolutionary operation, *AIIE Trans.*, **2,** 268, 269.

NERLOVE, M., and WAGE, S., 1964, On the optimality of adaptive forecasting, *Mgmt Sci.*, **10,** 207–24.

RAO, AMBAR G., and SHAPIRO, ARTHUR, 1970, Adaptive smoothing using evolutionary spectra, *Mgmt Sci.*, November.

ROBERTS, S. D., and REED, R., 1969, The development of a self-adaptive forecasting technique, *AIIE Trans.*, **1,** 314, 322.

SPENCER, M. H., CLARK, C. G., and HOGUET, P. W., 1961, *Business and Economic Forecasting* (Homewood, Illinois : Irwin).

TRIGG, D. W., and LEACH, A. G., 1967, Exponential smoothing with an adaptive response rate, *Ops. Res. Q.*, **18,** 53.

WHYBARK, D. CLAY, 1970, Comparing an adaptive decision model and human decisions, *Acad. Mgmt J.*, **16,** 700 ; 1973, A comparison of adaptive forecasting techniques, *Logistic Transpn. Rev.*, **8,** 13.

WINTERS, P. R., 1960, Forecasting sales by exponentially weighted moving averages, *Mgmt Sci.*, **6,** 324–42.

THE BOX-JENKINS FORECASTING TECHNIQUE

Vincent A. Mabert, Purdue University

Abstract

This paper describes the Box-Jenkins procedure for modeling univariate time series. The methodology contains three steps: Identification, Estimation, and Diagnostic checking. To illustrate the methodology, a case study is presented, where the reader moves through all three steps. With model development completed, single and multiple period forecasts are made.

The Box-Jenkins Forecasting Technique

Introduction

This paper presents an introductory description and application of the Box-Jenkins (BJ) technique of time series analysis for forecasting future events. The Box-Jenkins method represents a rather new and sophisticated approach to time series analysis that academicians have been using in recent years. However, little application has been found in the business community to data. This has been mainly due to its technical nature; precluding ease of understanding by the average practitioner.

While academic studies using the Box-Jenkins technique have shown it to be a highly successful short term forecasting tool, the author is aware of only a few companies who are presently using the technique or investigating its potential. General Telephone and Telegraph (5) appears to be one user. It has been applied to forecasts of telephone installations, electric power generation and sales, industrial company sales and common stock price moves by academicians. For example, see Tiao and Thompson (9) for forecasting applications in telephone call demand, Mabert and Radcliffe (7) for electrical peak load analysis, and Box and Jenkins (1) for stock price forecasts.

The Box-Jenkins methodology is not a radically new approach to forecasting. Rather, it represents an integration of a set of standard techniques into a framework for modeling univariate time series, based upon a combined autoregressive-moving average model. Historically, forecasting was done using either autoregression (3) or moving average (including exponential smoothing) (2) (10) model. However, there was no combined strategy in the past, until Box-Jenkins completed their work, that could capitalize upon the strengths of both approaches.

The Box-Jenkins methodology contains three basic steps:

1) Model Identification - by analyzing sample autocorrelations (SAC) and sample partial autocorrelations, the analysis identifies likely candidates for modeling the time series under investigation.

2) Non-Linear Estimation of Parameters - by minimizing the sum of the squared residuals, the appropriate parameter values are estimated.

3) Diagnostic Checking - by analyzing the pattern of the sample autocorrelation of the residuals, the analyst determines the direction of improvement that must be taken to improve the forecast model.

In the following sections, the Box-Jenkins model and three step procedure will be demonstrated. The discussion first covers the fundamentals of the Box-Jenkins model and common notation. The next section presents a detail example illustrating the application of the three step procedure. The paper concludes with an illustration of single and multiple period forecasts.

The Box-Jenkins Model Fundamentals

Assume that a production planner wishes to forecast sales by analyzing historical patterns. The Box-Jenkins technique does not attempt to analyse actual levels of the forecasted variable but, instead, to model the __difference__ between the variable level (Z_t) and its mean value (μ). We will continue to follow this convention, such that Y_t will refer __not__ to sales in any month but, instead, to the __difference__ in sales in month and the mean value of sales ($Y_t = Z_t - \mu$). The general Autoregressive Integrated Moving Average (ARIMA) model for sales can be expressed as:

ARIMA MODEL

$$Y_t = \Phi_1 Y_{t-1} + \Phi_2 Y_{t-2} + \ldots + \Phi_p Y_{t-p} \qquad [1]$$
$$+ \theta_0 - \theta_1 a_{t-1} - \ldots - \theta_q a_{t-q} + a_t$$

The Φ's and θ's respectively represent the autoregressive and moving average parameters which are estimated. The p and q terms represent the order of the model, the amount of historical information used, and a_t terms represent unforeseen random shocks or forecast errors occuring in period t. Finally, θ_0 represents a deterministic trend constant which is generally equal to zero since most series are dynamic and continually changing in trend.

A question may come to mind as to what a_t represents and why a negative weight ($-\theta$) is present in equation [1]. The a_{t-q}'s represent the forecast error, defined as $a_{t-q} = (Y_{t-q} - \hat{Y}_{t-q})$, where (^) indicates the forecasted value. The negative weights are the common nomenclature used, and is therefore employed, and the weight values need not be positive or sum to unity (1, p. 10).

Equation [1] can be rewritten into the general Box-Jenkins model of

$$\phi_p(B)Y_t = \theta_o + \theta_q(B)a_t \qquad [2]$$

The $\phi_p(B)$ and $\theta_q(B)$ are polynomials in B of order p and q respectively where

$$\theta_p(B) = 1 - \theta_1 B^1 - \theta_2 B^2 - \theta_3 B^3 - \ldots - \theta_p B^p,$$

and $\qquad\qquad\qquad\qquad\qquad [3]$

$$\theta_p(B) = 1 - \theta_1 B^1 - \theta_2 B^2 - \theta_3 B^3 - \ldots - \theta_q B^q$$

The B is a backshift operator such that $BY_t = Y_{t-1}$. The definition of a backshift operator provides a convenient means of noting manipulation of the series. For example

$$(1-B)Y_t = Y_t - Y_{t-1}$$

$$(1-B-B^2)Y_t = Y_t - Y_{t-1} - Y_{t-2} \qquad [4]$$

$$(1-B^4)Y_t = Y_t - Y_{t-4}.$$

As can be seen, the exponent of the backshift operator determines the appropriate amount of backward shifting.

The ARIMA model of equation [2] assumes that the times series is normally distributed around some constant mean. That is to say the time series is "stationary", as illustrated in Exhibit 1. Of course, stationary series are more the exception than the rule in most business situations due to existance of business cycles and changes in consumer preferences and desires.

Non-stationary series, which have changing means over time, can be converted into stationary ones by a simple transformation called "differencing." Using the differencing technique, one obtains the difference from a mean that changes over time. For example, assume June sales, Z_t, are 2500 units and July sales, Z_{t+1}, are 2700. The value plotted for July is not 2700 but, instead, the difference between the July and June receipts of 200. Such a transformation allows us to obtain a reasonably stationary series of sales, which is defined as Y_t (stationary sales in period t). Mathematically, one would calculate Y_t as

$$Y_t = Z_t - Z_{t-1} = (1-B)Z_t \qquad [5]$$

To see how such a differencing procedure transforms a non-stationary series into a stationary one, examine Exhibit 2. Section _a_ of the exhibit represents the historic values of sales as plotted over time. Section _b_ represents the plot of Y_t values over time, i.e., the plot of sales (from section _a_) minus the mean level of sales ($Y_t = Z_t - \mu$). The non-stationarity inherent in both sections a and b is quite apparent. However, by simply taking "first regular differences" ($Y_t = Z_t - Z_{t-1}$), a series with no trend has been created, as shown in section c. The desirability for having a stationary series is discussed in the next section. It turns out to be the crux of model identification procedure of the Box-Jenkins method.

There are a variety of non-stationary patterns, and first differencing may not always provide stationarity. Therefore, a combination of regular and seasonal differencing may be necessary. The following differencing function assists in obtaining stationary series

$$Y_t = (1-B)^d(1-B^s)^{d1}, \qquad [6]$$

where d (regular differencing) and d1 (seasonal differencing) control the order of regular and seasonal differencing, and s represents the length of a season.

Exhibit I. Stationary Time Series

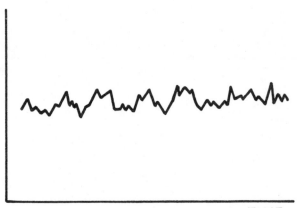

TIME

At this point, an example should help to illustrate how one moves from equation [2] to a specific forecast model. Assume that a first order autoregressive model with first regular differencing is the desired forecast equation. Based upon equation [2], the following model is specified.

$$(1-\phi_1 B)(1-B)^1(1-B^s)^0 Z_t = a_t \qquad [7]$$

This can be expanded and rearranged to give

$$(1-\phi_1 B)(1-B)^1 Z_t = a_t$$

$$Z_t - \phi_1 Z_{t-1} - Z_{t-1} + \phi_1 Z_{t-2} \qquad [8]$$

$$\hat{Z}_t = \phi_1 Z_{t-1} + Z_{t-1} - \phi_1 Z_{t-2}$$

where $\hat{Z}_t$ now becomes the period to be forecasted. Note that the final model need not include both autoregressive and moving average terms. In the next section, the determination of the appropriate order, p and q, for the general model will be demonstrated.

The general model of [2] can be expanded to represent seasonal series. Seasonal autoregressive and moving average operators $\phi_{p1}(B^s)$ and $\theta_{q1}(B^s)$ can be added so that the general model is of the form

$$\phi_p(B)\phi_{p1}(B^s)(1-B)^d(1-B^s)^{d1}Z_t =$$
$$\theta_o + \theta_q(B)\theta_{q1}(B^s)a_t. \qquad [9]$$

The seasonal operators are similar to the regular operators described in [3]

Exhibit 2. Sample Times Series

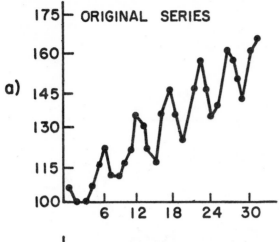

a) ORIGINAL SERIES

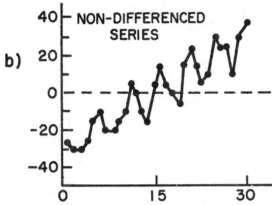

b) NON-DIFFERENCED SERIES

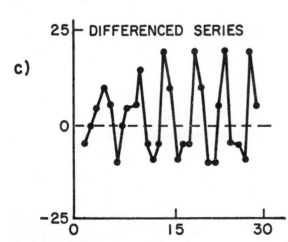

c) DIFFERENCED SERIES

The Box-Jenkins Methodology

Exhibit 3 presents ten years of monthly plastic pipe sales, in pounds, for a company which shall be referred to as PLACO Incorporated. The data is listed in Table 1. A review of Exhibit 3 indicates that there is an upward trend with occasional large moves away from the underlying trend. There also seems to be a small seasonal pattern present in the series over time occurring each twelve period interval.

The time series shall be broken into two parts. The first 96 months are used for identifying, estimating, and diagnostically checking the most appropriate parsimonious model. The second part, 24 observations, are a hold out sample, where forecasts from the selected model are compared against the actual observations.

Step 1:   Identification

Box and Jenkins have indicated that the general model, equation [9], provides too rich a class of models to permit immediate estimation. Therefore, experience and the data analysis allow the analyst to identify a subset of models worthy of investigation. To identify a tentative group, sample autocorrelations (SAC) and sample partial autocorrelations (SPAC) of the series are calculated. (References (1), (6) and (8) describe the calculation of these statistics).

Exhibit 3 indicates that plastic pipe sales are non-stationary, since a trend is present. Therefore, the series needs to be transformed through differencing. The appropriate differencing pattern is difficult to determine by reviewing the sample autocorrelations (SAC) of the differenced series. Non-stationary series exhibit sample autocorrelations (SAC) that fail to damp out quickly at increasing lags.

Stationary series are desired because they exhibit specific patterns in their autocorrelations (SAC) for particular models. These patterns are then compared against theoretical autocorrelation pa erns of various models of known p and q orders. For example, autoregressive models tend to exhibit theoretical autocorrelation patterns which dampen out. Moving average models exhibit patterns with large spikes at various lags. Exhibit 4 depicts the theoretical autocorrelation patterns of different known models. For example, a second order autoregressive model (p=2) tends to have a damped sine wave. Mathematically, the second order model is

$$(1 - \Phi_1 B - \Phi_2 B^2)Y_t = a_t$$

$$Y_t = \Phi_1 Y_{t-1} + \Phi_2 Y_{t-2} + a_t \qquad [10]$$

The plastic pipe time series was differenced with the combinations of first regular (d = 1, d1 = 0) and second regular (d = 2, d1 = 0) differencing first seasonal (d = 0, d1 = 1) differencing, and first regular-first seasonal (d = 1, d1 = 1) differencing. A review of the sample autocorrelations indicated that three candidates had good potential. The autocorrelations are shown in Exhibit 5 for first regular differencing, first seasonal differencing, and first regular-first seasonal differencing. Frame A (first regular differencing) of Exhibit 5 shows a large spike at lag one, indicating a first order moving average model, given by

$$(1-B)Z_t = a_t(1-\theta_1 B) \qquad [11]$$

Frame B (first seasonal differencing) shows a damped sine, indicating an autoregressive model of the second order. To confirm this, the analyst can calculate the sample partial autocorrelation (SPAC) of the differenced series. If a pure autoregressive model is present, the pattern of large values will

Exhibit 3. Plastic Pipe Sales

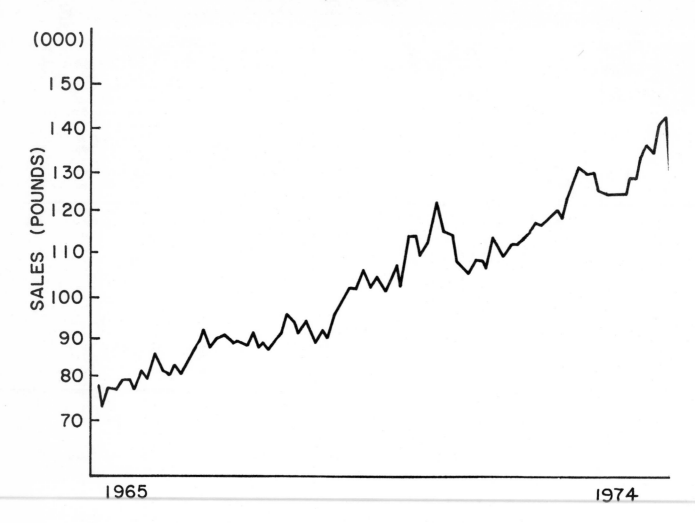

Exhibit 4. Theoretical Autocorrelation Functions

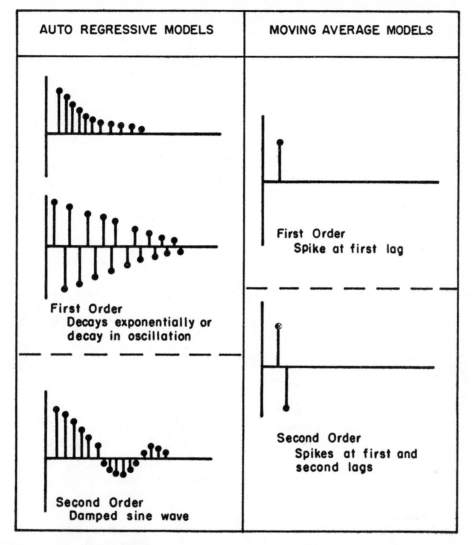

AUTO REGRESSIVE MODELS	MOVING AVERAGE MODELS
First Order Decays exponentially or decay in oscillation	First Order Spike at first lag
Second Order Damped sine wave	Second Order Spikes at first and second lags

indicate the order, with the reamining sample partial autocorrelations (SPAC) values being small. For example, a decaying SAC with a large SPAC at the first lag indicates a first order autoregressive model. Exhibit 6 depicts the sample partial autocorrelations (SPAC) for first seasonal differencing. Large values are present at a number of points and there is an oscillating pattern, indicating a mixed autoregressive-moving average model. Therefore, one uses the sample autocorrelation (SAC) function pattern as the prime indicator. The second order autoregressive model is given by

$$(1 - \phi_1 B^1 - \phi_2 B^2)(1 - B^{12})Z_t = a_t \qquad [12]$$

The addition of the appropriate moving average component occurs through diagnostic checking of the model.

The third frame, C, (first regular - first seasonal differencing) indicates large values at the first and twelfth lag. This indicates a model of the following form:

$$(1-B)(1-B^{12})Z_t = a_t(1-\theta_1 B)(1-\theta_{12}B^{12}) \qquad [13]$$

With identification complete, coefficient estimation follows.

Step 2: Estimation

Once a tentative model has been identified, the unknown parameters (ϕ, θ) are estimated by minimizing the squared forecast residuals, a_t.

$$s(\hat{\phi},\hat{\theta}) = \Sigma a_t^2 = \Sigma(Z_t - \hat{Z}_t)^2 \qquad [14]$$

Computer routines utilizing an iterative non-linear least squares procedure are used to minimize the sum of the squared residuals (9). The following parameter values, sum of squared errors, and standard deviation of errors were obtained for the three identified models.

Model 1 - Equation [11]

$$\hat{\theta}_1 = .316 \qquad \Sigma a_t^2 = 1.74 \times 10^9 \qquad \sigma = 4312$$

Exhibit 5.
Sample Autocorrelations of Differenced Series (SAC)

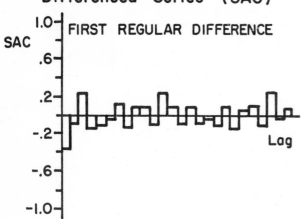

FIRST REGULAR DIFFERENCE

Exhibit 6.
Sample Partial Autocorrelation

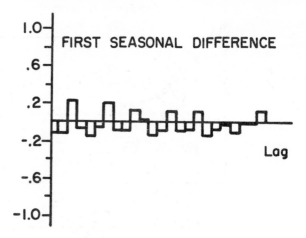

FIRST SEASONAL DIFFERENCE

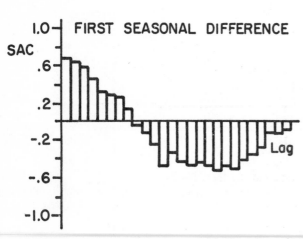

FIRST SEASONAL DIFFERENCE

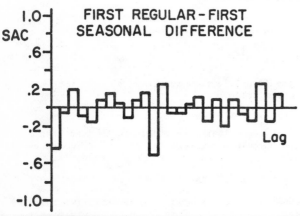

FIRST REGULAR – FIRST SEASONAL DIFFERENCE

Model 2 - Equation [12]

$$\hat{\Phi} = .551 \quad \hat{\Phi}_2 = .365 \quad \Sigma a_t^2 = 2.39 \times 10^9 \quad \sigma = 5450$$

Model 3 - Equation [13]

$$\hat{\theta}_1 = .518 \quad \hat{\theta}_{12} = .713 \quad \Sigma a_t^2 = 1.44 \times 10^9 \quad \sigma = 4230$$

The next step requires model evaluation.

Step 3: Diagnostic Checking

After estimation, the fitted model should be checked to see that it is an adequate representation of the observed series. Checking requires examination of the sample autocorrelations of the residual series, $\hat{a}_t$. Provided the model is adequate, the $\hat{a}_t$ will be independently distributed as $N(0, \sigma_a^2)$. If the $\hat{a}_t$ are not appropriately distributed, the pattern of sample autocorrelations should indicate the direction for improvement of the model. For example, a large spike at the kth lag would indicate the need for a moving average parameter of the form $(1 - \theta_k B^k)$.

Exhibit 7 presents the residual sample autocorrelations for the three models under investigation. A chi square test on the residual sample autocorrelation was conducted on all three (References (1) and (6) describe the chi square test). It was found that for models one and three, the assumption of a normally distributed residual pattern could not be rejected at the 95% confidence limit. Model two, on the other hand, was inadequate. A close review of Model 2's residual sample autocorrelation in Exhibit 7 indicates a large value at the twelfth lag. This indicates that the new model requires the addition of a moving average operation of the twelfth order, yielding Model 4 as:

$$(1 - \Phi_1 B - \Phi_2 B^2)(1 - B^{12})Z_t = a_t(1 - \theta_{12}B^{12}) \quad [15]$$

Model 4's parameters were then estimated, yielding the following results:

$$\hat{\Phi}_1 = .490 \quad \hat{\Phi}_2 = .501 \quad \hat{\theta}_{12} = .742$$
$$\Sigma a_t^2 = 1.42 \times 10^9 \quad \sigma = 4254$$

The residual sample autocorrelations, shown in Exhibit 7, for Model 4 indicates that the residuals are normally distributed and that the model is adequate.

To compare the three adequate models (1, 3 and 4), a review of the residual standard deviation for the models are in order:

Exhibit 7. Residual Sample Autocorrelations (SAC)

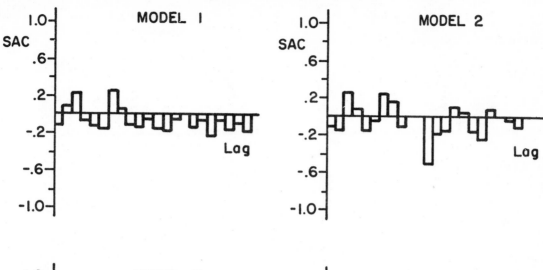

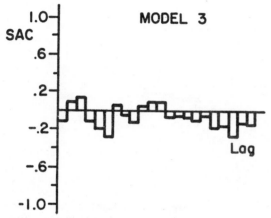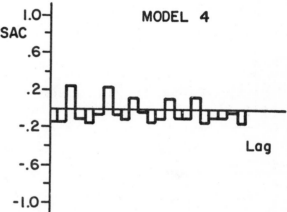

Model 1	σ	= 4312
Model 3	σ	= 4230
Model 4	σ	= 4254

You will notice that Models 3 and 4 have the lowest standard deviation, with 3's being slightly better. Also, Model 3 contains only two parameters compared to three for model 4. Therefore, Model 3 is selected as the appropriate parsimonious forecast equation.

Forecasting

Model 3 can be expanded and rearranged to obtain the following forecast equation.

Model 3 - Model Form:

$$(1 - B)(1 - B^{12})Z_t = a_t(1 - \hat{\theta}_1 B)(1 - \hat{\theta}_{12} B^{12}) \qquad [16]$$

Model 3 - Forecast Equation:

$$\hat{Z}_t = Z_{t-12} + Z_{t-1} - Z_{t-13} + a_t - \hat{\theta}_1 a_{t-1} - \hat{\theta}_{12} a_{t-12} + \hat{\theta}_1 \hat{\theta}_{12} a_{t-13} \qquad [17]$$

Where $\hat{Z}_t$ represents the period to be predicted, and the estimated values for $\hat{\theta}_1$ = .518 and $\hat{\theta}_{12}$ = .713 can be substituted into equation [17].

With December, 1972 as the time again, a single twenty-four period forecast was made, with two standard error limits. The actual, forecast, and error limit values are plotted in Exhibit 8. (References (1), (6), and (8) describe the error limit calculations). The mean absolute percent error for the twnety-four periods was 4.5% for this single origin forecast. A comparison of forecast error limits over time indicates that less reliability can be placed upon estimates that are farther into the future. Note that they spread farther apart in the future.

Adaptive forecasting in the Box-Jenkins framework indicates the use of interim data for forecast modification. Exhibit 9 illustrates forecast for 1973 and 1974 using such a procedure. The first forecast was made from December, 1972, the second from January, 1973, the third from February, 1973, and so on. Each forecast includes the most recent data possible, since changing the forecasting time origin each period brings the last available date point into the forecast. This procedure yielded a mean absolute percent error of 2.4% for the twenty-four period, using the same parameter estimates in the single origin example of Exhibit 8. Thus, the more recent information provided better forecasts.

Exibit 8. Single Origin Forecast

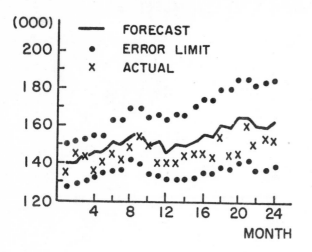

References

(1) Box, G. E. P. and Jenkins, G. M., <u>Time Series Analysis: Forecasting and Control</u>, San Francisco: Holden-Day, Inc., 1970.

(2) Brown, R. G., <u>Smoothing, Forecasting, and Prediction of Discrete Time Series</u>, Englewood Cliffs, N. J.: Prentice-Hall, 1963.

(3) Chisholm, R. K. and Whitaker, G. R., Jr., <u>Forecasting Methods</u>, Homewood, Ill.: Richard D. Irwin, Inc., 1971.

(4) Ferratt, T. W. and Mabert, V. A., "A Description and Application of the Box-Jenkins Methodology," <u>Decision Sciences</u>, Vol. 3, 1972.

(5) Harveston, M. F., Luce, B. J., and Smuczyaski, T. A., "Telephone Operator Management System-TOMS," Joint National Meeting of ORSA/TIMS/AIIE, November, 1972.

(6) Mabert, V. A., "An Introduction to Short Term Forecasting Using the Box-Jenkins Methodology," Monograph No. 2, Production Planning and Control Division Series, AIIE, 1975.

(7) Mabert, V. A. and Radcliffe, R. C., "A Forecasting Methodology as Applies to Financial Time Series," <u>The Accounting Review</u>, Vol. XLIM, 1974.

(8) Nelson, C. R., <u>Applied Time Series Analysis for Managerial Forecasting</u>, San Francisco: Holden-Day, Inc., 1973.

(9) Pack, D. J., Goodman, M. L., and Miller, R. B., "Computer Programs for the Analysis of Univariate Time Series Using the Methods of Box-Jenkins," Technical Report Number 296, Department of Statistics, University of Wisconsin, Madison, Wisconsin, April, 1972.

(10) Tiao, G. C. and Thompson, H. E., "Analysis of Telephone Data: A Case Study of Forecasting Seasonal Time Series," <u>The Bell Journal of Economics and Management Science</u>, Vol. 2, 1971.

(11) Winters, P. R., "Forecasting Sales by Exponentially Weighted Moving Averages," <u>Management Science</u>, Vol. VI, 1960.

Exhibit 9. Adaptive Forecasts

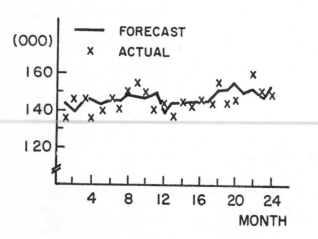

Conclusions

The Box-Jenkins methodology provides a structured approach to forecasting that this paper has attempted to demonstrate. Such an approach should prove useful to the analyst involved with forecasting. Due to space limitations, not all statistical procedures were presented. The reader has a variety of reference material available that describes this methodology and the techniques. The advanced reader should be able to use the original work by Box-Jenkins (1). However, for the individual with limited background, Mabert (6) provides an elementary description through reader exercises and many examples to help assist in understanding.

INT. J. PROD. RES., 1977, VOL. 15, NO. 2, 153–162

A combination projection — causal approach for short range forecasts†

VINCENT A. MABERT‡ and ARTHUR V. HILLS§

This paper illustrates a case study of forecasting daily traffic levels at branch banks, where many behavioural and business factors are present. Many influences are not equally spaced over, which reduces the effectiveness of traditional time series approaches. To handle this problem, a univariate time series ARIMA model is developed and then dummy variables are added to incorporate exogenous effects that are not captured by the projection ARIMA model. The results indicate that a more adequate representation of the customer traffic pattern has been obtained by combining the two modelling approaches.

Introduction

The forecasting of daily customer arrivals at six branch offices of Purdue National Bank‖ (PNB) is of prime interest to management. This information has significant impact on teller staffing decisions, since 25% of their work force are tellers. Also, both full and part-time tellers are employed, with part-time tellers used to handle peak traffic periods (Mabert and Raedels 1977). To use this work force effectively, good forecasts are required.

This paper illustrates a case study of how daily forecasts were developed for PNB. We start by describing the nature of the banking environment PNB management faces. Second, prior methods are reviewed for applicability to this problem. We next propose a method for modelling this environment, using a combined univariate ARIMA/dummy variable model. Finally, a series of tests were conducted to see if the combined model proved more accurate than the straight univariate model.

Branch banking

The arrival of customers to branch offices is controlled by many factors, such as custom, employer pay cycles and credit billing. Figure 1 presents 13 months of daily traffic levels for Branch One, which is representative of the other five. We noted that this branch, as well as the other five, exhibited no trend over time and had a strong weekly cycle where Mondays are correlated with Mondays, Tuesdays with Tuesdays, and so on. A monthly cycle was also

Received 6 May 1976.

†The original version of this paper appeared as ' A Combined Projection-Causal Approach for Short-Range Forecasts ', Working Paper No. 527, Krannert Graduate School of Management, Purdue University. (September 1975).

‡College of Business Administration, Bowling Green State University, Bowling Green, Ohio, U.S.A.

§College of Business Administration, University of Minnesota, Minneapolis, Minnesota, USA

‖The authors wish to express their appreciation to the management of Purdue National Bank of Lafayette, Indiana for providing this information, and Mr. Stan Calderon, Controller, for his assistance and support.

Published by Taylor & Francis Ltd, 10–14 Macklin Street, London WC2B 5NF.

Date	1973 October	November	December	1974 January	February	March	April	May	June	July	August	September	October
1	568	393	000		940	980	535	340		487	378		374
2	259	849		418			290	305		293	813		254
3	353		678	455			336	986	626	522		600	349
4	361		302	894	572	646	318		336			331	898
5	868	582	285		267	307	803		270	854	564	323	
6		295	272		207	233		483	305		271	825	
7		240	815	462	257	303		267	763		239		438
8	365	334		233	990	827	451	238		442	300	412	249
9	289	885		208			285	289		271	793	223	230
10	276		428	225			231	759	412	245		255	302
11	292		421	749	409	439	362		245	278	413	281	818
12	840	439	212		269	247	664		240	814	216	942	
13		263	257		227	250		422	278		218		
14		223	994	444	303	296		293	950		446		369
15	619	483		458	990	1010	584	289		562	779	406	444
16	287	933		309			295	350		276		256	268
17	226		458	269			243	834	446	256		216	307
18	269		246	857	418	438	252		234	286	392	249	828
19	843	453	130		265	290	843		234	839	274	714	
20		290	164		272	265		478	290		238		
21		406	714	409	268	278		256	816		263		389
22	392			250	810	773	406	227		408	802		234
23	242	749		193			241	276		219		355	232
24	225		400	269			230	478	422	217		183	249
25	303			883	468	356	269		235	208	263	221	750
26	762	428	321		247	245	748		221	750	404	293	
27		243	293		249	230			272		245	838	
28		199	794	433	496	248		432	1040		234		375
29	456	260		256		723	364	269		396	320		215
30	274	1031		243			431	290		253	857	581	232
31	393		396	437				1043		390			488

Figure 1.   Branch One daily traffic levels by calendar date.

116

evident. Higher customer traffic rates occurred around the end and middle of the month, which is coincident with pay-days.

Forecasting customer traffic requires knowing *when* changes occur, generally related to pay-days. Private and public organizations follow standard financial transaction cycles. First, mid month and end of month pay periods are common for salaried employees. Second, weekly and bi-weekly cycles are standard for paying bills and writing hourly employee pay-roll cheques. And third, the receipt of social security cheques around the third or fourth of a represents a major influence. These three effects combine to influence the month amount of customer traffic in a branch, as well as the customer's routine financial patterns.

Therefore, there are two time calendars present that an analyst must be concerned with. One, the weekly and/or bi-weekly pattern can be adequately handled by the time series projection technique because of the regular or equal spacing of the pay cycle. However, the second pattern, the calendar pay cycle, represents a different pattern. The monthly calendar is not of equal length. The influence of mid month and end of month pay-day does not occur at equal intervals. Weekends also cause actual pay-days to shift to either the previous Friday or following Monday.

How to accomodate such an occurrence represents a major problem that analysts face when multiple effects are present. We see that the presence of weekly and bi-weekly behaviour would allow the use of a projection technique, such as an ARIMA model. However, the handling of other events that influence traffic is of prime importance.

Prior forecasting studies

Prior researchers have investigated different ways of handling changes in the level of a time series. Box and Tiao (1975) discuss an area called 'intervention analysis', where a *single effect* creates a shift in a time series. They suggest a variety of models for representing ramp, step and impulse changes in the series. However, they only discuss the issue of modelling a time series under this approach. They do not cover how one uses this approach for forecasting periods when *multiple effects* are present.

Reinmuth and Wittink (1974) illustrate the use of a linear regression model with continuous variables and dummy variables with a tugonometric function to handle seasonal shifts in a time series. Tiao and Pack (1970) report the use of a dummy variable to handle weather effects in their time series analysis work of monthly concentrated orange juice consumption. Crane and Crotty (1967) use a two step procedure for prediction for monthly forecasting. First, project future requirements using an exponential smoothing model. This projection becomes an independent variable along with other causal variables in a multiple regression to derive a forecast. Berry *et al.* (1975) illustrate how one might modify an exponentially smoothing model to introduce non-time dependent events.

Hill (1975) illustrated the use of modified 'intervention analysis' (MIA) in a forecasting framework, which is extended in this paper for daily forecasts. *Stage One* uses the Box Jenkins methodology for univariate time series analysis

117

to identify the appropriate projection model. *Stage Two* requires the identification of the appropriate exogenous variables by examining residual patterns. The exogenous effects are introduced into the ARIMA model (Box–Jenkins) by means of dummy variables, with all coefficients being re-estimated.

Modelling procedure

In the following sections we shall illustrate the MIA procedure in detail, using the data from the six branches. Each of the six branch series contained 284 observations, which were broken into two parts. The first segment (184 observations) is used to identify the appropriate model and estimate model coefficients. The latter 100 data points are used later to evaluate forecast quality of the model under analysis allowing a valid comparative base.

Stage One: *ARIMA Model Estimation*

No attempt will be made to describe the Box–Jenkins univariate ARIMA modelling of the time series. A number of works have been written giving a complete description of the univariate modelling approach (Box and Jenkins 1971, Ferratt and Mabert 1972, Nelson 1973, Mabert and Radcliffe 1974). Rather, the functional form of the best univariate model is presented. It was found that the same functional form (eqn. (1)) proved best for all six series using the minimization of the variance as the selection criterion. This model, Model A, is given as

$$\hat{Z}_t = Z_{t-5} + \phi_1(Z_{t-1} - Z_{t-6}) + \phi_5(Z_{t-5} - Z_{t-10}) - \theta_5(Z_{t-5} - \hat{Z}_{t-5}) \tag{1}$$

where

$\hat{Z}_t$ = the forecast for period t,
Z_t = the actual observation in period t,
ϕ_p = autoregressive coefficient of order p to be estimated,
θ_q = moving average coefficient of order q to be estimated.

An analysis of the residual sample autocorrelation for eqn. (1) showed that no correlated behaviour was present at equally spaced intervals in the residual series. This was true for all six time series. However, exogenous variables are generally not spaced at even intervals over time.

Stage Two: *Exogenous Variable Analysis*

This stage requires the analysis of forecast errors to determine where improvement is possible. By the very nature of these series, the expected residual pattern, if present, would be related to calendar or operating days since the residual sample autocorrelations indicated an adequate model had been attained.

A 26 day operating month was created for the residual analysis. That is, all open branch days were evaluated in relation to the month's first and last day. The first 20 days reflected the time sequence using the beginning of the month as the time origin. The last 6 days reflected the time sequence using the end of month as the origin. This transformation meant that the eleventh operating day equated to the fifteenth of the month. The last operating day was the end of the month. The transformation was necessary because of unequal number of days in a month and weekend influences on calendar pay-days.

Using Branch 1 as an example, let us examine the results of using Model A. The estimated model yielded the following coefficient values.

$$\phi_1 = 0.2427$$
$$\phi_5 = 0.2335$$
$$\theta_5 = 0.9232$$

Figure 2 depicts the algebraic sum of errors $[\Sigma(Z_t - \hat{Z}_t)]$ for the 26 operating day month at Branch 1. You should note the substantial errors at the first, second, third, eleventh, and last operating day of the month. This reflects the univariate model's limited capacity to handle those times that coincide with calendar pay-days. Since we found similar behaviour at the other five branches, detail results have not been included for them.

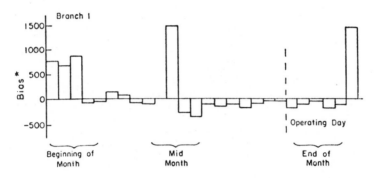

Figure 2. Model forecast bias by operating day. $*B_i = \sum_{t=1}^{m} (Z_{ti} - \hat{Z}_{ti})$, where:

B_i = bias for operating day i; Z_{ti} = the t observation in the set of the i operating day; $\hat{Z}_{ti}$ = the t forecast in the set of the i operating day; m = number of operating days of type i.

The observations at the first, fifth, sixth, and tenth period lags are occasionally disrupted by pay periods." When a pay-day occurs, the actual observation is inflated beyond the weekly cycle level. In order to compensate for inflated values and to incorporate the causal effects into the model, the following general model was proposed:

$$S_t = Z_t - (\psi_1 X_1 + \psi_2 X_2 + \ldots + \psi_n X_n) \tag{2}$$
$$\hat{Z}_t = S_{t-5} + \phi_1(S_{t-1} - S_{t-6}) + \phi_5(S_{t-5} - S_{t-10})$$
$$- \phi_5(\hat{Z}_{t-5} - \hat{Z}_{t-5})$$
$$+ \psi_1 X_1 + \psi_2 X_2 + \ldots + \psi_n X_n, \tag{3}$$

where ψs represent the coefficients for the dummy variables (X_1, X_2, ..., X_n) that reflect the pay-day effects. The S_t time series from eqn. (2) is the original time series adjusted for the pay-day effects. That is, S_t represents the expected level of traffic assuming no pay-day occurred.

Both a complete specification approach and a parsimonious approach were considered in specifying the dummy variables for eqns. (2) and (3). The complete specification model, Model B, required the addition of one X_i for all operating days with a large bias. For example, Branch 1 (Fig. 2) clearly has large residual biases on operating days 1, 2, 3, 11, and 26. Model B would require five dummy variables for this model, one for each of these days. A second model, guided by the rule of parsimony, would pool all consecutive dummy variables into a single dummy variable X_1. This model, Model C, would therefore use only one dummy variable to reflect the end of month–beginning of month pay period effect in days 26, 1, 2, and 3. Another dummy variable, X_2, would also be required when a large mid-month (day 11) effect was evident.

To summarize Models B and C, Table 1 specifies the number of dummy variables that each model contained and when they were applied. Both the completely specified and parsimonious models are included. Note that the completely specified models contain from four to five dummy variables, as indicated by the operating days that the variable is turned on to reflect the impact of that day. The parsimonious models contain only one or two variables for the middle and the end of the month.

Branch	Completely specified Model B	Parsimony Model C
1	1, 2, 3, 11, 26†	E and M‡
2	1, 2, 3, 11, 26	E and M
3	1, 2, 3, 26§	E§
4	1, 2, 3, 11, 26	E and M
5	1, 2, 11, 26	E and M
6	1, 2, 3, 11, 26	E and M

†Each number indicates the operating day that a single dummy variable was applied.

‡ ' E ' indicates the application of a single dummy variable for days 26, 1, 2, 3 for the four day period at the beginning and end of the month. ' M ' indicates the application of a mid month dummy variable.

§ Only at Branch 3, due to small errors, was there evidence that the mid-month variable may have minimal impact. Therefore, the mid-month variable was excluded from this branch.

Table 1. Models B and C dummy variable specification.

Results

A non-linear least squares search routine [10] was used to estimate the parameters for all three models by minimizing the variance. The estimation sample contained 184 observations. The remaining 100 observations were used as a hold-out sample to compare against forecasted values. Forecasts for each day in the holdout sample were made using the estimated parameters and using actual data when the forecasting origin made it available.

To evaluate the performance of Models A, B, and C, the variance and mean absolute deviation for the estimation (184 observations) and holdout sample (100 observations) were calculated. Table 2 summarizes the variance and MAD, with Table 3 containing the ratio Model A's variance to B's and C's variance to provide a measure of improvement, which is an F-test.

A review of Tables 2 and 3 indicates two interesting facts. First, the addition of dummy variables always provides an improvement. The combined models (B and C) performed significantly better (at the 90% confidence level) than the projection method (Model A) on the holdout samples of four of the six branches. In all six cases, the forecast error was reduced as measured by the MAD and variance, for both Models B and C.

Branch	Model	Estimation series		Hold-out series	
		MAD†	VAR‡	MAD	VAR
1	A	57·3	6 409	54·1	5 942
	B	50·9	5 114	42·7	4 041
	C	46·6	4 477	37·5	2 917
2	A	36·9	2 596	35·5	2 420
	B	32·6	2 034	33·0	1 997
	C	32·6	2 108	30·2	1 661
3	A	39·4	3 317	40·1	2 910
	B	35·0	2 924	36·8	2 686
	C	35·7	2 756	37·0	2 728
4	A	54·9	6 164	52·7	4 734
	B	50·3	5 317	45·7	3 348
	C	48·4	5 101	42·3	2 853
5	A	22·8	975	28·0	1 871
	B	21·4	924	28·8	1 797
	C	21·3	906	26·3	1 531
6	A	54·6	6 866	75·0	11 435
	B	49·8	6 019	58·0	7 245
	C	46·2	5 516	48·4	6 158

† MAD = Mean absolute deviation of forecast errors $= \dfrac{\Sigma|\hat{Z}_t - \hat{Z}_t|}{n}$.

‡ VAR = Variance of the forecast errors $= \dfrac{\Sigma(Z_t - \hat{Z}_t)}{n - k - 1}$, where: Z_t = actual observation for day t; $\hat{Z}_t$ = forecast for day t; n = number of observations; k = number of estimated coefficients.

Table 2. Forecast error mean absolute deviation and variance for estimation and hold-out series.

Branch	Variance model ratio	F Value estimation series	F Value hold-out series
1	A/B	1·25	1·47
	A/C	1·43	2·04
2	A/B	1·28	1·21
	A/C	1·23	1·25
3	A/B	1·13	1·11
	A/C	1·20	1·07
4	A/B	1·16	1·41
	A/C	1·20	1·65
5	A/B	1·06	1·04
	A/C	1·08	1·22
6	A/B	1·14	1·57
	A/C	1·24	1·86
Average of six Banks	A/B	1·17	1·30
	A/C	1·23	1·54

Table 3. *F*-Ratio calculations for the estimation and hold-out series. Table *F*-test values: $F_0|_{10} = 1·26$; $F_{0.05} = 1·35$; $F_{0.025} = 1·43$.

And second, performance using either approach yielded similar results, with the parsimonious approach being slightly better than the completely specified approach, as indicated in Table 3. The application of the F-test on the variances of Models B and C indicated that there is no significant difference in forecast errors. Figure 3 presents the cumulative forecast errors by operating day for Branch 1. The shaded blocks are Model B and the clear are C. Analysis of these residuals reveals no evident causal related pattern that would call for additional dummy variables.

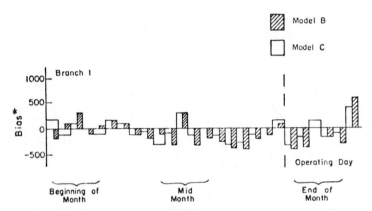

Figure 3. Model B and C forecast bias by operating day.

$$*B_i = \sum_{t=1}^{m} (Z_{ti} - \hat{Z}_{ti}),$$ where: B_i = bias for operating day i; Z_{ti} = the t observation in the set of the i operating day; $\hat{Z}_{ti}$ = the t forecast in the set of the i operating day; m = number of operating days of type i.

The coefficient values for Branch 1 using Model A or C, for example, provide some interesting insight into the behavioural process of customers. Listed below are the coefficients for both models.

Model A		Model C	
$\phi_1 =$	0·2427	$\phi_1 =$	0·1696
$\phi_5 =$	−0·2335	$\phi_5 =$	−0·2830
$\theta_5 =$	0·9232	$\theta_5 =$	0·7182
		$\psi_1 =$	97·5
		$\psi_2 =$	189·3

Note the values for ϕ_1, which operated on $(Z_{t-1} Z_{t-6})$ and $(S_{t-1} - S_{t-6})$ for eqns. (1) and (3), respectively. The addition of the ψ_i resulted in a reduction in ϕ_1, indicating that ϕ_1 is now filtering out more of the difference in $(S_{t-1} - S_{t-6})$.

The coefficient ϕ_5, on the other hand, is negative and has increased. It operates on $(Z_{t-5} - Z_{t-10})$ and $(S_{t-5} - S_{t-10})$, which represent the difference between weekdays 2 and 3 weeks past. This occurs due to a bi-weekly cycle in the data which results from bi-weekly pay periods. A negative ϕ_5 reduces estimates when $Z_{t-5} > Z_{t-10}$, because the forecasted day is between the pay period peaks. When $Z_{t-5} < Z_{t-10}$, then forecasts increase in value due to a negative ϕ_5.

The moving average operator θ_5 tracks the forecast error $(Z_t - \hat{Z}_t)$ like alpha in an exponential smoothing model. When overforecasting occurs $(\hat{Z}_t > Z_t)$, then forecasts in future periods are reduced. The addition of the ψ_i has caused a reduction in θ_5, indicating that forecasts have improved and less can be learned from prior forecast errors.

Finally, the dummy variable coefficients reflect interesting information. ψ_1 reflects the effects of financial transactions at the beginning and end of the month, where about 98 more customers per day can be expected. The same interpretation is possible for ψ_2 representing the mid-month effect, where 189 more customers per day can be expected. Such information allows for better staffing decisions.

We can see from the coefficient values that weekly, bi-weekly, and monthly behaviour is present in this branch. This parallels general experience in this industry. Similar behaviour was noted in the other five branches.

Conclusions

This paper demonstrates that the inclusion of simple calendar related causal variables to a time series projection forecasting model can provide significantly better forecasts. To include the exogenous variables with the projection model, it was necessary to adjust prior daily observations to create a new series (S_t). Now S_t represented the expected behavioural process of customers that followed a pattern on an equal spaced interval that was characterized by an ARIMA model. The ψ_is are then superimposed upon this process to capture the calendar related behavioural pattern.

The improvement was realized by identifying exogenous factors in the time series and building an ARIMA/Dummy variable model. The parsimonious approach to dummy variable specification proved to be no worse than a complete specification. Both the completely specified and the parsimonious combined models performed singificantly better on four of the six hold-out samples than the ARIMA model alone.

Ce document illustre une étude de cas pour la prévision quotidienne des niveaux de trafic dans des agences bancaires qui présentent de nombreux facteurs humains et commerciaux. De nombreuses influences ne sont pas réparties régulièrement ce qui réduit l'efficacité de la méthode traditionnelle des séries de temps. Pour traiter ce problème, il a été mis au point une maquette ARIMA à séries de temps mono-variable à laquelle sont ensuite ajoutées des variables factices destinées à incorporer les conséquences exogènes qui ne sont pas capturées par la maquette de projection ARIMA. Les résultats prouvent qu'une représentation plus adéquate du système de trafic du client a été obtenue grâce à la combinaison des deux ressources de maquettes.

Diese Untersuchung befaßt sich mit der Voraussage des täglichlichen Geschäfts-verkehrsvolumens in Bankfilialen, für den zahlreiche Verhaltens- und Geschäfts-faktoren eine Rolle spielen. Viele dieser Einflüsse sind nicht gleichmäßig verteilt, wodurch die Wirksamkeit der herkömmlichen Zeitfolgen-Verfahren herabgesetzt wird. Um dieses Problem zu lösen, wurde ein Zeitfolgen-Modell mit nur einer Variablen, ARIMA-Modell, entwickelt. Dann werden Scheinvariable eingeführt, um exogenen Wirkungen Rechnung zu tragen, die vom ARIMA Abbildungsmodell nicht erfaßt werden. Die Ergebnisse zeigen an, daß durch die Verbindung der beiden Modellverfahren eine angemessenere Darstellung des Kundenverkehrs-Musters erreicht wurde.

REFERENCES

BERRY, W. L., MABERT, V. A., and MARCUS, M., 1975, Forecasting teller window demand with exponential smoothing, Working Paper No. 536, Krannert Graduate School of Management, Purdue University.

BOX, G. E. P., and JENKINS, G. M., 1971, *Time Series Analysis Forecasting and Control* (San Francisco: Holden-Day).

BOX, G. E. P., and TIAO, G. C., 1975, Intervention analysis with applications to economic and environmental problems, *J. Am. statist. Ass.*, **70**, 70.

CRANE, D. B., and CROTTY, J. R., 1967, A two-stage forecasting model: exponential smoothing and multiple regression, *Mgmt Sci.*, B, **13**, 501.

FERRATT, T. W., and MABERT, V. A., 1972, A description and application of the Box–Jenkins methodology, *Decision Sci.*, **3**, 83.

HILL, A. V., 1975, Combining Time series and causal forecasting models: a case study, *Midwest AIDS Proceedings*, Indianopolis, Indiana, p. 217.

MABERT, V. A., and RADCLIFFE, R. C., 1974, A forecasting methodology as applied to financial time series, *Acct. Rev.*, **XLIM**, 61.

MABERT, V. A., and RAEDELS, A. R., 1977, Detail scheduling of a part-time work force: a case study of teller staffing, *Decision Sci.*, **8**, 109.

NELSON, CHARLES, R. 1973, *Applied Time Series Analysis* (San Francisco: Holden-Day).

PACK, D. J., GOODMAN, M. L., and MILLER, R. B., 1972, Computer programs for the analysis of univariate time series using the methods of Box–Jenkins, Technical Report No. 296, Department of Statistics, University of Wisconsin, Madison.

REINMUTH, J. E., and WITTINK, D. R., 1974, Recursive models for forecasting seasonal process, *J. Financial Quantitative Analysis*, **IX**, 659.

TIAO, G. C., and PACK, D. J., 1970, Modelling the consumption of frozen concentrated orange juice: a case study of time series analysis, Project Report, Bureau of Business Research and Service, University of Wisconsin, Madison.

5/Scheduling

Scheduling, in a broad sense, can encompass long or short time periods. For example, a typical, industrial master production schedule might look ahead one year into the future, while a shop schedule (which will help management realize the master schedule) may only be concerned with a one week, or even a one day time frame. The articles to be presented in this section deal primarily with short range scheduling.

Scheduling, then, in this short range manufacturing sense, can be defined as the allocation of jobs to specific machines within certain time frames. We will see that the goodness of the schedule can have a large influence on the effective utilization of the manufacturing facilities. Typical schedules of this type are concerned with the controlled movement of product components throughout a manufacturing facility. The usual input to a scheduling procedure (or algorithm) is demand for product. This demand will be broken down into many dependent, time phased demands of components on the production facilities.

We know that a computer directed production planning system such as MRP can convert the externally controlled independent demands for completed products to time phased demands on the production resources of the shop. These demands can be grouped into manufacturing batch sizes which make a good compromise between setup costs and storage costs.

If we say that external demand for product creates the need for schedules so that resources may be effectively utilized in satisfying that demand, one would not limit the topic of scheduling to machine scheduling only. Human resources may have to be scheduled, possibly at assembly benches or along assembly lines. One should also not limit the scheduling discipline to manufacturing only. As we will see in the following readings, service industries greatly benefit from the use of good scheduling systems. One attribute which is common to many of the current scheduling systems, however, is that they generally are amenable to computerization.

The utilization of computer based MRP systems has increased substantially during the decade of the 70's. It was during that time that the users of these systems learned how to work with the "exact" discipline of the digital computer for production planning and control systems. Coupe presents an excellent introductory paper on how data base management systems are used to support MRP systems by providing a scheduling procedure which considers utilization of resources. York provides a description of how one company, McDonnell-Douglas utilizes a specific software package for scheduling and control of in-process inventory. The paper by Jain describes how a company uses simulation to generate long range schedules which coordinate day-to-day activities of a machine shop.

Assembly line balancing models produce what could possibly be called a micro schedule: the sequence in which the work elements that are required for a product assembly are performed at individual stations on an assembly line. Schofield explains how computer-based assembly line balancing algorithms work by describing the logic of one specific method. Dar-El further defines the assembly line balancing problem by classifying mixed-model lines and describing how different models can be sequenced down the line to facilitate assembly by the sequential stations.

In many industrial, as well as non-industrial, situations it will be people, rather than facilities, which will be scheduled. Nurse scheduling in a health-care environment is an often studied example of this. Baker, Bodin, Finnegan and Ponder show how a heuristic scheduling procedure may be applied to the scheduling of airline crews. Keith shows how a heuristic solution methodology is used to obtain optimal or near optimal schedules for telephone operators at Illinois Bell Telephone Company.

APPLYING DATABASE MANAGEMENT

TO PRODUCTION SCHEDULING AND CONTROL

By **RICHARD J. COUPE,** Honeywell Information Systems Inc., Wellesley Hills, Mass.

TRADITIONALLY, production control has been compartmentalized into four discrete stages: routing, scheduling, dispatching, and expediting. Early production control systems usually resulted in a great amount of paper work and an excessive amount of manual dispatching and expediting. Integrating the production control function and other manufacturing business functions into one computer information system has not been accomplished, primarily because of the lack of a generalized database management software capability.

Each business function, such as product structuring and inventory control, has typically been performed by processing one application file within a stand-alone application subsystem. Data, such as part number, has to be stored redundantly and maintained in each file. Each application subsystem represents a suboptimum island of automation, from an EDP standpoint. Batch-oriented interface runs have to be processed to relate the contents of any two files. The business data is fragmented into many files, which makes it impossible to follow the pattern of information flow in the real world.

These application files were commonly stored on magnetic tape in first and second generation computer systems. Random access storage devices, such as disc storage drives, were introduced several years ago, along with file organization techniques to manage an application file in this environment.

▶ What Is Database Management?

Often the terms file management and database management are erroneously interchanged, because users consider their application files—both magnetic tape and disc—as their database. However, there is a fundamental difference between the two concepts. True database implies an integration of application files. Disc file organization and file management are concerned with the management and control of data records on a file-by-file basis. For example, an indexed sequential technique for control of data records in an inventory file is concerned only with the inventory file. It is not designed for handling the creation and maintenance

of relationships between the data records within the inventory file and the data records within another file. However, such relationships are precisely what database management software accomplishes.

Database management software provides the capability to store data records on random access storage devices and automatically create and maintain all the relationships that are required between data records. In the database environment, the application file may be said to disappear—actually, it exists in the form of linkage between some data records in the user database. Many other linkages may exist simultaneously for any particular type of data record. Thus, all the former application files have been merged into one database consisting of multiple data record types, each type having different relationships with other data records within the database.

This article defines the fundamental shop scheduling characteristics that can be incorporated with database management concepts. It is assumed that other business functions will be incorporated in a similar manner by building additional data records and relationships within the same database. The relationships a database system would form with basic business functions are depicted in *Fig.* 1.

▶ Scheduling System

The scheduling system must be designed to effectively encompass the following major elements involved in detailed scheduling and control of a production shop:

1. Prepare detailed production schedules and determine resource loads for each lot (order) in the shop. These considerations must include in-process loads, time-phased resource capacities, and infinite or finite capacity-loading.

2. Control the release (dispatch) of work on the shop floor and review planned lots to determine release point. This function includes the establishment of the priority sequence of operations within work centers and checking of release constraints.

3. Generate shop paper work including work-center release and expedite lists, shop order travel book, blueprint and tool requests, and materials accumulation book.

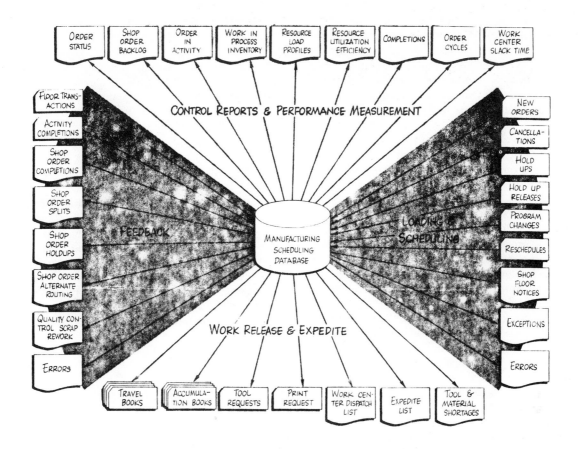

Fig. 1—Information flow diagram illustrates how a computerized database management system would interact with loading and scheduling, work release and expediting, feedback, and control and performance measuring functions of a business.

4. Monitor shop production performance by processing feedback to update the database. Resulting reports include order status, order completions, order cycles, and resource utilization and efficiency.

5. Implement corrective action as required, including rescheduling and reloading orders.

6. Maintain data required to support the scheduling system including resource capacities, operations planning, work-center slack cycles, work-in-process loads, and shop order backlog.

Levels of control. Detailed scheduling is essentially the establishment of operation routing plans, and start and complete dates for each production process required to satisfy the master schedule. The level to which detailed scheduling is accomplished depends on the degree of control needed to maintain a timely flow of orders within the shop.

In some shops, it may be necessary to assign only start and completion dates on the production order itself. Others may require the assignment of start and completion dates for groups of operations within the production process—each group usually incorporating the same class of operation or being

terminated by a critical operation where a material control checkpoint is desired. Of course, the ultimate in control would be the assignment of start and completion dates for each operation within the production process.

The level of control required will be highly variable by business and possibly by different shop areas within the same business. The flexibility to achieve varying levels of control must be built into the computer system. For example, it may be necessary to schedule each operation on orders flowing through a critical contributing shop area, while an assembly area may require only production order start and completion dates.

Within any business, the level of control depends on such factors as the complexity of the product, the nature and reliability of shop processes, and the discipline of management and shop personnel with regard to following established procedures designed to make the system work. Effective floor operating disciplines must be implemented before an automated shop scheduling system can function properly.

Basis of scheduling and loading. The foundation of detailed scheduling and loading consists of establishing the processing sequence of each item to be fabricated or assembled, the work centers where each process is done, and the load impact of each activity on shop resources. This information is typically supplied by operations planning sheets developed and maintained by manufacturing engineering personnel. Once captured, it is imperative that this information be maintained accurately and up to date.

Work center slack factors (i.e., queue) and resource capacities are also difficult to capture and maintain because of their dynamic nature. However, these items are all key ingredients in the detailed scheduling and loading function and, if necessary, must be approximated.

Detailed scheduling. The order cycle—which should be used for inventory planning purposes—includes the manufacturing cycle and a planning cycle time allowance for operations, quality planning development, and the procurement of any specialized tooling required. Items to be manufactured should be entered into the scheduling system as soon as their requirements are identified and validated. Although shop orders will not be released until the proper time, the system will have the data necessary to schedule and project future shop loads which will aid management in resource planning.

The earliest start date is the earliest planned time an activity can start in the shop. Under certain conditions (i.e., to balance resource underload), activities can be authorized to start earlier. The earliest start date of the first activity is the shop order release date. The latest start date is the latest planned time that an activity can start without jeopardizing its finish date. The difference between the two dates is the slack time allowance for various shop delays—such as queuing and machine breakdowns—that can occur at any work center.

Within the scheduling system, slack time may be a variable time interval assigned for each work center and, therefore, equal for all activities that are processed at a particular work center. A business optional override may be to assign a variable slack time interval depending on the inventory classification of the material item being scheduled. Using this option, high value items would have a smaller slack allowance relative to lower value items, thus, compressing the total cycle time during the scheduling process.

Slack time is different from the transit time for each activity and from the protection time for the overall shop order. Transit time is the interval allowed to move a job from one work center to another. It includes the time the job waits at a work center until it is moved, as well as the time the job actually spends in transit. The scheduling system should allow for a fixed transit time by work center or, optionally, a business may define a from/to matrix with corresponding transit times for all work centers.

Process cycle calculation. The normal mode of operation is to calculate a process time for each resource being utilized within each activity, de-

fined within the operations planning for a material item on a shop order. While calculating process time, the scheduling system should not consider the existing statuses of resource loads. Resource capacity, at this point, is considered infinite. During the loading phase, resource loads will be examined as each activity is being scheduled to determine whether or not activity start and finish dates are realistic—considering available capacity. It is within this subsequent loading phase that the system will accomplish finite capacity loading for critical resources.

Shop facilities model. Heading the organizational hierarchy in the shop facilities model should be an administrative center, which may represent a functional area of any size within the business. The number of administrative centers required depends on both the size of the organization and the level of control desired. Each administrative center should be composed of one or more work centers. Each work center should consist of one

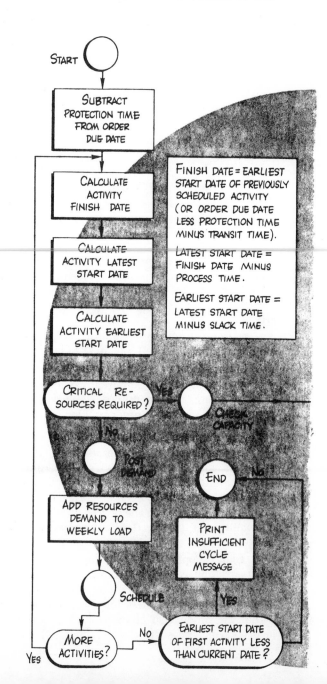

FINISH DATE = EARLIEST START DATE OF PREVIOUSLY SCHEDULED ACTIVITY (OR ORDER DUE DATE LESS PROTECTION TIME MINUS TRANSIT TIME).

LATEST START DATE = FINISH DATE MINUS PROCESS TIME.

EARLIEST START DATE = LATEST START DATE MINUS SLACK TIME.

or more facilities that represent the resources to be loaded and the detailed scheduling, resource loading, and priority sequencing parameters assigned by management. Multiple resources, such as labor and equipment, may be assigned and loaded into one work center. This structure also allows flexible resources, such as assembly labor, to be associated with multiple work centers.

Scheduling technique. A backward scheduling technique is normally used to assign tentative start and completion dates. This technique is accomplished by working backward from the shop order due date and—after assigning an order protection time, if desired—by scheduling each activity in reverse sequence from the last to the first. Transit time between work centers and the slack time associated with each activity are also factored in during this process. Backward scheduling is generally used in discrete-item manufacturing, since customers or stock replenishment calculations specify the due date for delivery.

Fig. 2—Chart shows recommended decision logic for determining scheduling and loading in a database management system.

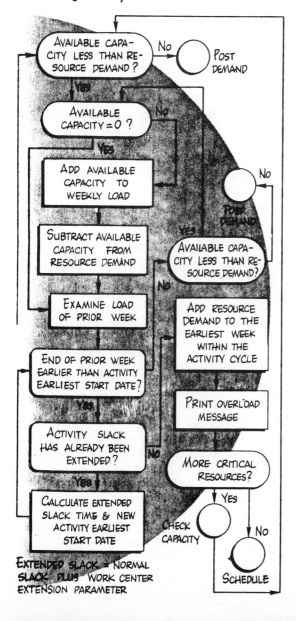

EXTENDED SLACK = NORMAL SLACK PLUS WORK CENTER EXTENSION PARAMETER

▶ Resource Loading

The complexity in scheduling stems from having to work within the capacity constraints imposed by limited critical resources, while attempting to minimize manufacturing cycles, costs, and inventory investment. Detailed scheduling and resource loading are two distinct but closely related processes. It is unrealistic to schedule activities without loading on critical resources, and it is equally unrealistic to establish dates only by loading.

After the scheduling process has utilized process time, slack time, and transit times to establish tentative start and completion dates for activities, resource loading may be used to validate these dates. This process is required on user defined critical resources only. In the typical shop, many resources may be defined as noncritical. In other words, loading noncritical resources without checking available capacity involves little risk and will save considerable computer processing time.

For each resource being utilized within an activity, the load impact represented by the activity is added to the total load for the week in which the activity finish date falls. While detailed scheduling is done on a daily basis, resource loading is done on a weekly basis. Considering the fact that the loading is being done for work that is not scheduled to reach the shop floor for days or weeks, it is not practical to attempt to predict daily load status that far in advance. The typical shop is too dynamic an environment for that kind of precision.

For noncritical resources, load demands are accumulated in order to produce time-phased load profiles. For critical resources, available capacity is compared with the total previous load plus the current resource demand. If the latter does not exceed available capacity, the earliest start date, latest start date, and finish date are validated and the system proceeds to schedule the next activity. However, if available capacity is less than the resource demand, the system attempts to find additional capacity for the activity in an earlier week within the activity cycle, extending the activity slack time to the predefined limit if necessary. This procedure essentially amounts to a trade-off of a longer activity cycle for a more balanced resource load. A flowchart of the system's recommended scheduling and loading logic is given in *Fig. 2.*

A key point is that the computer scheduling system should utilize a truly integrated manufacturing database via generalized database management software. An integrated database provides the capability for the scheduling system to model the actual business. The designs and relationships within the scheduling system database, coupled with options and parameters, are designed to process production control events as they occur in the user's actual shop floor environment.

Work release. Once detailed scheduling has been accomplished and the corresponding resource loads have been impacted, the shop order remains in a planned status until the appropriate release time.

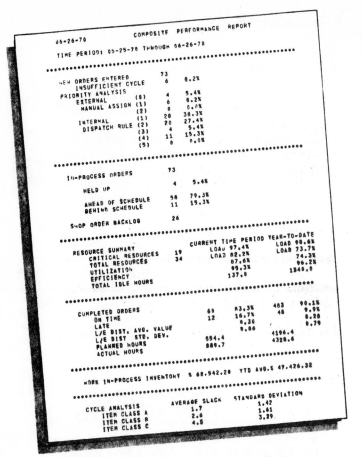

```
06-26-70          COMPOSITE PERFORMANCE REPORT
TIME PERIOD: 05-25-70 THROUGH 06-26-70

                                      73
NEW ORDERS ENTERED                     6      8.2%
    INSUFFICIENT CYCLE
PRIORITY ANALYSIS
    EXTERNAL          (0)               4      5.4%
    MANUAL ASSIGN (1)                   6      8.2%
                     (2)                0      0.0%
    INTERNAL          (1)              28     38.3%
    DISPATCH RULE (2)                  20     27.4%
                     (3)                4      5.4%
                     (4)               11     15.3%
                     (5)                0      0.0%


IN-PROCESS ORDERS                      73

    HELD UP                             4      5.4%
    AHEAD OF SCHEDULE                  58     79.3%
    BEHIND SCHEDULE                    11     15.3%
SHOP ORDER BACKLOG                     26


                            CURRENT TIME PERIOD    YEAR-TO-DATE
RESOURCE SUMMARY
    CRITICAL RESOURCES     19   LOAD 97.4%    LOAD 98.6%
    TOTAL RESOURCES        34   LOAD 82.2%    LOAD 73.7%
    UTILIZATION                      87.6%         96.2%
    EFFICIENCY                       95.3%       1840.0
    TOTAL IDLE HOURS                137.0


COMPLETED ORDERS           60   83.3%    403   90.1%
    ON TIME                12   16.7%     48    9.9%
    LATE                         0.30           8.20
    L/E DIST. AVG. VALUE         9.86           8.79
    L/E DIST STD. DEV.                   4196.4
    PLANNED HOURS        954.4          4328.6
    ACTUAL HOURS         889.7


WORK IN-PROCESS INVENTORY $ 68,542.28   YTD AVG.$ 47,426.32


CYCLE ANALYSIS      AVERAGE SLACK   STANDARD DEVIATION
    ITEM CLASS A         1.7              1.42
    ITEM CLASS B         2.6              1.61
    ITEM CLASS C         4.8              3.29
```

Fig. 3—Composite Performance Report helps top management keep track of major trends within a business.

Until work is released, the shop does not have authorization to begin processing. Therefore, work release performs the critical function of regulating the rate of work flow into the shop and, coupled with shop order completions, directly affects the level of work-in-process inventory represented by the backlog of orders at each work center.

At the time of work release, an important auxiliary function that must be performed is the preparation of shop paper work. Required paper work in the typical shop may include a dispatch list for each work center in priority sequence, labor vouchers, feedback cards, operation and routing sheets, travel cards, stock accumulation tickets, request cards for blueprints and/or special tooling, an expedite list, and shortage reports for material and/or tooling, if needed.

Release horizon. After work centers have been defined within the database, management must define a corresponding release horizon. This is a variable work center parameter that defines the number of work periods for which work is to be released. The release horizon is a function of order cycle time, order release rate, average activity process time, rate of change within the work center or shop area, user operating disciplines, etc. While the planning horizon used within scheduling and loading may be days or weeks, the work release horizon is normally a few shifts or days. It may approach one week in a fairly static shop. Care must be taken in defining the release horizon for the various work centers, since this minimum span

also determines the minimum frequency at which the work release and feedback processing functions must operate.

Review of planned shop orders. A scheduled and loaded shop order is stored in the database according to the earliest start date of the first activity on the order. The initial step within the work release function is to review these planned orders, comparing this date with the current date. Until this date arrives, the order remains in a planned, unreleased status. This mode of operation helps both the system and the shop personnel to accommodate changes without revising existing shop paper, dispersing and re-accumulating materials, scrapping materials, and experiencing other extra costs.

When the earliest start date of the first activity on a shop order falls within the release horizon, the shop order is released. Thus, all the activities associated with the order become candidates for release, awaiting a check of any release constraints —such as stock and tooling availability—that the user may have imposed. The release function should also allow release of any specific order ahead of the earliest start date of the first activity if management desires to relieve a resource underload situation or if the order has been manually assigned an urgent external priority.

Activities which become release candidates are stored by work center where they are accumulated with previously released activities. Therefore, when the activities are priority sequenced for a specific work center, all released work—including work physically located on the shop floor in queue—will be merged together. This method accounts for the fact that when an activity is completed within one work center or a new shop order is released, the shop order may move to a new work center and its priority will preempt the activities already in the queue.

▶ Priority Sequencing Strategies

Every time resources become available within a work center, a decision must be made as to which activity should be selected from among all the activities waiting in queue to be processed. To assist in this activity selection procedure, shop personnel must be guided by some type of priority scheme. Priority sequencing strategies can be devised to favor movement of orders through the shop on the basis of almost any desired criterion.

A variety of priority sequencing or dispatching rules can be utilized to meet the current objectives of management. Recognizing that management's objectives can and should vary with time, the scheduling system should have the flexibility to accept variable priority sequencing rules. Each priority rule will be applied to the queue of activities at each work center independently of the status of other work centers in the shop.

Before the business selects a specific priority rule for any work center, management should thoroughly understand the impact that this sequencing rule will have to assure that it is compatible with primary objectives—be they to minimize cycles, maximize resource utilization, maximize order completions, or minimize in-process inventory. Since the criterion selected will be based on the objectives for each business, management should consider those rules which are functions of dates established in detailed scheduling (i.e., slack time per activity and activity start date), and those which are oriented to an inherent characteristic of the shop order itself (i.e., shortest process time and shop order value).

The system should have the facility to incorporate the above rules and any unique rule developed to meet specific objectives. For example, a highly specialized rule may have to be developed to handle a unique process. At work centers where setup time is particularly critical and where partial setups can occur, a priority rule which minimizes setup time may be required. Each priority rule is applicable to any work center at any point in time.

Regardless of the strategy implemented, sequencing must ultimately be sensitive to meeting due dates—assuming that customer commitments are the primary business objective. How then can we capitalize on the best features of both due-date and non-due-date oriented rules? The answer lies in using a compound rule—one that is non-due-date to begin with but which will automatically switch to a due-date procedure for those shop orders which appear to be falling behind.

The implementation of a shop scheduling system requires selecting the final decision point for work activity sequence at each work center. The nature of most job shops renders unlikely the successful implementation of a system that makes rigid resource/activity assignments. For example, the system cannot evaluate the capabilities of operators on different machines for any given day. Neither can the system cope with short range problems that arise in the shop immediately after the system has finished feedback and new work-release processing.

Therefore, the system should provide relevant information to either the foreman or the dispatcher, who will make the final decision regarding resource/activity assignments. This man will be furnished a dispatch list, output by work release, previously sequenced to meet management's objectives. He can spend his time effectively in resolving floor problems, assigning activities to specific resources, training his men, and maintaining disciplines within his work center without being burdened with shop order priority decisions that will impact the total shop.

▶ Feedback and Control

Since events on the shop floor seldom occur exactly according to plan, a feedback function is needed to properly maintain the manufacturing system database. From strictly a scheduling function standpoint, the database must be updated for inventories, resource loads and unloads, hold-ups, cancels, modifications, etc., and new work must be made available for release as completions are reported.

All the variable parameters and options must also be updated to reflect current management objectives and to react to real world situations. The combination of actual feedback and parameter control will provide the system with a basis for taking corrective action if work is not being accomplished as scheduled, and will provide data for the system's decision making elements—such as priority sequencing activities within work centers.

The frequency of feedback reporting depends on a number of factors that make up the overall environment within a specific shop, including: the rate of materials flow; shop performance and reliability; the accuracy with which the planning elements of loading, scheduling, and sequencing are performed; and the time span defined as the release horizon. The shop environment may range from a periodic batch system to an on-line, real-time system without any fundamental changes in system architecture.

▶ Measuring System Performance

The principal objective of a shop scheduling and control system is to assist management in its efforts to control production effectively. Overall measurement and monitoring of shop performance are vital to assure that the production phase of the business is responding to current business objectives. There are many alternative approaches to measuring the aggregate performance of a shop, depending primarily on the philosophy of management in a particular organization.

The scheduling database must be structured to accommodate varying levels of information seekers across the various functions of the business. Utilizing database software, the capability exists to extract any information required by management. As long as this information is maintained in timely and accurate fashion, it is relatively easy to retrieve, manipulate, and generate reports of shop performance in terms meaningful to a particular business.

Certain types of measurements have come to be accepted in shop control including delivery performance, resource utilization, and work-in-process inventory. A characteristic of the above measurements is that they are all after the fact. The database also contains information which can be helpful in predicting future shop performance including size and trend of work backlogs, resource loads, and work center cycles. Many primary action, monitoring, and analysis reports can be outputted from a database management system.

The Composite Performance Report, *Fig. 3*, produced on request, is of special interest. For the time period specified, the report is designed to provide top management with concise information designed to aid in tracking major trends within the business.

TECHNICAL PAPER

INDEX TERMS

Management

1977 © (All Rights Reserved)

THE
COMPUTER AND
AUTOMATED SYSTEMS
ASSOCIATION OF SME
20501 FORD ROAD
P.O. BOX 930
DEARBORN
MICHIGAN 48128

AN APPROACH TO GAINING BETTER CONTROL OF THE JOB SHOP ENVIRONMENT

By

Ronald K. York
Associate Consultant
McDonnell Douglas Automation Company

ABSTRACT

This paper describes how McDonnell Douglas Astronautics Company - West is attempting to gain better control of its job shop environment. An IBM developed system called CAPOSS (Capacity Planning and Operation Sequencing System) is being implemented and interfaced with the company's own Parts Follow-up system to provide information that has traditionally been unavailable to many other companies with similar job shop environments.

This paper describes how McDonnell Douglas Astronautics Company-West is attempting to gain better control of its job shop environment. An IBM developed system called CAPOSS (Capacity Planning and Operation Sequencing System) is being implemented and interfaced with the company's own Parts Follow-up system to provide information that has traditionally been unavailable to many other companies with similar job shop environments.

INTRODUCTION

Companies with job shop characteristics have long struggled to maintain control of their operations in an effort to earn an acceptable level of profit. Manufacturing fabrication activities at McDonnell Douglas Astronautics Company-West (MDAC-W) have, in the past few years, changed from medium/high production of a few major products to medium/low production of many varied products. In this "job shop" type of environment, it is very important to respect production due dates, while at the same time, assure high utilization of equipment and machinery.

This paper describes, briefly, how MDAC-W is implementing an IBM-developed system called CAPOSS (Capacity Planning and Operation Sequencing System) in conjunction with its own system called PFU (Parts Follow-up System). It describes, in part, how the systems work and how they are logically tied to each other.

MDAC-W Environment

MDAC-W is the Western Division of one of five major companies within McDonnell Douglas Corporation (MDC). Its fabrication shop in Huntington Beach, California employs approximately 220 direct hourly people. At any one time, the shop has about 20,000 open fabrication orders with an average of 10 operations per order. The fabrication shop includes a machine shop, a sheet metal shop, a welding shop and areas that do metal processing, plastics fabrication and electrical work. The type of work performed by the fabrication shop in recent years has become largely job shop type work including parts for the DC-10, DC-9, DC-8, F-4, F-15, DELTA booster, AMARV (re-entry vehicle), SRB (Solid rocket booster), and some non-MDC commercial work. Because of this job shop environment, the efficient control of fabrication became increasingly difficult. It was because of this, that MDAC-W saw the potential in interfacing CAPOSS with its own PFU system.

CAPOSS and PFU Overview

CAPOSS is a capacity planning and shop floor scheduling system developed by IBM World Trade. Used primarily in job shop environments, CAPOSS has the following general capabilities:

o Capacity requirements planning

o Completion date estimating

o Load leveling
o Detailed operation scheduling
  - considers capacity limitations
  - supplies daily work lists for each work center in the shop
o Computation of cost statistics

CAPOSS is a third-generation scheduling system. Its predecessors are KRAUS and CLASS, both IBM products. The scheduling techniques of CAPOSS are advanced, and at present, few commercially available manufacturing systems have similar capabilities.

PFU is a production status system developed by McDonnell Douglas to provide immediate determination of

o Location.
o Schedule
o Quantity
o Shortages
o Status/Statistics

of all parts and their work orders, from the time of their release to their completion. Developed initially for McDonnell Douglas Aircraft Company, PFU is now also used by MDAC-W.

PFU is a real-time, on-line computerized system utilizing an IMS data base. PFU supports shop floor IBM 1031 Input Stations, TRIVEX Display Stations, and IBM 2740 Communication Terminals. The following MDAC-W files are maintained in an on-line mode:

o Open Order Master file
o Standards Operation Master file
o Operation Load Code/Department file.

The Open Order Master file contains all upcoming fabrication orders. Adds and changes are input by production control. Partial completions, completions and moves are input by either production control or manufacturing via the IBM 1031 Input Stations, an employee badge, and a traveler card. The Standards Operation Master file contains operation sequence routings by part number. The Operation Load Code/Department file is used by MDAC-W as primarily a work center cross-reference table.

One of the functions of PFU provides the capability of calculating the required start date of the current operation of every active fabrication order (F.O.) and also the estimated number of days required to complete each F.O. as shown in Figure 1. A backward scheduling technique is used to calculate the start date of the current operation. Operation set-up and run times together with wait times are used to back schedule from the required F.O. due date. The calculated start date, depending on actual schedule position can be either before or after the "now" date. A forward scheduling technique is used to calculate

the number of days required for completion. Starting from the "now" date, operation set-up and run times together with wait times are forward scheduled to calculate the completion date of the F.O. The completion date minus the "now" date equals the days to completion calculation. If the expedite code of the F.O. is equal to 3, the wait time in this calculation is reduced to 33% of its original value. It should be noted that these scheduling techniques do not consider capacity constraints. In addition, capacity requirements necessary to make these scheduling techniques do not consider capacity constraints. In addition, capacity requirements necessary to make due dates are not calculated by the system.

BACKWARD SCHEDULING TO CALCULATE START DATE OF CURRENT OPERATION:

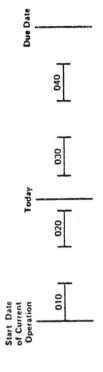

Start Date of Current Operation   010   Today   020   030   040   Due Date

FORWARD SCHEDULING TO COMPUTE NUMBER OF DAYS TO COMPLETION:

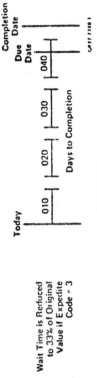

Wait Time is Reduced to 33% of Original Value if Expedite Code = 3

Today   010   020   030   040   Completion Date   Due Date

Days to Completion

FIGURE 1
PFU SCHEDULING TECHNIQUE

CAPOSS/PFU as a Team

The reasons for implementing CAPOSS were many, but the basic concepts and methods used by CAPOSS were not new to MDAC-W. Prior to the CAPOSS implementation, MDAC-W was using a combination of manual and small auxiliary computers to calculate long-term capacity requirements and to perform detailed machine loading and load leveling. They found, however, that these methods were too burdensome and could not react quickly enough to rapidly changing job shop conditions. As a result, the decision to implement CAPOSS was made with the intent to provide the following capabilities:

o long-term capacity requirements planning by work center
o improved short-term machine loading and load leveling
o improved "days-to-completion" calculation by considering actual shop capacity

o greater visibility to detect and correct potential problem areas

o ability to easily perform "what-if" exercises

o greater flexibility for future developments

To provide these capabilities, the implementation enables PFU and CAPOSS to work as a team. PFU maintains the IMS manufacturing data base (including routing and on-line fabrication order status information) and supplies to CAPOSS on a daily basis an activity file that contains fabrication order and operation adds, changes, partial completions, completions, and deletions. CAPOSS, in turn, replaces several PFU functions including production of daily work sequence lists, operation scheduling, and "days-to-completion" computation. CAPOSS additionally supplies long-term capacity requirements planning reports, load graphs, and cutter requirement dates. A general flow of the combined systems is shown in Figure 2.

During the initial implementation stages of CAPOSS, processing is restricted to just fabrication orders with routing through the machine shop (or about 12,000 fabrication orders and a corresponding 120,000 operations). There are plans to eventually expand CAPOSS processing to include all fabrication orders.

Basic Capabilities and Output

Functionally, as shown in Figure 3, CAPOSS at MDAC-W addresses five major areas:

o file maintenance
o order scheduling
o long-range capacity requirements planning
o short-range operation sequencing
o middle-range completion date estimating.

File maintenance refers to two major CAPOSS files; the work center and order file. The work center file is manually maintained and includes information for each work center such as work center number and description, number of machines, work center efficiency, inter-operation times, and number and length of shifts (see Figure 4). The order file is automatically maintained by PFU and contains fabrication order information including due date, quantity and part number, and operation information including operation number, work center number, set-up time, unit run time, and status information such as quantity completed. Transaction types can include adds, changes, partial completions, completions, and deletions.

Order scheduling calculates operation start and completion dates for each fabrication order. This scheduling technique uses CPM-like calculations, and ignores capacity constraints. CAPOSS also considers inter-operation time in the calculation of these dates. In addition to set-up and unit run times, the system allows an assortment of inter-operation times including work

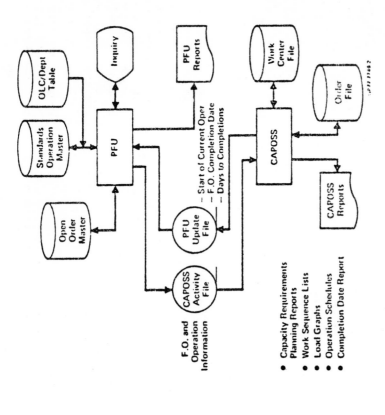

Inquiry

OLC/Dept Table

Standards Operation Master

PFU Reports

Work Center File

Open Order Master

PFU

CAPOSS

Order File

PFU Update File

CAPOSS Activity File

CAPOSS Reports

F.O. and Operation Information

— Start of Current Oper
— F.O. Completion Date
— Days to Completions

• Capacity Requirements Planning Reports
• Work Sequence Lists
• Load Graphs
• Operation Schedules
• Completion Date Report

FIGURE 2
PFU/CAPOSS SYSTEM FLOW

134

BASIC WORK CENTER INFORMATION

WORK CENTER NUMBER	DESCRIPTION	NO OF M/CS	W/C EFF %	C A P	INTER-OP TIME HRS T1	% T2	% T3	HRS T4	W/C LOC	SUB 06 CDE	SING GRP M/C NO. DESCRIPTN	MACHINE M/C NO.	SHIFT INFO # LNTH STRT	ALT FCD	ALT OFF SET	ALTERNATE WORK CENTER(S)	CALCULATED QUEUE TIMES FOR PRIORITY GROUPS 1	2	3	4
AA21	CLEEN NC	1	50	0	1	0	0	3	0	2	1		2 8.0 0.0	0	0		0.0	0.0	0.0	0.0
AA22.	M-218	2	82	0	1	0	0	3	0	2	1 2		3 7.5 0.0 3 7.5 0.0	0	0		0.0	0.0	0.0	0.0
AA23	MAZAK M4	1	67	0	1	0	0	3	0	2	1		2 8.0 0.0	0	0		0.0	0.0	0.0	0.0
AA24	CIN JSP1	1	64	0	1	0	0	4	0	2	1		3 7.5 0.0	0	0		0.0	0.0	0.0	0.0
AA25	NC VTL	1	75	0	1	0	0	3	0	2	1		2 8.0 0.0	0	0		0.0	0.0	0.0	0.0
AA27	OMA-5 NC	1	80	0	1	0	0	4	0	2	1		3 8.0 0.0	0	0		0.0	0.0	0.0	0.0
AA28	MILWMTIC	2	67	0	1	0	0	3	0	2	1 2		3 7.5 0.0 3 7.5 0.0	0	0		0.0	0.0	0.0	0.0
AA29	CIN JSP2	2	69	0	1	0	0	4	0	2	1 2		3 7.5 0.0 3 7.5 0.0	0	0		0.0	0.0	0.0	0.0
AA30	OMA-4 NC	1	69	0	1	0	0	4	0	2	1		3 8.0 0.0	0	0		0.0	0.0	0.0	0.0
AA31	SKINMILL	1	64	0	1	0	0	4	0	2	1		3 7.5 0.0	0	0		0.0	0.0	0.0	0.0
AA54	SLANTBED	1	56	0	1	0	0	3	0	2	1		2 8.0 0.0	0	0		0.0	0.0	0.0	0.0
AA57	NC AMER	1	92	0	1	0	0	3	0	2	1		3 7.5 0.0	0	0		0.0	0.0	0.0	0.0
AA77	P4 NC J8	1	67	0	1	0	0	1	0	2	1		1 8.0 0.0	0	0		0.0	0.0	0.0	0.0
AA84	DHUOP HN	1	67	0	1	0	0	3	0	2	1		3 7.5 0.0	0	0		0.0	0.0	0.0	0.0
AA98	CLEVELND	1	75	0	1	0	0	4	0	2	1		3 7.5 0.0	0	0		0.0	0.0	0.0	0.0
AB10	MYO 1 SP	2	67	0	1	0	0	2	0	2	1 2		2 8.0 0.0 2 8.0 0.0	0	0		0.0	0.0	0.0	0.0
AB11	MYO 2 SP	1	67	0	1	0	0	2	0	2	1		2 8.0 0.0	0	0		0.0	0.0	0.0	0.0
AB12	MYO 3 SP	1	67	0	1	0	0	2	0	2	1		2 8.0 0.0	0	0		0.0	0.0	0.0	0.0
AB74	MYO VERT	1	67	0	1	0	0	2	0	2	1		2 8.0 0.0	0	0		0.0	0.0	0.0	0.0
AB78	TRI8 JSP	1`	67	0	1	0	0	2	0	2	1		2 8.0 0.0	0	0		0.0	0.0	0.0	0.0
AC10	MILLS 18	18	67	0	1	0	0	1	0	2	1 2 3 4 5		2 8.0 0.0 2 8.0 0.0 2 8.0 0.0 2 8.0 0.0 2 8.0 0.0	0	0		0.0	0.0	0.0	0.0

FIGURE 4

MS77 - 775

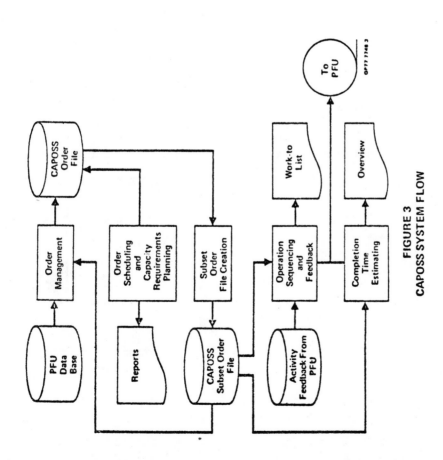

FIGURE 3
CAPOSS SYSTEM FLOW

center queue time (T1), pre-operation time (T2), post-operation time (T3), wait for move time (T4), and move time (T5) as shown in Figure 5. The user can specify an inter-operation time reduction percentage which allows T1, T4, and T5 to be reduced under certain situations to the percentage specified. The work center queue time (T1) used by the order scheduling function. The work center queue time individually specified for each work center. In short-term operation sequencing, the queue time is not actually calculated and the average queue time value is not used. The order scheduling function performs forward and backward scheduling calculations to produce early and latest start and completion dates for each operation. Where necessary, CAPOSS will compress inter-operation times up to the limit of the specified inter-operation time reduction percentage (MDAC-W uses 33%) in an effort to "squeeze" the fabrication order in-between its due date and the "now" date. In some cases, the inter-operation time reduction will not alleviate the problem, and a delay will exist for the fabrication order. After the order scheduling function is performed, CAPOSS records for each fabrication order the appropriate number of slack days, the actual inter-operation time reduction used, or the number of delay days. These factors are then used to calculate an order priority for each fabrication order. The greater the delay, the higher the order priority, and conversely the greater the slack, the lower the order priority. Both the calculated

operation start and complete dates and the order priorities are used later by the system (short-range operation sequencing and middle-range completion date estimating) to calculate additional dates that take into account actual capacity restrictions. An order schedule report is shown in Figure 6. Note that the dates shown on this report are represented by manufacturing day numbers instead of Gregorian dates.

Long-range capacity requirements planning uses the latest start and completion dates calculated by order scheduling to compute the load by period in hours necessary to satisfy the F.O. due dates (refer to Figure 7). This technique ignores existing capacity constraints and indicates ideally what the shop capacity levels should be. This technique provides significant visibility to help balance load against capacity. This allows for long-range management decisions to be made pertaining to the capital investment in machine tools and equipment, employment levels, and contract delivery feasibilities.

Through simulation, short-range operation sequencing produces detailed operation schedules and prioritized work-sequence lists to be used on the shop floor. The short term horizon used is normally 5 days. Work is scheduled to individual machine centers up to the limit of daily capacity. A characteristic of this scheduling technique is that simulated queue times are used rather than the average work center queue time values. The simulation technique used by operation sequencing uses queue files established for each work center. Queue file entry rules are used to determine how early an order can be released into the simulation. At MDAC-W, the first operation of an F.O. is released to its appropriate queue file 30 days before its latest start date, or the "now" date, whichever is latest. The second and succeeding operations of the F.O. are released to their appropriate queue files as soon as all previous operations of the F.O. have been scheduled. Each queue file is sorted in decending priority sequence resulting in highest priority operations being loaded first. Figure 8 shows the loading technique used. The cycle time shown in the figure is equal to 3 hours. This technique produces daily work-sequence lists by work center for MDAC-W (see Figure 9). These daily reports reflect the latest shop floor situation including such things as operation completions and partial completions, equipment downtime, and urgent orders and splits. The operation sequence reports provide visibility of the flow of eminent work through the shop.

The middle-range completion date estimating function of CAPOSS calculates the estimated completion date of fabrication orders. The computation of these dates takes into account actual capacity limits and the actual mix of work in the shop. Because completion date estimating is usually performed on a longer horizon than operation sequencing, the simulation used by completion date estimating is not as detailed as that used by operation sequencing. This enables the system to calculate

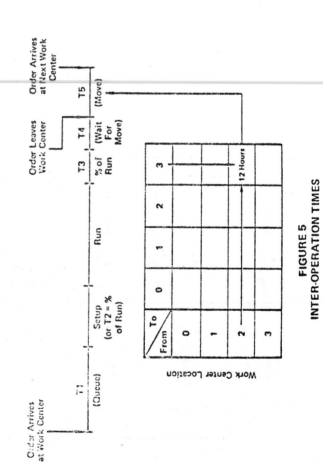

FIGURE 5
INTER-OPERATION TIMES

CAPACITY REQUIREMENTS PLANNING REPORT FOR WORK CENTER AA30   OM4-4 NC

NUMBER OF SINGLE MACHINES   ALTERNATE WC NO'S

PER NO	START DATE	PER LEN DAYS	AVAIL CAP HRS.	LOADED HOURS	0	50	100	150	200	OPEN HOURS	OVLD HOURS	CM OVLD HOURS
1	17DE6	5	80	131							51	51
2	03JA7	5	80	87							7	58
3	07JA7	5	80	102							22	80
4	14JA7	5	80	80								80
5	21JA7	5	80	93							13	93
6	29JA7	10	160	268							108	201
7	11FE7	10	160	185							25	226
8	25FE7	10	160	110						50		176
9	11MR7	30	480	490							10	186
10	25AP7	30	480	0						480		

TOTAL   113   1840   1546   PCT LOADED 84.0   PCT OPEN   16.0   530   236

WORK CENTER	NO. OF M/C S	AVG DAILY CAP PER M/C
AA30	1	16.0

OPERATIONS LIST - SCHEDULE SEQUENCE

MOD NO	PART NUMBER	FO SER NUMBER	OPR NO	SCHEDULE SSD	SCHEDULE SFD	EQUIP CODE	QTY	RUN TIME	S-U TIME	FROM WORK CNTR	FROM EQUIP CODE	FROM SFD	TO WORK CNTR	TO EQUIP CODE	TO SSD	E C	S C
25	AOG7009-501	6789000	005	17DE6	17DE6	1724XX	30	0.15	0.00				OT05	144CXX	17DE6		
20	3N4272	X FUTUR21A	010	17DE6	13JA7	172-XX	42	231.84	1.70				ZZZZ	1321XX	11FE7		
25	AOG7020-1	1234000	005	17DE6	17DE6	1723XX	30	0.15	0.00				OT05	144CXX	17DE6		
25	AOG7006-1	FUTUR22	050	17DE6	22DE6	1724XX	42	47.04	1.10				IT01	1911XX	03JA7		
25	AOG7007-7	2349000	005	17DE6	17DE6	1724XX	30	0.15	0.00				OT05	172JXX	17DE6		
25	AOG7007-8	3456000	005	17DE6	17DE6	1724XX	30	0.15	0.00				OT05	172-XX	17DE6		
25	AOG7007-3	3458000	005	17DE6	17DE6	1724XX	30	0.15	0.00				CT05	172-XX	17DE6		
25	AOG7007-6	3456000	020	20DE6	21DE6	1724XX	30	1.20	0.80	AM44	000200	20DE6	WT01	176J20	21DE6		
25	AOG7007-13	2347000	005	04JA7	04JA7	1724XX	30	0.15	0.00				ZZZZ	176J20	04JA7		
25	AOG7007-13	2347000	010	04JA7	04JA7	1723XX	30	0.15	0.00	ZZZZ	1621XX	04JA7	ZZZZ	176J20	04JA7		
25	AOG7020-1	1234000	090	04JA7	04JA7	1724XX	30	0.15	0.00	IT01	1013XX	04JA7	AF10	176J20	04JA7		
25	AOG7007-13	2347000	020	04JA7	04JA7	1724XX	30	0.15	0.00	ZZZZ	000360	04JA7	ZZZZ	172-XX	05JA7		
25	AOG7007-13	2347000	024	05JA7	05JA7	1724XX	30	0.15	0.00	ZZZZ	1724XX	04JA7	ZZZZ	176J20	05JA7		
25	AOG7007-13	2347000	028	05JA7	05JA7	1724XX	30	0.15	0.00	ZZZZ	000120	05JA7	IT01	176J20	05JA7		
25	AOG7014-501	1238000	005	06JA7	06JA7	1723XX	30	0.15	0.00	A152	163-XX	05JA7	OT05	176J20	06JA7		
25	AOG7007-13	2347000	050	06JA7	07JA7	1724XX	30	6.00	6.00	IT01	1623XX	05JA7	ZZZZ	176J20	10JA7		
25	AOG7017-1	1235000	005	07JA7	07JA7	1724XX	30	0.15	0.00				CT05	172-XX	07JA7		
25	AOG7007-13	2347000	055	07JA7	10JA7	1724XX	30	6.00	4.00	ZZZZ	172-XX	07JA7	ZZZZ	176J20	10JA7		
25	AOG7014-501	1238000	030	07JA7	07JA7	1724XX	30	2.10	0.70	OT05	1623XX	06JA7	AO71	172-XX	10JA7		
25	AOG7007-13	2347000	060	10JA7	10JA7	1724XX	30	4.50	2.00	ZZZZ	000J60	10JA7	AA30	176J20	12JA7		
20	3N4272	X FUTUR21A	020	13JA7	11FE7	172-XX	42	328.44	1.50	ZZZZ	164JXX	13JA7	WT01	176J20	21MR7		
25	AOG7020-1	1234000	160	24JA7	24JA7	1723XX	30	4.50	2.50	AZ14	1771XX	21JA7	AM10	1771XX	25JA7		
25	AOG7017-1	1235000	090	24JA7	24JA7	1724XX	30	4.20	2.00	AL10	1623XX	21JA7	AE10	176J20	26JA7		

FIGURE 7

INFINITE SCHEDULE - PART NUMBER SEQUENCE

MOD NO	PART NUMBER	FO SER NUMBER	OPR NO	WORK CNTH	SBGRP FR	SBGRP TO	EQUIP CODE	STANDARD SETUP (HRS)	STANDARD RUN (HRS)	OPR RED PCT	QUEUE TIME (T1)	(T2)	PLANNED SETUP (HRS)	PLANNED RUN (HRS)	(T3)	WAIT TIME (T4)	MOVE TIME (T5)	LSD	LFD
			0510	AC10			900640	0.10	0.01	0	.	0.0	0.15	0.45	0.0	.	.	4886	4886
			0530	AC10			000400	0.50	0.01	0	.	0.0	0.75	0.45	0.0	.	.	4886	4886
			0550	AC10			165160	0.30	0.01	0	.	0.0	0.45	0.45	0.0	0.00	0.00	4886	4886
			0600	AF55	1	2	164145	2.50	0.08	0	8.00	0.0	3.73	3.58	0.0	.	.	4888	4889
			0700	AF55	1	2	165160	0.80	0.05	0	.	0.0	1.19	2.24	0.0	8.00	0.00	4889	4889
			0800	AY70			165160	1.00	0.05	0	8.00	0.0	1.49	2.24	0.0	8.00	0.00	4890	4890
			0900	AZ14			131240	0.40	0.06	0	8.00	0.0	0.60	2.69	0.0	8.00	0.00	4891	4891
			1000	AZ11			114CXX	0.10	0.04	0	8.00	0.0	0.15	1.79	0.0	8.00	0.00	4892	4893
			1100	AZ14			165165	0.10	0.01	0	8.00	0.0	0.15	0.45	0.0	8.00	0.00	4894	4894
			1200	IT01			165160	0.00	0.50	0	8.00	0.0	0.00	0.15	0.0	8.00	0.00	4895	4895
			1300	IT01			114CXX	0.00	0.50	0	8.00	0.0	0.00	0.15	0.0	8.00	0.00	4895	4895
			1400	ZZZZ			165165	0.00	0.50	0	8.00	0.0	0.00	0.15	0.0	8.00	0.00	4896	4896
			1500	IT01			131240	0.00	0.50	0	8.00	0.0	0.00	0.15	0.0	8.00	0.00	4896	4896
			1600	WT01			165160	0.00	0.50	0	9.00	0.0	0.00	0.15	0.0	8.00	0.00	4897	4897
			1700	IT01			164145	0.00	0.50	0	8.00	0.0	0.00	0.15	0.0	8.00	0.00	4897	4897
			1800	IT01			165165	0.00	0.50	0	8.00	0.0	0.00	0.15	0.0	0.00	0.00	4898	4898
25	AOG7004-1	3457000	EXT PRI= INT PRI= 2				RED RATIO(%)= 0 RED USED(DAYS)= MAX RED POSS(DAYS)= 1 QTY= 30 EBD= DD=5001												
			0050	ZZZZ			194CXX	0.00	0.50	0	8.00	0.0	0.00	0.15	0.0	8.00	0.00	4892	4892
			0100	WT01			000300	0.00	0.50	0	8.00	0.0	0.00	0.15	0.0	8.00	0.00	4892	4892
			0200	AZ14			1724XX	0.00	0.08	0	8.00	0.0	0.30	3.58	0.0	8.00	0.00	4893	4893
			0300	AO71			1723XX	0.80	0.10	0	8.00	0.0	1.19	4.48	0.0	8.00	0.00	4894	4894
			0400	IT01			114CXX	0.00	0.50	0	9.00	0.0	0.00	0.15	0.0	8.00	0.00	4896	4896
			0500	AZ14			1724XX	0.10	0.04	0	5.00	0.0	0.15	1.79	0.0	8.30	0.00	4896	4896
			0600	IT01			1723XX	0.00	0.50	0	8.00	0.0	0.00	0.15	0.0	8.00	0.00	4897	4897
			0650	IT01			000180	0.00	0.50	0	8.00	0.0	0.00	0.15	0.0	0.00	0.00	4898	4898
25	AOG7004-3	3458000	EXT PRI= INT PRI= 8				RED RATIO(%)= 72 RED USED(DAYS)= MAX RED POSS(DAYS)= 1 QTY= 30 EBD= DD=4862												
			0050	ZZZZ			000120	0.00	0.50	24	9.00	0.0	0.00	0.15	0.0	0.00	0.00	4841	4841
			0100	CT05			1341XX	0.00	0.50	24	9.00	0.0	0.00	0.15	0.0	0.00	0.00	4841	4841
			0200	AF55	1	2	1623XX	3.50	0.07	24	9.00	0.0	5.22	3.13	0.0	.	.	4842	4843
			0300	AF55	1	2	1141XX	0.70	0.07	24	8.00	0.0	1.04	3.13	0.0	8.00	0.00	4843	4843
			0400	AY79			163-XX	0.80	0.10	24	9.00	0.0	1.19	4.48	0.0	24.00	0.00	4844	4845
			0450	AY79			1623XX	0.20	0.27	24	8.00	0.0	0.30	12.09	0.0	24.00	0.00	4846	4847
			0500	AF55	1	2	000140	0.80	0.05	24	8.00	0.0	1.19	2.24	0.0	.	.	4849	4849
			0600	AF55	1	2	163-XX	0.80	0.15	24	.	0.0	1.19	6.72	0.0	8.00	0.00	4849	4850
			0700	IT01			163-XX	0.00	0.10	24	9.00	0.0	0.00	3.00	0.0	0.00	0.00	4850	4850
			0800	OT10			000140	0.20	0.20	24	8.00	0.0	0.20	6.00	0.0	8.00	0.00	4851	4852
			0900	IT01			163-XX	0.00	0.50	24	9.00	0.0	0.00	0.15	0.0	0.00	0.00	4852	4852
			1000	AU96			1623XX	0.20	0.05	24	8.00	0.0	0.30	2.24	0.0	8.00	0.00	4853	4853
			1100	WT01			163-XX	0.00	0.50	24	9.00	0.0	0.00	0.15	0.0	0.00	0.00	4854	4854
			1120	WT01			1335XX	0.00	0.50	24	8.00	0.0	0.00	0.15	0.0	0.00	0.00	4854	4854
			1140	WT02			000120	0.00	0.50	24	8.00	0.0	0.00	0.15	0.0	0.00	0.00	4854	4854
			1160	WT01			162JXX	0.00	0.50	24	4.00	0.0	0.00	0.15	0.0	0.00	0.00	4855	4855
			1200	AF55	1	2	000140	1.00	0.15	24	8.00	0.0	1.49	6.72	0.0	.	.	4856	4857
			1250	AF55	1	2	000400	1.00	0.24	24	.	0.0	1.49	10.75	0.0	.	.	4857	4858

FIGURE 6

MS77 - 775

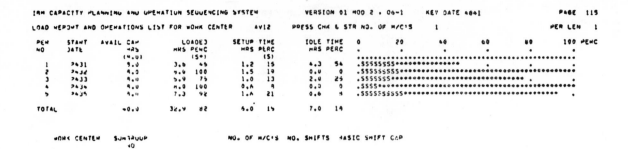

IBM CAPACITY PLANNING AND OPERATION SEQUENCING SYSTEM   VERSION 01 MOD 2 . 06-1   KEY DATE 4841   PAGE 115

LOAD REPORT AND OPERATIONS LIST FOR WORK CENTER   AV12   PRESS CHK & STR NO. OF M/C'S   1   PER LEN   1

PER NO	START DATE	AVAIL CAP HRS (%0)	LOADED HRS PERC (S%)	SETUP TIME HRS PERC (S)	IDLE TIME HRS PERC	0	20	40	60	80	100 PERC
1	2431	9.0	3.6 45	1.2 15	4.3 54	.SSSSSSSS•••••••••••••••••••••••••					
2	2432	9.0	9.0 100	1.5 19	0.0 0	.SSSSSSSSS••••••••••••••••••••••••••••••••					
3	2433	9.0	5.9 75	1.0 13	2.0 25	.SSSSSSS••••••••••••••••••••••					
4	2434	9.0	9.0 100	0.8 9	0.0 0	.SSSSSSSSS••••••••••••••••••••••••••••••••					
5	2435	9.0	7.3 92	1.8 21	0.6 8	.SSSSSSSSSS••••••••••••••••••••••••••					
TOTAL		40.0	32.9 82	6.0 15	7.0 14						

WORK CENTER	SUBGROUP		NO. OF M/C'S	NO. SHIFTS	BASIC SHIFT CAP
AV12	40		1	1	8.0

OPERATIONS LIST - WORK WOW SEQUENCE

MODEL NO	PART NUMBER	PU SER NUMBER	OPN NO	SCHEDULE CSD CFD	EQUIP CODE	QTY	RUN TIME	S-U TIME	FROM WORK CNTR EQUIP CODE	CFD	TO WORK CNTR EQUIP CODE	CSD	E C	S IN C PR
16	1-46780-1-	517557-	050	285E7 285E7	000190	180	1.34	0.4			AA23 164560			V
16	1-4947-0-1S	518143	050	285E7 285E7	000190	23	0.17	0.4			AA23 164550			V
16	1-44326-2-	5191H34	020	285E7 285E7	000180	1	0.60	0.3			AC10 172JAX			9
11	292-----5U1A	518U911	040	285E7 285E7	000180	44	0.33	0.0	WT01 000940	285E7	AG58 165160			V
25	444343-3-C	512245	080	285E7 285E7	0001A0	32	0.48	0.3	WT01 000940	285E7	WT01 000480	03UC7		9
25	AIM730-11Y	518730N	080	285E7 285E7	0001A0	24	1.43	0.4	IT01 000360	285E7	WT01 000450	03UC7		V
33	-356926-5U1F	50N3047	040	285E7 285E7	0001A0	6	1.61	0.3	ZZZZ 1643XX	285E7	AM44 151750	03UC7		V
25	470221-515M	5203560	050	285E7 285E7	000180	2	0.09	0.1	IT01 000360	285E7	WT02 000840	03UC7		V
33	-356926-5U1F	6100475	040	285E7 305E7	0001A0	11	2.94	0.3	ZZZZ 164-3XX	285E7	AM44 151750	04UC7 1		V
24	1441075-1-C	6133743	040	305E7 305E7	0001A0	16	2.39	0.4	WT02 000800	305E7	AC10 172JAX	04UC7 3		V
24	444651-3-C	6205447	140	305E7 305E7	000180	14	1.14	0.3	A714 132120	285E7	WT01 000400	04UC7		9
24	444651----C	6205447	140	305E7 03UC7	000180	17	1.27	0.3	A714 132120	285E7	WT01 000400			5
25	424643-3-1A	617-155	070	03UC7 03UC7	0001A0	1	0.01	0.1	IT01 000360	03UC7	AF55 164JAA	1		V
33	4912636-3-	6183970A	040	03UC7 04UC7	000180	22	4.21	0.3	WT02 000610	03UC7	AS32 134170			V
25	AIM7217-2-	5205414	030	04UC7 04UC7	0001A0	16	1.19	0.3	AC10 172AXX	03UC7	AC10 172AKX	1		V
25	AIM7217-5U1A	5205615	030	04UC7 04UC7	000180	14	1.19	0.3	AC10 172AXX	04UC7	AC10 172AXX	1		V
25	AIM7217-1A	520561A	030	04UC7 04UC7	000180	16	1.19	0.3	AC10 172AXX	305E7	AC10 172AXA	1		V
25	444A417-3A	4067924	080	04UC7 04UC7	0001A0	4	0.12	0.1	WT02 000820	04UC7	AF55 164JAA	1		V
25	AIM7353-1A	5191-24	100	04UC7 04UC7	000190	7	0.31	0.3	AX67 1221XY	305E7	A714 131JAX			V
33	-356926-5U1F	6043087	100	04UC7 05UC7	000180	4	0.40	0.1	AM44 151750	03UC7	AF55 164JAX			V

JOB QUEUE FOR WORK CENTER   AV12

33	-4944/4-5U1F	6174293	040		0001A0	11	2.94	0.3	ZZZZ 164-3XX	285E7	AM44 151750			V
25	AIM7353-5U1A	5167423	100		0001A0	33	1.44	0.3	AX67 1221AX	305E7	A714 131JAX			V
25	AIM7353-1A	5167422	100		0001A0	24	1.07	0.3	AX67 1221AX	305E7	A714 131JAX			V

FIGURE 9

MS77 - 775

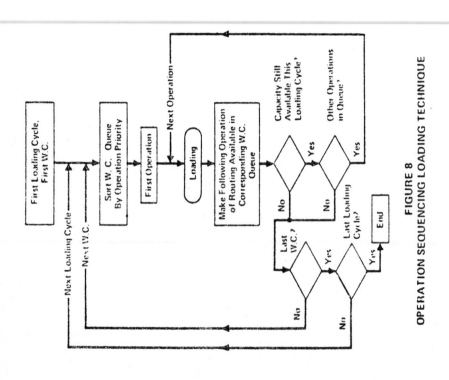

FIGURE 8
OPERATION SEQUENCING LOADING TECHNIQUE

138

realistic middle-range completion date estimates at practical data processing costs. Load calculations of the completion date estimator start from the last day considered by the short-term operation sequencer. The report produced by this technique shows for every F.O. in the middle-term (approximately 3 months), a comparison of required due date versus estimated completion date (see Figure 10). This report can help to highlight problem areas before they actually occur.

CAPOSS has many special capabilities that are optional to use and MDAC-W has elected to use several of these capabilities. MDAC-W uses the ability to specify routing information to more detail than just work center. In some cases, work center sub-groups have been specified and are used. Another capability in use is to assure that successive operations of the same F.O. on the same work center are loaded immediately after each other on the same machine. CAPOSS accomplishes this by temporarily raising the priorities of the successive operations in concern. An additional capability uses the MDAC-W expedite code as the CAPOSS external priority. Values used are 1 and 3, where 3 is the highest priority and overrides the system calculated order priority. A very important additional capability involves automatic partial completion. Normally, partial completions and completions are input daily to CAPOSS from PFU. However, for subcontracted operations and long operations that are sent to areas not maintained by PFU, daily partial completion status is not available. For these operations that are in process, and CAPOSS would not receive daily partial completion status, and therefore would produce daily reports that would not show realistic remaining operation times (upon receipt of completion transactions, large operation times would suddenly disappear). As a result, the automatic partial completion feature of CAPOSS is used for these types of operations. As soon as the operation is reported in process, a day's worth of work is automatically subtracted each day from the scheduled remaining time of the operation. An actual completion transaction is required, however, to record the operation fully completed. An additional capability to be used by MDAC-W is the networking capability within CAPOSS. This is used to generate cutter preparation and requirement dates.

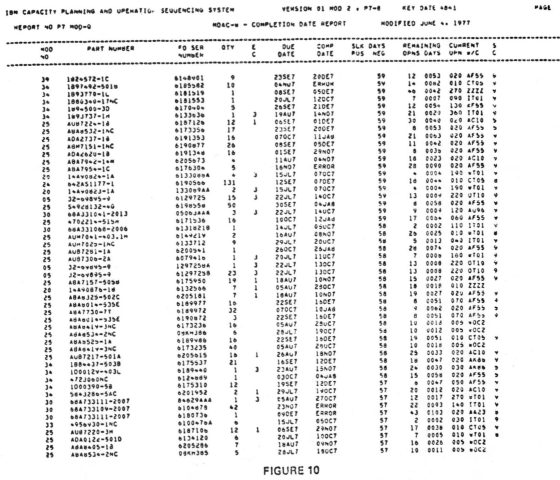

FIGURE 11
CUTTER REQUIREMENTS

MS77 - 775

MOD NO	PART NUMBER	FO SER NUMBER	QTY	E C	DUE DATE	COMP DATE	SLK DAYS POS NEG	REMAINING OPNS DAYS	CURRENT UPN W/C	S C
34	1824572-1C	6148901	9		23SE7	20DE7	59	12 0053	020 AF55	9
34	1897492-501B	6185582	10		04NU7	ERROR	59	14 0082	010 CT05	9
34	1893770-1L	6181519	1		08SE7	05OC7	59	40 0042	270 ZZZZ	9
34	1886340-17NC	6181553	1		20JL7	12OC7	59	7 0007	090 IT01	9
34	189-500-30	6170404	5		26SE7	21DE7	59	12 0054	130 AF55	
34	1893737-1M	6133636	1	3	19AU7	14NO7	59	21 0029	360 IT01	9
25	AU87224-1B	6187126	12	1	06SE7	01DE7	59	30 0040	020 AC10	9
25	ABA6532-1NC	6173356	17		23SE7	20DE7	59	8 0053	020 AF55	9
25	ADA2737-1B	6191353	16		07OC7	11JA8	59	21 0063	020 AF55	9
25	ABH7151-1NC	6190877	26		08SE7	05DE7	59	8 0036	020 AF55	9
25	ADA2620-1B	6191348	16		01SE7	29NO7	59	18 0023	020 AC10	9
25	ABA7942-14M	6205673	4		11AU7	04NO7	59	18 0023	020 AF55	9
25	ABA795-1C	6176304	5		16NO7	ERROR	59	28 0090	020 AF55	9
20	14AV0824-1A	6133088A	4	3	15JL7	07OC7	59	4 0004	190 WT01	9
24	6A2AS1177-1	6190566	131		12SE7	07OE7	59	18 0044	010 CT05	8
20	14AV0823-1A	133089AA	2	3	15JL7	07OC7	59	4 0004	190 WT01	9
05	32-048945-9	6129725	15	3	22JL7	14OC7	59	13 0009	220 OT10	9
25	S4928132-4G	6198556	50		30SE7	04JA8	59	8 0058	020 AF55	9
30	68A331041-2013	6050JAAA	3	3	22JL7	14OC7	59	9 0009	120 AU96	9
25	470221-515M	6171536	16		10OC7	12JA8	59	17 0084	060 AF55	9
30	68A331068-2006	6131821B	1		14JL7	05OC7	58	2 0002	110 IT01	9
25	AUM7041-403.1M	6144219	2		16AU7	08NO7	58	25 0025	040 WT01	8
25	AUH7025-1NC	6133712	1		29JL7	20OC7	58	5 0013	040 IT01	9
25	AU87281-1A	6200541	1		26OC7	26JA8	58	28 0074	020 AF55	9
25	AU87308-2A	6079416	1		20JL7	11OC7	58	7 0006	180 WT01	9
05	32-048945-9	129725BA	1	3	22JL7	13OC7	58	13 0008	220 OT10	9
05	J2-048945-9	6129725B	23	3	22JL7	13OC7	58	13 0008	220 OT10	9
25	ABA7157-505B	6175950	19	1	18AU7	10NO7	58	15 0027	020 AF55	9
20	14A90876-18	6132566	7	1	05AU7	28OC7	58	18 0018	010 ZZZZ	
25	ABA6325-502C	6205181	7	1	18AU7	10NO7	58	19 0027	020 AF55	9
25	ABA6014-535E	6189977	16		22SE7	16DE7	58	8 0051	070 AF55	9
25	ABA7730-7T	6189972	32		07OC7	10JA8	58	9 0062	020 AF55	9
25	ABA6014-535E	6190872	3		22SE7	16DE7	58	8 0051	070 AF55	9
25	ABA641V-3NC	6173236	16		05AU7	29OC7	58	10 0018	005 WOC2	
25	ADA653A-2NC	04KM386	10		28JL7	19OC7	58	10 0012	005 WOC2	
25	ABA6525-1A	6189986	16		22SE7	16DE7	58	19 0051	010 CT05	9
25	ABA641V-3NC	6173235	40		05AU7	28OC7	58	10 0018	005 WOC2	
25	AU87217-501A	6205615	16		26AU7	18NO7	56	25 0033	020 AC10	9
34	1884437-503B	6175537	21		16SE7	12DE7	58	18 0047	030 AK86	9
34	1000012V-403L	6189440	1	3	22AU7	15NO7	58	24 0030	030 AF55	9
34	472J000NC	6124889	1		030C7	04JA8	58	15 0058	020 AF55	9
34	1000390-5B	6175310	12		19SE7	12DE7	57	8 0047	050 AF55	9
34	58432B6-5AC	6201952	2	1	29JL7	19OC7	57	20 0012	020 AC10	9
30	68A733111-2007	84629AAA	1	3	05AU7	27OC7	57	12 0017	270 WT01	9
30	68A733109-2007	6104678	42		23NO7	ERROR	57	22 0093	140 IT01	9
30	68A733111-2007	6100478	1		04DE7	ERROR	57	43 0103	020 AA23	9
33	4956930-1NC	6100478A	1		15JL7	05OC7	57	2 0002	030 IT01	9
25	AU87220-3M	6187106	12	1	06SE7	29NO7	57	17 0038	010 CT05	9
25	ADA012C-501D	6134120	6		20JL7	10OC7	57	7 0005	010 WOC2	
25	ABA6405-1B	6205286	7		18AU7	04NO7	57	16 0026	005 WOC2	
25	ABA6534-2NC	03KM385	5		28JL7	19OC7	57	10 0011	005 WOC2	

FIGURE 10

139

MS77 - 775

There are several additional CAPOSS capabilities that could potentially be used by MDAC-W. One is the ability to group operations with similar set-up to reduce set-up times. Another is to group and sequence operations to increase utilization of machines, such as ovens, that can process many operations at the same time. The ability to specify capacity constraints on both machines and men for particular operations may be used in the future. Also, the capability to consider both alternate work centers and alternate operation sequences could potentially be used by MDAC-W.

Observations and Conclusions

Implementation of the system is now nearing completion. The long and medium-range capabilities have been installed and are showing great promise. The emphasis now is on installing the short-range operation sequencing capability. Although the implementation is not yet complete, there are a number of observations that can be made. First of all, streamlining and optimization of the processing of the system was found to be essential. The large amounts of data and calculations required can overwhelm computer capacity and budgets if not carefully controlled. Exception reports and acceptable horizons must be used when possible. The tendency is for the user to want large stacks of computer print-out of which most will not be used.

Like many other companies that have undertaken an implementation of this type, major obstacles have included data accuracy, shop discipline, and user education. As with most companies, it has taken unfaltering management commitment to overcome these obstacles. It is necessary that everyone involved with the system have good knowledge of how the system works and know how to use the information provided. More importantly, the user must feel like part of the "team" and must have a desire to make the system work. The system is not magic, it is only a very good bookkeeper, and the user must be made to realize that data integrity is mandatory. For many, it is difficult to adjust to a system that gives realistic information, when for years much information from computer systems has been either historic, or a statement of how things "should" have been done.

INTERFACES
Vol. 6, No. 1, Pt. 2
November 1975

A SIMULATION-BASED SCHEDULING AND MANAGEMENT INFORMATION SYSTEM FOR A MACHINE SHOP *

SURESH K. JAIN
Systems Analysis and Computation
Research Department, Bethlehem Steel Corporation
Bethlehem, Pennsylvania

ABSTRACT. This paper describes the design, working, performance, costs and benefits of a computerized scheduling and management information system that has been developed for a large, generalized m/n machine shop which had previously been a bottleneck facility in the Cast Roll Manufacturing complex of Bethlehem Steel Corporation. A flexible discrete-event simulation model, at the heart of the computer system, generates two types of schedules: Planning Schedules for making long- and medium-term planning and operating decisions, and Production Schedules for sequencing approximately 1000 rolls on 40 machines on a day-to-day basis.

A number of supporting programs perform data management, file management, and report-generation functions. Data-collection functions are deliberately performed manually to avoid the high costs associated with automatic data-collection equipment normally used in large computer systems. The computer programs are run in a time-sharing environment. A cathode ray tube and a medium-speed printer are the only hardware requirements of the system. With the implementation of the computer system, significant improvement is now being obtained as measured by productivity, labor and machine efficiencies, due date performance, and work-in-process inventory. The computer system is saving Bethlehem a substantial amount of money every year, and a notable feature of this system is its low annual operating cost.

Introduction

This paper describes how a simulation-based approach has been used at Bethlehem Steel to generate long-term plans and production schedules to coordinate the day-to-day activities of a large machine shop with over 35 machines. These machines process over 4000 cast iron and steel rolls per year for 100 mills located in about a dozen plants, and each of these rolls requires an average of 10 operations. This machine shop together with an iron roll foundry and a steel foundry comprise the Cast Roll Manufacturing (CAROM) complex, which is located at Bethlehem, Pa.

Roll purchases by plants are considered capital investments by the Bethlehem Steel Corporation, and each plant prepares an annual budget, which is approved in November for the following year. On approval of the budget, the plants transmit their anticipated roll requirements to CAROM, which must decide in a very short period of time which rolls it can manufacture and deliver on time throughout the following year. Since buying rolls from outside vendors involves cost in the way of foregone profits, it is desirable to make rolls in-house. On the other hand, if urgently required rolls are not delivered on time, the cost to Bethlehem may be substantial. Therefore, the objective is to make as many rolls as possible in-house and deliver them on time. The complexity of the problem renders it virtually impossible to use purely manual methods to determine how much to manufacture in-house and

*Acknowledgements. Thanks are due to C. F. Long and M. A. Ippoliti for their valuable suggestions during the development of the computer system, to L. E. Broadhead for his assistance in programming, and to B. S. Mikofsky for his help in preparing this paper.

how much to purchase from outside so as to be able to assure on-time delivery of rolls throughout the year.

Although problems can occur from time to time in any one of the components of the CAROM complex, our analysis of the overall operation pinpointed inherent difficulties in machine shop's scheduling practices. With the machine shop identified as the bottleneck facility, efforts to develop a solution were directed primarily to this part of the CAROM complex. Our objective was to develop a computer system that would enable CAROM to schedule the day-to-day activities of the machine shop and would at the same time provide information needed for the overall, long-term planning. In achieving this objective, our basic approach was computer simulation of the machine shop operations to determine, fast and accurately, the feasibility of producing a product mix at specified levels of manpower availability.

With this approach, we designed, built and implemented a low-cost computer scheduling and management information system that is now being used by management both to make planning decisions as well as to schedule the day-to-day activities of the machine shop. At present, the system is operating on a virtually troublefree basis in the batch processing mode. A second-generation design of this system has now been completed that will further increase smoothness of usage by incorporating time-sharing capabilities available within the company.

Roll Manufacturing Process

The roll manufacturing process involves casting a roll in either the iron or steel foundry, depending on the metallurgical requirements, and processing it for one or more of the following operations: cleaning, centering, turning, milling, drilling, shaping, treatment, grinding, and finishing. Over 500 types of iron and steel rolls, ranging in weight from 50 lbs. to 50 tons and in diameter from 6 in. to 6 ft., are cast in the two foundries.

Although the machine shop generally has about 35 machines, the number of machines varies as new and sophisticated equipment is added to replace the obsolete ones. There are no routing constraints in the machine shop. In other words, a roll can go on any one of the 35 machines any number of times for as many as 30 total operations. There are, however, other restrictions. For example, rolls of a particular type, say, strip mill rolls, must be finish-ground in pairs to meet the tolerance specifications. The processing time for a single operation can be as low as one-half hour and as high as 70 hours but is more or less constant for the same type of rolls. As far as possible, identical rolls are processed together, a procedure that results in fewer machine setups.

Manpower is scheduled on machines in multiples of 40 hours whenever possible, although overtime is permitted under certain circumstances. Most of the machines can be operated at a 20-shift, or 160-hour, per week level of operation. Uniform manpower levels are maintained on machines from one week to another, but it is of course possible to change the manpower level on any machine from week to week.

Method in Use Prior to Present System

Prior to the implementation of the computer scheduling system, CAROM did not have a sound basis for planning its operations. Machine loads were calculated manually by month on the basis of the roll requirements of the plants. If the machine load exceeded the available hours, a decision had to be made as to which orders it would be advisable to pull out of the machine load and purchase from outside vendors. Since it was not possible to assemble the whole complex of relevant data every time such a decision had to be made, some of the decisions resulted in either too few roll orders being pulled out and delivery dates not being met because of overload conditions, or too many roll orders being pulled out of the machine load with a concomitant drop in machine utilization and profits.

Another problem was that during the year plants would revise their roll requirements, sometimes drastically, based on the updated market research forecasts for their products. Such revisions in the roll requirements made it very difficult for CAROM management to keep abreast of the current state of operations, let alone predict and plan for the future. These were some of the major factors that led CAROM management to request that the Research Department develop a computer-based system.

In this paper a step-by-step account of the design developments that culminated in a computer system geared to the twofold objective of long-term planning and day-to-day scheduling are not discussed. However, the practical considerations that influenced the direction of our design efforts and a few illustrative examples of problems encountered and the resulting solutions will be highlighted.

Practical Considerations in System Design

The real problem in evolving a practical computer system for the machine shop was not the question of establishing the right theoretical foundation but rather the need to provide a practical solution for a real-world situation. That is, to be acceptable to management, the system would have to satisfy both the long-term planning and day-to-day scheduling requirements. The task of determining what would be acceptable to management is difficult. A primary reason is that in a complex situation with many conflicting dimensions, management certainly cannot specify the kind of computer system that would be acceptable before it has had a chance to explore with the system designer the range of problems and possible solutions. Indeed, just the first-stage objective of defining the problem may require a number of meetings.

A practical solution to any complex real-world problem is strongly evolutionary in its development. There is a creative give-and-take over a period of time during designer-management contacts, and management's needs and preferences take concrete shape as the designer provides information about specific problems and system solutions as they evolve.

Another key practical consideration in the design of any system is cost, i.e., the benefits of the projected system must pay for its costs. All too often, designers are inclined to build a complex system around a lot of fancy and expensive hardware — even in those cases where a more disciplined and determined analytical approach could lead to more economical design solutions. From the very beginning of our design program we were therefore guided by the basic economic consideration of avoiding sophisticated hardware when a simpler, less expensive solution procedure would do just as well. For example, analysis of the dynamics of the machine shop operations demonstrated that reporting timeliness would not suffer if operational data were collected manually, thus dispensing with automatic data collection equipment. Also, the frequency with which events take place in the machine shop ruled out the need for a dedicated computer. The scheduling programs could conceivably be run on an off-site computer. Consequently, we were able to design the system such that a cathode ray tube and a medium-speed printer will be the only hardware needed on-site to operate the system. This modest hardware requirement kept the initial outlay low. As to recurring costs, the programs were refined a number of times to improve their computational efficiency.

The selection and testing of individual design possibilities ran into the usual quota of problems. In an earlier version of the simulation model the intermachine delay time was assumed to be zero. Consequently, rolls finishing an operation on one machine were considered to be instantaneously available to begin processing on the next machine. With these assumptions, it became extremely difficult to follow the schedule in practice. Various intermachine delay times were then tested in the program and a four-hour intermachine delay time was found to adequately represent reality. Also, no provision had been made to group and process identical rolls together, since the prime consideration was the due-date performance. When the schedule coordinator started working with the schedules provided by the computer at that stage of the program, he deviated from them and scheduled rolls in such a way that identical rolls were processed one after another. It turned out that his divergence from these schedules was motivated by the desirability of reducing the number of setups. Some drastic changes had to be made in the simulation model to incorporate both the due-date and setup requirements of rolls.

Still another example of problems that had to be solved was the question of how frequently the production schedule would need to be updated. We first tried a weekly update, but after two days the computer schedule and the actual state of the machine shop were completely out of line with each other. Although twice-a-week updating turned out to be an entirely satisfactory practice, we refined the system design to provide the capability of an eight-hour update for atypical periods of extremely rapid and unusual changes.

Design of the Computer System

Beginning with a simple simulation model and proceeding through progressively more sophisticated models, we eventually developed a comprehensive system comprising the following subsystems:

1. *Planning Subsystem*: to generate planning schedules, and the associated reports for making long or medium-term planning and operating decisions.

2. *Production-Scheduling Subsystem*: to generate production schedules employed to determine the day-to-day activities of the shop and to maintain status of the machine shop.

3. *Information Subsystem*: to extract decision-making information from the data generated by the planning and the production subsystems and permanent files.

Employing a simulation-based predictive control approach, a flexible discrete-event simulation model dynamically generates both the production and the planning schedules. Activities for the machine shop are predicted by this control model for a period of 10 to 50 weeks for planning purposes and for 9 to 12 days for production scheduling, the maximum available manpower being supplied as input. Output from the model, in the form of predicted activities, is transformed into planning or production schedules for the actual scheduling of rolls in the machine shop. Data on activities that take place in the shop serve as feedback to the control model. This feedback provides a basis for updating the schedules generated by the computer. Control strategy is partially built in the form of a set of local sequencing rules used to select rolls for processing when machines become available. The process of schedule generation is shown schematically in Figure 1. To prepare data for the model, which is programmed in General Purpose System Simulation (GPSS), a data generator comprising a number of programs is employed to perform the following three functions:

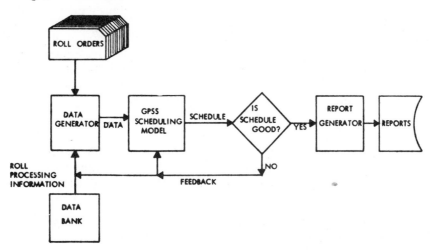

FIGURE 1. GENERATION OF THE MACHINE SHOP SCHEDULE

• *Initialization.* The simulation model is initialized with feedback from the shop floor so that at the start of the simulation the model represents the actual state of the machine shop. This function is accomplished in two steps: (a) rolls already on the machines in a semifinished state are released and scheduled first, and (b) all rolls present in the machine shop available for further processing are released and queued up in front of the machines on which the next operation is to be performed.

• *Roll arrangement by release time.* Once initialization is complete, all rolls on which no processing has yet started are arranged in ascending order of their release times on a temporary file for use in the simulation. Release time for a roll is calculated on the basis of its due date and the historical lead-time required to machine the roll.

• *Manpower input.* Maximum available manpower on each machine is read, interpreted and coded for use in the simulation model. Maximum available manpower is provided as input so that machines can be scheduled realistically within the constraints of manpower expected to be available.

The GPSS scheduling model simulates the operations of the machine shop for a given period of time using data generated by the data generator and referring to permanent computer files to access processing information during the course of the simulation. Rolls that have identical processing requirements are assigned a route number by the "schedule coordinator", who is responsible for coordinating the scheduling activities, and the relevant processing information is filed under this route number. Many different types of rolls can have the same route number.

The desired modes of operating the machine shop, e.g., grouping of identical rolls and processing them together on a machine to reduce the total number of setups, are programmed in the simulation model; and either a planning or a production schedule is generated using a set of complex local sequencing rules for the various processing stations. This set of rules had to be devised because the commonly used simple sequencing rules, e.g., "shortest processing time" and "slack per operation", aimed primarily at improving due-date performance were unsatisfactory for the machine shop in that they do so at the expense of the number of setups on machines. Indeed, almost everyone of the common rules tested presented problems. We therefore developed a comprehensive sequencing rule that achieves good due-date performance with as few setups on the machines as possible and uses the most efficient machines in a global sense. The way in which the rule works is detailed in the Appendix.

The scheduling model generates three types of data:

• For every operation performed on every roll during the course of the simulation a record is written on the output file for the purpose of report generation. This record contains the start and finish times for the operation in simulation clock, a numeric code of the machine on which the operation is scheduled, the operation number, and the process time for the operation performed.

• Machine or operator utilization during the simulation period is output by the week for planning purposes and by turns for production-scheduling purposes.

• Due-date performance statistics are calculated for eight major categories of rolls, e.g., small, large, extra-large.

Under the present setup, the output generated by the scheduling model is analyzed by the schedule coordinator to determine the quality of the schedule. He analyzes the schedule from the standpoint of due-date performance, manpower level, and operator utilization. If he considers that the schedule is good, he can then generate reports by means of the report generator. If the schedule is not considered good, changes are then made in maximum available manpower and/or the orderbook, and another schedule is generated.

Working of the System
Although each subsystem has its own distinct function, it is the integrated use of all three subsystems that results in a comprehensive planning and scheduling tool. However, the way in which the complete system operates can be best explained by describing how each of the three subsystems works in practice.

Planning Subsystem
The planning subsystem is used to generate long-term (10 to 12-month) plans used in the initial planning and to prepare medium-term (4 to 6-month) plans to plan and control shop operations over the medium term. Before going into the specifics of medium- and long-term planning, it will be useful to summarize the conditions and requirements of Bethlehem's planning process with respect to roll manufacturing.

Planning process. A complex planning process, spanning an initial planning period of 6 to 8 weeks followed by frequent updates of the plans, must be followed at Bethlehem because of the nature of the operations. The initial planning period begins in mid-October and ends in mid-December. Plans must be updated frequently, usually once a month, after the initial planning period to keep abreast of events in a dynamic environment.

At the beginning of the initial planning period, CAROM receives all the roll requirements for the following year from the plants. At that time, CAROM must plan its operations for the entire year within a very short period of time and decide after negotiating with each plant which rolls it can manufacture and deliver on time throughout the following year. The negotiation process is as follows: CAROM analyzes the roll requirements of a plant and, keeping in mind the requirements of other plants and the capacity to produce, decides which rolls it can make and deliver on time. It seeks a relaxation of due dates from the plant on rolls it cannot deliver on time. If the plant can live with the new due dates, the rolls are accepted. On the other hand, if the new due dates are not acceptable to the plant, the rolls are released to outside vendors. After negotiations with one plant are complete, CAROM must reanalyze the total roll requirements and negotiate with other plants one by one. In years when the demand for rolls exceeds the capacity to produce, the task of deciding how many and which rolls to produce in-house becomes extremely difficult. A computer-based solution is needed to handle this task.

Long- and medium-term planning. The process of generating medium- and long-term schedules proceeds as follows. When all the roll requirements for the following year are in, they are combined with the rolls already on order. The first step is to analyze the requirements to see whether processing them as they are will violate any policies laid down by CAROM. For example, as a matter of policy, the number of rolls in a given category manufactured during any month must fall between the minimum and maximum for that category. Another policy makes it mandatory that all rolls demanded by certain plants be manufactured in-house. The purpose of balancing the load is to determine the number of rolls required in each category by month for every plant. Then, if any of the several policies are violated, the due dates on rolls are changed and orders are dropped according to predetermined criteria until the policies are no longer violated.

A list showing the orders that should be dropped altogether and the orders on which due dates need to be revised is prepared for use by CAROM. CAROM uses this list to resolve the order distribution problem with the plants. Prior to this point, there has been no need to bring simulation into play, because the load-balancing program must first detect obvious flaws in the order distribution pattern before an accurate analysis of the order book begins. Once a fair and acceptable order distribution pattern has been achieved, the operations of the machine shop are simulated using the maximum available manpower estimates, and five types of reports are produced and used in planning. Brief characterizations of these reports and their uses are given in Table 1.

The Expected Machine Utilization Report (EMUR) is used in conjunction with the Group Report to arrive at suitable planning schedules and to determine manpower allocations. A good or suitable planning schedule is here defined as one that delivers near-100% machine utilization and over

TABLE 1. REPORTS GENERATED BY THE PLANNING SUBSYSTEM

Report	Data Arrangement	Contents	Functions
EXPECTED MACHINE UTILIZATION REPORT	By machine and by week	Manpower available. Manpower utilized. Work in front of machine at beginning of week.	Evaluating alternate manpower strategies. Determining suitability of the planning schedules. Scheduling maintenance.
GROUP REPORT	By route number and month	(a) Number of rolls ordered. (b) Number of rolls that can be delivered. Dumulative difference between (a) and (b).	Negotiating with individual plants. Isolating areas of abnormal demand. Testing manpower strategies. Evaluating due-date performance. Determining whether demand will be fulfilled.
SUMMARY OF EXPECTED SHIPMENTS	By plant and month for iron and steel rolls	Expected roll-tonnage shipment. Number of pieces to be shipped.	Providing management with a broad overview of schedule.
PLANT SCHEDULES	By plant, mill, and order number	Number of pieces demanded by month. Number of pieces to be shipped by month. Pieces that cannot be delivered. Total pieces on original order. Total pieces remaining to be shipped.	Informing the plants about the status of their orders.
SIX-WEEK LIST	By date on which first operation is scheduled	Full order information. Date on which first operation is scheduled. Machine on which first operation is scheduled.	Preparing foundry schedules. Informing the foundries about machine shop needs in the immediate future.

90% due-date performance. The Group Report presents a concise picture of the whole order book, due-date performance, and production capacity. A number of manpower allocation strategies — with and without overtime provisions — can be tested by repeated simulations until a strategy emerges that will require only a minimum of overtime but will deliver nearly 100% machine utilization and assure on-time delivery of over 90% of the rolls. This ability to rapidly evaluate alternate manpower strategies by computer simulation has saved the company money by reducing overtime on machines. The schedule corresponding to the optimum manpower strategy is used to negotiate the roll deliveries with the plants. An important application of the EMUR is in scheduling preventive maintenance. Slack periods are determined from the EMUR, and the machines are scheduled for maintenance during the slack periods, with the result that machines can be taken out of service with a minimum disruption to the operations.

The Summary of Expected Shipments provides management with a broad overview of the schedule. In the near future the computer system will also generate Plant Schedules showing complete details for every order of each plant; these will be prepared once at the end of the initial planning period and thereafter at the beginning of each month. They are transmitted to plants at the beginning of each month to keep them informed of the status of their orders. The Six-Week List shows the rolls that should be brought in from the two foundries during the first six weeks of the planning period. This list is used to order rolls from the foundries and to work out the schedules of the two foundries.

Production Scheduling Subsystem

The production scheduling subsystem: updates the state of the machine shop, schedules work onto each machine, and reschedules shop as necessary; and schedules manpower on a short-term basis.

For these key functions, the subsystem generates the Foreman's Report and the Short-Term Manpower Scheduling Report (Table 2). In addition, the computer provides a Roll Progress Schedule and a Nine-Day List.

Updating, scheduling, and rescheduling. For generating a production schedule, the current state of the shop must be known to initialize the simulation model. It would be impractical, if not impossible, to take a physical inventory of the machine shop to determine the actual state of each and every roll in the shop every time the schedule needs to be updated. Therefore, the method described below is being used to keep track of the state of the shop.

A physical inventory of the machine shop was taken when the computer system was implemented. Every roll on order has two status indicators; a status code and the number of operations completed on that roll. If kept current for all rolls on order, these indicators describe the state of the shop at any given time. The status code indicates whether the roll is available for further processing and, if it is not available, why it is not. If the number of operations completed is known, the next operations to be scheduled on the roll can be easily determined by accessing the routing and processing information stored under the route number of that roll. The state of the shop is kept current by means of the Foreman's Report, which is also used to schedule rolls on machines in the shop.

The Foreman's Report shows how, what and when rolls should be scheduled on each machine in the shop. The schedule coordinator issues a daily schedule based on the Foreman's Report to each of the shop's three foremen for operators or machines that the foremen supervise. Although the coordinator relies heavily on the Foreman's Report, he must of course use his discretion, for example, to accommodate last-minute changes. As operations are completed on rolls, the coordinator circles the roll code and the operation number on the Foreman's Report. The roll code identifies a given roll, and all computer records for that roll can be accessed if the roll code is known. If anything usual happens to a roll, e.g., there is a machining error and the roll has to be replaced, then the schedule coordinator changes the status code on the roll. Assigning an inactive status holds the roll up, and it will not be scheduled by the computer until the status code is revised.

Once the state of the shop is updated, a new production schedule can be generated by using the simulation approach described in Figure 1. As to rescheduling, the frequency of production-schedule updating depends on the nature and frequency of disturbances that occur in the system. We determined that the production schedules need to be updated at least twice a week — on Tuesdays and Fridays — to satisfy the requirements of short-term manpower scheduling described later. When a major disturbance occurs or the effect of minor disturbances builds up, the schedule coordinator has the option to generate a new schedule. The system is designed to provide him with flexibility for rescheduling the shop at the beginning of any eight-hour turn. For practical purposes, however, he does not need to update the schedule more than once a day.

Short-term manpower scheduling. The same principles that govern the determination of long-term manpower requirements also apply to the short-term situation. A work force of approximately 120 men has to be scheduled in the machine shop, and exact manpower assignments for the following week must be posted in the shop by Thursday in accordance with the union rules. On Tuesdays the maximum manpower expected to be available during the following week is input to the system for all 21 turns of the week. A production schedule is generated for 12 days, the machine utilization is analyzed for every eight-hour turn, and the decision to change the manpower allocation is made in terms of the expected machine utilization. The exact manpower levels for the following week are established and posted in the machine shop by Thursdays. On Fridays the exact manpower scheduled during the following week is used as input to generate a revised production schedule.

Other reports. As already mentioned, the production scheduling subsystem also generates two other types of reports: the Roll Progress Schedule, which is helpful in answering the questions plants may have about individual rolls, and the Nine-Day list, showing which rolls must be received from the foundries during the following week. A brief description of these is given in Table 2.

Information Subsystem. The information subsystem comprises all programs that extract information for use by management. Thus, some of the components of the other two subsystems, e.g., the report generating programs, can also be viewed as being part of the information subsystem. The information subsystem has three major functions: to provide routine reports, to answer management inquiries, and to calculate statistics and performance measures.

TABLE 2.   REPORTS GENERATED BY THE PRODUCTION SUBSYSTEM

Report	Data Arrangement	Contents	Functions
FOREMAN'S REPORT	By foreman's area of supervision, machine and scheduled start time of operations	Full order information. Roll identification. Operation Number. Starting time of operation. Finishing time of operation. Operation time. Last operation completed. Next operation scheduled.	Updating machine shop status. Scheduling work onto machines. Rescheduling shop as needed.
SHORT-TERM MANPOWER SCHEDULING REPORT	By machine and by turn	Manpower available. Manpower utilized. Work in front of machine at beginning of turn.	Scheduling manpower on a short-term basis.
ROLL PROGRESS SCHEDULE	By roll code	Full order information. Roll identification. Operations to be performed. Start, finish, and process times for all operations.	Predicting and monitoring progress of rolls. Answering queries of plants on specific rolls.
NINE-DAY LIST	By date on which first operation is scheduled	Full order information. Date and machine on which first operation is scheduled.	Letting foundries know what to deliver the following week.

Management frequently asks typical questions such as: "How many rolls are due to the Lackawanna plant in June?", "What kind of order distribution pattern do we have as of today?" However, inquiries of a nonroutine nature are bound to be made from time to time, and it would be difficult, if not impossible, to provide unlimited capabilities in the system to answer every conceivable question. Consequently, a reasonable range of capabilities has been provided that enables management to access those types of information needed for effective decision-making. At regular intervals the information subsystem also calculates performance measures, such as due-date performance and man-hours per ton, as well as other statistics. It stores operational data and provides management with capabilities for extracting historical information.

System Performance and Benefits

In evaluating the effectiveness of a computer system in use under conditions where it directly affects the attitudes and reactions of a sizable complement of personnel, as is the case in the machine shop, one has to consider not only the performance of the system as such but also the impact of the system on the human beings with whom the system interfaces. To evaluate the performance of the computer system as a whole, a four-month test was conducted beginning in February 1974. Four basic measures of performance — Man-hours per ton, Work-in-process inventory, Due-date performance, Grouping factor, i.e., number of setups/number of operations completed — were chosen and monitored during the test period.

Man-hours per ton and the grouping factor are measures of efficiency. Any increase in efficiency permits additional business, if the demand exists, to be contracted, with resulting higher profits for the company. An improvement in these two measures also reduces direct labor costs. A reduction in work-in-process inventory ties up less working capital in production. Improved due-date performance, though very important to plants, is difficult to translate into dollars.

During the test period, production schedules were generated as required and plans were updated once a month. The performance data collected from this test period were compared with similar data for the last six months of 1973 mainly because the product mixes during the two periods were almost identical and the production conditions were quite similar.

TABLE 3. COMPARISON OF PERFORMANCES WITH AND WITHOUT COMPUTER SYSTEM: MAN-HOURS PER TON

	Prior to computer: Base Period 7/73–12/73	Computer System: Test Period 2/74–5/74
Tons Worked	10,092	8,313
Hours Required	70,811	54,427
Man-Hours per Ton	7.02	6.55
Decrease in man-hours per ton from Base Period		0.47
% Decrease in man-hours per ton from Base Period		6.7%

Man-hours per ton figures for the base and the test periods are shown in Table 3. During the test period, a 6.7% decrease in man-hours per ton was achieved. To interpret the effect of this improvement in efficiency on direct labor costs and profits, one needs to know: (1) the direct labor cost per hour, (2) the total shop capacity, and (3) the contribution margin to profits and fixed costs. Because of the proprietary nature of the information, we cannot disclose the exact figures. However, the magnitude of savings may be judged from an example based on typical figures current in the industry. The average direct labor cost for the steel industry is approximately $10/hr. Using shop capacity of 30,000 tons/year, a 0.47 decrease in man-hours per ton would be equivalent to annual cost savings of about $140,000 (10 x 30,000 x 0.47). Assuming a 6.7% increase in business to utilize the man-hours saved, this increase in business would add about $500,000 (250 x 30,000 x 0.067) to profits per year based on a reasonable contribution margin of $250/ton. Therefore, in summary, we're looking at savings in excess of $600,000.

Table 4 shows the work-in-process inventory for the base and the test periods. Savings due to reduction in the work-in-process inventory are non-recurring and are treated as one-time savings. During the test period the inventory turnover ratio, defined as the number of times the inventory is used up in a year, increased by 6.2%. Work-in-process inventory in the machine shop is very valuable, and every percentage point reduction is equivalent to a one-time saving in excess of $40,000.

TABLE 4. COMPARISON OF PERFORMANCES WITH AND
WITHOUT COMPUTER SYSTEM: WORK-IN-PROCESS INVENTORY

	Prior to Computer: Base Period 7/73–12/73	Computer System: Test Period 2/74–5/74
Average Inventory	7,428	7,350
Average Monthly Shipments	1,705	1,791
Turnover Ratio	2.75	2.92
Improvement in Turnover Ratio		+6.18%

Table 5 compares the monthly due-date performance of rolls for the base period and the test period. During the months of February and March, only one-half of the rolls were delivered on time. This deterioration in the due-date performance was caused by an unrealistic order book. A balanced order book can become unrealistic if a number of unusual major disturbances occur within a short period of time. Any scheduling system loses its effectiveness under such circumstances unless the older book is revised so that the due-date requirements are made realistic. Such a condition existed in February and March. This was corrected in April by revising the order book. Due-date performance improved immediately and went up to 96.3%. In fact, subsequent experience demonstrated that with a realistic order book, computerized scheduling makes it possible to deliver about 90% of the rolls on time.

INTERFACES   Practice of MS

TABLE 5. COMPARISON OF PERFORMANCES WITH AND WITHOUT COMPUTER SYSTEM: DUE-DATE PERFORMANCE

	Prior to Computer: Base Period	Computer System: Test Period			
	7/73–12/73 %	2/74 %	3/74 %	4/74 %	5/74 %
On or Before Time	63.8	42.3	50.1	96.3	88.2
1 Month Late	30.4	47.5	33.0	1.2	11.6
2 Months Late	5.0	2.3	11.6	1.5	0.2
3 or More Months Late	0.8	2.9	5.3	1.0	0.0

Analysis of data on the grouping factor revealed that most of the week-to-week variations in the grouping factor are caused by changes in the product mix, and improvements in the grouping factor can be obtained up to a certain level only, further improvements being achieved at the expense of due-date performance. The savings due to better grouping of rolls are reflected in the decrease in man-hours per ton, and therefore no separate savings are cited here.

We have seen what the quantifiable benefits of the computer system are, but there are also intangible benefits. Thus, the computer system makes it possible to:

- Make good decisions regarding outside purchases;
- Plan preventive maintenance to coincide with slack periods, thereby reducing machine downtime during normal and peak operations;
- Reduce manpower costs by testing several manpower allocation strategies, with and without overtime provisions;
- Meet plant requirements more effectively;
- Provide faster response to capital requests and disturbances to the system;
- Make available a large amount of important information to aid management in better decision-making.

Finally, in terms of the human impact, the computer system had a significant effect on the thinking of the personnel in the machine shop. During the development stage some of the people who were working with us at the shop level had some misgivings about the changes that might come in with the introduction of a computer system. Their reservations stemmed largely from the fact that they had not yet become knowledgeable about the capabilities and limitations of a computer in general and the projected computer system in particular. As the system developed and demonstrated its effectiveness, acceptance by the machine shop personnel as a whole increased. In fact, the situation now is exactly the opposite of what it was during the earlier periods of the program. Even former skeptics have become "addicted" to the system and vouch for its benefits.

Conclusion

A sizeable proportion of the ORSA/TIMS community has been of the opinion that the simulation approach is restricted to the analysis type of situations only. The project described in this paper demonstrates how a simulation-based computer system can be used effectively to perform both the long-or medium-term planning and the day-to-day scheduling functions for a machine shop. The successful implementation and use of this kind of system in Bethlehem's cast roll-processing machine shop proves that simulation can be employed as a predictive control tool to provide dynamic scheduling in a fairly complex situation. This has resulted in increased efficiency, reduction of work-in-process inventory and direct labor costs. Important operating and statistical information now exists, which is of considerable value to management in routine and nonroutine decision making.

APPENDIX
SEQUENCING RULE BUILT INTO SCHEDULING MODEL

GLOSSARY

Choice: One of those machines on which the current operation can be performed. A roll can have up to five machine choices for an operation.

Cutoff Point: Hours of work that can be accumulated in a machine queue without making the queue excessively long.

Identical Rolls: Rolls having the same route number, due date, and priority.

Slack: $S = D - C - P$

where S = Slack in hours

D = Due date in simulation clock hours

C = Current simulation clock in hours

P = Processing time remaining on the roll in hours

Latest Start Time: $L = (S + C)/24$

where L = Latest start time in simulation clock days.

Group One: All rolls with priority higher than normal. There are a limited number of rolls in this group. Ties between rolls having the same priority are broken by route number.

Group Two: All rolls with nonpositive slack arranged according to due month. Overdue rolls are considered due in the current month.

Group Three: Rolls with positive slack arranged according to the latest start time. Ties for rolls having the same latest start time are broken by route number.

MACHINE ASSIGNMENT

Step 1. If the roll has only one choice, go to Step 6.

Step 2. Check queues in front of all *choices* for an identical roll. If check is positive, go to Step 6.

Step 3. Check queue in front of first choice. If the queue is less than the *cutoff point*, go to Step 6.

Step 4. Check queues in front of the second through fifth choices. If any one of the queues is less than the *cutoff point*, go to Step 6.

Step 5. Raise *cutoff point* for the queues. Repeat Steps 3 through 5 until the choice of machine is made.

Step. 6. Assign roll to the *choice*. Classify roll into one of the three groups.

ROLL SELECTION PROCESS AT EACH STATION

Step 1. When a machine becomes available, search groups One through Three for a roll identical to the one just finished. If an identical roll is found, go to Step 3.

Step 2. Pick first roll in Group One for processing. If Group One is empty, try Group Two and then Group Three. If all three groups are empty, go to Step 4.

Step 3. Check the number of rolls identical to the roll just finished that have been processed in the same setup. If the number is five or more, go to Step 2. Otherwise, pick identical roll, selected in Step 1, for processing.

Step 4. Wait for the arrival of work at the machine. When work arrives, go back to Step 1 again.

Comput. & Indus. Engng. Vol. 3, pp. 53–69
Pergamon Press Ltd., 1979. Printed in Great Britain

ASSEMBLY LINE BALANCING AND THE
APPLICATION OF COMPUTER TECHNIQUES

NORMAN A. SCHOFIELD[†]

Department of Production Engineering and Production Management, Nottingham University, England

(*Received October* 1978)

1. INTRODUCTION

1.1 *Assembly lines*

Assembly lines are commonly used to assemble consumer durable items such as cars, radios and domestic appliances. Interchangeable parts are assembled together at a set of sequential work stations at each of which is performed a prespecified part of the total work content. The assembly is usually moved mechanically, e.g. by belt, conveyor or indexing line. Provided that parts are available and that demand for the product is adequate, these traditional assembly lines can be highly efficient. The well defined sequence of operations minimizes the need for control documentation. Manual handling is reduced. Work in progress is small and as each operator is responsible for only a limited amount of the work, training time can be reduced and semi-skilled labor used.

However, assembly lines have several disadvantages. First, the stringent requirements placed on component availability make assembly lines vulnerable to disruptions by internal and external suppliers. The short cycle work with a low skill requirement can lead to poor job satisfaction, and there may be high labor turnover and absenteeism. Thirdly, many of the mass production industries have had quality problems. In an attempt to overcome these difficulties, several organizations have increased cycle times and moved to team working. Whatever approach is adopted, good balancing of individual or team work is essential and helpful to all concerned and so current conditions have, if anything, increased the need for good assembly line design or re-design.

In this paper I shall look at the problems involved in balancing assembly lines in the realistic industrial environment and then examine the types of approach adopted to date. The main part of the paper describes the NULISP computer system which has been devised at Nottingham University, England after extensive research. Since completing the development of NULISP it has been used commercially in a range of industries with successful results. Therefore, the author hopes that the paper will be useful for both the student and the industrial engineer since it describes recent research which can be judged in the light of its practical implementation.

1.2 *Line balancing*

Line balancing is an important production planning function because the efficiency of assembly lines is directly linked to the quality of the balance. It is a job requiring knowledge of the product, layout, processes, materials, tools, labor and rules for combining this information. In addition the engineer responsible must have an aptitude for fast accurate computing and detailed paper work. The balancing process and the subsequent evaluation of the assignment are often highly subjective and balances often have to be produced to some deadline.

It is usual to begin with the production schedule, a table of standard performance times for operations, a list of all the operations in fairly broad outline and a desk calculator. Experience and logic is brought to bear on this information and, after considerable expenditure of time and effort, a line balance can be produced.

---

†Dr. Schofield is a Research Fellow in the Department of Production Engineering and Production Management at Nottingham University, Nottingham, England.

Although relatively few sequences can be studied using this method, it has one very great advantage. It allows the engineer to use his experience while balancing, in that he may sub-divide tasks, change tools or methods and other interactions may occur which cannot easily be achieved using a computer.

Whatever methods are employed, it is clear that there are a multitude of companies involved in assembling products and there is a real need for balancing techniques that reduce the time and tedium of preparing balances and improve the quality of the balanced line itself. In this situation computer aided assembly line balancing offers many advantages in that it enables far more possibilities to be investigated and thus increases the chance that good solutions will be found. It also enables the engineer to obtain balances for differing production rates and to prepare contingency balances for lower manning levels due to sickness or absenteeism. In addition, with the widespread availability of timesharing facilities, it is now possible to put much of the engineer's experience to good use by enabling him to interact with the line balancing program via a small computer terminal.

1.3 The balancing problem

We can illustrate an assembly line by the following simplified diagram.

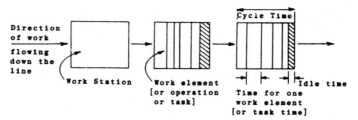

Fig. 1. A diagrammatic representation of an assembly line.

Each WORK STATION consists of WORK ELEMENTS which have been previously derived from a breakdown of the assembly of a particular product. These work elements are usually defined in such a way that they are indivisible into smaller elements. Therefore no element of work will be split between operators because to do so would incur extra work in the form of handling time.

The assembly line balancing problem is basically to pack these work elements into each work station, while obeying precedence constraints on the order in which the tasks can be accomplished, in such a way that the load on each operator is evenly balanced and there is as little idle time as possible. As an example, if we take the case of assembling a signal lamp for an automobile, then we may find a list of 20–30 work elements such as:

(1) assemble bulb holders to lamp base,
(2) assemble bulbs to holders,
(3) assemble reflectors,
(4) assemble lens to base,
etc.

Depending on the times for each of these tasks, they would be allocated to operators so that the station times do not exceed the chosen cycle time (the regular time interval at which each newly completed product will come off the end of the line). Precedence constraints are relatively clear for this simple product, since we can see immediately that the holders and bulbs and reflectors must be fitted to the base before access is obscured by covering the base with the lens. This is shown in Fig. 2.

We are now in the position to say that the rudimentary knowledge necessary to balance a line consists of:

(1) task times,
(2) precedence relationships,
(3) desired output rate or cycle time.

Armed with this information, the problem becomes one of combinatorial mathematics, the solution to which is far from trivial. A line with n tasks, without precedence constraints has $n!$

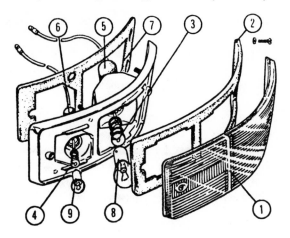

Key to some of the parts in the lamp assembly
(1) Lens,
(2) Lens rubber,
(3) Cable contact assembly, flasher,
(4) Cable contact assembly, slide,
(5) Grommet, cable entry, flasher,
(6) Grommet, cable entry, side,
(7) Base rubber,
(8) Flasher bulb (Sp),
(9) Side bulb (Min).

Fig. 2. Sketch of a stylised signal lamp for an automobile showing the main parts.

possible sequences of its tasks. If n were 15, this would mean that there were 1,307,674,368,000 possible sequences, the evaluation of which would be impractical for man or computer. As the assembly line increases in size, the number of feasible solutions rapidly increases.

Fortunately there are many solutions which would be equivalent, involving the minimum number of operators or work stations, and when precedence constraints are included the number of feasible sequences is dramatically reduced. Nevertheless, for all but the shortest of lines it is necessary to use a computer and special methods of evaluation in order to be able to evaluate a sufficient number of sequences that a good balance is likely to be present in that set.

1.4 *Practical considerations for line balancing in industry*

The realistic assembly line balancing problem is one of assigning work elements (operations) to work stations in such a way as to produce a "sensible" work content at each work station. This requires that the assembly line will meet the desired production rate, is compatible with any balancing restrictions and that there is a "reasonable" balance between the work allocated to each work station.

Examples of some balancing restrictions are:

(a) Technological; e.g. a bolt should be put through the hole before the nut is put on. These technological restrictions define a precedence relationship, which may be shown diagrammatically as a precedence graph or specified by means of data.

(b) Zoning constraints. Zoning constraints are restrictions which make it desirable that two specific operations should not be performed at the same work station, and contrariwise that two operations *should* be performed at the same work station.

(c) Restrictions imposed by fixed facilities on the line, which require that certain operations must be performed at specific work stations. Some tasks may need to be fixed at specified locations because the related equipment is immovable except at prohibitive cost. Fixing a task involves placing all its predecessors at work stations before that at which the fixed task must occur.

(d) Tasks exceeding the cycle time. It may be possible to sub-divide jobs with times greater than the cycle time, but often it may be better that the worker who begins a task should complete the whole of it. In consequence, the worker is no longer confined to the station as previously assumed.

There are other complications with a real assembly line. These include manning the line with varying operator availability, dealing with the line changes involved in the multi-product situation, sequencing the work down a mixed model line and coping with line stoppages. There is also the problem of variability in work element times, skills and performance. The assembly line planner has to make some simplifying assumptions in order to make any progress with the problem.

For an interesting summary of current practice in the United States, the reader is referred to Chase[3] who conducted a survey of assembly line operations in 111 manufacturing plants. The survey shows that formalized published line balancing algorithms are not being used, primarily because practitioners are not familiar with them. Chase concludes that there is a definite need for usable balancing procedures as evidenced by the large number of major rebalances undertaken each year in many categories of industry.

2. TECHNIQUES AVAILABLE TO SOLVE THE PROBLEM

We have already said that other than for very simple products the number of possible ways in which work elements can be assigned to work stations is immense. In practice, therefore, the manual balancing process is often based on an inspection of the precedence diagram.

The various line balancing techniques available include:
—enumerating all sequences,
—selecting the best from a set of randomly chosen sequences,
—selecting a solution consistent with current company practice,
—deriving a solution by mathematical programming,
—deriving a solution by mathematical methods,
—deriving a solution by using heuristic rules,
—using rules which take account of the problem structure.

All of these approaches have been investigated by different workers. Enumeration is impractical except for trivial problems. Jackson[6] used enumeration but takes account of the problem structure to restrict the number of choices and so produce a practical method for deriving hand solutions to simple lines. Held et al.[4] used dynamic programming to obtain optimal solutions but this is computationally expensive. Helgeson and Birnie[5] and Kilbridge and Wester[7] used heuristic methods as the basis of practical computer systems. Arcus[1] used heuristic methods in conjunction with random selection procedures to produce a method which Mastor[9] showed to perform well in the comparative study of methods. The Nottingham University program NULISP, described in greater detail later, also uses heuristics to weight random selection procedures which produce several good, usually optimal, solutions quickly, cheaply and efficiently.

In addition to the operation assignment algorithm, a realistic assembly line balancing program requires to take account of the practical restrictions to handle the data effectively and to produce results in a form and with timeliness appropriate for the practical user. The timeliness constraint may often raise a requirement for on-line processing. Mixed models will raise a further requirement for mixed model balancing, i.e. assigning operations of several different models in a way which is consistent with skill and facility location. In turn, there is a requirement for sequencing, say, a shift's work of models in such a way as to ease the work flow. All of these facilities are available in NULISP.

3. A PRACTICAL COMPUTER SYSTEM—NULISP

3.1 Introduction

The NULISP (Nottingham University LIne Sequencing Program) suite of programs described more fully in Schofield[10] will assign operations onto work stations so that the work content is balanced between operators. The programs are available in batch or interactive mode and their flexibility enables them to be used for the day to day sequencing of tasks on a flowline production system and to aid the designer when planning the positioning of facilities and setting of team sizes for future production lines. The complete assembly is specified to the computer as a set of tasks with associated times, technological precedence relationships and line restrictions. The desired production rate may be specified in terms of a cycle time or a range of team sizes and the NULISP system will then produce a balanced line, splitting the tasks between work stations so as to minimize the total idle time for the job. There are two main versions of the NULISP program, designed to provide solutions to the two forms of the line balancing problem:

—given a cycle time, find the least number of work stations to do the job;

—given an available number of operators, minimize the cycle time.

The approach used in NULISP is to generate, using a weighted random selection procedure, a sufficient number of solutions that there is a high probability of obtaining an optimal result. Each task is weighted in priority according to such factors as task time, number of "followers" in the precedence diagram, the times of the followers, etc. Unfortunately, owing to copyright protection, the full extent of the weighting procedures cannot be described in detail.

Because the process is iterative there is a good chance that many alternative line balances are obtained. The industrial engineer may then choose between these on the basis of other criteria, such as the ease of setting up the line in the factory.

The output is a fully annotated breakdown of the total operation by work stations showing the tasks occurring at each station, the idle time, team size, production rate and an indication of the evenness of the balance of work between operators. Small changes in the data allow assessment of a variety of possible circumstances to be made quickly and easily by the line designer.

Thus, savings can be made in the time taken to produce realistic balanced lines and the resulting decreases in line idle time can lead to large cost savings during the lifetime of a product.

In generating this output, NULISP can allow for:

—normal precedence constraints as indicated in Fig. 3,

—work element times which are greater than the cycle time,

—handling time to and from a conveyor,

—variable inspection times,

—grouping of tasks for a variety of reasons,

—separation of one group of tasks from another group for reasons of skill differences, cleanliness, safety considerations, etc.,

—fixing of tasks at particular work stations to account for fixed facilities on the line,

—time for changing the orientation of the assembly.

3.2 Data specification for a single-model assembly line

3.2.1 *The task description data.* The source of the basic data for all the NULISP programs is the precedence diagram which is usually expressed as a network. This describes the technological precedence relationships between the various tasks that make up the full assembly of the product.

The user can then express the information on this diagram in a form suitable for the computer. Each task is defined in the input data by a unique task number, a task description, a standard time and a list of its "followers" obtained from the precedence diagram. In this context we interpret followers as those tasks which cannot be started until the preceding task has been completed. For flexibility the task numbers need not be sequential and the times may be specified in whatever unit system is desired.

3.2.2 *Restriction data.* The practical constraints within which the engineer has to obtain a balance are far more extensive than just those described by the precedence diagram. He may, for instance, have to work within the limitations of an existing layout and also within strict rules governing the way he may allocate labour. Furthermore, each line is likely to have its own unique set of constraints. Any program which is developed to aid in the design of assembly lines must be capable of working within these restrictions.

To deal with these situations, NULISP contains a set of facilities which have been developed as a result of applying the program to the assembly of a wide range of products including auto products, telecommunications equipment, diesel engines, excavators and many others. Experience gained in these applications shows that the program is capable of dealing with the majority of assembly line constraints, some of the more common examples of which are discussed below.

Grouping of tasks. In many assemblies, different tasks use common tooling, or require the

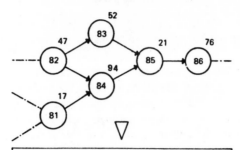

NULISP TASK DESCRIPTION DOCUMENTS			
Task	Description	Time	Followers
81	FEED JIG*	17	84
82	SEAL*	47	83 84
83	LABEL TOP*	52	85
84	CAP J/7*	94	85
85	STACK*	21	86

Fig. 3. Precedence diagram translated into input for NULISP.

same specialized skill. It is obviously desirable that such tasks are grouped together at the same station. The instruction:

JOIN* ⟨the joined task numbers⟩

is used in the NULISP programs to ensure that the string of tasks following the word JOIN* are placed together at the same station.

Separation of tasks. The reverse situation, where one group of tasks cannot occur at the same station as another group of tasks is also common. This separation may be necessary for a variety of reasons.

—A line has clean and dirty jobs which should be separated.
—Operations clash in their use of machine resources which cannot be placed together at one station.
—Tasks or groups of tasks separately require so much storage space for stock that they cannot be placed together.

The instruction:

SEP* ⟨task numbers⟩ FROM* ⟨task numbers⟩

ensures that in the computer balance none of the tasks in the first list occur at a station with any tasks from the second list.

Fixing tasks at particular stations. Tasks may also be constrained to a station, or range of stations, for reasons such as immovable machine facilities or a mechanised part supply system. To deal with this situation the instruction:

$$\text{FIX* ⟨task numbers⟩} \begin{Bmatrix} \text{AT*} \\ \text{AFTER*} \end{Bmatrix} \text{⟨station number⟩}$$

is used to indicate to the problem that the relevant tasks have restricted mobility in the balance and must be allocated at or after a particular station.

Withholding tasks from certain stations. The existence of a "special facility" at a station may in turn reduce the range of tasks that can be assigned to it, for reasons of safety, cleanliness or limited access. To cope with this situation the following instruction is used:

WITHHOLD* ⟨task numbers⟩ FROM* ⟨station numbers⟩.

Multi-manning. In the assembly of large products it is common to have more than one operator at some stations. This occurs usually because the product is sufficiently large to allow more than one operator access to it, or the nature of the work makes it necessary for two or more operators to be available to accomplish certain tasks. The instruction:

MULTI* ⟨no. of operators⟩ AT* ⟨station number⟩

allows the engineer to set the manning levels to suit the need of the product and the particular assembly line set-up.

Each of the above restriction statements may be used as many times as is required to define fully the constraints within which a balance can be sought.

3.2.3 *Basic NULISP data.* This data provides the remaining information needed by the NULISP programs. Much of it may be omitted and the program will assume standard values.

Assembly title. The assembly name or code is input to the program by use of the statement:

ASSY* ⟨description⟩*.

This description is then automatically added to the titling of every sheet of output.

Definition of time units. As has been mentioned previously, the tasks' times may be specified in whatever units the user requires. The final output is annotated with the information contained in the instruction:

UNITS* ⟨description⟩* ⟨units⟩.

Number of iterations. NULISP is an iterative program, and the user is required to define the number of sequences to be evaluated by the program in its search for the optimum. The instruction:

ITERAT* ⟨number of iterations⟩

is used to set the number of iterations. As a rough guide this should be about 20 for lines with less than 50 work elements and 10 or less for larger lines. Optimum sequences can usually be found within a very short time.

Station handling allowance. It is preferable to omit routine handling tasks from the precedence diagram, since these are likely to be relevant only to a specific assembly line set-up. For example, where the operator picks a sub-assembly from a band-line and returns it to the conveyor after the work has been done, this handling time cannot be associated with any particular task, but rather with the station. To cater for this a handling allowance can be introduced by a statement of the form:

HAND* ⟨description⟩* ⟨time⟩ AT* ⟨station number⟩.

This enables the user to allocate a constant handling allowance to each station on the line, or by using more than one HAND* statement, to allocate a handling allowance that varies from station to station. The latter case arises if the increase in product weight is significant, or the station layouts vary down the line.

3.2.4 *The two modes of use.* As mentioned earlier, the assembly line balancing problem is generally expressed in one of the following forms.

(a) Given a cycle time C, find the least number of work stations to do the job. This will design the line to match the desired output.

The NULISP 2 program will accept the production rate implicitly specified by means of the cycle time. The CYCLE* statement is followed by a time in the same units as the task times, e.g. CYCLE* 1.80. More than one cycle time may be specified per run of the program and line balances will be printed for each production rate.

(b) For a given number of stations, minimize the cycle time. This will design the line to maximize the output for a given number of operators.

The NULISP 3 and NULISP 4 programs require that the user specifies the number of work stations required on the line. The statement has the general form:

STATIONS* ⟨lower station limit⟩⟨upper station limit⟩.

NULISP 3 then calculates and prints out the theoretical cycle times for perfect balances with each of the desired work station counts. It also produces on the line printer a graph showing the theoretical variation of balance delay (the idle time expressed as a percentage of the total work station time over the line) with cycle time. This may be used to select realistic cycle times for feeding into NULISP 2.

NULISP 4 also calculates the theoretical minimum cycle times corresponding to the range of work station numbers specified by the user. For each stated "team size" the program then has four attempts, using times near the minimum cycle time, to obtain a balanced line with the desired number of stations.

3.3 An example NULISP run for a small product

The following pages illustrate the input to NULISP 2 and output for a small assembly line. The number of tasks has been kept low in order to make the illustration as clear as possible.

The first step is to define the technological precedence relationships of the tasks comprising the assembly by drawing the precedence diagram. This information, together with the restriction and basic data is then written out on the NULISP input forms. The total data set is then punched onto cards and submitted to the computer for a "batch" run. Alternatively the data could be set up in a file in preparation for an "on-line" run.

Some output in the form of a station breakdown for the line follows the figures describing input.

The product is a small signal lamp for an automobile, as previously shown in Fig. 2. This example was provided by the kind permission of The Lucas Electrical Company and is realistic as a representation of a line balancing problem, although the actual task times have been replaced by notional times.

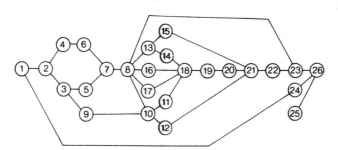

Fig. 4. A typical precedence diagram for a simple assembly.

3.4 Mixed model lines—A summary

3.4.1 *Introduction.* The assembly lines discussed so far have all been dedicated to the manufacture of a single product. However, in many cases one line is used to assemble more than one model of the same general product. The extreme example of this is in the automobile industry where one basic model can have thousands of combinations of customer variations, all of which have to be catered for using the same set of manufacturing facilities. When Henry Ford introduced the concept of assembly lines he avoided this problem by saying "You can have any colour you like, as long as it's black!". Unfortunately, for manufacturers of automobiles and most other products nowadays, the novelty of the "basic model" is past and customers demand their own personal mix of requirements.

Depending on the complexity of the product and the type of variations, companies using

NULISP LINE BALANCING PROGRAM – TASK DESCRIPTIONS

USER: J.M. SCHOFIELD   DATE: 1.7.77
OPERATION: LAMP ASSEMBLY   REF: L.732

NEWBAL: 26 – Only on 1st sheet

TASK NO.	TASK DESCRIPTION	TIME	FOLLOWING TASKS					
1	BASE TO PRESS	.46	2	24				-99
2	BOLTS TO BASE & AIR PRESS	.99	3	4				-99
3	SP HOLDER TO TOOL	.32	5	9				-99
4	MIN HOLDER TO TOOL	.32	6					-99
5	SEALING WASHER OVER SP HOLDER	.32	7					-99
6	SEALING WASHER OVER MIN HOLDER	.32	7					-99
7	BASE OVER HOLDERS	.46	8					-99
8	REFLR. TO BASE ETC.	.71	10	13	16	17	23	-99
9	SPRING TO SP HOLDER	.38	10					-99
10	SP CABLE TO HOLDER	.59	11	12				-99
11	SP BULB TO HOLDER	.54	18					-99
12	SP GROMMET TO HOLDER	.152	21					-99
13	MIN CABLE TO HOLDER	.59	14	15				-99
14	MIN BULB TO HOLDER	.54	18					-99
15	MIN GROMMET TO HOLDER	.152	21					-99
16	LENS RUBBER TO BASE	.60	18					-99
17	BASE TO FIXTURE	.46	18					-99

Form N.1.
Revised 2/4/76

Fig. 5. The first sheet of the NULISP task description.

NULISP LINE BALANCING PROGRAM – RESTRICTION DATA

USER: J.M. SCHOFIELD   DATE: 1.7.77
OPERATION: LAMP ASSEMBLY   REF: L.732

ASSY: L.732   UNITS: MIN   .001

LIMIT: 15   ITERAT: 10

TRACE/~~NOTRACE~~   STANDBY: 1   5

CYCLE: 176   OR   STATIONS: ———

HAND: ~~HANDLING TIME FOR ASSEMBLY~~   13   AT: ALLA

JOIN: 1   2
JOIN: 3   4   5   6   7   8
JOIN: 12   15
JOIN: 17   18   19   20

SEP: 2   FROM: 3
SEP: 8   FROM: 17
SEP: 11   14   FROM: 12   15
SEP: 23   FROM: ALL

FIX: ———   AT: / AFTER: ———

MULTI: ———   AT: ———

BALANCE: Any of the above instructions may be repeated here, to give different conditions for a new balance. If new restrictions occur in this section, they must be preceded by a RESET card.

ENDBAL: (to terminate the run)

Form N2.
Revised 10/11/75

Fig. 6. The restriction data.

```
N U L I S P-2   P R O G R A M
*******************************
********** 10/08/78 *********

STATION BREAKDOWN      ASSEMBLY NAME  L.732    SHEET NUMBER  1
*****************      ***********************    **************

** TIMES ARE IN MIN   UNITS **

NO. OF ITERATIONS      10
NO. OF TASKS           26
NO. OF WORK STATIONS   14
NO OF OPERATORS        14.00

STATION  1 ( 1.00 OPERATOR )    TIME=  0.1580      IDLE TIME=   0.0150
***********   ***********************   ***************   *********************

ELEMENT     DESCRIPTION                     TIME  FREQ  ACT. TIME    FOLLOWERS
            HANDLING TIME FOR ASSEMBLY      0.0130 1/ 1  0.0130
    1   BASE TO PRESS              *J  1*   0.0460 1/ 1  0.0460      2   24
    2   BOLTS TO BASE & AIR PRESS  *J  1*   0.0990 1/ 1  0.0990      3    4

STATION  2 ( 1.00 OPERATOR )    TIME=  0.1650      IDLE TIME=   0.0080
***********   ***********************   ***************   *********************

ELEMENT     DESCRIPTION                     TIME  FREQ  ACT. TIME    FOLLOWERS
            HANDLING TIME FOR ASSEMBLY      0.0130 1/ 1  0.0130
    3   SP HOLDER TO TOOL              *J  2*   0.0320 1/ 2  0.0160   5    9
    4   MIN HOLDER TO TOOL             *J  2*   0.0320 1/ 2  0.0160   6
    5   SEALING WASHER OVER SP HOLDER  *J  2*   0.0320 1/ 2  0.0160   7
    6   SEALING WASHER OVER MIN HOLDER *J  2*   0.0320 1/ 2  0.0160   7
    7   BASE OVER HOLDERS              *J  2*   0.0460 1/ 2  0.0230   8
    8   REFLR. TO BASE ETC.           *J  2*   0.0710 1/ 2  0.0355   10  13  16  17  23
   13   MIN CABLE TO HOLDER                    0.0590 1/ 2  0.0295   14  15
```

Fig. 7. Part 1 of the station breakdown output.

```
                        ASSEMBLY NAME  L.732    SHEET NUMBER  2
                        ***********************    **************
STATION  3 ( 1.00 OPERATOR )    TIME=  0.1650      IDLE TIME=   0.0080
***********   ***********************   ***************   *********************

ELEMENT     DESCRIPTION                     TIME  FREQ  ACT. TIME    FOLLOWERS
            HANDLING TIME FOR ASSEMBLY      0.0130 1/ 1  0.0130
    3   SP HOLDER TO TOOL              *J  2*   0.0320 1/ 2  0.0160   5    9
    4   MIN HOLDER TO TOOL             *J  2*   0.0320 1/ 2  0.0160   6
    5   SEALING WASHER OVER SP HOLDER  *J  2*   0.0320 1/ 2  0.0160   7
    6   SEALING WASHER OVER MIN HOLDER *J  2*   0.0320 1/ 2  0.0160   7
    7   BASE OVER HOLDERS              *J  2*   0.0460 1/ 2  0.0230   8
    8   REFLR. TO BASE ETC.           *J  2*   0.0710 1/ 2  0.0355   10  13  16  17  23
   13   MIN CABLE TO HOLDER                    0.0590 1/ 2  0.0295   14  15

STATION  4 ( 1.00 OPERATOR )    TIME=  0.1700      IDLE TIME=   0.0030
***********   ***********************   ***************   *********************

ELEMENT     DESCRIPTION                     TIME  FREQ  ACT. TIME    FOLLOWERS
            HANDLING TIME FOR ASSEMBLY      0.0130 1/ 1  0.0130
   16   LENS RUBBER TO BASE                    0.0600 1/ 1  0.0600   18
    9   SPRING TO SP HOLDER                    0.0380 1/ 1  0.0380   10
   10   SP CABLE TO HOLDER                     0.0590 1/ 1  0.0590   11  12

STATION  5 ( 1.00 OPERATOR )    TIME=  0.1650      IDLE TIME=   0.0080
***********   ***********************   ***************   *********************

ELEMENT     DESCRIPTION                     TIME  FREQ  ACT. TIME    FOLLOWERS
            HANDLING TIME FOR ASSEMBLY      0.0130 1/ 1  0.0130
   12   SP GROMMET TO HOLDER           *J  3*   0.1520 1/ 2  0.0760   21
   15   MIN GROMMET TO HOLDER          *J  3*   0.1520 1/ 2  0.0760   21

STATION  6 ( 1.00 OPERATOR )    TIME=  0.1650      IDLE TIME=   0.0080
***********   ***********************   ***************   *********************

ELEMENT     DESCRIPTION                     TIME  FREQ  ACT. TIME    FOLLOWERS
            HANDLING TIME FOR ASSEMBLY      0.0130 1/ 1  0.0130
   12   SP GROMMET TO HOLDER           *J  3*   0.1520 1/ 2  0.0760   21
   15   MIN GROMMET TO HOLDER          *J  3*   0.1520 1/ 2  0.0760   21
```

Fig. 7. Part 2 of the station breakdown output.

manual techniques approach mixed model line balancing in different ways. These approaches break down into three major types.

(1) The "bolt it on afterwards" method. For some medium sized products, the variations between models consist of different sub-assemblies to be bolted on near the end of the assembly track. For example generators may be built with a range of mechanisms such as cooling or filter devices for use in desert conditions, etc.

In this situation, it is possible for the production planner to balance the assembly line for the basic model and plan his team of operators accordingly. When small batches of the variants are being run down the line, he can introduce one or more extra stations at the end of the line and call on "utility" operators to work on the variations at these positions.

This approach is, therefore, for variations representing discrete portions of work, which can be conveniently located at one or more stations. If the total time for the variation elements is close to the cycle time then this is preferable, otherwise we shall incur large idle times by running the line with mixed models. Where the variations for different models cause many small tasks to be performed throughout the assembly process, we can see that the "bolt it on afterwards" method would be impracticable.

(2) The approach which says "I haven't really got a mixed-model problem". Many companies with complex variations in different models, affecting most work stations on the line decide to ignore the problem. This is particularly common where the size of batch for each model produced is very small, while the total number of all models still justifies the use of an assembly line.

Under these circumstances, the manufacturing manager usually finds that his most difficult problems are the supply of appropriate parts to each work station and the production of paperwork to issue to each operator to tell him what to do for each model. These considerations

```
                    ASSEMBLY NAME   L.732    SHEET NUMBER 3
                    **********************    *************
STATION   7 ( 1.00  OPERATOR )     TIME=   0.1570     IDLE TIME=   0.0160
***********  *************************   ****************   ********************

ELEMENT      DESCRIPTION                         TIME   FREQ  ACT. TIME    FOLLOWERS
             HANDLING TIME FOR ASSEMBLY          0.0130 1/ 1  0.0130
    11   SP BULB TO HOLDER                       0.0540 1/ 1  0.0540        18
    14   MIN BULB TO HOLDER                      0.0540 1/ 1  0.0540        18
    25   FIX DATE LABEL                          0.0360 1/ 1  0.0360        26


STATION   8 ( 1.00  OPERATOR )     TIME=   0.1620     IDLE TIME=   0.0110
***********  *************************   ****************   ********************

ELEMENT      DESCRIPTION                         TIME   FREQ  ACT. TIME    FOLLOWERS
             HANDLING TIME FOR ASSEMBLY          0.0130 1/ 1  0.0130
    17   BASE TO FIXTURE            *J  4*       0.0460 1/ 2  0.0230        18
    18   LENS TO BASE               *J  4*       0.0400 1/ 2  0.0200        19
    19   WASHERS TO LENS            *J  4*       0.0640 1/ 2  0.0320        20
    20   SCREWS THROUGH LENS ETC.   *J  4*       0.1480 1/ 2  0.0740        21


STATION   9 ( 1.00  OPERATOR )     TIME=   0.1620     IDLE TIME=   0.0110
***********  *************************   ****************   ********************

ELEMENT      DESCRIPTION                         TIME   FREQ  ACT. TIME    FOLLOWERS
             HANDLING TIME FOR ASSEMBLY          0.0130 1/ 1  0.0130
    17   BASE TO FIXTURE            *J  4*       0.0460 1/ 2  0.0230        18
    18   LENS TO BASE               *J  4*       0.0400 1/ 2  0.0200        19
    19   WASHERS TO LENS            *J  4*       0.0640 1/ 2  0.0320        20
    20   SCREWS THROUGH LENS ETC.   *J  4*       0.1480 1/ 2  0.0740        21


STATION  10 ( 1.00  OPERATOR )     TIME=   0.1730     IDLE TIME=   0.0000
***********  *************************   ****************   ********************

ELEMENT      DESCRIPTION                         TIME   FREQ  ACT. TIME    FOLLOWERS
             HANDLING TIME FOR ASSEMBLY          0.0130 1/ 1  0.0130
    24   BACK RUBBER TO BASE                     0.0850 1/ 2  0.0425        26
    21   P.V.C. TUBE ADDITION                    0.1810 1/ 2  0.0905        22
    22   COIL CABLES                             0.0550 1/ 2  0.0275        23
```

Fig. 8. Part 3 of the station breakdown output.

```
                    ASSEMBLY NAME  L.732   SHEET NUMBER  4
                    ***********************  ****************
STATION  11  ( 1.00  OPERATOR  )   TIME=   0.1730    IDLE TIME=   0.0000
************  *********************  ***************  ********************

ELEMENT      DESCRIPTION                        TIME  FREQ  ACT. TIME   FOLLOWERS
             HANDLING TIME FOR ASSEMBLY        0.0130  1/ 1  0.0130
     24  BACK RUBBER TO BASE                   0.0850  1/ 2  0.0425       26
     21  P.V.C. TUBE ADDITION                  0.1810  1/ 2  0.0905       22
     22  COIL CABLES                           0.0550  1/ 2  0.0275       23


STATION  12  ( 1.00  OPERATOR  )   TIME=   0.1730    IDLE TIME=   0.0000
************  *********************  ***************  ********************

ELEMENT      DESCRIPTION                        TIME  FREQ  ACT. TIME   FOLLOWERS
             HANDLING TIME FOR ASSEMBLY        0.0130  1/ 1  0.0130
     23  VIEW &TEST                            0.1600  1/ 1  0.1600       26


STATION  13  ( 1.00  OPERATOR  )   TIME=   0.1490    IDLE TIME=   0.0240
************  *********************  ***************  ********************

ELEMENT      DESCRIPTION                        TIME  FREQ  ACT. TIME   FOLLOWERS
             HANDLING TIME FOR ASSEMBLY        0.0130  1/ 1  0.0130
     26  PACK AND BOX HANDLE                   0.2720  1/ 2  0.1360


STATION  14  ( 1.00  OPERATOR  )   TIME=   0.1490    IDLE TIME=   0.0240
************  *********************  ***************  ********************

ELEMENT      DESCRIPTION                        TIME  FREQ  ACT. TIME   FOLLOWERS
             HANDLING TIME FOR ASSEMBLY        0.0130  1/ 1  0.0130
     26  PACK AND BOX HANDLE                   0.2720  1/ 2  0.1360


EVALUATION TIME      4  SECS.
******************************

THE STANDARD DEVIATION OF STATION IDLE TIMES IS   0.0076  MIN
```

Fig. 8. Part 4 of the station breakdown output.

```
     TIME SUMMARY           ASSEMBLY NAME   L.732
     ************           *********************



     ACTUAL CYCLE TIME   =      0.1730
     NO. OF WORK STATIONS=        14        ( WITH 14.00  OPERATORS )
     TOTAL WORK CONTENT  =      2.2860
     BALANCE DELAY       =      0.1360      ( 5.6 %)
     TOTAL TIME          =      2.4220
     STAND-BY ALLOWANCE  =      0.1211      ( 5.0  % FOR  1 STANDBY OP(S))
     STANDARD TIME TOTAL =      2.5431

     PRODUCTION RATE AT STANDARD =  330.31    PCS./HOUR
     ***********************************************************
     TIME PER PIECE            =    0.0030   HRS./PIECE
     ***********************************************************

     NO. OF  L.732 PER 8 HR. SHIFT = 2642.4
     ****************************************************
```

Fig. 9. The summary information for the line balance.

make it practically impossible for him to plan a properly balanced line and to carefully sequence models so that a heavy load on one station is followed by a light load for a model requiring less work. Instead the models are sequenced down the line on an *ad hoc* basis which is decided by the line supervisor hour by hour. Models for which parts are unavailable are held back until a later date, or partially assembled and put into temporary storage.

The problem remaining is how to decide on an appropriate cycle time. If we are expecting a fixed number of operators to deal with all variations on the line and the work content for different models varies considerably then we cannot set the cycle time to that which would cope with the "average" model. Since we have abdicated responsibility for sequencing models we must assume that large idle times and overloads will result and the "average" cycle time will be higher than expected, but not through any fault of the operators. The common solution to this is to set the cycle time to the maximum that could be expected if the most complex model was always being assembled. This "standard" is then used for production planning and wage payment calculations. In this situation idle times of 30% or more are not uncommon.

The effect of this approach can be modified somewhat by having a buffer stock of part-completed assemblies between each work station. This decouples the operators so that variations in work content do not immediately hit the next station, but are soaked up by the buffer, thus spreading the load. Operator instructions are usually attached to each model, and often the non-standard parts travel with the model in a "kit" rather than being supplied in tote bins at the work station.

These sorts of solutions are found in industries making engines, particularly larger diesel engines to specific customers' orders. Other examples are the assembly of luxury automobiles, truck chassis and caravans.

(3) The "set it up and start again" approach. Another case that is quite common is the assembly of small to medium sized products for which the different models are required in reasonable batch sizes. "Reasonable" may be from a few hundred to a few thousand. The company may then decide to set up the assembly line for one model, run it until the batch is complete and then set it up again for the mext model. The other characteristics of this situation are that:

—cycle times are low (<1 min);

—the number of operations is small (<100);

—the number of operators is small (<15);

—no special machine facilities are required other than those that are common to all models and can be left positioned at the same place on the line;

—parts for different models can be supplied easily and quickly in bulk, to shorten the set-up time;

—there are usually several similar assembly lines running in parallel, with operators who have a range of skills and can be moved from one station to another and one line to another;

—the skills required from one model to the next are very similar so that no significant learning period is needed after changeover between batches;

—often one or more automatic or semi-automatic machines perform the work at some stations. The "balancing" is usually done to fit in with the machine cycle times although variable speeds can sometimes be provided.

Having decided to deal with mixed models in this way, the planner needs to produce only single model balances but because of the frequency of changeovers he must anticipate a variety of conditions and plan his balances in advance. The change from one model to another then becomes a matter of routine.

The author has seen this sort of solution adopted in packaging lines for frozen food, bottling and packing of perfumes and the assembly of small auto accessories such as lamps and generators. A special situation where it can happen is in the assembly of small diesel engines which may be built with two, three or four cylinders but in other respects are identical. This means that the central section of the line is "elastic" and can cope with the assembly of cylinder barrels and pistons for the necessary number of cylinders.

So, these are some of the ways in which manufacturing industries are forced to deal with their mixed model line balancing, using manual methods. Some of the problems encountered, particularly relating to parts supply as mentioned in (2), will not be solved by clever balancing techniques.

However, for the manufacturer who makes a basic product which has a variety of different models each required in reasonable quantities, we need to provide a system for balancing a line to deal with all the model variations. These variations will probably effect the work content of every station on the line and so the resulting load variability needs to be spread evenly by sequencing the models into a suitable order for starting them off down the line. The next section summarizes briefly the approach used in NULISP. A detailed description appears in Schofield[10, Chapter 4].

3.4.2 *Mixed model line balancing using NULISP.* In balancing a mixed model assembly line it is necessary to ensure that for each model the balancing criteria are met. These are that the line will meet the desired production rate and that, while all restrictions of technological precedence and line layout are obeyed, there is a "reasonable" balance of work between work stations. However, since every model is made on one line, it is also desirable that each model requires the same number of stations and the same disposition of special skills and facilities, and that work which is common to several models is always performed at the same station. These criteria have been incorporated into the NULISP package along with a simple method of specifying the different models and their frequency of manufacture so that for the given model mix an overall balance for the line may be produced.

As one would expect, there is more data to be processed by the computer and the problem is more difficult to solve. However, the data specification has been eased by making it similar to that for the single model case. The work on the line is described in terms of the basic model and a number of variations which are combined to make up the different models. The total number of tasks and number of models are specified. All of the tasks included in the basic model are specified first and are introduced by the instruction BASIC* MODEL*. Each variation is described in terms of new tasks which must be included and tasks in the basic model which should be omitted. Each variation is introduced by an instruction of the form:

VARIATION* ⟨variation number⟩ ⟨description⟩.

The specification of a complete variation might be:

VARIATION* 2   FIT HIGH SPEED BEARING*

OMIT*   15
OMIT*   16
OMIT*   17
OMIT*   18

INCLUDE*   28 FIT SPACER*   63 29   30   −99
INCLUDE*   29 FIT H/S BEARING*   189 31 −99
INCLUDE*   30 ADJUST*   148 31 −99
INCLUDE*   31 SECURE H/S BEARING*   93 21 −99

To explain the above set of data, let us describe in words what we are telling the computer:

"Variation number 5 which is called "sound proofing for cab" consists of the following alterations to the basic model:

include new task 402 which is called "wadding to roof interior" and is followed in the precedence diagram by tasks 39 and 403

Include new task 403...
Omit task 69,
etc."

Ater specifying all the variations we need to tell the computer how to use these to make up the different models of the product. An example is as follows:

Model no.	Description	Number required	Variation numbers			
1	BASIC MODEL*	20				
2	HIGH SPEED MODEL*	30	1	2		
3	VARIABLE SPEED MODEL*	10	1	2	3	
4	DELUXE MODEL*	20	1	2	4	5
5	EXPORT MODEL*	50	1	2	3	5

For this production schedule of models, NULISP will balance the assembly line so that *on average* each station is not overloaded and that peak loads for certain models can be catered for. A typical output for a station dealing with work related to several different models will appear as follows.

```
STATION   1  (  1.0  OPERATOR  )
***********  *******************

ELEMENT        DESCRIPTION                              TIME      MODEL OCCURRENCE
               HANDLING TIME FOR ASSEMBLY               0.013
      1   SHAFT TO CASE                   *F**J  1*     0.058     ALL
      2   SPACER                          *F**J  1*     0.058     ALL
      3   SECURE PLUG                     *F**J  1*     0.042     ALL
      4   FIT CIRCLIP                     *F**J  1*     0.035     ALL
      5   USE PRESS                       *F**J  1*     0.030     ALL
     24   PUMP TO JIG                     *J  5*        0.032     2    3
     25   INSERT DIAPHRAM                 *J  5*        0.053     2    3
     26   CLIP ON PUMP COVER              *J  5*        0.058     2    3

STATION TIME FOR EACH MODEL :
MODEL       TIME      PER MAN
    1       0.125     0.125
    2       0.197     0.197
    3       0.197     0.197

TOTAL STATION TIME PER MAN FOR COMPLETE PRODUCTION SCHEDULE =    0.644   MIN

AVERAGE STATION TIME PER MAN FOR THE GIVEN SCHEDULE          =    0.161   MIN

(SEE END OF BALANCE PRINTOUT FOR A COMPARATIVE ASSESSMENT OF AVERAGE STATION TIMES)
```

Fig. 10. Typical NULISP output for a mixed model line balance.

3.4.3 *Mixed model line sequencing.* A separate program has been written which will determine a good sequence in which to process a group (e.g. a shift) of models down the line. The requirements of this program are that the imbalance of work associated with the different models is distributed in sensible ways. The criteria for distribution will vary between organizations, some preferring similar models to appear close together others requiring that they should be well separated. For this reason a variety of algorithms are available which give different emphasis between total makespan and balance of work and which enable the production sequencer to determine a sequence to match his current requirements.

A fuller report of a comparative study of these methods appears in Bonney[2]. An interesting point is that the mixed model sequencing problem has the same structure as the flowshop sequencing problem which has been analyzed by many workers but which still in general defies mathematically optimal solution. The heuristic methods examined bridge the normal gap between theory and practice.

4. THE INTERACTIVE VERSION OF NULISP

So far NULISP has been described as a suite of programs which would be "batch processed" on a computer. That is, the user would complete his data forms, get the data punched onto cards, and submit the cards to the computing centre for processing. Results would be returned to him overnight or after several days, depending on the priority given to his job.

However, it is desirable, particularly when designing an assembly line, to shorten this lead time and to maximize the interaction between man and the computer. With this objective in mind, the NULISP programs have been modified to allow the user to run each program "on line" using a "teletype terminal" in or near his office. This modified "interactive" version of NULISP has been called IDEAL—Interactive Design and Evaluation of Assembly Lines. Using the IDEAL system the industrial engineer may judge the consequences of data changes, e.g. to cycle time or restrictions; and reevaluate an assembly line within minutes. The non-expert user is guided through the use of IDEAL by means of a set of computer-generated prompts and responses, which can be suppressed as the user gains in experience.

The system is now available in the United Kingdom via the General Post Office Datel 200 System to a national computer bureau, and some users are accessing the programs on their own company's computer. The programs have also been converted to other computer languages to make them compatible with world-wide computing facilities.

5. CONCLUSIONS

We have seen that other than for very simple products the number of possible ways in which work elements can be assigned to work stations is immense. There are formalized rules for the manual solution of the line balancing problem, and these aim to reduce the number of possibilities considered. In practice, however, they soon become computationally infeasible and the manual balancing process is usually based on inspection of the precedence diagram. The balances obtained are highly subjective and involve a considerable expenditure of time and effort on the part of someone with product knowledge. Other disadvantages of the manual approach are the physical impossibility of considering other than a limited selection of work task arrangements and the error-prone nature of the work.

Since the purpose of this paper was to acquaint the first-time reader with *a* computer approach to line balancing, the author has not spent time drawing comparisons with other systems that have been developed. There are a range of such systems described in the literature. Many have been designed for special purposes and others will only cope with trivial line balancing situations. Some adopt a simulation approach which enables the user to try out various solutions which he has previously derived by manual methods.

NULISP comes under the heading of a "general-purpose line balancing program" and the only comparable systems known to the author are COMSOAL and CALB.

COMSOAL (Computer Methods of Sequencing Operations for Assembly Lines) described fully in Arcus[1], was developed at the University of California, Berkeley. This program uses biased random sampling techniques to provide a good chance of an optimal result within a small set of solutions. It is iterative and so it is possible to achieve several good answers with relatively small expenditure of computer time. It was originally designed in cooperation with the Chrysler Corporation, but the author is not sure of the extent of its development or commercial application since that time.

CALB (Computer Aided Line Balancing), described in Magad[8], was devised at the IIT Research Institute, Chicago, Illinois as part of their Advanced Assembly Methods Program. The balancing procedure in CALB assigns work elements to each station in accordance with their availability by time and precedence. A special de-assignment procedure allows the computer to find an assignment of elements to satisfy cycle time tolerances, if such a solution exists. The user specifies the degree of balance desired rather than the computer trying to find the best solution possible. CALB deals with most practical restrictions required and its designers claim many successful applications.

It is clear that the use of the computer for assembly line balancing enables the industrial engineer to accomplish many things that were not practicable before. Systems such as NULISP are providing beneficial results in a variety of industries, for the large or small user.

Such clear savings may be demonstrated that NULISP and similar packages will be found increasingly in the "tool boxes" of industrial engineers to help with their everyday work situations. The industrial engineering revolution is here at last!

Acknowledgements—The copyright to NULISP is owned by the National Research Development Corporation, Kingsgate House, 66/74 Victoria Street, London SW1, who funded the development of the program following research sponsorship by the Science Research Council under grant number B/RG/504.

The author would like to acknowledge the help and advice given by Maurice C. Bonney, Senior Lecturer in the Department of Production Engineering and Production Management at Nottingham University, England.

The Lucas Electrical Company has been associated with the development of NULISP at Nottingham University over a period of several years and the author is particularly grateful to the Company for the provision of data for testing and improving the program, and for inclusion in this paper.

REFERENCES

1. A. L. Arcus, COMSOAL: A computer method of sequencing operations for assembly lines, *Int. J. Prod. Res.* **4**(4) (1966).
2. M. C. Bonney, Some Heuristic Algorithms for the Flowshop sequencing problem. Proceedings of 5th International Seminar, Algorithms for Production Control and Scheduling, Karlovy Vary, Czechoslovakia (September, 1976).
3. R. B. Chase, Survey of paced assembly lines, *Ind. Engng* (February, 1974).
4. M. Held, R. M. Karp & R. Sharesian, Assembly line balancing—Dynamic programming with precedence constraints, *Ops Res.* **2**(3) (1963).
5. W. B. Helgeson & D. P. Birnie, Assembly line balancing using the ranked positional weight technique, *J. ind. Engng* **12**(6) (1961).

6. J. R. Jackson, A computing procedure for a line balancing problem, *Mgmt Sci.* **2**(3) (1956).
7. M. D. Kilbridge & L. Wester, A heuristic method of assembly line balancing, *J. ind. Engng* **XII**(4) (1961).
8. E. L. Magad, CALB—Systematic assembly management, *Assembly Engng* (September, 1969).
9. A. A. Mastor, An experimental investigation and comparative evaluation of production line balancing techniques, *Mgmt Sci.* **16**(11) (1970). Reported also in E. S. Buffa & W. H. Taubert, Production Inventory Systems: Planning and Control, Richard D. Irwin Inc. (1972).
10. N. A. Schofield, *NULISP Users Manual*, 3rd Edn (1975).

OMEGA. The Int. Jl of Mgmt Sci., Vol. 6, No. 4, pp. 313 323
© Pergamon Press Ltd 1978. Printed in Great Britain

0305-0483 78 0901-0313S02.00 0

Mixed-Model Assembly Line Sequencing Problems

EZEY M DAR-EL

Israel Institute of Technology

(Received December 1977; in revised form February 1978)

The paper develops a comprehensive classification of mixed-model assembly lines from which four categories of model sequencing are derived. Each category aims at satisfying one or both of two objective criteria, the one minimizing the overall line length, and the other minimizing the thruput time. Approaches for solving the sequencing problem in each category are presented. The paper suggests a design strategy that can be followed by designers of mixed-model assembly lines. Specific topics requiring further research are also defined.

1. INTRODUCTION

THE MIXED-MODEL line sequencing problem was first enunciated in 1963 by Kilbridge and Wester [4], yet, until today, some 14 years later, only a few papers on this topic have appeared in professional journals. While mixed-model lines are found in many manufacturing plants, a practical method for tackling the attendant sequencing problem has still to be developed for adoption by industry. However, a comprehensive classification of mixed-model assembly lines is needed in order to clearly distinguish between the different types of sequencing problems that may arise.

This paper presents a classification of mixed model assembly lines and their main design features. Various approaches for solving the appropriate sequencing problem are discussed.

2. CHARACTERISTICS OF MIXED-MODEL LINES

Many types of Mixed-Model assembly lines exist in industry [7] and developing a classification system is best approached through identifying and distinguishing between several important design features. These are discussed below.

(1) *The conveyance system*

This can either be a *conveyor* moving at uniform speed, or else a *stationary system* where the product remains stationary at each station, and only transferred to the next station after completion of the station's task. Alternatively, the next station's operators may replace the current ones, as in the assembly of large products, such as with aircraft, ships, etc.

(2) *The product's link to the conveying system*

Specifically, the question is whether or not the product can be moved independent of the conveyor movement, i.e. if the product can be removed from the conveyor, or else held stationary relative to the conveyor movement. Products that cannot be moved independently of the conveyor movement are referred to as being *Products Fixed*, whereas those with independent movement are called *Products Movable*. Products that are fixed may be rotated in any direction but may not be removed from their respective positions on the conveyor. Large products, such as washers and refrigerators, would be included in this category since these are often simply placed on the conveyor and rely on their weight to maintain their respective locations. Usually, there is no provision for buffer stock between stations in 'Products Fixed' assembly lines where operators

174

generally work under *paced* conditions. On the other hand, 'Products Movable' lines allow buffer stock to accumulate between stations, with the consequence that operators work under *unpaced* conditions.

(3) *The stations*

Stations can be *closed* or *open*. It is undesirable, or else impossible, for operators from adjacent stations to violate the boundaries of a closed station (e.g. the station could be a pit area, a spray paint booth, a dip tank, heating chamber, and so on). Therefore, the times available for completing work tasks allocated to stations in a 'Product Fixed–closed station' line, are constrained. Open station boundaries can be crossed, but the extent of the crossing can be either *restricted* (e.g. due to the limited range of powered tools, materials handling equipment, etc.) or *unrestricted*. In both cases, the requirement is that no interference occurs between adjacent operators. Clearly, there is flexibility in the times available for completing tasks allocated to open stations. A stationary line is an example of an assembly line having open stations, since a product 'completed' at one station can immediately be collected for processing by the downstream operator.

(4) *The launching discipline*

Kilbridge and Wester [4] described two launching disciplines: The first is *fixed rate launching* (FRL), where the launching period γ is the weighted average of the total assembly time for all products to be assembled, over all stations. The second discipline is *variable rate launching* (VRL), where the launching period is the first station's task time of the last product launched, i.e. on completing work on the current product, the first station's operator can immediately begin working on the next product. Selecting between these two launching disciplines, implies that *no* buffer stock exists between work stations. The launching discipline becomes irrelevant to the analysis when buffer storage is allowed. All researches on this topic have adopted the FRL (fixed) discipline for their models, assuming it to be the more practical of the two [1, 2, 5]. Not only is this unproven, but the VRL (Variable) discipline is used quite frequently with manual lines [7].

3. THE MIXED-MODEL SEQUENCING PROBLEM

Two approaches have been proposed so far for solving the mixed-model sequencing problem. One is by Thomopoulos [5, 6] who assumes a given facility (station lengths) and finds the sequence that minimizes the total penalty for a number of "inefficiencies" (operator idle time, utility work, work congestion and deficiency). This approach fails on two counts: it provides no help for determining station lengths (i.e. for a new design), and depending on the assumed dimensions of the station lengths, *any* sequence can be made to look good!

The second approach was proposed by Dar-El and Cother [1]. They select the sequence that minimizes the overall assembly line length for no operator idle time (discussed later) or other inefficiencies. This approach also determines the major facility dimensions (i.e. station lengths). Their method transforms all task processing times into operator movements on the assembly line, so that station lengths can be determined. However, neither approach makes the distinction between two objective criteria which can be identified in mixed-model sequencing problems.

Objective I to find the sequence that minimizes the overall facility length (cf. [1]); and

Objective II to find the sequence that minimized the thruput time (i.e. the typical flow-shop sequencing problem).

The physical description of these two objectives is illustrated in Fig. 1 which shows the operator movement for a closed station assembly line using the FRL discipline. If the conveyor speed is taken as unity, then the task processing times can represent the operator movement, i.e. the movement of the product fixed to the conveyor. Station lengths are then found by placing boundaries on the extreme operator movement locations (e.g. as with station 1 in Fig. 1). Actual station lengths are found as follows:

if

V_c = the conveyor speed (ft/min);

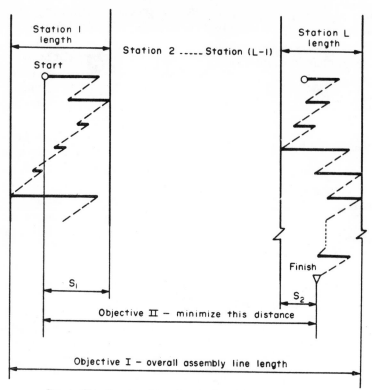

FIG. 1. *Objectives in solving the mixed-model sequencing problems.*

V_0 = the walking speed of the operator (ft/min), i.e. walking upstream to start work on the next product;

L = the number of work stations;

γ = the launching period (min.);

SLONG = the overall line length (min.),

then SLONG* = the actual line length, given by

$$\text{SLONG*} = (\text{SLONG})\, V_c + \frac{\gamma V_c^2}{(V_0 + V_c)}. \quad (1)$$

The second term in the equation accounts for the time taken for operators to walk upstream to start work on the next product.

Minimizing the overall facility length does not necessarily minimize the thruput time. Consequently, a trade-off between these two objectives may need to be considered when determining the minimum cost solution for a particular problem. Figure 2 illustrates the independence of those two objectives. Data for the sequencing problem given in Table 1 includes 3 models involving a total of 7 products to be processed over 2 stations.

$$\text{FRL period } \gamma = \frac{42}{7 \times 2} = 3$$

Figures 2(a) and 2(b) respectively represent the optimal sequence for Objective I (A.A.B.B.B.C) and Objective II (B.A.B.C.B.A.B), and are drawn for the open station case with products fixed to the conveyor (see Section 4). It is observed that overall line lengths and thruput times have different values in the two configurations.

4. A CLASSIFICATION OF MIXED MODEL PROBLEMS

A proposed classification of mixed-model sequencing problems is shown in Fig. 3. It ranges from conveyor lines on which products are fixed with closed stations and no buffer capacity, to lines on which the products are movable, buffer stocks exist (VRL discipline) and station boundaries can be crossed by adjacent operators.

It is observed that when products are not fixed to the conveyance system, there is no need to be concerned with station lengths.

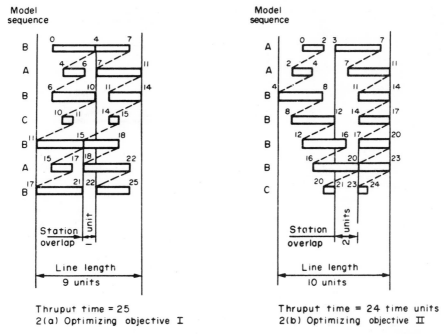

FIG. 2. *Optimal solutions for Objectives I and II—'products fixed-open stations' conditions.*

Whenever a product is completed at one station, it immediately becomes available for the downstream operator, who either straightaway works on it, or else, the product is held in temporary storage. Under these conditions, the station lengths should be determined according to proper workplace design principles and the mixed-model problem is reduced to one of finding a sequence that minimizes the thruput, i.e. the flow-shop sequencing problem.

On the other hand, both objectives apply to problems included in the 'Fixed' product category and cost trade-off conditions between these two objectives may need to be investigated.

Figure 3 also suggests that the station types are either all open, or all closed. This is not the case in practice, since station mixes (i.e.

hybrids) do occur. The case of hybrid lines is discussed later.

5. ANALYSIS OF MIXED-MODEL SEQUENCING PROBLEMS (see Fig. 3)

(a) *Products fixed to conveyor–closed stations– VRL and FRL disciplines*

Both objectives defined earlier apply to this category, but it will be argued that minimizing the facility length is an overiding consideration, thus eliminating the need to consider the influence of thruput times.

The effect of closed stations is to make it *very unlikely* for the completion time of a product on one station, to coincide with the start time for work (on the same product) at the next station. For example, Fig. 4(a) illustrates the closed station version of the case given in Fig. 2(b). The overall line length is

TABLE 1. DATA FOR A SIMPLE MIXED-MODEL SEQUENCING PROBLEM

Model	Products required	Task times allocated to: Station 1	Station 2	Total assembly time
A	2	2	4	12
B	4	4	3	28
C	1	1	1	2
Total	7			42

177

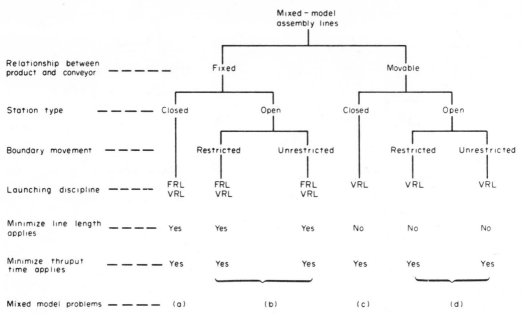

FIG. 3. *A proposed classification of mixed-model sequencing problems.*

increased to 12 units (from 10 units) and the thruput time is increased to 26 time units (from 24 time units). Figure 4(b) shows the Gantt chart version Fig. 4(a) and illustrates the point, that products are unlikely to be worked upon continuously by adjacent operators.

Figure 4(b) also illustrates another feature of mixed-model lines with closed stations. For any station, once work is started, that station remains *continuously* occupied until all products are completed, i.e. with no operator idle time. The price paid for this 'ideal situ-ation' is for station lengths to be increased un-til continuous operations can be maintained for each station.

Where there are many stations in the assem-bly lines, it becomes evident that a reduction in thruput time is better effected by station compression, i.e. by satisfying objective I only. Thus, referring to Fig. 1, to minimize TP (the thruput) means:

$$\text{Min(TP)} = \text{Min}\left\{S_1 + \sum_{i=2}^{L-1} (\text{Station length})_i + S_2\right\} \quad (2)$$

where L is the maximum number of stations.

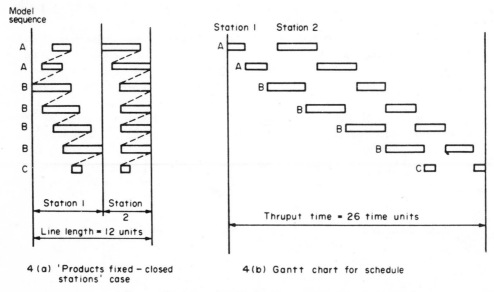

4 (a) 'Products fixed – closed stations' case

4 (b) Gantt chart for schedule

FIG. 4. *Illustrating the 'closed station' version of Fig. 2(b).*

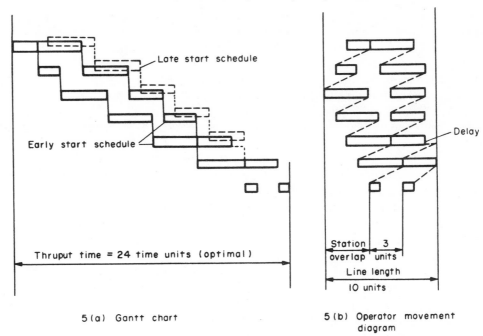

5(a) Gantt chart   5(b) Operator movement diagram

FIG. 5. *Open station version of Fig. 4 (see also Fig. 2(b)).*

Equation 2 is only marginally different from the expression for minimizing SLONG, the overall line length (Objective I), which is given by:

$$\text{Min(SLONG)} = \text{Min}\left\{ \sum_{i=1}^{L} (\text{Station length})_i \right\}. \quad (3)$$

Consequently, it is assumed that the sequencing solution to 'Products Fixed—Closed Stations' problems should only aim at minimizing the overall station length. If L were small (say 4 or 5 stations), then a trade-off between the two objectives may need to be considered, as discussed, under problem (b) below.

The Dar-El–Cother model [1] is suggested as an appropriate method for solving this problem (a brief description is given in the Appendix). Fairly good results were obtained in applying this sequencing model to large lines—the final overall line lengths measuring between 5 and 15% above the appropriate $(\text{SLONG})_{LB}$ dimension. The Dar-El–Cother model can be used with either the FRL or VRL disciplines, there being no evidence to suggest that any one method is superior to the other. However, the FRL discipline is more likely to be used since it better suits the characteristics of several conveyor types (e.g. overhead and tow-line conveyors). It is an appropriate

method to use when several lines are synchronized to feed into a main line which is used for the assembly of some large product (e.g. motor cars). On the other hand, if all models are approximately well balanced over all L stations, then there are advantages in choosing the VRL discipline, since *any* sequence would minimize both the overall line length as well as the thruput time. However, in the final analysis, the choice between the two disciplines may well be determined by the *cost* of the conveyor system.

(b) *Products fixed to conveyor–open stations– VRL and FRL disciplines*

For this category, both Objectives I and II should be considered for determining the assembly sequence, since each operation can begin at its *early start* time. On a Gantt chart this means that all jobs are moved as far to the left as possible as in Fig. 5(a) which illustrates the open station solution for the problem in Fig. 4(b). The solution shown in Figs 5(a) and 5(b) are identical to that in Fig. 2(b), although operations in the latter are drawn at their *late start* positions (as per the dotted schedule in Fig. 5(a). However, the Fig 2(b) version is preferred since it simplifies the analysis for the 'restricted movement' case (discussed later in this section).

The Dar-El–Cother algorithm for open stations by itself is inadequate, since no account is taken of the thruput time. Instead, the following approach is proposed.

First, determine a relationship equating the incremental cost of extending the facility length by one unit, with its equivalent value in reduced thruput time (i.e. increased production).
Let

P = total production required over a planned period;

Δt = time units (e.g. in centi-mins) be the equivalent value in thruput time for one unit of the facility length;

u = the unit labor cost ($/hr);

F = the incremental cost per unit (0.01 V_c if time is measured in centi-mins) of facility length; F includes the additional facility cost and floor space required, as well as the extra power need to drive the system;

$u.P.\ \Delta t/6000$ is the $ savings when TP is reduced by Δt (centi-mins). Then $\Delta t = 6000F/u.P.$

Example:
If

P = 10,000 products, produced over 1 year.

u = $10 per h.

V_c = 4 ft. per min.

Cost per ft. of facility plus floor space taken, is estimated at $2,500.

Then $F = 0.01 \times 4 \times 2500 = \$100$ per 'unit' of facility length. Hence, $\Delta t = 6$ time units (i.e. 0.06 min). Thus the cost of reducing SLONG by 1 unit is equivalent to reducing the thruput time by 6 units

The second step is to generate a number of solutions, each one having an overall line length (SLONG) and its associated thruput time (TP). These are plotted on a 'SLONG–TP' diagram (as in Fig. 6) and the first point that touches an upward moving 'equivalent cost' line provides the minimum cost solution.

Several methods can be used for generating solution sequences—some directed towards meeting Objective I while others, to Objective II. The Dar-El–Cother algorithm for open stations can be used as an example of the first method. Its results may be improved if the 'selection heuristic' can somehow take into account lower bound overall time estimates, such as used in solving flow-shop problems.

Sequences which satisfy Objective II could be obtained through any of the methods used in solving flow-shop problems, though the size of most industrial mixed-model problems may necessitate the use of heuristic methods. Treating mixed-model sequencing as a flow-shop problem, implies that the VRL discipline is utilised. The FRL discipline simply introduces unnecessary constraints [4] which requires that for any product in the sequence at any station i:

$\gamma \leqslant$ average task time for all launched products up to (and including) station i.

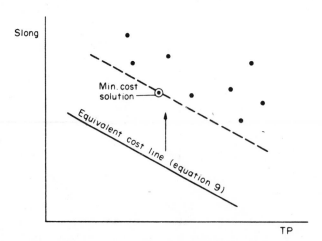

FIG. 6. *Relationship between SLONG and TP*

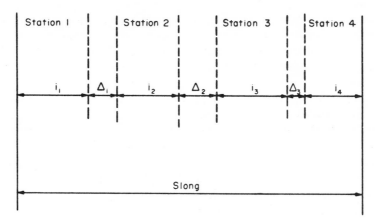

FIG. 7. *Illustrating the 'products fixed–open stations' case.*

The restricted movement case can be readily obtained from the unrestricted movement solution. Simply ensure that the overlap dimension (Δ_i) between adjacent stations (i and ($i + 1$)), is less than or equal to the allowable movement by elongating the line length where necessary. This procedure is illustrated in Fig. 7 which is drawn for a 4 station line.

If Δ_i overlap distance between stations i and ($i + 1$) and design requirements specifies that the allowable movements be d_i, $d_i > 0$, $i = 1, 2 \ldots, (L - 1)$.
Then the 'corrected' overall line length, SLONG', would be:

$$\text{SLONG}' = \text{SLONG} + \sum_{i=1}^{L-1} \Delta_i - d_i$$

(only $\Delta_i > d_i$ terms included) (5)

(c) *Products movable–closed stations–VRL discipline*

The overall line length is not influenced by the sequence in cases where the product is free to move independently of the conveyor. This is because the product can always be held stationary upstream of an occupied work station. Station layouts are therefore designed according to proper plant layout principles.

This category is appropriate to the assembly of smaller and less expensive products which can be held as buffer stock between stations. It also applies to larger products when the conveyor system allows these to be held stationary at each station, e.g. with some types of tow-line conveyors. Closed station conditions (pit area, spray chamber, etc.) may also apply. Best results would be obtained with the VRL disci-

pline. In fact, the FRL discipline would straightaway be 'transformed' to the VRL discipline since the products can move independent of their launched positions on the conveyor.

Assembly sequences for problems in this category are determined according to Objective II which corresponds to flow-shop problems. Thus, any algorithm that can produce good solutions to large flow-shop problems can also be utilized for mixed-model sequencing. One possible outcome is that the solution may require the segregation of all models, i.e. all products of one model assembled first, followed by all products of a second model, and so on. (This is likely to occur when each model is evenly balanced over the L stations.) There could be some advantage to production if this arrangement could be tolerated from marketing and warehousing considerations. This is because the 'learning factor' could play a dominant role in reducing performance time, when all product A's are assembled consecutively as against their being distributed over the production period (a day, 2 days, or, even a week).

The only effect on the analysis that closed stations has, is to increase the thruput times, i.e. to include the time taken for a 'completed' product to arrive at the downstream boundary. Closed stations have no influence on the assembly sequence.

(d) *Products movable–open stations–VRL discipline*

This arrangement gives the maximum flexibility in the design for mixed-model assembly.

Operators can cross upstream stations boundaries to collect and transfer the next product for processing at their own stations. This category also applies to the 'stationary' assembly line.

Stations are again designed according to proper plant layout principles and the assembly sequence selected should minimize the thruput time. The VRL discipline is the only meaningful launching discipline and the only influence that 'restricted operator' movement has, is to lengthen the thruput time, i.e. it does not affect the assembly sequence in any way.

6. HYBRIDS—ASSEMBLY LINES HAVING BOTH OPEN AND CLOSED STATIONS

Mixing open and closed stations in assembly lines does occur in practice. Most stations in such lines have open boundaries except those few that are closed for technological or safety considerations. However, only the 'Product Fixed' category of lines are affected, i.e. Cases (a) and (b).

Hybrid lines can be solved on a cumulative basis, applying the models (a) and (b) to the appropriate places on the assembly line. Consider for example, a 12 station assembly line having the following composition of open and closed stations:

Station:	(1)(2)(3)(4)	[5]	[6)(7)(8]	[9]	[10)(11)(12]
Case:	(b)	(a)	(b)	(a)	(b)

Key: [ ] closed station. [ ) closed upstream, open downstream. ( ) open station. ( ] open upstream, closed downstream.

Then the lower bound of the overall assembly line, $(SLONG)_{LB}$ would comprise the following terms:

$$(SLONG)_{LB} = (LB)_{1 \to 4} + (LB)_5 + (LB)_{6 \to 8} + (LB)_9 + (LB)_{10 \to 12}$$

The approach proposed in problem (b) should be used for generating several solution sequences which are evaluated to obtain the least cost solution.

Choosing the launching discipline is not so simple. Keeping in mind that hybrids apply only to the 'products fixed' category, it is more likely that industrial practice would lean towards employing the FRL discipline,

whereas it is suggested that the VRL discipline could produce more efficient solutions. However, the ultimate choice is more likely to be made on the basis of a cost analysis of alternative conveyor systems.

7. DISCUSSIONS AND CONCLUSIONS

It is hoped that this paper has succeeded in incorporating all mixed-model assembly line types likely to be found in practice. Illustrations of the various assembly line categories were given and their behaviour analysed. It was shown that two design criteria exist in mixed-model sequencing problems:

● to find the sequence that minimizes the overall facility length

● to find the sequence that minimizes the thruput time.

Although the analysis for the different catergories have led to possible solution methods, more importantly, it has provided an insight as to what design decisions ought to be made in the first place. The designer should initially enquire whether a 'Product Movable' arrangement (models (c) and (d)) is feasible, since the resulting layout is likely to be far less expensive than for the 'Product Fixed' arrangement. Also, the possibility of a buffer stock occurring with 'Product Movable' lines means that a shorter cycle time can be used.

However, the greatest advantage for using 'Product Movable' lines lie in its flexibility to cope with changes in production, since the layout is *independent* of the sequence. This is not the case with 'Product Fixed' lines, which requires a 'new solution' to be produced for each production change.

If the product *must* be fixed to the conveyor, then as many stations as possible should have open boundaries, with the VRL discipline selected as the preferred launching system. These design factors are summarised in Table 2.

Research efforts are needed in two main areas (marked ** in the table):

● In formalising a method for solving the sequencing problem in 'Product Fixed–Open Station' lines (including hybrids)

TABLE 2. SUMMARY OF DESIGN FACTORS

Station type (case)	Products fixed		Products movable	
	Closed (a)	Open (b)	Closed (c)	Open (d)
Launching system	Fixed rate Launching(FRL) or Variable Rate Launching(VRL)	FRL or VRL†	VRL†	VRL†
Movement across boundaries	—	Restricted or unrestricted	—	Restricted or unrestricted†
Sequencing criteria	Min. line length	Min. line length and min. thruput time	Min. thruput time	Min. thruput time
Relative Facility Length (RFL)	$(RFL)_a$	$(RFL)_b < (RFL)_a$	$(RFL)_c < (RFL)_b$	$(RFL)_d = (RFL)_c$
Relative Thruput Time (TP)	TP_a	$TP_b < TP_a$	$TP_c < TP_b$	$TP_d < TP_c$ (marginally)
Flexibility in coping with Production changes	None	None	Maximum	Maximum
Preference based on Total Cost	2nd Preference (closed stations used only when essential)		1st Preference (closed stations used only when essential)	
Future research effort	*	**	**	

† Preferred

● In developing inexpensive means for transposing 'Product Fixed' designs into the 'Product Movable' mode.

Of less urgency, though still important, is the search for a more efficient solution to the 'Product Fixed–Closed Station' category (marked * in the table). Attention could also be directed towards tackling problems in which the overall line length is given, as input data. This problem is only relevant to the 'Products Fixed–Open Stations' category (case (b)) and to hybrid lines (case (a) would be insolvable and cases (c) and (d) are not affected). It is hoped that this paper enhances the contribution that industrial engineering practitioners can make to designers of mixed-model assembly lines.

REFERENCES

1. DAR-EL EM & COTHER RF (1975) Assembly line sequencing for model-mix. *Int. J. Prod. Res.* **13**(5), 463–477.
2. DAR-EL EM & CUCUI S (1977) Optimal mixed-model sequencing for balanced assembly lines. *Omega* **5**(3), 333–342.
3. DAR-EL EM & NADIVI A (1977) A mixed-model sequencing application. *Technion-III*. Operations Research, Statistics and Economics Mineograph Series No. 193.
4. KILBRIDGE MD & WESTER L (1963) The assembly line model-mix sequencing problem. *Proc. of the Third Int. Conf. Op. Res.* English Universities Press; (Paris: Dunod Editeur).
5. THOMOPOULOS NT (1967) Line balancing sequencing for mixed-model assembly. *Mgmt Sci.* **14**(2), 59–75.
6. THOMOPOULOS NT (1970) Mixed-model line balancing with smooth station assignments. *Mgmt Sci.* **16**(9), 593–603.
7. WILD R (1972) *Mass Production Management.* John Wiley, Chichester, UK.

ADDRESS FOR CORRESPONDENCE: *Professor Ezey M Dar-El, Technion, Israel Institute of Technology, Haifa, Israel.*

APPENDIX

The following is a brief description of the Dar-El–Cother method for determining the assembly sequence in mixed-model problems.

The method starts by making the length of each station equal to its lower bound. Products are then sequenced in a specific manner which always aims at minimizing the sum of station length increments. The lower bound $(LB)_i$

for each station i is found as follows:

let

$\bar{t}_i$ be the largest task time allocated to station i.

t_i the smallest task time allocated to station i.

γ the FRL period.

T_i the total work allocated to station i.

P the total number of products to be assembled over the shift (or planned period).

Then three lower bounds can be defined:

$$(lb)_1 = 2\gamma - t_i \qquad (A1)$$

$$(lb)_2 = \bar{t}_i \qquad (A2)$$

$$(lb)_3 = t_i + |T_i - \gamma \cdot p| \qquad (A3)$$

Then $(LB)_i = \max \{(2\gamma - t_i), \bar{t}_i, (t_i + |T_i - \gamma p|)\}$ (A4)

$(SLONG)_{LB}$, the lower bound for the overall assembly line length is then given by:

$$(SLONG)_{LB} = \sum_{i=1}^{L} (LB)_i \qquad (A5)$$

The third lower bound $(lb)_3$, only applies when $T_i \neq \gamma P$ (Dar-El and Nadivi [3]) implying that the starting position of the operator in station i *does not* coincide with his finishing position (when work on all P products are completed).

Selecting candidates for the sequence depends on a 'Selection Heuristic' which is briefly described below:

If $M = (M_1 : M_2 : \ldots : M_k)$ is the 'proportional vector' between models $1, 2, \ldots, k$ that are to be assembled, then the model selected for the next place on the sequence should aim at maintaining as near as possible, the vector M among the pool of products yet to be allocated.

Operator Scheduling

ELBRIDGE GERRY KEITH

Illinois Bell Telephone Company
225 W. Randolph Street - HQ 15C
Chicago, Illinois 60606

Abstract: The development of mechanized scheduling of operators at Illinois Bell Telephone Company is discussed in this paper. The solution of the scheduling problem using integer linear programming was uneconomical so that a two step procedure was developed to solve the problem. First, the optimal solution with fractional operators is found by linear programming. Then a heuristic algorithm is used to find an integer solution close to this optimal solution. This method is in use at all Illinois Bell Telephone operator offices.

■ In the telephone business, providing the proper number of operators to handle customer calls for long distance, directory assistance, and other services is essential to the twin requirements of customer service and efficiency. A daily forecast of quarter-hour operator requirements is made for each operator office. Then a schedule of operator work-hours or tours is developed that closely matches the forecasted quarter-hour requirements. The task of drawing a good daily work schedule for the operator office is difficult, since an operator may work any one of thousands of combinations of start times, lunch times, and early and late relief (break) periods. The allowable combinations of work-hours or tours are determined from sets of rules described in the union contracts and Illinois Bell practices.

The operator scheduling problem is the selection of operator tours to closely match the operator requirements.

The manual solution broke the problem into two parts. A basic schedule was drawn to match 70% to 90% of the expected requirements. This basic schedule would remain in effect for up to six months. Each day a new supplemental schedule would be drawn to match the difference between the latest forecast and the basic schedule. The manual method depended on the skill of the operator office employee, and the results were often adversely affected by the basic schedule, which determined most of the schedule, but was based on a traffic distribution several months old. The mechanization of the scheduling process eliminated the basic schedule. It also resulted in savings involving schedule preparation and savings due to more efficient schedules.

Linear Programming Model

The initial method used to solve this problem was integer linear programming. The forecasted quarter-hourly operator requirements were taken as the minimum number of operators to be on duty each quarter-hour. This model takes the form:

Integer Programming Model

Minimize
$$Z = \sum_{j=1}^{n} C_j X_j \tag{1}$$

Subject to $\sum_{j=1}^{n} X_j a_{jr} \geq f_r \qquad r = 1,96 \tag{2}$

X_j non-negative integer for $j=1,n$ $\tag{3}$

Received December 1977; revised August, October and November 1978. Paper was handled by Development and Implementation Department.

Where

   Z is the objective function,

   n is the number of permissible tours or individual operator work-hours,

   C_j is the cost, which can be the number of hours worked, the daily operator wage or the desirability associated with the jth tour,

   X_j is the number of operators working the jth tour,

   a_{jr} is the element of the zero-one matrix describing when the jth tour is on duty for the rth quarter-hour with a one entry, and

   f_r is the forecasted number of operators required in the rth quarter-hour.

During the testing phase of this model, it was determined that integer programming failed to produce operator schedules at reasonable costs [2].

The next approach was to apply a heuristic rounding procedure to the optimal, non-integer linear programming solution of the above problem. The heuristic algorithm consists of two parts. The first part rounds all fractional activities in the original solution to the closest integer. For some unknown reason, this solution often results in too few tours, since, in a majority of cases, most of the fractions are less than one-half. The second portion of the heuristic algorithm attempts to add or remove tours from the initially rounded solution. The effect of adding a tour is computed for each unique tour in the original linear programming basis. If any tour reduces the amount of shortage between the forecast and the schedule, it is a candidate to enter the solution. A slight change was made in the problem definition to select among possible candidates. The operator office management may select the minimum number of quarter-hours of shortage a tour must cover before being entered into the solution. The tour with the maximum reduction in shortage is used unless it does not cover the minimum number of quarter-hours specified by the user. If more than one tour is equally qualified, that tour is selected whose choice would result in creating the lowest sum of squares of surplus quarter-hours.

The addition criterion is reapplied until no tour can be added. A subtraction routine is then applied. The subtraction routine logically removes each tour in the solution and determines whether it should be added back according to the above logic. If more than one tour may be removed from the solution, the tour that introduces the smallest number of quarter-hours of shortage and provides the greatest reduction of the sum of squares of surplus quarter-hours is removed from the solution.

Field Testing

After the completion of the first economical schedules, the quality of the schedules was discussed with the operator office management. The operator office or "field" management indicated that the so-called requirements are treated only as estimates and some shortage is acceptable. Two parameters were added to the rounding routine to restrict the amount of shortage. The first parameter forces the addition of tours until the acceptable level of shortage is reached. The second parameter gives the amount of shortage that a tour should reduce in order to be economically justified.

A serious problem was the quality of the manually forecasted operator requirements. A mechanized forecasting program was written to improve the quality of the forecasted operator requirements. The initial program estimated both the daily traffic volume into the operator office and its distribution pattern. A comparison of the mechanized estimation of daily work volumes with the manual estimates revealed that the manual estimates were more accurate. The manual method was better able to consider the numerous periodic activities that affect traffic volumes such as school calendars, religious calendars, and special events. The program was revised to accept manual input of daily work volume estimates, distribute work volumes throughout the day, and convert the quarter-hourly work volumes into the number of operators required each quarter-hour. Modified linear interpolation was used to convert the half-hourly measurements into quarter-hourly forecasts. The daily distribution factors are maintained using an adaptive exponential smoothing technique. The forecasting program incorporating these features provides the accurate forecasted requirements necessary to provide good quality schedules.

Another serious problem with the quality of the schedules remaining at this point was the distribution of the surplus. The initial linear programming solution tended to bunch the surplus so that one quarter-hour would have a surplus of seven operators while the adjoining quarter-hours had a surplus of only one operator even though it was possible to spread the surplus evenly while maintaining the same value of the objective function. Analysis of this problem revealed that the initial model form was unsatisfactory and caused Illinois Bell to investigate alternative model forms.

Second Linear Programming Model

The search for a model to more evenly distribute the surplus and shortage led to the introduction of a major revision of the initial linear programming model. The linear programming model was changed to:

Second Linear Programming Model

Minimize

$$Z = \sum_{j=1}^{n} C_j X_j + \sum_{r=1}^{96} (CLU\,LU_r + CLB\,LB_r + CUU\,UU_r$$

$$+ CUB\,UB_r) \qquad (4)$$

Subject to

$$\sum_{j=1}^{n} X_j a_{jr} + LU_r + LB_r - UU_r - UB_r = f_r \qquad r = 1,96 \qquad (5)$$

$$LB_r \leqslant L_r \qquad r = 1,96 \qquad (6)$$

$$UB_r \leqslant U_r \qquad r = 1,96 \qquad (7)$$

$$X_j \geqslant 0 \qquad j = 1,n \qquad (8)$$

$$LU_r, LB_r, UU_r, UB_r \geqslant 0 \qquad r = 1,96 \qquad (9)$$

where

Z is the objective function,

n is the number of operator work tours,

C_j is the cost associated with the jth tour,

CLU is the arbitrary cost associated with the unbounded slack variables,

CLB is the arbitrary cost associated with the bounded slack variables,

CUU is the arbitrary cost associated with the unbounded surplus variables,

CUB is the arbitrary cost associated with the bounded surplus variables,

X_j is the number of operators working the jth tour,

a_{jr} is the element of the zero-one matrix describing when the jth tour is on duty for the rth quarter-hour with a one entry,

LU_r is the unbounded slack variable for the rth quarter-hour,

LB_r is the bounded slack variable for the rth quarter-hour,

UU_r is the unbounded surplus variable for the rth quarter-hour,

UB_r is the bounded surplus variable for the rth quarter-hour,

f_r is the forecasted requirement for the rth quarter-hour,

L_r is the lower bound of the bounded slack variable for the rth quarter-hour, and

U_r is the upper bound for the bounded surplus variable.

This model controls the amount of surplus and shortage for each quarter-hour using the four slack and surplus variables. The bounded slack and surplus variables form a tolerance band. If the tolerance band for all quarter-hours is three operators for the surplus variable and two operators for the slack variable, the solution tends to keep surpluses to three operators or less and shortages to two operators or less because the unbounded slack and surplus variables always have a higher cost than the corresponding bounded variable. The costs used in this model are 100 for both bounded variables, 200 for the unbounded surplus variable and 300 for the unbounded slack variables. The boundaries of the bands, L_r and U_r, are controlled by the user. The offices are better able to administer the shortage and surplus when it occurs during certain periods of the day. When the surplus or shortage occur during the late evening, night, or very early morning, no adjustment can be made in the operator schedule, since supervision may not be present. The size of the operator team also affects whether a shortage or surplus is acceptable. A shortage of two operators when four are scheduled is unacceptable while a shortage of two when 200 are scheduled might be acceptable.

Surpluses that occur in the late afternoon, for example, can be force-adjusted by allowing operators to volunteer to leave early without pay. Similarly, shortage can be force-adjusted by scheduling overtime. The relative amount of surplus to shortage and the placement of that surplus and shortage can be controlled by the setting of the boundaries of the tolerance bands. The major success of the bands has been the elimination of bunched surplus and shortage. It is not practical for the office to force-adjust when the amount of shortage or surplus varies significantly from quarter-hour to quarter-hour, but force-adjustment is effective when the surplus or shortage extends an hour or longer.

The tolerance bands were not successful in removing substantial natural periods of surplus or shortage that were created by the contractual tour limitations and by the traffic pattern. For example, if surpluses occur in the early morning and late afternoon and shortages occur during the late morning busy period, these surpluses and shortages cannot both be eliminated from the solution with the given traffic distribution and contractual tour limitations.

The bands work due to a two-tiered pricing. Inside the bands, a shortage or surplus has a lower cost. These slack and surplus variables are bounded so that only the first few units of slack or surplus can enter the solution at the lower cost. After the upper bound is reached, any additional surplus or shortage brings the higher unbounded slack or surplus variable into the solution. Thus, the isolated bunching of surplus is reduced, since a lower cost solution is achieved by spreading the surplus over several quarter-hours in order to stay inside the upper bounds. The two-tiered pricing is better than a single bounded surplus or slack variable, since, if the upper bounds are not properly chosen for the single slack or surplus variables, the solution would be infeasible. It is impossible to continually review these fixed upper bounds individually by operator office and maintain them in view of traffic changes and tour limitation changes, which seem to occur with every new contract agreement.

The operation of the system was changed so that an operator office can access the system from its remote location rather than via a batch program run at the computer center. The time sharing programs allow the operator office the flexibility to modify the computer-drawn schedules. An allocation routine was added to the scheduling system. A group of offices or complex has the scheduling system treat the complex as one entity and produces a combined schedule for all offices. The allocation program splits this overall schedule into separate sub-schedules for each office according to the office's hours of operation, operator force size and number of installed operator positions.

Improvement in Computational Efficiency

The linear programming solution requires a significant amount of computer time, since each operator office (there were over ninety Illinois Bell offices) uses a different schedule every day. Several different linear programming solution strategies were tried in an attempt to improve the solution time. A previous solution was used as the starting basis along with several dual and primal solution strategies. Unfortunately, starting with the standard artificial basis yielded the fastest solution time. Another solution strategy was to randomize the variables and use the multiple cycling and pricing techniques of the Mathematical Programming System (MPS) from IBM [3]. No significant improvement was found. Finally, restructuring the linear programming model in conjunction with some special solution strategies greatly reduced the solution time. Mr. R. Frank from the IBM Scientific Center suggested transforming the linear programming matrix to make the data matrix more sparse. The transformation consists of premultiplying both sides of the system of constraint equations (5) for the second linear programming model by a nonsingular matrix consisting of ones along the diagonal and minus ones above the diagonal. The resultant constraint equation becomes:

$$\sum_{j=1}^{n} X_j a_{j1} + LU_1 + LB_1 - UU_1 - UB_1 = f_1 \qquad (10)$$

$$\sum_{j=1}^{n} X_j(a_{jr} - a_{jr-1}) + LU_r - LU_{r-1} + LB_r - LB_{r-1} - UU_r + UU_{r-1}$$

$$-UB_r + UB_{r-1} = f_r - f_{r-1} \quad r = 2,96 . \quad (11)$$

All other equations remain the same. The constraint equation for the first quarter-hour is identical while in subsequent quarter-hours ($r = 2,96$) the a_{jr} and slack and surplus variables are replaced with the difference between the current value and the value for the previous quarter-hour. This form produces more zero elements in the a matrix since operators are on duty for four to eighteen quarter-hours consecutively. Each consecutive string is reduced from four to eighteen ones to a one and a minus one. The slack and surplus variables are increased from a single one to a one and a minus one. The net result is to reduce the number of non-zero elements

in the data matrix to one-third of the previous total. This sparsity reduces the time per iteration by 30%. However, the amount of time to reach a feasible solution was increased by about ten-fold, since the form of the data matrix no longer contained the explicit shortage and surplus variables which provide a simple method for achieving a feasible solution. The net result of the increased feasibility time and the reduced iteration time was an increase in solution time. To counteract this increase, a feasible starting basis of shortage and surplus variables was inserted which totally eliminated the solution time to become feasible and in addition, the amount of iteration time during feasibility was reduced slightly. The overall reduction was about 50% in solution time.

The restructured model essentially schedules the net change in operators for each quarter-hour. Each constraint equation (11), except the first, represents the number of operators coming on duty minus the number leaving the switchboard. The right-hand side of the constraint equation (11) is the number of additional operators required in the current quarter-hour. The slack variables are represented by a phantom operator coming on duty for one quarter-hour, while the surplus variables are represented by a phantom operator who leaves the switchboard for a quarter-hour. Thus the entries in the a matrix represent the number of operators entering or leaving the switchboard. The first period is unchanged so that the base level of operators can be established.

Relief Shifting

Another aspect of the scheduling problem was investigated in order to reduce the total solution time as well as to improve the quality of the solution. A major revision was made in the heuristic rounding routine. Another step was added to this procedure which adjusts the placement of the operator reliefs. The adjustment step actually consists of two procedures. After the completion of the rounding routine, the first procedure completely reassigns the reliefs without regard to their initial placement. The second procedure adjusts the placement of reliefs in an attempt to better match the required number of operators. The detailed procedures are Illinois Bell proprietary information and will not be discussed in detail here. Because the reliefs are readjusted, the tour matrix can be smaller since only one relief combination need be provided for each tour. Smaller data matrices can be used and still produce schedules of higher quality.

Operation of the Scheduling System

The scheduling software at Illinois Bell Telephone is on a combination of inhouse time sharing and batch operations. The operator office forecasts its operator requirements using programs running on the time sharing system. After the office reviews the forecast, it stores the forecasted requirements for overnight schedule drawing and stores any specific tours that the office management wishes to include in the schedule.

The forecasting generally occurs on Friday, and the batch linear programming run is made over the weekend when the computer time is more available. The linear programming code uses a linear programming matrix containing a list of tours for a specific operator office or group of offices. The following Monday the operator office clerk retrieves the schedules and reviews them with local management. Some tours are added to the schedule to care for expected absence, etc. These adjustments may be made Monday afternoon or Tuesday and the revised schedule for the following week listed.

The list of tours and the boundaries of the bands, which form the linear programming matrix, vary between operator offices due to differing office hours and union agreements. The tour files are maintained by staff personnel along with the boundaries of the tolerance bands, since these data are not frequently changed and clerical turnover in the operator office makes it difficult to keep the operator office clerk trained on the infrequently executed update programs.

The packaging of the scheduling programs was vital to the success of the scheduling system. The programs must be easily run by operator office clerks who are physically remote from the support groups and may not have been fully trained.

Program Availability

After Illinois Bell had successfully completed the development of the scheduling programs for the initial linear programming model, these programs (excluding the forecasting program) were given to AT&T. These original programs ran on a batch computer rather than interactively from the operator offices.

AT&T repackaged these programs and released them to several outside commercial time sharing vendors. These vendors, including McAuto, CSC, and GE, modified and added their own enhancements to the scheduling programs. These versions are currently available from various vendors.

Future Developments

A mechanized assignment system which associates a specific operator with each tour, and a payroll system are being developed to further process the scheduling output. The assignment system will list the appropriate operator's name beside the list of hours and will produce many other reports. The assignment system has required the use of many mathematical programming techniques. The assignment will become the basic data for payroll.

Conclusion

The operator scheduling system has been successfully used in all Illinois Bell operator offices for several years. In order to validate the high regard of the mechanized schedules by the operator office managers a goodness-of-fit test was made comparing the forecasts and schedules. That test indicated that mechanized schedules have a substantially better fit to the forecast than manual schedules. All other Bell System Operating Companies are either using other versions of the same linear programming formulation or using an iterative network algorithm and a different heuristic rounding algorithm developed by Bell Telephone Laboratories [1]. The network algorithm was developed to permit the scheduling on minicomputers, which did not have efficient linear programming codes.

The forecasting and scheduling system has resulted in better utilization of operators, in clerical savings, and has provided a planning tool. The improved scheduling efficiency results in annual operator savings of two and one-half percent or about one and one-half million dollars. The clerical savings are ninety thousand dollars annually. The mechanized scheduling has provided a planning tool to estimate the number of operators necessary under various assumptions. The system has been used to price out changes in work-hours and to determine office sizes and hours. These savings are for Illinois Bell Telephone Company and do not include the savings for other companies.

Acknowledgment

I would like to especially thank Mary Haugk of Illinois Bell Operator Services, who for many years suggested improvements in the system and worked with the operator offices to make the system implementation a success. A special thanks is given to James Kennedy who began the project and directed the effort and to Gary Gilleland and George Sereikas who made numerous significant contributions to the system. I would also like to thank the many others in Operator Services, Interdepartmental Systems and Management Sciences who made helpful suggestions in the development and implementation of the system. Finally, I would like to thank the referees and others who made helpful suggestions regarding the exposition of this paper.

References

[1] Segal, M., "The Operator-Scheduling Problem: A Network-Flow Approach," *Operations Research*, **22**, 808-823 (1974).

[2] Woolsey, R.E.D., "A Candle to Saint Jude, or Four Real World Applications of Integer Programming," *Interfaces*, **2**, 20-22 (1972).

[3] *Mathematical Programming System—Extended (MPSX) and Generalized Upper Bounding (GUB) Program Description* SH20-0968, IBM, White Plains, New York (1972).

Mr. Elbridge Gerry Keith is a Staff Statistician in the Management Sciences Division of Illinois Bell Telephone Company. His current research interests include work measurement and simulation studies. He received his BA degree from Lawrence University and his MS from Iowa State University. He is a member of ASA.

Efficient Heuristic Solutions to an Airline Crew Scheduling Problem

EDWARD K. BAKER
Department of Management Science
School of Business Administration
University of Miami
Coral Gables, Florida

LAWRENCE D. BODIN
College of Business and Management
University of Maryland
College Park, Maryland 20742

WILLIAM F. FINNEGAN
Manager of Flight Operations Planning
Federal Express Corporation
Memphis, Tennessee

RONNY J. PONDER
Director of Operations Research and Planning
Federal Express Corporation
Memphis, Tennessee

Abstract: This paper presents an application of efficient, heuristic solution procedures to the airline crew scheduling problem of the Federal Express Corporation. It is demonstrated that near-optimal solutions to this class of very large airline crew scheduling problems may be obtained by using heuristic procedures similar to those used in vehicle routing and scheduling. As a result of this research, the procedures developed here have been implemented and are in use, on a monthly basis, at the Federal Express Corporation.

■ This paper presents an application of efficient, heuristic solution procedures to the airline crew scheduling problem at the Federal Express Corporation of Memphis, Tennessee. Federal Express is an airline which specializes in the overnight, door-to-door transportation of small packages. In order to provide this service for the major cities in the United States, Federal Express operates its own fleet of jet aircraft from a single hub at Memphis. Each evening, packages, which are collected in the field, are flown to Memphis, sorted, and flown on to their destination for delivery the next morning. The assignment of crews to the required aircraft flight legs comprises the Federal Express crew scheduling problem.

The Federal Express Corporation is one of the most innovative and fastest growing organizations in the package airline industry. In order to provide a rapid response to demand for its services, Federal Express required the development of an effective computer based system for scheduling their air crews. Due to operational deadlines, it was desired that near-optimal solutions to very large (ap-

proximately 1,000 flight) crew scheduling problems be obtained in less than one hour of in-house (Burroughs 6700) computer time. These and other factors, discussed in detail below, suggested the investigation of efficient, heuristic solution procedures. The results of this study are presented in this paper.

Description of the Problem

The airline crew scheduling problem is described in detail by Arabeyre, et al. [1]. Briefly, the problem assumes that there exists a fixed set of aircraft flight legs, each of which must be assigned a crew. (A flight leg is an airborne trip between an origin-destination city pair.) Among the cities visited on the aircraft itineraries are one or more cities designated as crew bases, or domiciles. Each crew schedule, or "pairing" as they are called, consists of a sequence of flight legs, the first of which originates at the crew base and the last of which terminates at the crew base.

In addition, the pairings must be formed so that no FAA, labor, or company regulations are violated. These regulations impact the formation of the crew schedules by governing maximum flight hours, maximum duty hours, minimum crew rest, and other factors which affect the feasibility of linking two or more flight legs into a sequence which forms

Received March 1978; revised October 1978. Paper was handled by Applied Optimization Department. Paper was presented at the ORSA/TIMS/AIIE Distribution Conference, Hilton Head, SC, February 1978.

a pairing. Company policies and labor agreements may also affect the cost of each crew pairing by providing minimum pay guarantees for the crew schedules. These minimum guarantees, which supersede actual flight time as a base for cost calculations, may be related to the number of duty periods on a pairing or to the time the crew is required to be away from its home base. Within this framework, the airline crew scheduling problem is then to find the set of legal crew pairings which covers every flight leg at a minimum total cost.

The existing crew scheduling problem at Federal Express has several facets which distinguish it from other airline crew scheduling problems. First, all crews are based at a single crew domicile at Memphis, Tennessee. As a result, all crew pairing must originate and terminate in Memphis. Second, crew personnel are paid per time credited for operating specific pairings, rather than by salary. Hence the minimization of the number of crews required over the scheduling period is not a consideration. Additionally, the current crew scheduling problem at Federal Express does not place a maximum or a minimum value on the total number of flight hours which can be operated from the single crew base at Memphis. The total number of flight hours at a base or domicile can be a major constraint when there are crews based at more than one domicile.

Survey of the Literature

The airline crew scheduling problem can be formulated as the following set partitioning problem:

$$\text{Minimize } Z = \sum_{j=1}^{N} c_j\, x_j$$

$$\text{s.t. } \sum_{j=1}^{N} a_{ij}\, x_j = b_i, \qquad i = 1,2,\ldots, m \text{ flight legs}$$

where:

N = the number of legal pairings that can be enumerated

c_j = the cost of pairing j

$$x_j = \begin{cases} 1, & \text{if pairing } j \text{ is used in the solution} \\ 0, & \text{otherwise} \end{cases}$$

$$a_{ij} = \begin{cases} 1, & \text{if flight leg } i \text{ is on pairing } j \\ 0, & \text{otherwise} \end{cases}$$

$$b_i = \begin{cases} \text{the number of crews required on flight leg } i; \text{ typi-} \\ \text{cally } b_i = 1 \text{ for all } i. \end{cases}$$

In this formulation, the deadheading of crews is not allowed. The solution is a subset of the pairings. This subset covers each flight leg exactly once and minimizes cost.

The solution procedure for the set partitioning formulation of the airline crew scheduling problem is a three-stage process: enumeration, reduction, and selection. In the enumeration stage, all feasible pairings, the columns of the constraint matrix, are generated. This is accomplished by a straight forward enumeration procedure. Due to the combinatorial nature of the problem, however, one finds that a problem of 100 flights may generate several thousand columns; a problem of 1,000 flight legs may generate several million feasible pairings. As a result, the reduction stage of the solution procedure is applied within the enumeration process in an attempt to reduce the problem size and total time required to obtain a solution. The reduction procedures may be either objective or subjective. Objective reduction procedures, as in Balinski [2] or Garfinkel and Nemhauser [9], use both dominance and logical comparisons to reduce the number of pairings. Subjective reductions may include limits on the maximum length of a pairing or elimination of all pairings with layovers at an undesirable station. These procedures can be very effective in reducing the size of the problem. Kolner [14] notes that after application of the reduction procedures, a problem with 100-120 flight legs may generate only 2,000-3,000 pairings, as opposed to the original hundred thousand.

The final stage of the set partitioning solution procedure is the selection of those pairings (columns) which satisfy all the constraints at a minimum cost. A comprehensive survey of solution procedures for the set partitioning problem is given by Balas and Padberg [2]. Various solution techniques which have been applied specifically to the airline crew scheduling problem include cutting plane algorithms [11, 13, 18], implicit enumeration procedures [17, 19], a group theoretic approach [6, 23], and various heuristics [21, 22]. Although the computational success of each procedure may vary, the experience of American Airlines [6], as shown in Table 1, provides a good overall summary of the enumeration-reduction-selection solution procedure to the airline crew scheduling problem.

Table 1: Summary of Experience at American Airlines			
Number of Daily Flights	Estimated number of pairings	Approximate IBM 360/65 time to Generate pairings	Solve problem
6	18	1 sec	2 sec
25	128	10 sec	25 sec
125	350,000	40 mins	2 hrs
600	2,000,000	4 hrs	30 hrs

Proposed Solution Procedures

In this paper, vehicle routing and scheduling heuristics are proposed as possible solution procedures for the Federal Express airline crew scheduling problem. Cassidy and Bennett [7], Christofides [8], Golden [10], and others have demonstrated the effectiveness of heuristic techniques in "solving" large, complex routing and scheduling problems. This paper demonstrates that the application of heuristic procedures to the airline crew scheduling problem can provide near-optimal solutions in a reasonable amount of computer time.

The interpretation of the airline crew scheduling problem as a vehicle routing or scheduling problem is very intuitive. Let each flight leg represent a customer whose demand is equal to the number of crews the flight leg requires. Let each crew be a delivery vehicle, of some finite capacity, able to deliver only one unit to each customer visited. Each crew base will correspond to a vehicle depot, hence each pairing will correspond to a vehicle tour originating and terminating at its depot. The problem is to find the minimum cost set of vehicle routes which meet the customer demands and satisfy all route constraints (i.e., FAA, labor, and company regulations). Strictly speaking, the crew pairing problem is more closely aligned with the problems of vehicle scheduling than those of vehicle routing. The presence of the time element which establishes precedence relationships for sequencing the flight legs is much more directly related to scheduling than to routing. There are, however, insights to be gained from either interpretation. It is noted that a concise formulation of the vehicle scheduling problem is as a set partitioning problem (see Balinski and Quandt, [4]), however, almost all large scale vehicle routing or scheduling problems reported solved in the literature use heuristic rather than exact methods.

The solution procedures developed in this paper fall into three categories: pairing construction, pairing improvement, and composite procedures. The pairing construction procedures use the flight leg data generated by the aircraft routing as input and construct a feasible set of crew pairings. The pairing improvement procedures use a feasible set of crew pairings as input and attempt to generate an improved set of pairings. The construction of an initial feasible solution and the application of one or more improvement procedures is defined as a composite procedure.

The pairing construction procedures utilized in this research are adaptations of the scheduling heuristics proposed by Bodin, Kydes, and Rosenfield [5]. In their paper on automated manpower scheduling, the authors propose several scheduling mechanisms which may be useful in solving problems classically formulated and solved as set partitioning problems. The scheduling mechanism implemented here is a variation of what is termed the concurrent scheduler.

The concurrent scheduler begins by extracting all crew base departure flights from the flight leg data file. Each of the base departures is used as a seed to begin a crew pairing. Each unassigned flight leg is then selected, in order of departure time, to be assigned to a partially completed pairing. A candidate flight leg may be assigned to a partially formed pairing if the assignment will not violate any of the FAA, labor, or company regulations. Therefore, the concurrent scheduler tests each of the work rules for the proposed assignment of the given flight leg to the partially formed pairing. If one of the work rules is violated, the proposed assignment is declared infeasible. The candidate flight leg is then considered for assignment to the next partial pairing. Typically, a flight leg may be legally assigned to several partially formed pairings. The selection of the most effective assignment is determined by utilizing one of the various criteria for assignment cited below. If the flight

leg cannot be legally assigned to any partial pairing, then this pairing goes to the bottom of the pairings list to be handled in the following week. Since no deadheading is allowed and each city has the same number of arrivals as departures, each pairing is guaranteed to return to the home domicile of the crews albeit several weeks from when they departed their home base.

The criteria for assignment which provided the most consistent results are described in detail below:

a. First feasible assignment—

The next candidate flight leg is assigned to the first feasible pairing which is found. If no feasible fit is found, the arrival and departure times of the flight leg are incremented by one week (the scheduling period) and the flight leg is placed at the end of the unassigned flight leg list.

b. First feasible assignment with the same aircraft flight number—

The next candidate flight leg is assigned to the first feasible pairing for which the aircraft flight number of the partially formed pairing and the candidate flight leg are the same.

c. First crew in takes first flight out—

The next candidate flight leg is assigned to the pairing for which the time between the departure of the candidate flight leg and the arrival of last flight leg on the pairing is a maximum. This criterion uses a first in first out procedure to assign flight legs to the crew pairing that has been waiting the longest.

d. Last crew in takes first flight out—

The next candidate flight leg is assigned to the pairing for which the time between the departure of the candidate flight leg and the arrival of the last flight leg on the pairing is a minimum over all pairings considered. This criterion minimizes the time each crew is on the ground by assigning flight legs to pairings so that the last crew in takes the first flight out.

e. Minimum cost assignment—

The next candidate flight leg is assigned to the pairing for which the total additional cost for handling the leg is a minimum over all pairings considered.

The results of using these criteria to form initial feasible solutions are shown in Table 2. This table is discussed in the next section.

Although the pairing construction procedures produced feasible solutions, the total cost of these solutions was typically above the desired level of operating efficiency. In order to reduce the total cost of a set of crew pairings, several pairing improvement procedures were developed. Most of the improvement procedures used in this crew scheduling application possess thoroughly tested vehicle routing counterparts.

Perhaps the best known vehicle routing improvement procedures are the 2-opt and 3-opt procedures of Lin [15] and the K-opt procedures of Lin and Kernighan [16]. A

Table 2: Concurrent scheduler pairing construction procedure.					
Start Time	Objective				
	A	B	C	D	E
0	108,799	107,871	108,968	101,115	103,745
1440	109,753	108,745	111,642	102,952	103,745
2880	108,730	107,834	112,980	102,952	103,745
4320	108,565	107,750	112,896	102,952	103,745
5760	106,366	105,476	112,866	102,952	103,745
7200	107,486	104,959	112,937	102,952	103,745
Processor Time (min:sec) for six solutions					
	(12:49)	(12:50)	(15:59)	(15:52)	(16:04)

Objective:
  A—first feasible assignment
  B—first feasible assignment with same aircraft flight number
  C—first crew in takes first flight out
  D—last crew in takes first flight out
  E—minimum cost assignment

K-opt route improvement procedure attempts to obtain a reduced cost route by exchanging any K branches in the route with any K branches not in the route. When all possible exchanges are attempted and improvements made, the algorithm terminates and the solution is considered K-optimum.

In the airline crew scheduling problem, the 2-opt procedure can be extended to provide a very efficient pairing improvement procedure. Suppose two pairings from the same crew base both transit a particular city, say Dallas. If it is feasible (legal) to split each of these pairings into two pieces and exchange their completions from Dallas to the crew base, such that a reduced cost configuration results, then a cost effective 2-opt exchange can be made. Since any such exchange must take place at a stop common to all candidate pairings, this 2-opt procedure is readily extended to the case where K pairings transit a particular city. In this situation, a $K \times K$ assignment problem may be solved to find the minimum cost configuration of all current pairings through that city. This extended 2-opt procedure was found to be much more effective, in terms of computation time required, than the standard 2-opt procedure which considers only one possible improvement at a time. In this case, a $K \times K$ cost matrix had to be computed in order to price out all potential changes.

A second pairing improvement procedure which was employed was the MERGE technique of Hinson and Mulherkar [12]. The MERGE technique is a heuristic set partitioning algorithm which exploits the availability of feasible solutions to the crew pairing problem. Given an initial set of feasible solutions as input, the MERGE procedure compares the first two solutions to see if a reduced cost composite solution can be found. The resultant minimum cost partition is then compared to the third solution for possible improvement. This procedure continues until all feasible solutions have been utilized. This procedure is not exact since the final set of pairings obtained will be a function of the initial ordering of the set of feasible solutions used as input. The MERGE technique, which was originally developed to solve the Federal Express vehicle scheduling problem, was found to be effective in this crew scheduling application.

The final improvement procedure employed is known as hubturning. A hubturn is the transit of the crew base on a crew pairing. To this point in the crew scheduling process, all pairings terminate when the crew returns to the crew base. We now wish to allow pairings to continue through the crew base, terminating when the crew returns to the base for the second time. Due to the nonlinear nature of the cost associated with each crew pairing, it may be possible to combine two non-hubturned pairings into a single pairing which transits the crew base at a reduced total cost. Hubturns can significantly reduce the cost of forming two non-hubturned pairings together if the cost of one non-hubturned pairing is based on time away from base while the other is based on block time (or time in the air). Once a final set of non-hubturned pairings is obtained, a one-match algorithm is used to put together feasible hubturned pairings.

Computational Results

Aircraft routing data and operational requirements for the crew pairings were obtained from the Federal Express Corporation. The data set consisted of 964 flight legs which comprised one week of flight operations during July 1977. Since the aircraft routings varied throughout the week, the scheduling period was assumed to be one week rather than one day.

Two benchmarks, which were available for this data set, allowed comparisons to be made as to the effectiveness and computational efficiency of the proposed heuristic procedures. The first benchmark was the actual operating schedule used by Federal Express during the period. This schedule was manually generated. The time required to create this schedule was three days, however, it is difficult to evaluate how similarities to previous operating schedules may have guided its formation. The total number of credit minutes for the week required (paid) in the manual solution was 102,324. (Each credit minute costs slightly more than one dollar.) The second benchmark solution was obtained from a commercially available version of American Airline's crew pairing program. Given the manually generated solution of 102,324 as a starting point, the overall credit was improved to 97,440 in approximately one hour of IBM 370/158 computer time. This solution was thought to be within one percent of the optimum solution.

Table 2 presents the results of the concurrent scheduling mechanism for various objective functions. Since varying results were obtained for different start times, the results are shown for six different start positions in minutes over the week. The processor time listed below each column indicates the time required in minutes and seconds to generate each set of six solutions. The machine used in these calculations was the Burroughs 6700 at the Federal Express Corporation. The Burroughs 6700 is approximately five times slower than the IBM 370/158 for these particular FORTRAN programs.

Table 3 displays the results of applying the extended 2-opt procedure to each of the initial feasible solutions

Table 3: Extended 2-OPT Procedure applied to initial feasible solutions.					
Start Time	A	B	Objective C	D	E
0	104,539	104,535	104,862	99,245	101,064
1440	105,239	105,202	108,988	100,434	101,010
2880	104,682	104,768	110,458	100,434	101,010
4320	103,513	103,647	110,369	100,434	101,010
5760	103,482	103,558	110,043	100,434	101,010
7200	103,509	102,876	110,362	100,434	101,010
Processor Time (min:sec) for six solutions	(21:46)	(23:01)	(21:09)	(19:52)	(20:11)

Objective
A—first feasible assignment
B—first feasible assignment with same aircraft flight number
C—first crew in takes first flight out
D—last crew in takes first flight out
E—minimum cost assignment

produced by the concurrent scheduler. The improvements ranged from two to four percent with an average processor time of 3.53 minutes required per improved solution.

Table 4 presents the results of the MERGE and hubturn improvement procedures. The six initial feasible solutions plus the six solutions improved by the extended 2-opt procedure were used as input to the MERGE heuristic set partitioning technique. The maximum improvement found by the MERGE procedure was one half of one percent. In cases D and E no improvement was found over the best solution obtained by the extended 2-opt improvement procedure. Once a final set of non-hubturned crew pairings was selected, the hubturn improvement procedure was applied. In a rather amazing result, four of the five cases converged to the same local minimum value of 98,666. This represented an improvement of almost six percent in case C. This can be explained, to some extent, by the high degree of degeneracy present in the crew scheduling problem. Experience with these types of problems has shown that many pairing configurations yield the same objective function value. As the pairings are allowed to increase in length, as in the hubturn procedure, the possibility of alternative pairing configurations with the same total cost increases.

Table 4: Results of MERGE and Hubturn improvement procedures.					
	A	B	Objective C	D	E
MERGE Procedure	103,162	102,386	104,106	99,245	101,010
Processor Time (Min:sec) required for MERGE	(3:28)	(2:47)	(2:29)	(1:37)	(1:53)
Hubturn Procedure	98,666	98,666	98,666	98,666	99,267
Processor Time (min:sec) required for Hubturns	(0.40)	(0:40)	(0:41)	():41)	(0:41)

Objective
A—first feasible assignment
B—first feasible assignment with same aircraft flight number
C—first crew in takes first flight out
D—last crew in takes first flight out
E—minimum cost assignment

Summary and Conclusions

As the number of flight legs to be scheduled becomes large, the airline crew scheduling problem requires a great deal of computer time to be solved by standard integer programming techniques. Good approximate solutions may be obtained, however, by viewing the crew scheduling problem as a vehicle routing or scheduling problem and by adapting various vehicle routing and scheduling techniques to its solution. Using combinations of schedule construction and schedule improvement procedures, solutions were obtained for a 964 flight leg problem which were greater than three percent below the actual schedule operated for the period and within two percent of a commerically generated benchmark solution. The time required to produce these solutions is on the order of minutes rather than hours.

The procedures developed in this paper have subsequently been implemented and are in use at Federal Express. The programs have been designed to be used in either the interactive or the batch mode. In the interactive mode, a single set of crew pairings is constructed and improved by the extended 2-opt and hubturn procedures. The current version of the pairing construction procedure uses the first feasible objective to assign the flight legs to the partially formed pairings. In addition, file data manipulation capabilities were incorporated to allow the crew scheduler to preset any flight connections he desires. Since the processor time required by these algorithms is approximately proportional to the square of the number of flight legs to be scheduled, any presetting greatly reduces the total run time of the program. In the batch mode, the user specifies the number of initial feasible solutions to be constructed and the program proceeds with the generation and improvement procedures, including the MERGE technique, and produces a single best solution. Operationally, both modes of the system are usually employed. The program is initially run in the interactive mode to allow the crew scheduler to make a preliminary evaluation of the crew pairings and to preset the data file as he feels is appropriate. The preset data file is then run in the batch mode, for 10 initial solutions, which requires approximately one hour of computer time, and the final crew pairings are printed in a format suitable for distribution to the flight crew personnel.

In addition to the savings in monthly crew costs, the implementation of the crew pairing model has greatly increased the flexibility of the crew scheduling process. Prior to the development of the model, the formation of the Federal Express crew pairings was done manually with occasional use of commerically available crew scheduling codes. The logistics of keypunching the aircraft routing data, hand carrying the data to the contractor's location, and then manually interacting with the contractor's model until a satisfactory set of pairings was obtained required two to three days. Since only five days were allotted within the monthly aircraft routing-crew scheduling operation for the formation of the crew pairings and the creation of the monthly crew rosters, no preliminary evaluation of the crew schedules was possible. In addition, with only two days to manually construct the monthly crew rosters, the rosters were often a major source of dissatisfaction among flight crew personnel. With the implementation of the crew pairing model, the crew schedules can be obtained in a single day. This efficiency allows for a preliminary evaluation of the pairings and allows a greater portion of the crew scheduling time to be spent forming monthly crew rosters which are more desirable to the flight crews. Although the initial users of this model were instrumental in its development, new flight operations personnel have mastered its use in less than one month of experience.

The success of the vehicle routing and scheduling heuristics applied to airline crew scheduling in this paper may, in part, be due to the special nature of the Federal Express crew scheduling problem. The Federal Express system operates from a single hub and crew domicile located at Memphis, Tennessee. The scheduling of its aircraft routes, and hence crew pairings, is dependent upon the fact that packages require linear journeys rather than the typical circuitous passenger journey. As a result, the aircraft itineraries tend to be very similar with respect to departure and arrival times at the crew base. This fact, combined with only a moderate amount of interaction between aircraft routes, provides a structure which is well suited to solution by heuristic procedures. The general applicability of these procedures to passenger airline crew scheduling problems is a matter for further research.

Acknowledgment

We wish to thank Bruce Casper, Joseph Hinson and Kelly Frey of the Federal Express Corporation for their assistance on this project.

References

[1] Arabeyre, J. P., Fearnley, J., Steiger, F. C., and Teather, W., "The Airline Crew Scheduling Problem: A Survey," *Transportation Science,* **3**, 2, 140-163 (May 1969).

[2] Balas, E. and Padberg, M. W., "Set Partitioning: A Survey," *SIAM Review,* **18**, 4, 710-760 (October 1976).

[3] Balinski, M. L., "Integer Programming: Methods, Uses, Computation," *Management Science,* **12**, 3, 253-313 (Nov. 1965).

[4] Balinski, M. L. and Quandt, R. E., "On An Integer Program for a Delivery Problem," *Operations Research,* **12**, 2, 300-304 (1964).

[5] Bodin, L. D., Kydes, A. S. and Rosenfield, D. B., "Approximation Techniques for Automated Manpower Scheduling," Program for Urban and Policy Sciences Research Paper UPS/UMTA-1 State University of New York, Stony Brook, New York (1975).

[6] Bornemann, D. R., "A Crew Planning and Scheduling System," *AGIFORS,* **10** (1970).

[7] Cassidy, P. J. and Bennett, H. S., "TRAMP-A Multi-Depot Vehicle Scheduling System," *Operational Research Quarterly,* **23**, 2, 151-163 (1975).

[8] Christofides, N., "The Vehicle Routing Problem," NATO Conference on Combinatorial Optimization, Paris (Sept. 1974).

[9] Garfinkel, R. S. and Nemhauser, G. L., *Integer Programming* John Wiley and Sons, New York (1972).

[10] Golden, Bruce L., "Vehicle Routing Problems: Formulations and Heuristic Solution Techniques," Technical Report No. 113, Operations Research Center, M.I.T. (August 1975).

[11] Gomory, R., "An Algorithm for Integer Solutions to Linear Programs," in Graves and Wolfe (Eds.) *Recent Advances in Mathematical Programming,* McGraw-Hill, New York (1963).

[12] Hinson, J. and Mulherkar, S., "Improvements to the Clarke and Wright Algorithm as Applied to an Airline Scheduling Problem," Technical Report, Federal Express Corp., (1975).

[13] House, R. W., Nelson, L. D. and Rado, T., "Computer Studies of a Certain Class of Linear Integer Problems" in *Recent Advances in Optimization Techniques,* Lavi and Vogl (Eds.), John Wiley and Sons, Inc., New York, 241-281 (1966).

[14] Kolner, T. K., "Some Highlights of a Scheduling Matrix Generator System," *AGIFORS,* **6** (1966).

[15] Lin, S., "Computer Solutions of the Traveling Salesman Problem," *Bell System Technical Journal,* 2245-2269 (1965).

[16] Lin, S. and Kernighan, B. W., "An Effective Heuristic Algorithm for the Traveling-Salesman Problem," *Operations Research,* **21**, 2, 498-516 (March 1973).

[17] Marsten, Roy E., "An Algorithm for Large Set Partitioning Problems," *Management Science,* **20**, 5, 774-787 (January 1974).

[18] Martin, Glenn T., "An Accelerated Euclidean Algorithm for Integer Linear Programming" in *Recent Advances in Mathematical Programming,* Graves and Wolfe (Eds), McGraw-Hill, 311-317 (1963).

[19] Pierce, John F., "Application of Combinatorial Programming to a Class of All-Zero-One Programming Problems," *Management Science,* **15**, 3, 191-209 (Nov. 1968).

[20] Ponder, R., Hinson, J., Tsai, D., Finnegan, W., and Sternad, M. "Federal Express, The Small Package Airline," *AGIFORS,* **17**, (1977).

[21] Rubin, Jerrold, "A Technique for the Solution of Massive Set Covering Problems, with Application to Airline Crew Scheduling," *Transportation Science,* **7**, 1, 34-48 (Feb. 1973).

[22] Steiger, F., "Activity Report of the Agifors Study Group 'Crew Scheduling'," Agifors Symposium, 120-134 (1967).

[23] Thiriez, Hervé, "Airline Crew Scheduling: A Group Theoretic Approach," M.I.T. Department of Aeronautics and Astronautics, Report No. R69-1 (1969).

Edward K. Baker is an Instructor in Management Science in the School of Business Administration at the University of Miami. He is also currently researching his DBA dissertation in operations research at the University of Maryland. Baker's research on the topic "Efficient Heuristic Solutions to Airline Crew Scheduling Problems" is being supported by a contract with the Federal Express Corporation of Memphis, Tennessee. His other research interests include integer programming, networks, and applications of operations research to problems in transportation and finance. Mr. Baker received his BES and MS degrees from Johns Hopkins University. He is a member of ORSA and ASA.

Dr. Lawrence D. Bodin is an Associate Professor of Management Science and Statistics in the College of Business and Management at the University of Maryland. Professor Bodin's primary research are networks, vehicle routing, and manpower scheduling. He has published numerous papers in these areas. Professor Bodin received his AB degree in mathematics from Northeastern University and his MS and PhD in operations research from the University of California at Berkeley. He is a member of ORSA and SIGMAP.

William F. Finnegan is Manager of Flight Operations Planning at the Federal Express Corporation. Mr. Finnegan is currently responsible for long and short range crew planning and development of crew pairings and monthly crew rosters. Mr. Finnegan received his BS degree at Villanova University and holds an MS in applied mathematics and an MS in urban and policy science from SUNY, Stony Brook. He is also a member of ORSA and AGIFORS.

Dr. Ronny J. Ponder is Director of Operations Research and Planning at the Federal Express Corporation. Dr. Ponder is responsible for Operations Planning and Corporate Planning for Federal Express where he supervises a staff of 20 professionals. Dr. Ponder received his BBA Degree at Southern State University, MBA at Louisiana Tech University, and DBA at Mississippi State University. He is a member of ORSA, TIMS, AGIFORS, AIIE, and other professional organizations.

Appendix

Production Planning

Adam, Nabil, and Surkis, Julius, "A Comparison of Capacity Planning Techniques in a Job Shop Control System," *Management Science*, Vol. 23, No. 9, 1977, pp. 1011-1015

Baker, K.R., "Work Force Allocation in Cyclical Scheduling Problems: A Survey," *O.R. Quarterly*, Vol. 27, No. 1, 1976, pp. 155-168

Baker, Kenneth R., "An Experimental Study of the Effectiveness of Rolling Schedules in Production Planning." *Decision Sciences*, Vol. 8, No. 1, January, 1977, pp. 19-27

Baker, Kenneth R., "Scheduling a Full-time Workforce to Meet Cyclic Staffing Requirements," *Management Science*, Vol. 20, No. 12, 1974, pp. 1561-1568

Baker, Kenneth R., and Magazine, Michael, "Workforce Scheduling with Cyclic Demands and Day Off Constraints," *Management Science*, Vol. 24, No. 2, 1977, pp. 161-167

Baker, Kenneth R., and Peterson, David, "An Analytic Framework for Evaluating Rolling Schedules," *Management Science*, Vol. 25, No. 4, 1979, pp. 341-351

Baker, Kenneth R. and Damon, William W., "A Simultaneous Planning Model for Production and Working Capital," *Decision Sciences*, Vol. 8, No. 1, January, 1977, pp. 95-108

Beenhakker, Henri L., and Sirdeshpande, Jayant G., "Planning Procedures For A Process Industry," *AIIE Transactions*, Vol. 6, No. 2, pp. 126-134

Bitran, Gabriel R. and Hax, Arnoldo C., "On the Design of Hierarchical Production Planning Systems," *Decision Sciences*, Vol. 7, No. 1, January, 1977, pp. 28-55

Buffa, Elwood S., Cosgrove, Michael J., and Luce, Bill J., An Integrated Work Shift Scheduling System," *Decision Sciences*, Vol. 7, No. 4, October, 1976, pp. 620-630

Buxey, G.M., "Assembly Line Balancing with Multiple Stations," *Management Science*, Vol. 20, No. 6, 1974, pp. 1010-1021

Buxacott, J.A., "The Production Capacity of Job Shops with Limited Storage Space," *International Journal of Production Research*, Vol. 14, No. 5, 1976, pp. 597-606

Daellenbach, H.G., "Note On A Stochastic Manpower Smoothing and Production Model," *O.R. Quarterly*, Vol. 27, No. 31, 1976, pp. 573-580

Doyle, P. Fenwick, II, and Savage, G.P., "Management Planning and Control In Multi-Branch Banking," *O.R. Journal*, Vol. 30, No. 2, 1979, pp. 105-112

Ebert, Ronald J., "Aggregate Planning With Learning Curve Productivity," *Management Science*, Vol. 23, No. 2, 1976, pp. 171-182

Elmaleh, J., and Eilon, Samuel, "A New Approach To Production Smoothing," *International Journal of Production Research*, Vol. 12, No. 6, 1974, pp. 673-182

Erlenkotter, Donald, "Capacity Planning for Large Multilocation Systems: Approximate and Incomplete Dynamic Programming Approaches," *Management Science*, Vol. 22, No. 3, 1975, pp. 274-285

Folic, Michael, and Tiffin, John, "Solution for a Multi-Product Manufacturing and Distribution Problem," *Management Science*, Vol. 23, No. 3, 1976, pp. 286-296

Fryer, John S., "Effects of Shop Size and Labor Flexibility in Labor and Machine Limited Production Systems," *Management Science*, Vol. 21, No. 5, 1975, pp. 507-515

Goodman, David A., "A Goal Programming Approach to Aggregate Planning of Production and Work Force," *Management Science*, Vol. 20, No. 12, 1974, pp. 1569-1575

Grinold, Richard C., "Manpower Planning with Uncertain Requirements," *Operations Research*, Vol. 24, No. 3, 1976, pp. 387-399

Gupta, S.K., and Sengupta, J.K., "Decision Rules in Production Planning Under Chance-Constrained Sales," *Decision Sciences*, Vol. 8, No. 3, July, 1977, pp. 521-533

Hamner, W. Clay and Carter, Phillip L., "A Comparison of Alternative Production Management Coefficient Decision Rules," *Decision Sciences*, Vol. 6, No. 2, April 1975, pp. 324-336

Hitomi, K., and Nakamura, N., "Optimal Production Planning for A Multiproduct, Multistage Production System," *International Journal of Production Research*, Vol. 14, No. 2, 1976, pp. 194-214

Kennay, G.A., Morgan, R.W., and Ray, K.H., "An Analytical Model For Company Manpower Planning," *O.R. Quarterly*, Vol. 28, No. 411, 1977, pp. 983-996

Kleindorfer, P.R., Kriebel, C.H., Thompson, G.L., and Kleindorfer, G.B., "Discrete Optimal Control of Production Plans," *Management Science*, Vol. 22, No. 3, 1975, pp. 261-273

Koragaonker, M.G., "Integrated Production Inventory Policies for Multistage Multiproduct Batch Production Systems," *O.R. Journal*, Vol. 30, No. 4, 1979, pp. 155-162

Koyano, E., "A Study of Measuring Methods For The Number of Personnel Required In An Office Based On Imput and Output Relations Analysis," *International Journal of Production Research*, Vol. 16, No. 6, 1978, pp. 509-520

Krajewski, Leroy, and Ritzman, Larry P., "Disaggregation in Manufacturing and Service Organizations: Survey of Problems and Research," *Decision Sciences*, Vol. 8, No. 1, January 1977, pp. 1-18

Lee, William B., and Khumawala, Basheer M., "Simulation Testing of Aggregate Production Models In An Implementation Methodology," *Management Science*, Vol. 20, No. 6, 1974, pp 903-911

Lockett, A.G., and Muglemann, A.P., "A Problem of Aggregate Scheduling, An Application of Goal Programming," *International Journal of Production Research*, Vol. 16, No. 2, 1978, pp. 127-136

McClain, John O., and Thomas, Joseph, "Horizon Effects in Aggregate Production Planning with Seasonal Demand," *Management Science*, Vol. 23, No. 7, 1977, pp. 728-736

Mabert, Vincent A., "A Case Study of Encoder Shift Scheduling under Uncertainty," *Management Science*, Vol. 25, No. 7, 1979, pp. 623-631

Markland, Robert E., and Newett, Robert J., "An Application of Mathematical Programming to Soybean Processing," *Omega*, Vol. 3, No. 3, June 1975, pp. 313-319

Markland, Robert E., and Newett, Robert J., "Production Distribution Planning in a Large Scale Commodity Processing Network," *Decision Sciences*, Vol. 7, No. 4, October, 1976, pp. 579-594

Moskowitz, Herbert, and Miller, Jeffrey G., "Information and Decision Systems for Production Planning," *Management Science*, Vol. 22, No. 3, 1975, pp. 359-370

Nutt, Paul c., "An Experimental Comparison of the Effectiveness of Three Planning Methods," *Management Science*, Vol. 23, No. 5, 1977, pp. 499-511

Ritzman, Larry P.; Krajewski, Leroy J.; and Showalter, Michael J., "The Disaggregation of Aggregate Manpower Plans," *Management Science*, Vol. 22, No. 11, 1976, pp. 1204-1214

Sanderson, I.W., "An interactive production planning system in the chemical industry", *O.R. Journal*, Vol. 29, No. 8, 1978, pp. 731-740

Singhal, K., "Integrating production decisions," *International Journal of Production Research*, Vol. 16, No. 5, 1978, pp. 383-394

Sugimori, Y.; Kusunoki, K.; Cho, F.; and Uchikawa, S., "Toyota production system and Kanban system. Materialization of just-in-time and respect-for-human system," *International Journal of Production Research*, Vol. 15, No. 6, 1977, pp. 552-564

Vajda, S., "Mathematical aspects of manpower planning, *O.R. Quarterly*, Vol. 26, No. 3i, September 1975, pp. 527-542

Wagner, Harvey M. "The Design of Production and Inventory Systems for Multifacility and Multiwarehouse Companies," *Operations Research*, Vol. 22, No. 2, 1974, pp. 278-291

Weeks, James K.; and Fryer, John S., "A Simulation Study of Operating Policies in a Hypothetical Dual-constrained Job Shop," *Management Science*, Vol. 22, No. 12, 1976, pp. 1362-1371

Young, Andrew; and Abodunde, T., "Personnel recruitment policies and long-term production planning," *O.R. Journal*, Vol. 30, No. 3, 1979, pp. 225-236

Forecasting

Adam, Everett E.; and Ebert, Ronald J., "A Comparison of Human and Statistical Forecasting," *AIIE Transactions*, Vol. 8, No. 1, 1976, pp. 120-127

Bestwick, Paul F., "A forecasting monitoring and revision system for top management," *O.R. Quarterly*, Vol. 26, No. 2ii, July 1965, pp. 419-430

Buffa, Frank P., "The Application of a Dynamic Forecasting Model with Inventory Control Properties," *Decision Sciences*, Vol. 6, No. 2, April, 1975, pp. 298

Bunn, D.W., "A Bayesian approach to the linear combination of forecasts," *O.R. Quarterly*, Vol. 26, No. 2I, June 1975, pp. 325-330

Dancer, Robert E., and Gray, Clifford F., "An Empirical Evaluation of Constant and Adaptive Computer Forecasting Models for Inventory Control," *Decision Sciences*, Vol. 8, No. 1, January, 1977, pp. 227-238

Dickinson, J.P., "Some comments on the combination of forecasts," *O.R. Quarterly*, Vol. 26, No. 1ii, April 1975, pp. 205-210

Fogler, H. Russell, "A Pattern Recognition Model for Forecasting," *Management Science*, Vol. 20, No. 8, 1974, pp. 1178-1189

Gilchrist, Warren, "Statistical Forecasting – The State of the Art," *Omega*, Vol. 2, No. 6, Dec. 1974, pp. 733-761

Gold, Bela, "From Backcasting towards Forecasting," *Omega*, Vol. 2, No. 2, April 1974, pp. 209-223

Golder, E.R., Settle, J.G., "Monitoring schemes in short-term forecasting," *O.R. Quarterly*, Vol. 27, No. 2ii, 1976, pp. 489-502

Kwak, N.K.; Garrett, Walter A.; and Barone Sam, "A Stochastic Model of Demand Forecasting for Technical Manpower Planning," *Management Science*, Vol. 23, No. 10, 1977, pp. 1089-1098

Mabert, Vince A., "Forecast Modification Based Upon Residual Analysis: A Case Study of Check Volume Estimation," *Decison Sciences*, Vol. 9, No. 2, April 1978, pp. 285-296

Mabert, V.A.; and Hill, A.V., "A combination projection-casual approach for short-range forecasts," *International Journal of Production Research*, Vol. 15, No. 2, 1977, pp. 153-162

McKenzie, Ed, "The monitoring of exponentially weighted forecasts," *O.R. Journal*, Vol. 29, No. 5, 1978, pp. 449-458

Montgomery, Douglas C.; and Contreras, L.E., "A note on forecasting with adaptive filtering," *O.R. Quarterly*, Vol. 28, No. 1i, 1977, pp. 87-88

Oller, L.E., "A method for pooling forecasts," *O.R. Journal*, Vol. 29, No. 1, 1978, pp. 55-64

Sarin, Rakesh K., "An Approach for Long Term Forecasting with an Application to Solar Electric Energy," *Management Science*, Vol. 25, No. 6, 1979, pp. 543-554

Wecker, William E., "Predicting Demand from Sales Data in the Presence of Stockouts," *Management Science*, Vol. 24, No. 10, 1978, pp. 1043-1054

Winkler, Robert L.; Smith, Wayne, S.; and Kulkarni, Ram B., "Adaptive Forecasting Models Based on Predictive Distributions," *Management Science*, Vol. 24, No. 10, 1978, pp. 977-896

Wood, Steven D.; and Steece, Bert M., "Forecasting the Product of Two Time Series With a Linear Asymmetric Error Cost Function," *Management Science*, Vol. 24, No. 6, 1978, pp. 690-701

Inventories

Aggarwal, Sumer C., "A review of current inventory theory and its applications," *International Journal of Production Research,*, Vol. 12, No. 4, 1974, pp. 443-482

Aggarwal, Sumer C., and Dhavale, Dileep G., "An Empirical Study of an Inventory-Distribution System," *Omega*, Vol. 3, No. 2, April, 1975, pp. 203-211

Ahluwalia, Krishen G.; Saxena, Umesh, "Development of an Optimal Core Steel Slitting and Inventory Policy," *AIIE Transactions*, Vol. 10, No. 4, 1978, pp. 399-408

Axsater, S., "Coordinating control of production-inventory systems," *International Journal of Production Research*, Vol. 14, No. 6, 1976, pp. 669-688

Berry, William L.; Marcus Myles; Williams, Greg, "Inventory Investment Analysis Using Biased Sampling Techniques," *Management Science*, Vol. 23, No. 12, 1977, pp. 1295-1306

Boche, Raymond E., "The Interdependence of Industrial Engineering and Computing: Some Inventory Models for Information Systems," *AIIE Transactions*, Vol. 8, No. 3, 1976, pp. 328-335

Brodheim, Eric; Derman, Cyrus; Prastacos, Gregory, "On the Evaluation of a Class of Inventory Policies for Penshable Products such as Blood," *Management Science*, Vol. 21, No. 11, 1975, pp. 1320-1325

Buffa, Frank P., "A Model for Allocating Limited Resources When Making Safety-Stock Decisions," *Decision Sciences*, Vol. 8, No. 2, April 1977, pp. 415-426

Das, Chandrasekhar, "An Improved Formula for Inventory Decisions Under Service and Safety Stock Constraints," *AIIE Transactions*, Vol. 10, No. 2, 1978, pp. 217-219

Das, Chandrasekhar, "Some Aids for Lot-Size Inventory Control Under Normal Lead Time Demand," *AIIE Transactions*, Vol. 7, No. 1, 1975, pp. 77-79

Davis, K. Roscoe, and Taylor III, Bernard W., "A Heuristic Procedure for Determining In-Process Inventories," *Decision Sciences*, Vol. 9, No. 3, July 1978, pp. 452-466

Fortuin, L., "A survey of literature on reordering of stock items for production inventories," *International Journal of Production Research*, Vol. 15, No. 1, 1977, pp. 87-106

Gardner, Everette S.; Dannenbring, David G.; "Using Optimal Policy Surfaces to Analyze Aggregate Inventory Trade-offs," *Management Science*, Vol. 25, No. 8, 1979, pp. 709-720

Gelders, Ludo F.; Van Looy, Paul M., "An inventory policy for slow and fast movers in a petrochemical plant: A case study," *O.R. Journal*, Vol. 29, No. 9, 1978, pp. 867-874

Goyal, S.K.; Belton, A.S., "On A Simple Method of Determining Order Quantities in Joint Replenishments under Deterministic Demand," *Management Science*, Vol. 25, No. 6, 1979, p. 604

Ladany, S.; and Sternlieb A., "The Interaction of Economic Ordering Quantities and Marketing Policies," *AIIE Transactions*, Vol. 6, No. 1, 1974, pp. 35-40

Lockett, A.G., and Muhlemann, A.P., "The Use of Formal Inventory Control Models: A Preliminary Survey," *Omega*, Vol. 6, No. 3, 1978, pp. 227-230

Meyer, Robert R.; Rothkopf, Michael H.; Smith, Stephen A., "Reliability and Inventory in a Production-Storage System," *Management Science*, Vol. 25, No. 8, 1979, pp. 799-807

Naddor, Eliezer, "Optimal Heuristic Decisions for the s,S Inventory Policy," *Management Science*, Vol. 21, No. 9, 1975, pp. 1071-1073

Northcraft, L.P., "Computerized Cable Inventory," *Industrial Engineering*, Vol. 6, No. 2, 1974, pp. 45-49

Oral, Muhittin; Malouin, J.L.; and Hobbs, J. Brian, "An Inventory Control Policy of the (Q.S.R.) Type for Manufacturing Industries: Simulation Analysis Approach," *AIIE Transactions*, Vol. 6, No. 4, 1974, pp. 345-353

Paul, R.J.; Thomas, R.C., "An Integrated Distribution, Warehousing and Inventory Control System for Improved Books," *O.R. Quarterly*, Vol. 28, No. 311, pp. 629-640

Perreault, William D. Jr., and Russ, Frederick A., "Quantifying Marketing Trade-Offs in Physical Distribution Policy Decisions," *Decision Sciences*, Vol. 7, No. 2, April 1976, pp. 186-201

Schneider, Helmut, "Methods for Determining the Re-Order Point of an Ordering Policy When A Service Level is Specified," *O.R. Journal*, Vol. 29, No. 12, 1978, pp. 1181-1194

Shorrock, Brian H., "Some Key Problems In Controlling Component Stocks," *O.R. Journal*, Vol. 29, No. 7, 1978, pp. 683-690

Silver, Edward A., "A Control System For Coordinated Inventory Replenishment," *International Journal of Production Research*, Vol. 12, No. 6, 1974, pp. 647-672

Silver, Edward A., Smith, Stephen A., "A Graphical Aid For Determining Optimal Inventories in a Unit Replenishment Inventory System," *Management Science*, Vol. 24, No. 3, 1977, pp. 358-359

Steudel, H.J., "Monitoring and Controlling In-Process Inventories With Highrise Storage Via Time Series Analysis," *International Journal of Production Research*, Vol. 15, No. 4, 1977, pp. 383-390

Stohr, Edward A., "Information Systems For Observing Inventory Levels," *Operations Research*, Vol. 27, No. 2, 1979, pp. 242-259

Whybark, Clay D.; Williams, J. Gregg, "Materials Requirements Planning Under Uncertainty," *Decision Sciences*, Vol. 7, No. 4, October, 1976, pp. 595-606

Scheduling

Baker, Kenneth R., "A Comparitive Study of Flow-Shop Algorithms," *Operations Research*, Vol. 23, No. 1, 1975, pp. 62-73

Ben-Bassat, Moshe and Borovits, "Computer Network Scheduling," *Omega*, Vol. 3, No. 1, Feb. 1975, pp. 119-131

Bodin, Lawrence D. and Kursh, Samuel J., "A Computer-Assisted System for the Routing and Scheduling of Street Sweepers," *Operations Research*, Vol. 26, No. 4, 1978, pp. 525-537

Boebion, J.; Almar, A. and Pun, L., "Scheduling Method Synchronizing Two Lines of Activities and Minimizing Waiting and Pass-Time," *International Journal of Production Research*, Vol. 16, No. 4, 1978, pp. 321-334

Bonney, M.C.; Gundry, S.W., "Solutions to The Constrained Flowshop Sequencing Problem," *O.R. Quarterly*, Vol. 27, No. 41, 1976, pp. 869-884

Booler, J.M.P., "A Method for Solving Crew Scheduling Problems," *O.R. Quarterly*, Vol. 26, No. 11, March, 1975, pp. 52-62

Buxey, G.M.; and Sadjadi, D., "Simulation Studies of Convey or Paced Assembly Lines With Buffer Capacity," *International Journal of Production Research*, Vol. 14, No. 5, 1976, pp. 607-624

Carnall, C.A.; Wild, R., "The Location of Variable Work Stations and The Performance of Production Flow Lines," *International Journal of Production Research*, Vol. 14, No. 6, 1976, pp. 703-710

Caswell, W.M.; Rao, A., "A Practical Approach to the Large-Scale Forest Scheduling Problem," *Decison Sciences*, Vol. 5, No. 3, July 1974, pp. 364-373

Dannenbring, David G., "An Evaluation of Flow Shop Sequencing Heuristics," *Management Science*, Vol. 23, No. 11, 1977, pp. 1174-1182

Dar-El, E.M., and Cucuy, S., "Optimal Mixed-Model Sequencing for Balanced Assembly Lines," *Omega*, Vol. 5, No. 3, 1977, pp. 333-342

Davies, Samuel G.; Swanson, Lloyd A., "A Computerized Operations Scheduling Model for the Reduction of Commercial Bank Float," *O.R. Journal*, Vol. 29, No. 6, 1978, pp. 559-564

Davis, Edward W., "Project Network Summary Measures and Constrained-Resource Scheduling," *AIIE Transactions*, Vol. 7, No. 2, 1975, pp. 132-142

Deane, Richard H.; White, Emett R., "Balancing Work Loads and Minimizing Setup Costs in Parallel Processing Shop," *O.R. Quarterly*, Vol. 26, No. 11, March 1975, pp. 45-54

Delporte, Christian M.; Thomas, L. Joseph, "Lot Sizing and Sequencing for N Products on One Facility," *Management Science*, Vol. 23, No. 10, 1977, pp. 1070-1079

Dhall, Sudarshan K.; Lin, C.L., "On a Real-Time Scheduling Problem," *Operations Research*, Vol. 26, No. 1, 1978, pp. 127-140

Dhavale, D.; Aggarwal, S., "An Investigation of Multiproduct, Multimachine Production Scheduling and Inventory Control of a Flow-shop System," *International Journal of Production Research*, Vol. 16, No. 6, 1978, pp. 477-492

Dorsey, Robert C.; Hodgson, Thomas J.; Ratliff, A. Donald, "A Network Approach to a Multi-Facility Multi-Product Production Scheduling Problem Without Backordering," *Management Science*, Vol. 21, No. 7, 1975, pp. 813-822

Eilon, S.; and Chowdhury, I.G., "Due Dates in Job Shop Scheduling," *International Journal of Production Research*, Vol. 14, No. 2, 1976, pp. 223-238

Elmaghraby, Salah E.; Park, Sung H., "Scheduling Jobs on a Number of Identical Machines," *AIIE Transactions*, Vol. 6, No. 1, 1974, pp. 1-13

Elmaghraby, Salah E., "The Economic Lot Scheduling Problem (ELSP): Review and Extensions," *Management Science*, Vol. 24, No. 6, 1978, pp. 587-598

Flowers, A. Dale; Preston, Stephen E., "Work Force Scheduling with the Search Decision Rule," *Omega*, Vol. 5, No. 4, 1977, pp. 473-479

Fryer, John S., "Organizational Structure of Dual-Constraint Job Shops," *Decision Sciences*, Vol. 5, No. 1, January 1974, pp. 45-57

Gelders, L. and Kleindorfer, P.R., "Coordinating Aggregate and Detailed Scheduling in the One-Machine Job Shop: II-Computation and Structure," *Operations Research*, Vol. 34, No. 2, 1975, pp. 312-324

Gelders, L.F.; and Sambandam, N., "Four Simple Heuristics for Scheduling a Flow Shop," *International Journal of Production Research*, Vol. 16, No. 3, 1978, pp. 221-232

Godin, Victor B., "Interactive Scheduling: Historical Survey and State of The Art," *AIIE Transactions*, Vol. 10, No. 3, 1978, pp. 331-337

Gonzales, Teofilo; Sahni, Sartaj, "Flowshop and Job Shop Schedules," *Operations Research*, Vol. 26, No. 1, 1978, pp. 36-52

Goodwin, James C., Jr.; Elvers, Douglas; and Goodwin, Jack S. "Overtime Usage in a Job Shop Environment," *Omega*, Vol. 6, No. 6, 1978, pp. 493-500

Graves, Stephen C., "On the Deterministic Demand Multi-Product Single-Machine Lot Scheduling Problem," *Management Science*, Vol. 25, No. 3, 1979, pp. 276-279

Henderson, William B.; Berry, William L. "Determining Optimal Shift Schedules for Telephone Traffic Exchange Operators," *Decision Sciences*, Vol. 8, No. 1, January 1977, pp. 239-255

Hershaur, James C.; Ebert, Ronald J., "Search and Simulation Sections of a Job Shop Sequencing Rule," *Management Science*, Vol. 21, No. 7, 1975, pp. 833-843

Holloway, C.A.; Nelson, R.T., "Job Shop Scheduling with Due Dates and Variable Processing Times," *Management Science*, Vol. 20, No. 9, 1974, pp. 1264-1275

Holloway, C.A.; Nelson, R.T., "Job Shop Scheduling with Due Dates and Overtime Capability," *Management Science*, Vol. 21, No. 1, 1974, pp. 68-78

Holloway, C.A.; and Nelson, Rosser T., "Job Shop Scheduling with Due Dates and Operation Overlap Feasibility," *AIIE Transactions*, Vol. 7, No. 1, 1975, pp. 16-20

Hoogson, Thom J., "A Note on Single Machine Sequencing with Random Processing Times," *Management Science*, Vol. 23, No. 10, 1977, pp. 1144-1146

Jones, G.A.; Wilson, J.G., "Optimal Scheduling of Jobs on a Transmission Network," *Management Science*, Vol. 25, No. 1, 1979, pp. 98-104

Latecoere, L.; and Boebion, J. Pun, L., "Model Adaptive Scheduling for Solving Perturbation Problems in the Cloth Industry," *International Journal of Production Research*, Vol. 14, No. 2, 1976, pp. 239-250

Lowerre, James M., "Work Stretch Properties for the Scheduling of Continuous Operations Under Alternative Labor Policies," *Management Science*, Vol. 23, No. 9, 1977, pp. 963-971

Mabert, Vincent A.; and Raedels, Alan R., "Detail Scheduling of a Part Time Work Force," *Decision Sciences*, Vol. 8, No. 1, January, 1977, pp. 109-120

Miller, Holmes E.; Pierskalla, William P.; and Rath, Gustave J., "Nurse Scheduling Using Mathematical Programming," *Operations Research*, Vol. 24, No. 5, 1976, pp. 857-870

Miller, Jeffrey G.; and Berry, William L., "Heuristic Methods for Assigning Men To Machines: An Experimental Analysis," *AIIE Transactions*, Vol. 6, No. 2, pp. 99-104

Miller, Jeffrey G.; and Berry, William L., "The Assignment of Men to Machines: An Application of Branch and Bound," *Decision Sciences*, Vol. 8, No. 1, January 1977, pp. 56-72

Moore, Laurence J.; and Taylor III, Bernard W., "Experimental Investigation of Priority Scheduling in a Bank Check Processing Operation," *Decision Sciences*, Vol. 8, No. 4, October, 1977, pp. 692-710

Morton, Thomas E.; Dharan, Bala Ganga, "Algoristics for Single-Machine Sequencing with Precedence Constraints," *Management Science*, Vol. 24, No. 10, 1978, pp. 1011-1020

Nelson, Rosser T.; Holloway, Charles H.; Wong, Ruby Mei-Lun, "Centralized Scheduling and Priority Implementation Heuristics for a Dynamic Job Shop Model," *AIIE Transactions*, Vol. 9, No. 1, 1977, pp. 95-102

New, C.C., "Job Shop Scheduling: Is Manual Application of Dispatching Rules Feasible," *O.R. Quarterly*, Vol. 26, No. 11, March 1975, pp. 35-44

Newson, E.F. Peter, "Multi-item Lot Size Scheduling By Heuristic," *Management Science*, Vol. 21, No. 10, 1975, pp. 1186-1203

Olsen, E.D., "Shop Control System Far Cry From Job Jar Approach," *Industrial Engineering*, Vol. 10, No. 12, 1978, pp. 16-20

Panwalkar, S.S.; and Khan, A.W., "An Ordered Flow-shop Sequencing Problem with Mean Completion Time Criterion," *International Journal of Production Research*, Vol. 14, No. 5, 1976, pp. 631-636

Panwalkar, S.S.; and Iskandar, Wafik, "A Survey of Scheduling Rules," *Operations Research*, Vol. 25, No. 1, 1977, pp. 45-61

Patterson, James H.; and Albracht, Joseph J., "Assembly Line Balancing: Zero-One Programming with Fibonacci Search," *Operations Research*, Vol. 23, No. 1, 1975, pp. 166-172

Paul, R.J., "A Production Scheduling Problem in the Glass-Container Industry," *Operations Research*, Vol. 27, No. 2, 1979, pp. 290-302

Prabhakar, T., "A Production Scheduling Problem with Sequencing Considerations," *Management Science*, Vol. 21, No. 1, 1974, pp. 34-42

Rand, Graham K., "A Manual Production Scheduling Algorithm," *O.R. Quarterly*, Vol. 25, No. 4, December 1974, pp. 541-552

Randolph, Paul H., "Job Shop Scheduling A Case Study," *Omega*, Vol. 4, No. 4, 1976, pp. 463-477

Sato, S.; Yamaoka, T.; Aoki, Y.; and Veda, T., "Development of Integrated Production Scheduling for Iron and Steel Works," *International Journal of Production Research*, Vol. 15, No. 6, 1977, pp. 539-552

Schwarz, Leroy B.; Graves, Stephen C.; Hausman, Warren H., "Scheduling Policies for Automatic Warehousing Systems: Simulation Results," *AIIE Transactions*, Vol. 10, No. 3, 1978, pp. 260-270

Segal, M., "The Operator-Scheduling Problem: A Network-Flow Approach," *Operations Research*, Vol. 22, No. 4, 1974, pp. 808-823

Smith, M.L.; Panwalkar, S.S.; Dudek, R.A., "Flowshop Sequencing Problem with Ordered Processing Time Matrices," *Management Science*, Vol. 21, No. 5, 1975, pp. 544-549

Solem, Olav, "Contribution to the Solution of Sequencing Problems in Process Industry," *International Journal of Production Research*, Vol. 12, No. 1, 1974, pp. 55-76

Stainton, R.S., "Production Scheduling with Multiple Criteria Objectives," *O.R. Quarterly*, Vol. 28, No. 21, 1977, pp. 285-292

Stinson, Joel P.; Davis, Edward W.; and Khumawala, Basheer M., "Multiple Resource-Constrained Scheduling Using Branch and Bound," *AIIE Transactions*, Vol. 10, No. 3, 1978, pp. 252-259

Thesen, Arne, "Heuristic Scheduling of Activities Under Resource and Precedence Restrictions," *Management Science*, Vol. 23, No. 4, 1976, pp. 412-422

Weeks, James K., "A Simulation Study of Predictable Due Dates," *Management Science*, Vol. 25, No. 4, 1979, pp. 363-373

Yoshida, Teruhiko; and Nakamura, Nobuto; Hitom, Katsundo, "Group Production Scheduling for Minimum Total Tardiness Part (1)," *AIIE Transactions*, Vol. 10, No. 2, 1978, pp. 157-162

Yuan, John, S.C.; Horen, Jeffrey H.; Wagner, Harvey M., "Optimal Multi-Product Production Scheduling and Employment Smoothing with Deterministic Demands," *Management Science*, Vol. 21, No. 11, 1975, pp. 1250-1262

MORE FROM IIE...

PRODUCTIVITY—A series from INDUSTRIAL ENGINEERING

This is a collection of nineteen articles directed at various levels of productivity and levels of impact. It serves as a beginning approach to the massive problem of improving overall productivity while keeping the industrial engineer's role in focus.

The varied aspects of productivity improvement in this publication include a general discussion of the productivity problems; the definition and measurement of productivity; specific ways of improving productivity in the manufacturing sector as well as service, clerical and government sectors; and the relationships between productivity improvement and education.

Edited by Marvin E. Mundel
ISBN # 0-89806-004-4
ORDER # 240

PRODUCTIVITY FROM THERE TO HERE...BUT WHAT'S AHEAD? THREE STEPS TO IMPROVED PRODUCTIVITY

Two dynamic, non-technical slide-sound presentations that give you and your organization a way to tell why productivity gains are essential to American livelihood! Geared to all levels of the working force, these presentations clearly show, to workers and managers alike, why productivity growth is mandatory to maintain an improved standard of living.

Each presentation is 24 minutes in length and includes 140 35mm color slides and cassette tape narration. Packaged in a three-ring binder with instructions, script and equipment checklist.
ORDER # 241

For ordering and pricing information, contact:
Institute of Industrial Engineers
c/o Technical Services Department
25 Technology Park/Atlanta
Norcross, GA 30092
(404) 449-0460